WOMEN & AGING

WOMEN & AGING

A GUIDE TO THE LITERATURE

HELEN RIPPIER WHEELER

LYNNE
RIENNER
PUBLISHERS

BOULDER
LONDON

Published in the United States of America in 1997 by
Lynne Rienner Publishers, Inc.
1800 30th Street, Boulder, Colorado 80301

and in the United Kingdom by
Lynne Rienner Publishers, Inc.
3 Henrietta Street, Covent Garden, London WC2E 8LU

Library of Congress Cataloging-in-Publication Data
Wheeler, Helen Rippier.
     Women and aging : a guide to the literature / by Helen Rippier
Wheeler.
     p. cm.
    Includes indexes.
    ISBN 1-55587-661-7 (alk. paper)
    1. Aged women—United States—Bibliography. 2. Middle aged women—
United States—Bibliography. 3. Gerontology—United States—
Bibliography. I. Title.
Z7963.A4W54 1997
[HQ1064.U5]
016.30526—dc20   96-41175
                                          CIP

British Cataloguing-in-Publication Data
A Cataloguing-in-Publication record for this book
is available from the British Library.

Printed and bound in the United States of America

     The paper used in this publication meets the requirements
 ∞ of the American National Standard for Permanence of
     Paper for Printed Library Materials Z39.48-1984.

5 4 3 2 1

Contents

Foreword

The words "women" and "aging" go together very well—in a demographic sense, that is. The older women become, the more their numbers increase relative to men. Women outlive men by an average of seven years, and the ratio of women to men increases sharply among older persons. For example, for every 100 men 65 years of age and older, there are about 150 women. By the age of 85, this ratio becomes about 100 to 250. Aging is definitely a women's issue.

Over the past couple of decades, more and more scholars in a number of fields have been focusing on women in mid- and late life and have been conducting studies and publishing more books and articles about them. As interest grows, so does the need for guidance through the growing number of publications on women and aging. Although there are useful bibliographies on the subject, few are comprehensive and current guides. In contrast, Helen Rippier Wheeler's book *Women and Aging* is a true guide. It covers 2,260 titles published between the years 1980 and 1994, all critically selected by Dr. Wheeler according to their usefulness to scholars, educators, and the informed public. With its built-in cross-referencing system and advice for researching further in the reader's chosen topic, the book should become an important source in libraries and schools throughout the country.

Dr. Wheeler's strong commitment to gender and age equity comes through in *Women and Aging.* Her feminist orientation is welcome, since societies around the world are growing older and the territory of old age is largely populated by women. Helen Rippier Wheeler's book is a valuable road map that can help guide the reader through this new landscape. I hope that it will stimulate even more research and writing on the subject.

Robert N. Butler, M.D.

Introduction

The older woman is all of us.
Ti-Grace Atkinson, 1939– ,
responding to the question,
"How old is 'older'?"

The aged—referred to variously as elderly, seniors, and in other ways—currently constitute the most rapidly expanding part of the population. The aging of women should be considered, if only because the proportion of very old women to very old men has increased faster than any other age group. By way of introduction to knowing about females' aging, here are four concepts for consideration:

• We (society) are all aging, all of the time.
• The way a society or dominant culture perceives a person or groups of people can influence available opportunities for education, employment, and health; it can restrict them by assigning them to certain roles. And myths and stereotypes can influence the way people see themselves. The mass media serve to perpetuate the status quo.
• Age and gender biases combine to make this a women's issue. To paraphrase Martin Luther King, Jr.: what happens to one happens to all. To prioritize which group or person "has it worse" is divisive.
• Females are perceived by society to age at a different rate than males, namely the double double standard that a woman should be younger than a man as well as young. This business of being a disadvantaged statistical majority is familiar to many women. The confluence of age and sex is a gigantic topic, and it is important to clean up the water while changing the direction of the stream. "The problems of old age in America are largely the problems of women," according to former National Institute on Aging director Robert N. Butler, M.D.[1]

Researchers, scholars, professionals, politicians, educators, and other groups rely on standard (and standardizing) definitions in carrying out and applying influential works. Elderly men have been much more studied than elderly women, and men have constituted the "representative" populations in numerous aging-related action researches, despite the expectation that women 65 and over will constitute more than 60 percent of the United States elderly population by the year 2000, while elderly—85 and over—women will make up more than 73 percent. (Unless otherwise noted, statistics are derived from the Bureau of the Census' *Statistical Abstract of the United States.*) The problem of selection and formulation of related topics and methodology, when acknowledged, is too often attributed to lack of needed information, resources, and publications. More than twenty-five years ago the situation was described as self-perpetuating in the sense that researchers tend to study populations about which considerable knowledge already exists.[2]

Because public policy and government action are based on these attitudes, disparate treatment takes its toll on females throughout their lives, but particularly as they approach mid-life, enter their 60s, and when they are old. Social, health, housing, and other welfare provisions are directly affected.

During the 1970s, a growing consensus perceived over-40 women as "older women." At the 1973 annual conference on aging held at the University of Michigan, it was decided that "older woman" refers to any woman past menopause. (Rarely does one hear reference to an "older man.")

Today's middle aged women are the future majority within the aged. ERIC[3] provides a Middle-Age scope note of 45–65 years. Harris considers middle age a relatively recent development in the life course, which has come about with the increase of life expectancy; it begins between age 35 and 40 and ends between 60 and 65.[4]

Gerontology—the scientific study of the biological, social, and psychological aspects of aging—was coined in 1903 as a term from the Greek geront, meaning old man, and logos, meaning study of. Geriatrics is the medical study of the physiology and pathology of old age.

Aging is the process of becoming mature or old, as well as any artificial process for imparting the characteristics and properties of age. Harris refers to the regular changes that occur in mature, genetically representative organisms living under representative environmental conditions as they advance in chronological age; biological, psychological, and social aging are involved.

Within mid-life and older women populations, the possibility of membership in one or more of several other groups should be recognized. These other groups include:

- Single, never-married, or without family
- Employed, unemployed, or unemployable
- Feminist: aware of ageism, discrimination, unenforced law and divisiveness, and perceptive of responsibility for some response

A woman may make her primary commitment or allegiance to population groups in terms of her ethnicity, life style, national origin, race, religion, etc. Some sociologists argue that economic class, race, and sex/gender must be considered in analyzing the status of females. A few recognize that these factors as well as age must be considered in their welfare and oppression.

The assumption that women have primary responsibility for the household (not part of government's workplace definition) continues to thrive, overlaid with the general expectation that they will also work, i.e., be employed for wages outside the home—quite aside from having a "career"—in order to support themselves, their children, and others. When these two types of labor are totaled, women work many more hours than men, often with no personal pension provision, or one based on lower wage rates.

The highly referenced Baltimore Longitudinal Study of aging did not include women until 1978, having examined men only for more than twenty years. A landmark report on healthy aging published by the National Institute of Mental Health involved only men. Medical textbooks often provide so-called unisex coverage, as if there were no significant differences between the aging of women and of men. Until very recently, the over-65 woman has been concealed within the generics of "he/his/him" or the less biased but euphemistic doublespeak of "older person."

Women are organizing in order to fight unfair budget cuts, abuse of the elderly, and negative stereotypes as they impact upon them disparately and especially in terms of their age. At the first Conference on Midlife and Older Women (1983), topics of concern included sexuality, abuse of the elderly, mental health, and independent living. Recommendations included creation of a national health plan, elimination of gender as a factor in setting insurance rates and pension benefits, and the elimination of negative sexual images of older women.[5] The same year, the second National Conference on Lesbian and Aging's considerations included health workers' prejudices against sexually active elders and the inordinate struggle to secure legal rights for partners.[6]

More recently, U.S. Representative Patricia Schroeder's support for legislation that seeks to address the appalling lack of attention provided American women's healthcare needs includes extra funds for research on osteoporosis.[7] Dr. Kathy S. Brenneman, director of the Washington Hospital geriatric medicine section, was among those providing testimony on this legislation. She has heard one common theme in the numerous arguments against including women in clinical trials: men are considered easier research subjects than women. Aside from the sexism inherent in such a contention, several of the aspects on which its advocates rely disappear when applied to older women. Women, who make up 51 percent of the U.S. population, tend to live longer than men. Some medical conditions (arthritis, for example) strike women more often than men, making women the biggest consumers of prescription medications. But women have often been excluded from clinical trials of new medications because what may harm a woman may also harm her unborn offspring. The men-are-easier theorists contend that women are more likely to drop out of studies, with pregnancy cited as a reason women allegedly do not finish what they start.[8] Concern about including women of childbearing age in trials is legitimate but fails to account for the lack of trials involving older women.

Researchers have been inflexible in the way they have designed protocols. They have failed to adapt to an aging society. Because women generally live longer than men and develop disease later in life, and because the U.S. population is increasingly dominated by older persons, more research needs to be done on the illnesses of old age, and particularly those of elderly women.[9] The effectiveness of many treatments for heart disease in women remains largely unknown because so few women are included in heart-disease research, a particularly lamentable fact because surgery has been shown—in men—to ease symptoms and improve heart function.[10]

Women and Aging: A Guide to the Literature considers the aging of women, beginning at approximately age 35, as it takes place and is perceived by the social and behavioral sciences and the humanities, and including gerontology as well as interdisciplinary women and gender studies. *The Thesaurus of ERIC Descriptors* defines "women's studies" as a curriculum or subject area encompassing the history and contemporary social, political, and cultural situation of women. Feminists reason that "women's studies" is prescriptive, and that this field of study is more accurately called "women studies" or "feminist studies." Women studies is not merely *for* ladies—it is about females, and for people. The focus of this book is on a configuration of related problems and the methods of researching them.

As their numbers increase, older people are increasingly regarded commercially, as markets and consumers. Popular, professional, and scholarly publications are being contracted by trade publishers. Standardized textbooks are a growing market, with distribution at the undergraduate level and to professional programs. Some edited collections relating to females' aging experiences have made their way through the gatekeepers of academic publishing and the conglomerate trade-book marketplace since the beginning of the contemporary women's movement, and particularly in the 1980s.[11] During that decade, the number of edited compilations of original essays and reprinted articles published as books about mid-life and older women increased. Collections such as Baruch's *Women in Midlife,* Fuller's *Lavender Rose or Gray Panther,* Lesnoff-Caravaglia's *The World of the Older Woman,* and Markson's *Older Women: Issues and Prospects* provide consensus of the particular concerns of these women and these writers. Total health maintenance, housing, and income are often considered. Journals and other types of serials also publish occasional topical issues and articles.

This guide accesses information about contemporary developments in the fields of aging, gerontology, and gender needed by people and groups consisting of and representing mid-life and older women. Leads to representative, reliable, up-to-date, and available information and publications are provided by means of book annotations and subject analyses and cross-referenced indexing, as well as the subcategories within each of the thirteen chapters of the collection itself, as listed in the table of contents. But many publications interrelate topics, consider cause and effect, and may also provide geographic or other focus. Occasionally a publication's title may not exactly convey its contents, or may not be completely revelatory. Full exploitation of the *see* and especially *see also* cross-references will generate a harvest of the most useful documents. Guidance in further research is provided in Chapter 13, and clarifying notes are interspersed.

USING THE GUIDE

Selection

Borenstein's *The Older Woman in 20th-Century America: A Selected Annotated Bibliography,* published in 1982, is available in many libraries. Dr. Borenstein identified 885 titles, most published in the 1960s and 1970s. Dolan and Gropp identified 420 items from 1979–1982 in their bibliography, *The Mature Woman in America,* published in 1984. Few of their selections are duplicated in *Women and Aging: A Guide to the Literature.*

This collection's emphases are on available, English-language publications and doctoral dissertations of the years 1980–1992, and the aging of females in mid-life and old age as viewed in the social-behavioral sciences and humanities literature, including gerontology and interdisciplinary women studies. Some master's degree–level theses are included. Most titles are nonfiction, although fiction and poetry by and about women as they age are included. The guide also identifies some relevant bibliographies, serials, indexes, reviews, and biographies.

The 1980s abounded with "life skills guides" (an established subject heading in the Library of Congress thesaurus) directed at the popular market and often created by the many mid-life women who had been displaced from homemaker roles. The 1990s market is glutted with books pandering to many widowed women's lack of self-reliance and personal independence. In a typical 1990 example, subtitled *A Woman's Guide to Widowhood,* an attorney advises her readers to volunteer, to dress neatly and be on time for a job interview, to try freelance work—flower arranging or party planning, for example. And when alone in the car, don't keep your purse on the seat beside you, or when using a public toilet stall, don't hang it on a door hook. . . . Many of these guides deny or ignore disparate treatment of women in terms of their sex/gender and age. There are so many such publications that an extensive listing would be neither possible nor desirable, even though they are part of the literature of women and aging.

Also not included in the guide's scope are comprehensive reference books, unless they provide specific articles or extensive material related to women's aging and aged women. Many of the statistics and data about the world's aging populations are compiled as parts of government publications; for example, the United States Bureau of the Census's Current Population Reports Series P. . "How to" get-stay-act young publications intended to exploit the "seniors" consumer market are not included. Nor, with few exceptions, are such works as guides (to skills, Social Security, Medicare, etc.), directories (of medical specialists, retirement places, etc.), handbooks, and manuals. Books about "man's" (i.e., humankind's) aging have not been selected unless there is comparison or specific consideration of female sex/feminine gender concerns and issues.

Arrangement

The guide consists of chapters representing broad fields and areas as they relate to aging of women, mid-life women, and elderly women. Each is organized alphabetically by topics, which are listed in the table of contents and at the beginning of each chapter. It is important to use the subject index at the end of the volume in order to obtain complete access to information on topics of interest. Each title is displayed once within the chapter section that best represents its primary concern. Many topical subsections have been provided with notes placing them in context and enabling further research. These may include established subject headings (descriptors) useful in locating additional and post-1992 documents and information.

Alphabetization "as is," rather than based on assumptions or rules, is used. For example, McCarthy is listed as McCarthy, after MacDonald, and not before MacCarthy. The only exception is the conventional disregard of the articles (a, an, the) when they are the first word of a title.

Each entry consists of:

1. Its sequential *entry number*.

2. The *author*'s full name. Where there are two authors, editors, or compilers, both names are provided, but "et al" is used when there are more than two. Authors' and biographees' years of birth and death are frequently provided.

3. The full *title* in italics for books and periodicals. Chapters in books and articles in periodicals are displayed within quotation marks.

4. *Publication data* for books consist of city of publication, publisher, and date of publication, usually the latest copyright date. There follow: "bib" if there is significant bibliographic support; "il" if illustrated or provided with charts, diagrams, illustrations, tables, etc.; and "index" if indexed. If the book is part of a numbered series, that information may complete the publication data display.

Publication data for special issues of periodicals and articles and parts of books (usually a chapter) consist of inclusive pagination or chapter number, the article's title and author(s), volume and issue (if any) numbers, and the date and title of the publication in which the article or chapter appeared. Contents of some edited collections and volumes 1–4 (1989–1992/93) of the *Journal of Women & Aging* are analyzed. The following abbreviations as part of the bibliographic data display are used:

bib = bibliography
ed = editor, edition

il   = illustrated
index = index, indexed
J   = Journal
Q   = Quarterly
U   = University

ERIC is part of the National Institute of Education, a nationwide information system acquiring, indexing, abstracting, storing, and disseminating significant reports and projects. It defines education so broadly as to make these tools and documents relevant to social and behavioral scientists. Many of the indexed publications are available in microform in academic and large public libraries. The following entry illustrates the form used in the guide for documents available through ERIC:

> (2252) Mathews, Virginia H. "Libraries: Aids to Life Satisfaction for Older Women: A 1981 White House Conference on the Aging Background Paper." ERIC, September 1981. ED #215289. 97 pages.

- (2252) refers to its sequential entry number.
- Mathews, Virginia H. is the author.
- "Libraries: Aids to Life Satisfaction for Older Women: A 1981 White House Conference on the Aging Background Paper" is the title.
- ERIC, September 1981. ED #215289. 97 pages. These data locate and retrieve the document. They communicate the date the document was issued, the "ED" (education) document number, and the number of pages in the document.

The following entry illustrates the form used for doctoral dissertations included in the guide. (A few master's degree–level theses are also cited.) It is based on standard form in use internationally.

> (1743) Rosenberger, Nancy Ross. *Middle-Aged Japanese Women and the Meanings of the Menopausal Transition.* U of Michigan, 1984. 45/07A.

- (1743) refers to its sequential entry number.
- Rosenberger, Nancy Ross is the writer of the dissertation and recipient of the doctorate.
- *Middle-Aged Japanese Women and the Meanings of the Menopausal Transition* is the full title of the dissertation.
- U of Michigan is the institution granting the doctorate.
- 1984 is the year the degree was granted.
- 45/07A locates an abstract of this dissertation in Volume 45, Part A, Issue 7 of *Dissertation Abstracts International.* These abstracts are also accessible online.

5. A brief *annotation* is part of each book's entry to provide an idea of content, point of view, and place in the literature. Related readings, something about the author, special features, and possible limitations may be included.

The guide concludes with two alphabetical indexes, of authors and subjects. Indexing refers to entry numbers. Subject indexing relies on keywords derived from the sections and titles, supplemented by numerous cross-references (*see* and *see also*) and enhanced where necessary. Subject indexing also includes formats and genres so that there is access beyond subject matter per se to such things as bibliographies, biographies, diaries, fiction, and reviews.

Acquisition Information

Some books may be available in several versions, e.g., text, abridged, edited for various grade-level or age-ranges, etc.; and several formats, e.g., large print or type, illustrated, bindings, etc., in addition to hardcover and/or paperback. Consult the current edition of *Books in Print* ("BIP") for a full selection. A few entries for publications or publishers not available in standard reference tools are provided with source addresses. Addresses of most sources represented in the guide are listed in the BIP publishers' volume. Other standard tools available in many libraries and bookstores that provide bibliographic and/or source information include *The Directory of Little Magazines and Small Presses, The Small Press Record of Books in Print*, and *The Literary Market Place.*

University libraries have copies of doctoral dissertations written by their students, and other dissertations may also be found in their collections. Many can be borrowed by means of interlibrary loans. Reference to the *Comprehensive Dissertation Index* (to *Dissertation Abstracts International*) will provide information on how to purchase a microfilm or printed copy. Before doing this, consult your library's catalog, because the dissertation may be in its collection. The work may also have been published in trade-revision as a book with the same or a somewhat different title. For example, Phyllis Kernoff Mansfield's 1983 Ph.D. thesis, *Advanced Maternal Age and Pregnancy Outcome: A Critical Appraisal of the Scientific Literature,* may have such a relationship to her 1985 book *Pregnancy for Older Women: Assessing the Medical Risks.*

1
Gerontology and Women's Aging

*Beyond the age of twenty-one, apart from medical people who are in-
terested only in our gradual decay, we are left to fend for ourselves on
the way downstream to senescence, at which point we are picked up
again by the gerontologists.*

Gail Sheehy, 1937– , *Passages* (1976)

DEMOGRAPHIC PERSPECTIVES

1   **McLaughlin, Steven D., et al.** *The Changing Lives of American Women.* Chapel
Hill: U of North Carolina Press, 1988. bib, il, index.
      Many useful tables tracing twentieth-century changes in educational attain-
ment, marriage, divorce, premarital sexual behavior, labor force participation, child
bearing, etc. make this useful for current demographics and discussion of human life
cycle and attitudes toward and of women across three generations.

2   **O'Rand, Angela M.** "Women." In Erdman Palmore, ed. *Handbook of the Aged in
the U.S.* New York: Greenwood, 1984. Chapter 8.

3   **Rossi, Alice S.,** 1922– . "Demographic Dimensions of an Aging Population."
In Alan J. Pifer and Lydia Bronte, eds. *Our Aging Society.* New York: Norton, 1986.
79–110.

4   **U.S. Congress. Senate. Special Committee on Aging.** *Aging America: Trends and
Projections.* Washington: Department of Health and Human Services, 1990. bib, il.
      Each year beginning in 1984 this statistical compilation has been prepared in
conjunction with the American Association of Retired Persons. The Bureau of the Census's *Projections of the Population of the U.S. by Age, Sex, and Race: 1983–2080* in its Current Population Reports Series P25 (1984) is also useful.

5   **Zopf, Paul E., Jr.** *America's Older Population.* Houston: Cap and Gown Press,
1986.

Professor Zopf believes misconceptions include an American older population abandoned by adult offspring, living in nursing homes, poor, senile, and sexless. *See* Chapters 3 and 4, "Sex Composition of the Older Population" and "Marriage and Family Status of the Elderly."

Health and Health Care

Calcium and bone density

See also Health and Health Care: Osteoarthritis; osteoporosis (20–39).

6 **Gleeson, Margaret Mary Blake.** *The Effects of Weight-Lifting on Bone Mineral Density in Premenopausal Women.* Texas Woman's U, 1988. 49/10B.

7 **Kanders, Beatrice Stefannie.** *The Effect of Diet and Physical Activity on Bone Density in Females Ages 24 to 35.* Columbia U Teachers College, 1985. 46/03B.

8 **Loker, Sevim Fatima.** *Effect of Calcium-Carbonate Fortified Baked Products on Calcium Balance and Related Metabolism in Elderly Females.* Texas Woman's U, 1980. 41/05B.

9 **Reed, Judith Ann.** *Dietary Calcium and Bone Changes in Late Elderly Caucasian Women.* U of North Carolina at Chapel Hill, 1991. 51/10B.

10 **Riis, Bente, et al.** "Does Calcium Supplementation Prevent Postmenopausal Bone Loss? A Double-Blind, Controlled Clinical Study." *New England J of Medicine* January 22, 1987 316: 173–177.

11 **Tylavsky, Frances A.** *Determinants of Bone Mass in Elderly Women.* U of North Carolina at Chapel Hill, 1985. 47/01B.

Collections and compilations

12 **Doress-Worters, Paula Brown, and Diana Laskin Siegal.** *Ourselves, Growing Older: Women Aging with Knowledge and Power.* New York: Simon and Schuster, 1987. bib, il, index.
　　Prepared by the Midlife and Older Women Book Project in cooperation with the Boston Women's Health Book Collective, like *Our Bodies, Ourselves,* this deserves to be published in national editions and other languages. The aging and growing during the second half of life theme is organized in three sections: aging well; living with ourselves and others as we age; and understanding, preventing, and managing medical problems. The final chapter is by Tish Sommers, "Changing Society and Ourselves." *See also* #1423.

13 **Freedman, Rita Jackaway, and Sharon Golub, eds.** "Health Needs of Women as They Age" issue. *Women & Health* 10(2/3) 1985.

14 **Henig, Robin Marantz, et al.** *How a Woman Ages.* New York: Ballantine, 1985. bib, index.
　　Following Gail Sheehy's introduction, Henig and the editors of *Esquire* consider "Teeth, Bones, and Joints," "Babies and Beyond," the "Sensuous Woman," "Still Sexy at Sixty," and the "Myth of Senility."

Handicapped women

15   Armstrong, M. Jocelyn. "Friends as a Source of Informal Support for Older Women with Physical Disabilities." *J of Women & Aging* 1991 3(2): 63–83.

16   Browne, Susan E., et al. *With the Power of Each Breath: A Disabled Women's Anthology*. Pittsburgh: Cleis Press, 1985.
        A significant number of the fifty-four physically handicapped contributors of fiction, nonfiction, and poetry are middle-aged and old women.

17   Garner, Myrna B., and Vickie L. Douglass. "Apparel Needs of Aging and/or Disabled Women." *J of Women & Aging* 1991 3(4): 23–35.

18   Kinderknecht, Cheryl H., and J. Dianne Garner. "Living Productively with Sensory Loss." *J of Women & Aging* 1993 5(3/4): 155–180.

19   Kunkel, Suzanne Rose. *Gender Differences in Disability Among the Older Population*. U of Cincinnati, 1990. 52/02A.

Osteoarthritis; osteoporosis

See also this chapter: Health and Health Care: Calcium and bone density (6–11); this chapter: Health and Health Care: Physical activity; exercise; weight and strength training; athletics (40–69); Chapter 6, Health and Health Care: Estrogens; E.R.T.; Hormone replacement therapy (1172–1186).

> *Osteoporosis is a crippling, disfiguring disease due to bone loss in both sexes, although women are much more likely to be affected by it. After menopause, women lose bone mass six times more rapidly than men. Around age 65 the rate of bone loss slows. Related terms are* menopause *and* dowager's hump—*a stooped posture and characteristic sign resulting from vertebrae collapse (the term originated when the condition was most prevalent among old, upper-class women apt not to exercise).*

20   Downe-Wamboldt, Barbara L. *Stressors, Coping Strategies and Life Satisfaction of Elderly Women with Osteoarthritis*. U of Texas, Austin, 1990. 51/04B.

21   Farquhar, Diana Marie. *The Availability of Ready-to-Wear Clothing Incorporating Design Features Preferred by Elderly Arthritic Women*. Florida State U, 1981. 42/11B.

22   Kaplan, Frederick S., M.D. "Osteoporosis." *Women & Health* 1985 10(2/3): 95–114.

23   Kelsey, Jennifer L. "Epidemiology of Osteoporosis." In Ellen B. Gold, ed. *The Changing Risk of Disease in Women: An Epidemiological Approach*. Lexington: Heath, 1984. Chapter 21.

24   Kinderknecht, Cheryl H. "Social Work with the Osteoporotic Woman." *J of Women & Aging* 1992 4(1): 57–76.

25   Lindsay, Robert. "The Aging Skeleton." In Marie R. Haug, et al, eds. *The Physical and Mental Health of Aged Women*. New York: Springer, 1985. Chapter 45.

26   Lindsay, Robert, and Felicia Cosman. "Estrogen in Prevention and Treatment of Osteoporosis." In Marcha Flint, et al, eds. *Multidisciplinary Perspectives on*

Menopause: Annals of the New York Academy of Sciences (Volume 592). New York: The Academy, 1990. 326–333.

27   **MacPherson, Kathleen I.** "Osteoporosis and Menopause: A Feminist Analysis of the Social Construction of a Syndrome." *Advances in Nursing Science* 1985 7(4): 11–22.

28   **Mayes, Kathleen,** 1931– . *Osteoporosis: Brittle Bones and the Calcium Crisis.* Santa Barbara: Pennant, 1986. bib, index.

    Mayes considers risks, preventions, and cautions of osteoporosis, although she provides little information about estrogen replacement therapy.

29   **Melton, L. Joseph, III.** "Epidemiology of Osteoporosis: Predicting Who Is at Risk." In Marcha Flint, et al, eds. *Multidisciplinary Perspectives on Menopause: Annals of the New York Academy of Sciences* (Volume 592). New York: The Academy, 1990. 295–306.

30   **Notelovitz, Morris, M.D., and Marsha Ware.** *Stand Tall! The Informed Woman's Guide to Preventing Osteoporosis.* Houston: Triad, 1982. bib, il, index.

    Notelovitz and Ware discuss different types of calcium supplements and emphasize the great variety of osteoporosis and appropriate treatments—including hormone therapy—and prevention by means of diet, exercise, and lifestyle.

31   **Olson, Amy Clarke.** "Osteoporosis [review essay]." In Carol J. Leppa, ed. *Women's Health Perspectives: An Annual Review,* Volume 2. Phoenix: Oryx, 1989. Chapter 8.

32   **Roberto, Karen A.** "Adjusting to Chronic Disease: The Osteoporotic Woman." *J of Women & Aging* 1990 2(1): 33–47.

33   **Roberto, Karen A.** "Stress and Adaptation Patterns of Older Osteoporotic Women." *Women & Health* 1988 14(3/4): 105–120.

34   **Roberto, Karen A., and Shelley McGraw.** "Self-Perceptions of Older Women with Osteoporosis." *J of Women & Aging* 1991 3(1): 59–70.

35   **Silbergeld, Ellen K., et al.** "Lead and Osteoporosis: Mobilization of Lead from Bone in Postmenopausal Women." *Environmental Research* October 1988 47(1): 79–94.

36   **Smith, Wendy,** 1956– . *Osteoporosis; How to Prevent the Brittle-Bone Disease.* New York: Simon & Schuster, 1985. bib, il, index.

    Smith and consultant Stanton H. Cohn's guide emphasizes prevention of the disease for which there is no cure, only treatment.

37   **Tiffany, Joyce Ethel.** *The Older Woman and the Experience of Osteoporosis.* Texas Woman's U, 1988. 50/04B.

38   **Watts, Nelson B., M.D.** "Intermittent Cyclical Etidronate Treatment of Postmenopausal Osteoporosis." *New England J of Medicine* July 12, 1990 323(2): 73–79.

39   **Whatley, Marianne H., and Nancy Worcester.** "The Role of Technology in the Co-Optation of the Women's Health Movement: The Cases of Osteoporosis and Breast Cancer Screening." In Kathryn Strother Ratcliff, et al, eds. *Healing Technology: Feminist Perspectives.* Ann Arbor: U of Michigan Press, 1989. 199–220.

Physical activity; exercise; weight and strength training; athletics

See also Health and Health Care: Osteoarthritis; osteoporosis (20–39).

40   **Aldrich, Joanne.** *The Relationship Between Health Perceptions and Exercise Habits in Elderly Females.* Boston U, 1986. 47/05A.

41   **Baker, Marshina.** *Physiological Effects of Exercise upon Females Aged 55 and Above.* North Carolina Central U, 1984. M.S. thesis.

42   **Brown, Rebecca D.** *Effects of a Strength Training Program on Strength, Body Composition, and Self-Concept of [Middle-Aged] Females.* Brigham Young U, 1985. 46/09A.

43   **Caramelli, Kim Ellen,** 1959– . *Effect of Load Bearing During Treadmill Walking in Women Aged 57 to 67.* U of Florida, 1984. M.A. thesis.

44   **Carpenter, James Richard, Jr.** *The Effect of Exercise on Several Physiological and Psychological Variables Among Three Elderly Female Subjects.* West Virginia U, 1982. 43/11A.

45   **Cosky, Alicia C.** *The Effect of Aerobic Exercise on Fitness Status, Cognition, and Health Locus-of-Control in Older Women.* Northern Illinois U, 1989. 51/01A.

46   **Daly, Janice Ann.** *Effect of Exercise on Indices of Bone Integrity in Postmenopausal Women.* Florida State U, 1987. 49/03B.

47   **Dan, Alice J., et al.** "Lifelong Physical Activity in Midlife and Older Women." *Psychology of Women Q* December 1990 14(4): 531–542.

48   **Dowdy, Deborah Belle.** *The Effects of Aerobic Dance on Physical Work Capacity, Cardiovascular Function and Body Composition of Middle-Aged Women.* U of Georgia, 1982. 43/11A.

49   **Eggers, Jean Lee.** *Well-Elderly Women's Entrance and Adherence to Structured Physical Fitness Programs.* U of Cincinnati, 1986. 47/07A.

50   **Fegan, Debra Lyn.** *Cross-Validation of the American College of Sports Medicine's Metabolic Prediction Equation for Walking in Older Females.* San Jose State U, 1992. M.A. thesis.

51   **Fonda, Jane,** 1937– . *Women Coming of Age.* New York: Simon & Schuster, 1984. il, index.
      Written with Mignon McCarthy, Fonda's second workout book is intended to meet the special needs of mid-life women, and is one of the better examples of this genre. Fonda and McCarthy consider the aging female body, menopause, nutrition, grooming, and working out as well as personal reminiscences.

52   **Foster, Vicky Lynn.** *VO(2)Max Test-Retest Reliability and Alteration in Aerobic and Anaerobic Metabolism in Elderly Women Resulting from an Individualized Exercise Program.* U of Colorado at Boulder, 1983. 44/09A.

53   **Fournier, Susan M., and Gary A. Fine.** "Jumping Grannies. Exercise as a Buffer Against Becoming 'Old.'" *Play & Culture* November 1990 3(4): 337–342.

54   **Heislein, Diane M.** *Strength Training in Aging Women: A Pilot Study.* MGH Institute of Health Professions, 1991. M.S. thesis.

55   Johnson, Sandra Kay. *Time-Series Analysis of Individual Performances of Older Women on a Serial Gross Motor Task*. U of North Carolina at Greensboro, 1982. 43/07A.

56   Khoury-Murphy, Milady, and Michael Dean Murphy. "Southern Bar(Belles): The Cultural Problematics of Implementing a Weight Training Program Among Older Southern Women." *Play and Culture* 1992 5(4): 409–419.

57   Lenzini, Kathy L. *Cross-Validation of the Rockport Fitness Walking Test in Females 65 Years and Older*. Northern Illinois University, 1989. M.S. thesis.

58   McLaughlin, William Kirk-Patrick. *The Effects of an Age-Specific Exercise Program on Aerobic Capacity, Body Composition, Body-Image and Exercise Behavior in 42–77 Year-Old Women*. U of Maryland, College Park, 1983. 44/12A.

59   Meyer, Nancy Lynn. *The Effects of Ten Weeks of Strength and Flexibility Training on the Strength, Flexibility, Body Circumferences, and Self-Perceptions of Middle and Late-Middle Aged Women*. U of Northern Colorado, 1986. 47/12A.

60   Morocco, Kathleen M. *Age, Physical Activity Patterns, Estrogen Levels and Central Circulatory Responses of Postmenopausal Women to Acute Submaximal Exercise*. U of North Carolina at Greensboro, 1986. 48/02B.

61   O'Brien, Sandra J., and Patricia A. Vertinsky. "Elderly Women, Exercise, and Healthy Aging." *J of Women & Aging* 1990 2(3): 41–65.

62   Owens, J. F., et al. "Can Physical Activity Mitigate the Effects of Aging in Middle-Aged Women?" *Circulation* April 1992 85(4): 1265–1270.

63   Peiffer, Roxane Ethlyn. *Effects of Aging on Selected Measures of Muscular Strength and Endurance, Physical Activity Level and Body Composition Between Men and Women*. U of Pittsburgh, 1986. 47/10A.

64   Pepe, Margaret Veronica. *An Exploration of the Differences Between Adult Women Who Participated in the 1985 State-Level Ohio Senior Olympics and Adult Women Nonparticipants Utilizing Social Exchange Theory*. Kent State U, 1986. 47/09A.

65   Richardson-Lehnhard, Holly Jo. *The Effects of Training on Selected Steroid Hormones: Response to Exercise in Postmenopausal Women*. Ohio State U, 1984. 45/08A.

66   Stillman, Rachel Bryan. *The Influence of Physical Activity on Bone Mineral Content in Women over Eighteen Years of Age*. U of Illinois at Urbana-Champaign, 1988. 49/09B.

67   Swan, Pamela Diane. *The Effect of Habitual Physical Activity on Left Ventricular End Diastolic Diameter and Left Ventricular Posterior Wall Thickness: In Postmenopausal Women as Measured by M-Mode Echocardiography*. U of North Carolina at Greensboro, 1987. M.S. thesis.

68   Titzel, Melanie R. *The Effects of a Dance-Movement Program on the Self-Concept of Institutionalized, Intermediate Care, Female, Elderly*. Pennsylvania State U, 1986. M.S. thesis.

69   Upton, Sarah Jill. *A Comparison of Cardiorespiratory Fitness of Trained and Untrained Middle-Aged Women*. Texas Woman's U, 1981. 42/08A.

INTERDISCIPLINARY COLLECTIONS

70   Abel, Emily K., ed. "Women and Aging" issue. *Women's Studies Q* Spring/Summer 1989 17(1/2).

71   Alexander, Jo, 1910– , et al, eds. *Women and Aging: An Anthology by Women.* Corvallis: Calyx, 1986. bib, il.
The Calyx Editorial Collective produced this very positive anthology of photographs, essays, fiction, poetry, profiles, art, and reviews, with an extensive bibliography. Essays reprinted from *Broomstick, Equal Times, Sinister Wisdom, Sojourner,* etc. and contributions by Ursula K. LeGuin, Marge Piercy, Margaret Randall, Mary Tallmountain, May Sarton, Elizabeth Layton, Barbara Macdonald, etc., make this enjoyable and useful in the classroom. *Library Journal's* reviewer referred to this as "strong stuff from old women" (April 1, 1986).

72   Garner, J. Dianne, and Susan O. Mercer, eds. "Women as They Age: Challenge, Opportunity and Triumph" issue. *J of Women & Aging* 1989 1(1/2/3).

73   Gee, Ellen Margaret Thomas, 1950– , and Meredith M. Kimball. *Women and Aging.* Toronto: Butterworths, 1987. bib, index.
The authors provide an overview of social science literature on Canadian women's middle and old age; they believe that "the lack of power and status characteristics of older women results from limited options open to them earlier in their lives." Needed are pension reform, preventive self-directed health care, retirement planning, support for caregivers, mass-media monitoring, and greater integration into society (equality).

74   Gold, Ellen B., ed. *The Changing Risk of Disease in Women: An Epidemiological Approach.* Lexington: Heath, 1984. bib, index.
Almost all of these papers from a symposium held at Johns Hopkins University in 1981 relate to women's age and aging, e.g., E. Goldberg's "Health Effects of Becoming Widowed" and J. Kelsey's "Epidemiology of Osteoporosis."

75   Grau, Lois, and Ida Susser, eds. "Women in the Later Years: Health, Social and Cultural Perspectives" issue. *Women & Health* 1988 14(3/4). Also New York: Harrington Park Press, 1989. il.

76   Lesnoff-Caravaglia, Gari, ed. *The World of the Older Woman: Conflicts and Resolutions.* Frontiers in Aging Series, Volume 3. New York: Human Sciences Press, 1984. bib, il, index.
All older women are recognized as a special segment of the population, with special needs, interests, and concerns. Suggestions are provided for the resolution of some of the problems and development of needed services. Some of these papers have appeared elsewhere. Topics include rape and other abuse, cross-cultural experiences, the double standard, policy and legal issues, menopause, and widows.

77   Markson, Elizabeth W., ed. *Older Women: Issues and Prospects.* Lexington: Heath, 1987. bib, index.
This collection of original essays includes "The Crossroads of Menopause"; "The Sexuality of Older Women"; "Beyond the Sweatshop: Older Women in Blue-Collar Jobs"; "Shopping Bag Women: Aging Deviants in the City"; and "Suburban Older

Women." Sociologist-gerontologist Markson contends that as women age, they become more dominant and assertive, while men become less so.

78   **McCarthy, Mary Sue, et al, eds.** "Growing into Age" issue. *Canadian Woman Studies/Les Cahiers de la Femme* Winter 1992 12(6–9).

79   **Ory, Marcia G., and Huber R. Warner, eds.** *Gender, Health, and Longevity: Multidisciplinary Perspectives.* New York: Springer, 1990.
         The specialist writers surpass the usual single-discipline study that emphasizes one factor over another to explain the gender gap in mortality and morbidity—why women have higher levels of illness and disability than men, yet live longer.

2
Psychological Perspectives on Women's Aging

The nurse I spoke to said sedation had no effect; the new patient was "having some trouble adjusting." "Adjusting" and "adjustment" were words much in use by the staff at Golden Mesa [nursing home]. Patients were always perfectly happy once they had "made a proper adjustment."

Anthropologist Carobeth Laird, 1895–1983, *Limbo* (1979)

ANDROGYNY

From the Greek andros *(man, male) and* gyne *(woman)—possessing both traditionally masculine and feminine characteristics—and thus, a psychological consideration related to gender rather than to sex. Sex and gender are also terms that are damaging when confounded: sex defines male and female, usually biological; gender describes masculine and feminine, usually acquired characteristics.*

80   Grober, Susan E. *Androgyny and Adjustment to Aging: A Study of Sex Roles in Later Life.* New School for Social Research, 1988. 47/08B.

81   **Gutmann, David L.,** 1925– . *Reclaimed Powers: Toward a New Psychology of Men and Women in Later Life.* New York: Basic Books, 1987. bib, il, index.

Chapters 6, "The Inner Liberation of the Older Woman: Psychological and Fantasy Measures," and 7, "The Virile Older Woman: Across History and Across Cultures," argue for realizing the potentials denied women and men prior to the childrearing period of life—women can assume the assertive, competitive stance held by their spouses, and men can become contemplative as well as assertive.

82   **Rasmussen, Susan J.** "Interpreting Androgynous Woman: Female Aging and Personhood Among the Kel Ewey Tuareg." *Ethnology: An International J of Cultural and Social Anthropology.* January 1987 26(1): 17–30.

83   **Tucker, Trent Cowan.** *The Perceived Attractiveness of Sex-Typed and Androgynous Sex-Role Qualities in Males and Females Across the Life Span.* U of Kentucky, 1987. 49/02B.

Appearance; Clothing
See also Chapter 4: Consumerism; Credit (718–722).

84   **Baruch, Grace Kesterman,** 1936–1988. *Lifeprints: New Patterns of Love and Work for Today's Woman.* New York: McGraw, 1982. bib, index.
        Numerous studies and surveys consisting of questionnaires and some follow-up interviews have been made by social scientists interested in middle-aged women's "problems" assumed to be associated with the aging process. Baruch and Rosalind Barnett and Caryl Rivers's study focused instead on the causes of mid-life women's feelings about themselves and their well-being. Their population consisted of Caucasian women aged 35–55 in the United States.

85   **Berkun, Cleo S.** "Changing Appearance for Women in the Middle Years of Life: Trauma?" In Elizabeth W. Markson, ed. *Older Women: Issues and Prospects.* Lexington: Heath, 1987. Chapter 1.

86   **Berkun, Cleo S.** *Perception of Changing Appearance, Aging and Mood in Middle-Aged Women.* U of California, Berkeley, 1981. 42/07A.

87   **Cole, K. C.** "Aging Bull: Is It Possible to Stave Off the Inevitable? Or Merely Foolish to Try?" *Ms* April 1989 17: 44+.

88   **Freedman, Rita.** "Myth America Grows Older." In her *Beauty Bound: Why We Pursue the Myth in the Mirror.* Lexington: Lexington Books, 1986. Chapter 9.

89   **McGovern, Susan Rose.** *The Value of Thinness in Females: Age and Sex-Role Factors.* Emory U, 1988. 49/07B.

90   **Melamed, Elissa,** 1931– . *Mirror, Mirror: The Terror of Not Being Young.* New York: Linden Press/Simon & Schuster, 1983. bib.
        Dr. Melamed recognizes the power of the media (Chapter 6, "Mixed Messages: Older Women and the Media"), and she acknowledges that negative responses to older women constitute discrimination. In this work based on interviews of middle-aged women, she contends that women can and must change the ageism/sexism double standard if they are to achieve equity.

91   **Oldman, Marilyn.** *The Application of Rational-Emotive Therapy to the Middle-Aged Woman's Distress About Looking Older.* Fairleigh Dickinson U, 1987. 47/12A.

92   O'Sullivan, William Mitchell. *A Study of the Relationship Between Life Satisfaction of the Aged and Perceptions They Hold Concerning Their Own Masculinity or Femininity.* New York U, 1980. 41/02B.

93   Simons, Nancy Jane. *The Differential Effects of Declining Attractiveness on Pre-Middle-Aged, Middle-Aged and Advanced-Middle-Aged Women.* SUNY at Buffalo, 1984. 45/11B.

94   Spruiell, Phyllis R., et al. "Clothing Preferences of Older Women: Implications for Gerontology and the American Clothing Industry." *Educational Gerontology* September-October 1982 8(5): 485–492.

95   Stimpson, Catharine R. "The Fallacy of Bodily Reductionism." In Ann Mae Voda, et al, eds. *Changing Perspectives on Menopause.* Austin: U of Texas Press, 1982. Chapter 19.

96   VanItallie, Theodore B., M.D. "The Perils of Obesity in Middle-Aged Women [editorial]." *New England J of Medicine* March 29, 1990 322(12): 928–929.

COUNSELING AND THERAPIES
See also this chapter: Mental Health (235–261).

97   Banks, Martha E., et al. "Elderly Women in Family Therapy." *Women & Therapy* Summer/Fall 1986 5(2/3): 107–116.

98   Bocksnick, Jochen Gerd. *Effectiveness of a Physical Activity Adherence Counseling Program with Older Females.* U of Alberta (Canada), 1991. 53/02A.

99   Brown, Nancy Eynon. *Psychosocial Variables That Discriminate Between Midlife Homemakers and Homemaker–Graduate Students as an Aid to Lifespan Counseling.* U of Akron, 1985. 45/09A.

100   Burnside, Irene M. "Group Work with Older Women: A Modality to Improve the Quality of Life." *J of Women & Aging* 1989 1(1/2/3): 265–290.

101   Cavallaro, Marion L. "Curriculum Guidelines and Strategies on Counseling Older Women for Incorporation into Gerontology and Counseling Coursework." *Educational Gerontology* March-April 1991 17(2): 157–166.

102   Chandler, Judith Babb. *A Comparison of the Self-Expressed Counseling Needs of Mid-Life and Older Women Enrolled in Four Georgia Adult Basic Education Settings Based on the Perceptions of Coordinators, Teachers, Aides, and Counselors.* U of Georgia, 1984. 45/09A.

103   Collier, Helen V. *Counseling Women: A Guide for Therapists.* New York: Free Press, 1982. bib, index.
    Includes "Older Women, Lesbians, and Female Offenders" and "What Is 'Sex-Fair' Therapy?" Naomi Gottlieb's *Alternative Social Services for Women* (New York: Columbia U Press, 1980) also considers older women, women in midstream, and displaced homemaker client groups. Carol Tavris and Dianne L. Chambless include mid-life, old age, and depression in *Everywoman's Emotional Well-Being* (New York: Doubleday, 1986).

104   Crose, Royda. "What's Special About Counselling Older Women?" *Canadian J of Counselling* October 1991 25(4): 617–623.

105   **Ferguson, James Dominic.** *Reminiscence Counseling to Increase Psychological Well-Being of Elderly Women in Nursing Home Facilities.* U of South Carolina, 1980. 41/09B.

106   **Hebl, John H.** *Forgiveness as a Counseling Goal with Elderly Females.* U of Wisconsin, 1990. 51/04A.

107   **Larimore, Helen,** 1928– . *Older Women in Recovery: Sharing Experience, Strength, and Hope.* Deerfield Beach: Health Communications, 1992. bib.
      Larimore is an addictions therapist consultant in Chicago; she recognizes the damage done by ageism and sexism as well as the need for responsible caretakers. These interviews urge getting on with life.

108   **Patten, Pamela C., and Fred P. Piercy.** "Feminist Therapy: Theoretical Considerations for Elderly Couples." *J of Feminist Family Therapy* 1989 1(3): 57–72.

109   **Schlesinger, Rachel A.** "Midlife Transitions Among Jewish Women: Counseling Issues." *Women & Therapy* 1990 10(4): 91–100.

110   **Stern, E. Mark, ed.,** 1919– . "Psychotherapy and the Widowed Patient" issue. *The Psychotherapy Patient* 1990 6(3/4).

Death and Dying
See also this chapter: Grief and Bereavement (153–174); Chapter 3: Self-Deliverance; Assisted Suicide; Right to Die (627–636).

111   **Marzen, Thomas J.** "In the Matter of [84-year-old] Claire C. Conroy." *Issues in Law and Medicine* July 1985 1(1): 77–84.

112   **McKinley, James C., Jr.** "Retired Nurse [83-year-old Gladys H. Queen] Is Bludgeoned to Death in Brooklyn." *New York Times* November 18, 1990 140(1): 38.

113   **O'Laughlin, Kay.** "The Final Challenge: Facing Death." In Elizabeth W. Markson, ed. *Older Women: Issues and Prospects.* Lexington: Heath, 1987. Chapter 13.

114   **Richter, Judith Anne M.** *Perceptions of Resources That Helped Widows and Widowers During the Dying Process of Their Mates.* U of Colorado Health Sciences Center, 1984. 45/05B.

115   **Stillion, Judith M.,** 1937– . *Death and the Sexes: An Examination of Differential Longevity, Behaviors, and Coping Skills.* Washington: Hemisphere, 1985. bib, index.
      Stillion reviews possible causes for the sex differential in death from biological, psychosocial, and environmental perspectives, including "Sex Roles and Death Attitudes Across the Life Span" and "Murder, Suicide, and the Sexes."

Dementia
See also this chapter: Mental Health (235–261).

116   **Danforth, Art.** *Living with Alzheimer's: Ruth's Story: The Personal Story of Two Victims of Senile Dementia.* Falls Church, Virginia: Prestige Press, 1984. bib.
      A husband's frank account of daily life as he coped with his wife's physical and mental deterioration is an expression of fear and concern as well as anger and guilt.

117   **Edwards, Henry.** *What Happened to My Mother.* New York: Harper, 1981.
Changes in behavior and even a mental breakdown went unnoticed by both her husband and son (the writer), as the wife/mother deteriorated. Hospitalized, she was faced additionally with Parkinson's disease. Ultimately, a different physician and hospital led to her recovery.

118   **Gutmann, David L., 1925–** . "Developmental Perspectives on the Diagnosis and Treatment of Psychiatric Illness in the Older Woman." In Marie R. Haug, et al, eds. *The Physical and Mental Health of Aged Women.* New York: Springer, 1985. Chapter 8.

119   **Holland, Gail Bernice, 1940–** . *For Sasha with Love: An Alzheimer's Crusade: The Anne Bashkiroff Story.* New York: Dembner, 1985.
In a 1990 interview Anne Bashkiroff declared, "Looking back, I am appalled at my memories of being a caregiver. . . . It was nothing to do with love. Whatever a caregiver feels for her partner, she will feel more if she feels good about herself." Her ordeal led her to work for change, including this book that includes a research update. This is the candid account of her experiences and emotions during the eight years she cared for her spouse as Alzheimer's disease took his memory, his intellect, and his control over his body.

120   **Karlin, Nancy J., and Paul A. Bell.** "Self-Efficacy, Affect, and Seeking Support Between Caregivers of Dementia and Non-Dementia Patients." *J of Women & Aging* 1992 4(3): 59–77.

121   **Kawai, Makoto, J., M.D., et al.** "Five Elderly Dementia Patients Who Played with Dolls." *J of Women & Aging* 1990 2(1): 99–107.

122   **Powell, Lenore S.** "Alzheimer's Disease: A Practical, Psychological Approach." *Women & Health* Summer/Fall 1985 10(2/3): 53–62.

123   **Rubin, Judith A.** *Comparisons of Marital Relationship Measures Among Elderly Wives of Alzheimer's, Chronically Ill and Healthy Spouses.* U of Wisconsin, Madison, 1991. 53/03A.

124   **Rusk, Carla Lee.** *Alzheimer's Disease: Effects on the Family.* U.S. International U, 1986. 47/05B.

DEPRESSION; TERMINAL ILLNESS
See also this chapter: Mental Health (235–261).

125   **Adams, Sheryl Lee.** *Depression and Marital Satisfaction, Among Married Women Ages 25 to 44, as a Function of Intimacy, Control, and Interpersonal Dependency.* Florida State U, 1989. 50/06A.

126   **Baker, Robert Norman.** *The Interpersonal Dimensions of Geriatric Depression: A Structural Analysis of Mother-Daughter Relationships.* U of Rosemead School of Psychology, 1988. 49/08B.

127   **Carr, Meredith Ann.** *The Effects of Aging and Depression on Time Perspective in Women.* Columbia U, 1985. 46/08A

128   **Davis-Berman, Jennifer.** "Physical Self-Efficacy and Depressive Symptomatology in Older Women: A Group Treatment Approach." *J of Women & Aging* 1989 1(4): 29–40.

129   Fiorot, Michele Anne. *Personality, Depression, and Response to Psychotherapy in Elderly Female Patients.* U of Miami, 1987. 49/01B.

130   Formanek, Ruth, and Anita Gurian, eds. *Women and Depression: A Lifespan Perspective.* New York: Springer, 1987. bib, index.
       Part 4 is devoted to "Depression in the Aging Woman." Chapters 16, "Depression and Menopause: A Socially Constructed Link," and 17, "Depression and the Older Woman," are by Formanek. Chapter 18, "'Old Wives' Tales': Retrospective Views of Women over 65," is by Lisa R. Greenberg.

131   Gardner, Margaret A. *Prevalence and Correlates of Depressive Symptoms in Aged Black Females: Some Preliminary Findings.* U of Kentucky, 1990. 50/12B.

132   Handmaker, Muriel Beton. *The Effects of Early Parental Death and Exit Events on Depression in Older Men and Women.* U of Louisville, 1984. 45/11B.

133   Holzer, Charles I., III, et al. "Living with Depression." In Marie R. Haug, et al, eds. *The Physical and Mental Health of Aged Women.* New York: Springer, 1985. Chapter 7.

134   Krames, Lester, et al. "The Role of Masculinity and Femininity in Depression and Social Satisfaction in Elderly Families." *Sex Roles* December 1988 19: 713–721.

135   Kusama, Susan McGuire. *The Activities of Depressed Women Aged 30–60: Behavioral Cognitive and Affective Meaning Perspectives.* Washington U, 1987. 48/07B.

136   Lipkin, Laura Robin. *Rorschach Performance as a Test of a Theory of Late Onset Depression in Women.* Temple U, 1988. 49/07B.

137   Louie, Douglas. *Sex Difference in the Life Experience: Depression Relationship Among the Elderly.* Syracuse U, 1984. 46/02A.

138   Mader, Shirley Titcomb. *Depression as Loneliness in Post-Generative Women: A Crisis of Faith Development.* Boston U, 1986. 47/07A.

139   Martinez, Eduardo M. *Social Support and Life Events as Predictors of Quality of Life and Depression in a Sample of Retired Women.* George Peabody College for Teachers of Vanderbilt U, 1986. 47/07B.

140   Mastrogeorge, Barbara Lee. *The Effects of Locus-of-Control and Chronic Illness Status on Geriatric Depression Scale Scores in Communities of Elderly Women.* Fielding Institute, 1990. 51/12A.

141   McKinlay, John B., and Sonja M. McKinlay. "Depression in Middle-Aged Women: Social Circumstances Versus Estrogen Deficiency." In Mary Roth Walsh, ed. *The Psychology of Women: Ongoing Debates.* New Haven: Yale U Press, 1987. 157–161.

142   McKinlay, John B., et al. "The Relative Contributions of Endocrine Changes and Social Circumstances to Depression in Mid-Aged Women." *J of Health & Social Behavior* December 1987 28(4): 345–363.

143   Pilgram, Beverly Oretha. *Depression in Elderly Black Women.* Memphis State U, 1991. M.S. thesis.

144   Thomas, Dona Neal. *Influence of Creativity, Depression, and Psychological Well-Being on Physiological and Psychological Symptoms in Midlife Women.* Texas Woman's U, 1988. 49/10B.

145   **Thomas, Joyce Ann.** *The Effect of a Life Management Skills Program on Depression and Grief in Widows.* Michigan State U, 1982. 43/05B.

146   **Ungerstedt-Savage, Lena Therese.** *Giving Voice to Hope in the Despair of Aging Women: An Approach to Despair, Depression and Anxiety.* Boston U, 1987. 47/11A.

147   **Wasson, Wendy.** *The Dynamisms of Depressive Experience Among Women in Late Life.* Northwestern U, 1986. 47/06B.

148   **Weaver, Dolores Custer.** *A Study to Determine the Effect of Exercise on Depression in Middle-Aged Women.* Tennessee State U, 1984. 45/07A.

149   **Zappone, Karen Krabacher.** *The Relationship of Sex-Role Identity, Perception of Husbands' Attitudes Toward Women and Marital Adjustment to Depression in Reentry Women.* California School of Professional Psychology, San Diego, 1987. 48/09A.

GENERATION GAP; "SANDWICH GENERATION"

Sandwich generation *usually refers to adult children of the aged who are sandwiched between parents and children. A closely related term is* women in the middle—*females who have responsibilities for both their dependent children and parents and parents-in-law.*

150   **Older Women's League.** *Failing America's Caregivers: A Status Report on Women Who Care.* Washington: OWL, 1989.
        OWL reports on the sandwich generation—those who care for children and elderly relatives. The typical woman can expect to spend seventeen years caring for children and eighteen years caring for older family members.

151   **Sloan, Bernard.** *The Best Friend You'll Ever Have.* New York: Crown, 1980.
        A Neil Simon–like photo of the author appears with ad-writer Sloan's personal narrative of the final stage of his widowed, Jewish American mother's life—her death from cancer. The generation gap between mother and son, who has been married for twenty years to a Protestant, is clear; and the reader comes to feel for both.

152   **Zal, H. Michael.** "The Sandwich Generation." In his *The Sandwich Generation: Caught Between Growing Children and Aging Parents.* New York: Insight Books/Plenum Press, 1992. Part III.

GRIEF AND BEREAVEMENT

See also this chapter: Death and Dying (111–115).

153   **Abramson, Jane Beber.** *Evaluation of the Effects of Separation on Adaptation to Loss in Older Women Who Have Lost Their Mothers.* Northwestern U, 1984. 45/12B.

154   **Baugher, Robert James, Jr.** *Perception of the Widow's Bereavement Process by Her Adult Child.* Vanderbilt U, 1986. 47/08B.

155   **Baugher, Robert James, Jr., and Naftali G. Berrill.** "Perceptions of the Widow's Bereavement Process by Her Adult Children." *J of Women & Aging* 1991 3(3): 21–38.

156   **Bennett, Gillian.** "Heavenly Protection and Family Unity: The Concept of the Relevant Among Elderly Urban Women." *Folklore* 1985 96(1): 87–97.

157   **Biggers, Trisha A.** *The Relationship Between the Grief Reaction of Older Widows and Their Level of Ego Development.* U of Florida, 1981. 43/01A.

158   **Bright, Carole Katherine.** *A Study of the Impact of Normal and Atypical Grief Patterns on the Health and Living Environment of Institutionalized and Non-Institutionalized Elderly Widows.* U of San Francisco, 1985. 47/04A.

159   **Burnside, Irene.** "Adjustment to Family Losses: Grief in Frail Elderly Women." In Marie R. Haug, et al, eds. *The Physical and Mental Health of Aged Women.* New York: Springer, 1985. Chapter 11.

160   **Caserta, Michael S., et al.** "Older Widows' Early Bereavement Adjustments." *J of Women & Aging* 1989 1(4): 5–27.

161   **Duvall, Richard Leigh.** *Method of Burial and Its Relationship to the Intensity of Widows' Grief.* U.S. International U, 1983. 44/11B.

162   **Ferraro, Jerrold Samuel.** *Psychological Variables Affecting the Grief of Variably Aged Widows.* U of Texas at Austin, 1984. 45/08B.

163   **Gallagher, Dolores E., et al.** "Effects of Bereavement on Indicators of Mental Health in Elderly Widows and Widowers." *J of Gerontology* September 1983 38: 565–571.

164   **Gass, Kathleen Ann.** *Appraisal of Bereavement, Coping Counterharm Resources, and Health Status of Conjugally Bereaved Aged Widows.* Case Western Reserve U, 1984. 45/09B.

165   **Golden, Clifford Stephan.** *The Effect of a Structured Group Training Program upon the Bereavement Syndrome of Volunteer Widowed Participants.* U of Miami, 1984. 46/01B.

166   **Julius, Nancy.** *Conjugal Bereavement in the Elderly: Medical and Psychological Outcomes.* Yeshiva U, 1985. 46/11B.

167   **LeShan, Eda J.** "Widowhood: Loss, Grief, and Letting Go." In her *Oh, to Be 50 Again! On Being Too Old for a Mid-Life Crisis.* New York: Times Books, 1986. 314–332.

168   **Lund, Dale A., ed.** *Older Bereaved Spouses: Research with Practical Applications.* New York: Hemisphere, 1989. bib, il, index.
        The influence of gender on the bereavement process shows these psychologists that there are more similarities than differences between males and females. None of their eight conclusions refers to significant difference between women and men as bereaved spouses, although widows reported significantly more difficulty than divorced women with their social adjustment.

169   **Petiet, Carole Anne.** *Grief in Divorcees and Widows: Similarities, Differences, and Treatment Implications.* California School of Professional Psychology, Berkeley, 1982. 43/06B.

170   **Robbins, Martha Ann,** 1942– . *Midlife Women and Death of Mother: A Study of Psychohistorical and Spiritual Transformation.* New York: Peter Lang, 1990. bib, index.
        Robbins examines the experience of maternal bereavement for middle-aged women in this volume based on her 1988 Harvard University doctoral thesis (49/07A) of the same title.

171   **Scadron, Arlene.** "Letting Go: Bereavement Among Selected Southwestern Anglo Widows." In her *On Their Own: Widows and Widowhood in the American Southwest, 1848–1939.* Champaign-Urbana: U of Illinois Press, 1989. Chapter 10.

172   **Silverman, Phyllis R.** *Helping Women Cope with Grief.* Beverly Hills: Sage, 1981. Intended to provide information about services in the United States for helping grieving widows, this somewhat mistitled book is a tool for social welfare work.

173   **Stillion, Judith M.** "Women and Widowhood: The Suffering Beyond Grief." In Jo Freeman, ed. *Women: A Feminist Perspective, 3d ed.* Palo Alto: Mayfield, 1984. 282–293.

174   **Warner, Sandra Lou Easton.** *A Comparative Study of Widows and Widowers Based upon Measurements of Grief and Social Support (Gender-Role).* U of Texas at Austin, 1985. 46/12A.

LIFE SATISFACTION AND WELLBEING; CONTROL
See also Chapter 11.

175   **Abu-Laban, Sharon McIrvin.** "Women and Aging: A Futurist Perspective." *Psychology of Women Q* Fall 1981 6(1): 85–98.

176   **Baglioni, Anthony John, Jr.** *A Structural Equation Approach to Life Satisfaction Among Elderly Migrant Women.* U of Virgina, 1986. 48/02B.

177   **Bearon, Lucille Beth.** *No Great Expectations: The Nature of Life Satisfaction in a Sample of Elderly Women.* Duke U, 1982. 43/05A.

178   **Bearon, Lucille Beth.** "No Great Expectations: The Underpinnings of Life Satisfaction for Older Women." *Gerontologist* December 1989 29(6): 772–778.

179   **Blaker, Karen.** *Celebrating Fifty: Women Share Their Experiences, Challenges, and Insights on Becoming 50.* Chicago: Contemporary Books, 1990. bib. Psychologist Blaker's reader survey of fifty women is presented as an affirmation of American middle-aged women.

180   **Burnside, Irene Mortenson.** *The Effect of Reminiscence Groups on Fatigue, Affect, and Life Satisfaction in Older Women.* U of Texas at Austin, 1990. 51/09B.

181   **Cartland, Barbara Hamilton,** 1902– . *Getting Older, Growing Younger.* New York: Dodd, Mead, 1984. Cartland is the prolific English writer of romantic fiction and advice books, such as this cliched title about her health foods devotion. Her multi-volume autobiography concludes with *I Seek the Miraculous,* published in 1978 (London: Sheldon).

182   **Cotroneo, Maria Louise.** *A Comparison of Life Satisfaction of Single and Married Women After Retirement.* D'Youville College, 1988. M.S. thesis.

183   **Downey, Nancy.** "Mindfulness Training: The Effect of Process and Outcome Instructions on the Experience of Control and the Level of Mindfulness Among Older Women." *Educational Gerontology* March-April 1991 17(2): 97–109.

184   **Fletcher, Shirley.** *An Investigation of the Relationship of Locus of Control and Social Opportunity to Life Satisfaction and Purpose in Life Among Elderly Women.* New York U, 1981. 42/12B.

185   **Ford, Marsha S.** *The Relationship of Self-Concept and Self-Direction to Life Satisfaction in Elderly Women.* Texas A & M U, 1988. 49/06A.

186   Gaylord, Susan. "Women and Aging: A Psychological Perspective." *J of Women & Aging* 1989 1(1/2/3): 69–94.

187   Gee, Ellen Margaret Thomas, 1950– . "Preferred Timing of Women's Life Events: A Canadian Study." *International J of Aging and Human Development* 1990 31(4): 279–294.

188   Gordon-Jackson, Patricia Ann. *Life Satisfaction of Retired Married and Single Women.* U.S. International U, 1988. 49/07A.

189   Gutmann, David L., 1925– . "Beyond Nurture: Developmental Perspectives on the Vital Older Woman." In Virginia Kerns and Judith K. Brown, eds. *In Her Prime: New Views of Middle-Aged Women, 2d ed.* Urbana: U of Illinois Press, 1992. Chapter 15. (Also Brown and Kerns's *In Her Prime: A New View of Middle-Aged Women,* 1985.)

190   Hailstorks, Robin Jean. *Life Satisfaction Among Black Elderly Women—A Retrospective Analysis.* Ohio State U, 1983. 44/04B.

191   Henry, Mary E. *The Relationships Among Life Satisfaction, Life-Work Role Pattern and Perceived Functional Health in Older Women.* New York U, 1990. 50/09A.

192   Jackson, Beryl Bernice Haughton. *Life Satisfaction in Black Climacteric Women in Relation to Specific Life Events.* U of Pittsburgh, 1982. 43/10A.

193   Lippard, Lucy R., and Mary Mizenko. "'Right Now Is Always the Best Age.'" "Coming of Age" issue. *Heresies* 1988 23: 12–19.

194   Liss, Barbara Ellen. *Life Satisfaction: A Comparison of Retired and Employed Women.* U of Texas Health Sciences Center at Houston School of Public Health, 1982. 43/11A.

195   Meiner, Sue Ellen Thompson. *Life Satisfaction, Perceived Health Status, and Activities of Young-Old and Old-Old Women Living in Urban and Rural Areas.* Southern Illinois U at Edwardsville, 1991. 52/04A.

196   Phillipson, Chris. "Women in Later Life: Patterns of Control and Subordination." In Bridget Hutter, ed. *Controlling Women: The Normal and the Deviant.* London: Croom Helm, 1981. Chapter 9.

197   Riddick, Carol Cutler. "Life Satisfaction Among Aging Women: A Causal Model." In Maximiliane E. Szinovacz, ed. *Women's Retirement: Policy Implications of Recent Research.* Beverly Hills: Sage, 1982. Chapter 3.

198   Riddick, Carol Cutler. *The Life Satisfaction of Retired and Employed Older Women: A Re-Examination of the Disengagement Theory.* Pennsylvania State U, 1980. 41/05A.

199   Robinson, Teresa Braswell. *Clothing Attitudes of Elderly Female Tennesseans as Related to Life Satisfaction and Social Participation.* U of Tennessee, 1984. 45/06A.

200   Rosenquist, Lawrence Karl. *Life Satisfaction of Elderly Females Who Are Overweight as Compared to Elderly Females of Ideal Weight.* U of Arizona, 1989. M.S. thesis.

201   Sanders, Gregory Frank. *Life Satisfaction of Older Couples: A Family Strengths Perspective.* U of Georgia, 1983. 44/05A.

202   Sarrel, Lorna J., and Philip M. Sarrel, M.D., 1937– . *Sexual Turning Points: The Seven Stages of Adult Sexuality.* New York: Macmillan, 1984. bib, index.

This social worker–physician team has prepared a life-cycle perspective; of particular interest are Chapters 20, "Menopause"; 21, "Male Sexuality and Aging"; and 23, "Widowhood."

203   **Spitze, Glenna, and J. Logan.** "More Evidence on Women (and Men) in the Middle." *Research on Aging* June 1990 12(2): 182–198.

204   **Steitz, Jean A.** "The Female Life Course: Life Situations and Perceptions of Control." *International J of Aging and Human Development* 1981–1982 14(3): 195–204.

205   **Stull, Donald Edgar.** *Predicting Husbands' and Wives' Well-Being in Later Life: A Dyadic Approach (Retirement).* U of Washington, 1986. 47/08A.

206   **Tate, Lenore Artie.** *Life Satisfaction and Death Anxiety in Aged Women.* California School of Professional Psychology, Fresno, 1980. 41/07B.

207   **Tate, Nellie P.** *Social Interactional Patterns and Life Satisfaction of a Group of Elderly Black Widows.* Brandeis U, 1981. 42/05A.

208   **Teuter, Ursula.** *Goal Development and Activity Patterns in a Group of Elderly Women Experiencing High Life Satisfaction.* U of Pittsburgh, 1982. 43/09B.

LIFESPAN DEVELOPMENT AND THEORIES; LIFE CYCLE

209   **Allatt, Patricia, et al, eds.** *Women and the Life Cycle: Transitions and Turning Points.* Women and the Life Cycle Series, #26. New York: Macmillan, 1987. bib, index.
      These papers were presented at the 1986 British Sociological Conference on the sociology of the life cycle: Part I, "Social Categories: Exploring the Conventions"; Part II, "Historical Time and Private Lives"; Part III, "The Displacement of the Structural to the Personal." The editors are social workers, sociologists, and researchers at British universities.

210   **Allen, Cynthia Clapp.** *Career Plans and Life Patterns of College-Educated Women: A Twenty-Year Follow-Up Study.* Temple U, 1985. 46/03B.

211   **Bank, Lewis Israel.** *Sex Differences in Cognitive Abilities Among the Middle-Aged and Elderly.* U of California, Los Angeles, 1982. 43/06B.

212   **Deem, Rosemary.** "'My Husband Says I'm Too Old for Dancing': Women, Leisure and Life Cycles." In Patricia Allatt, et al, eds. *Women and the Life Cycle: Transitions and Turning Points.* New York: Macmillan, 1987. Chapter 8.

213   **Edinburg, Golda M.** "Women and Aging." In Carol C. Nadelson and Malkah T. Norman, eds. *The Woman Patient. Volume 2: Concepts of Femininity and the Life Cycle.* New York: Plenum, 1982. 169–194.

214   **Fisher, Jerilyn.** "Teaching 'Time': Women's Responses to Adult Development." In Frieda Johles Forman and Caoran Sowton, eds. *Taking Our Time: Feminist Perspectives on Temporality.* New York: Pergamon, 1989. Chapter 12.

215   **Gould, Joan, 1927– .** *Spirals: A Woman's Journey Through Family Life.* New York: Random, 1988.
      Gould perceives a life cycle of roles—daughter, mother, and widow.

216   **Gould, Ketayun H.** "A Minority-Feminist Perspective on Women and Aging." *J of Women & Aging* 1989 1(1/2/3): 195–216.

217   **Hubbs-Tait, Laura.** "Coping Patterns of Aging Women: A Developmental Perspective." *J of Women & Aging* 1989 1(1/2/3): 95–122.

218   **Huyck, Margaret Hellie.** "Gender Differences in Aging." In James E. Birren and Klaus Warner Schaie, eds. *Handbook of the Psychology of Aging, 3d ed.* San Diego: Academic Press, 1990. Chapter 7.

219   **Jeffries, Dorothy Louise.** *An Exploratory Study of Black Adult Development Among Forty Females Ages Twenty to Forty Years.* George Peabody College for Teachers of Vanderbilt U, 1985. 46/06A.

220   **Lachman, Margie E.** "Methods for a Life-Span Development Approach to Women in the Middle Years." In Grace Kesterman Baruch, ed. *Women in Mid-Life.* New York: Plenum, 1984. Chapter 2.

221   **LeVine, Sarah, and Robert A. LeVine.** "Age, Gender, and the Demographic Adaptation: The Life Course in Agrarian Societies." In Alice S. Rossi, ed. *Gender and the Life Course.* New York: Aldine, 1985. Chapter 2.

222   **Mercer, Ramona Thieme, et al.** *Transitions in a Woman's Life: Major Life Events in a Developmental Context.* Focus on Women, #12. New York: Springer, 1989. bib, index.
    Dr. Mercer's collection of case studies considers psychological aspects of the human life cycle and life change events of American women in middle and old age.

223   **Nadelson, Carol C., and Malkah T. Notman, eds.** *Concepts of Femininity and the Life Cycle.* Volume 2 of *The Woman Patient.* New York: Plenum, 1982. index.
    Contents include: "Midlife Concerns of Women: Implications of Menopause" by Notman; "Marriage and Midlife: The Impact of Social Change" by Nadelson, et al; "Separation: A Family Developmental Process of Midlife" by Joan J. Zilbach; and "Women and Aging" by Golda M. Edinburg.

224   **Parks, Carlton Wheatley, Jr.** *Dimensions of Thought in Adulthood as a Function of Age, Sex, Position, and Task Complexity.* U of Minnesota, 1986. 47/09B.

225   **Riley, Matilda White.** "Women, Men, and the Lengthening Life Course." In Alice S. Rossi, ed. *Gender and the Life Course.* New York: Aldine, 1985. Chapter 18.

226   **Roberts, Helen.** "The Social Classification of Women: A Life-Cycle Approach." In Patricia Allatt, et al, eds. *Women and the Life Cycle: Transitions and Turning Points.* New York: Macmillan, 1987. Chapter 3.

227   **Romer, Nancy.** *The Sex-Role Cycle: Socialization from Infancy to Old Age.* New York: Feminist Press/McGraw Hill, 1981. il, index.
    Chapters are devoted to reevaluating life choices in middle adulthood and to later diminishing importance of sex roles.

228   **Sanderson, Kay.** *Social Mobility in the Life Cycle of Some Women Clerical Workers.* U of Essex (United Kingdom), 1988. 49/07A.

229   **Schnabel, Paula Lyn.** *A Comparison of the Level of Differentiation Among Three Successive Generations of Related and Unrelated Women.* New York U, 1987. 49/01B.

230   **Silver, Margery Hunter.** *Life Review as a Developmental Process: Themes of Caring, Mourning, and Integrity in Group and Individual Therapy with Low-Income Elderly Women.* Harvard U, 1982. 43/11B.

231   **Simmons, Diane O.** *A Life-Span Developmental Approach Toward Building a Theory of the Elderly African-American Female.* Rutgers State U of New Jersey, 1990. 51/07B.

232   **Spanier, Graham B., and Paul C. Glick.** "The Life Cycle of American Families." *J of Family History* Spring 1980 5: 97–111.

233   **Steele, Marilyn.** *Life in the Round: A Model of Adult Female Development.* Wright Institute, Berkeley, 1986. 47/07B.

234   **Teed, Sharon Ann.** *Women Now at Midlife—A Follow-Up Study Expanding the Perspective of Woman's Adult Life Cycle.* California School of Professional Psychology, Berkeley, 1986. 47/09B.

MENTAL HEALTH
See also this chapter: Dementia (116–124).

235   **Bassett, Susan S., et al.** "Reliability of Proxy Response on Mental Health Indices for Aged, Community-Dwelling Women." *Psychology and Aging* March 1990 5(1): 127–132.

236   **Beck, Cornelia M., and Barbara P. Pearson.** "Mental Health of Elderly Women." *J of Women & Aging* 1989 1(1/2/3): 175–194.

237   **Benzies, Bonnie Jeanne.** *Maternal Status and Mental Health in Later Life.* Illinois Institute of Technology, 1980. 41/12B.

238   **Carmen, Elaine Hilberman, M.D., et al.** "Inequality and Women's Mental Health: An Overview." *J of Psychiatry* 1981 138(10): 1319–1330.

239   **Eckels, Elaine Traugot.** *Stress and Coping in Middle-Aged and Older Women.* U of Wisconsin, Madison, 1980. 41/10B.

240   **Feinson, Marjorie Chary.** "Mental Health and Aging: Are There Gender Differences?" *Gerontologist* 1987 27(6): 703–711.

241   **Garrone, Linda A.** *Object Relations as Reflected in Psychological Testing of Older Women: Paraphrenic Inpatients, Depressed Outpatients, and Normal Controls.* Northwestern U, 1990. 50/08B.

242   **Gatz, Margaret, et al.** *Health and Mental Health of Older Women in the 1980s: Implications for Psychologists.* ERIC, April 1982. ED #221802. 11 pages.

243   **Gatz, Margaret, et al.** "Older Women and Mental Health." In Annette U. Rickel, et al, eds. *Social and Psychological Problems of Women: Prevention and Crisis Intervention.* Washington: Hemisphere, 1984. Chapter 15.

244   **Gentner, Lorraine Marie.** *The Effects of Back Massage on the Psychological Well Being of Elderly Women.* U of Texas at Austin, 1980. 41/11B.

245   **Grau, Lois.** "Mental Health and Older Women." *Women & Health* 1988 14(3/4): 75–92.

246   Hayslip, Bert, Jr., et al. "Older Women's Perceptions of Female Counselors: The Influence of Therapist Age and Problem Intimacy." *Gerontologist* April 1989 29(2): 239–244.

247   Hooper, Judith O., et al. "Older Women, the Student Role and Mental Health." *Educational Gerontology* March-June 1983 9(2–3): 233–242.

248   Junge, Maxine, and Vernett Maya. "Women in Their Forties: A Group Portrait and Implications for Psychotherapy. *Women & Therapy* Fall 1985 4(3): 3–19.

249   Kaas, Merrie J. *Emotional Referencing: The Definition and Management of Mental Health by Older Women.* U of California, San Francisco, 1987. 48/08B.

250   Levy, Sandra M. "The Aging Woman: Developmental Issues and Mental Health Needs." *Professional Psychology* February 1981 12(1): 92–100.

251   Lewis, Myrna. "Sex Bias Dangerous to Women's Mental Health." *Perspectives on Aging* 1987 16: 9–11.

252   National Institute on Aging and National Institute of Mental Health. *The Older Woman: Continuities and Discontinuities: [Workshop] Report.* Washington: U.S. Department of Health, Education, and Welfare, 1980.

253   Osborn, Marilyn Elizabeth. *Psychological Adjustment to Aging in Older Women.* California School of Professional Psychology, Los Angeles, 1983. 44/08B.

254   Rathbone-McCuan, Eloise, et al. "A Pilot Training Program in the Mental Health of Older Women." *Educational Gerontology* June 1981 6(4): 353–363.

255   Riddick, Carol C., et al. "The Relative Contribution of Leisure Activities and Other Factors to the Mental Health of Older Women." *J of Leisure Research* 1984 16(2): 136–148.

256   Rosenauer, Libby Lois. *Stress in Middlescent Women: A Comparison of the Perceptions of Therapists and Middlescent Women.* U.S. International U, 1982. 43/02B.

257   Ruth, Jan-Erik, and Peter Oberg. "Expressions of Aggression in the Life Stories of Aged Women." In Kaj Bjorkqvist and Pirkko Niemela, eds. *Of Mine and Women: Aspects of Female Aggression.* San Diego: Academic Press, 1992. 133–146.

258   Sheehan, Susan. *Is There No Place on Earth for Me?* New York: Houghton Mifflin, 1982.
        Miss Sylvia Frumkin (Maxine Mason 1952–1995)—heavy, ungainly, said to be schizophrenic—is Sheehan's subject. She was a patient at Creedmore, a state mental institution located in Queens County. The epilogue suggests improvement: Frumkin says "Getting well is growing up." The original account appeared in slightly different form in four Spring 1981 issues of *New Yorker* magazine, where Sheehan was a staff member; she received a Pulitzer Prize and National Mental Health Association Award for this work.

259   Taylor, Sue Perkins. "Mental Health and Successful Coping Among Aged Black Women." In Ron C. Manuel, ed. *Minority Aging: Sociological and Social Psychological Issues.* Westport: Greenwood, 1982. Chapter 9.

260   Walton, Valerie A., et al. "The Mental Health of Elderly Women in the Community." *International J of Geriatric Psychiatry* July-August 1990 5(4): 257–263.

261   Wisniewski, Wendy, and Donna Cohen. *Older Women: A Population at Risk for Mental Health Problems.* ERIC, November 1984. ED #258073. 21 pages.

SELF-ESTEEM; SELF-ACTUALIZATION

262   **Bryant, Karen Lee.** *Examining Typological Characteristics of Women at Mid-Life: Relationships Between a Theory of Individuation and Self-Actualization.* Pacific Graduate School of Psychology, 1987. 48/09B.

263   **Conway-Turner, Katherine.** "Sex, Intimacy and Self-Esteem: The Case of the African-American Woman." *J of Women & Aging* 1992 4(1): 91–104.

264   **Ellett, Susan Elizabeth.** *An Investigation of Identity and Self-Esteem in Traditional Married Women During Their Middle Years, and the Impact of the Life Planning Seminar.* Virginia Commonwealth U, 1981. 42/07B.

265   **Erdwins, Carol J., et al.** "A Comparison of Different Aspects of Self-Concept for Young, Middle-Aged, and Older Women." *J of Clinical Psychology* July 1981 37(3): 484–490.

266   **Frevert, Rita Lundt.** *Effects of Life Career Pattern on Self-Esteem and Life Satisfaction of College-Educated Women in the Middle Years.* Iowa State U, 1982. 43/05B.

267   **Giltinan, Janice M.** "Using Life Review to Facilitate Self-Actualization in Elderly Women." *Gerontology & Geriatrics Education* 1990 10(4): 75–83.

268   **Goldberg, Stephen Alan.** *An Investigation into the Usefulness of Gender Typing as a Construct in Understanding Self-Esteem in Old Age.* Temple U, 1985. 46/08A.

269   **Jacobs, Ruth Harriet,** 1924– . *Be an Outrageous Older Woman—A R*A*S*P (Remarkable Aging Smart Person).* Order from: Knowledge, Ideas & Trends, Inc., 1131-0 Tolland Turnpike #175, Manchester, CT 06040. 1991.
    Sociologist and gerontologist Jacobs provides "how to" on surviving and thriving as an older woman within the constraints that exist for many in housing and health, and making one's political voice heard.

270   **Klemesrud, Judy.** "Improving the Self Image of Older Women." *New York Times* November 2, 1981: B9, columns 2–5.

271   **Miller, Karen R.** *Midlife Women and Self-Esteem.* California School of Professional Psychology, Berkeley, 1980. 41/12B.

272   **Moss, Willodean Daniel.** *An Assessment of Self-Esteem and Perceived Needs of Widowed and Divorced Women.* U of Kentucky, 1981. 42/10A.

273   **Myers, Carol Lynn.** *Gender Role Attitude, Current Life-Style, Self-Esteem, and Role Satisfaction in College-Educated Men and Women 10 and 15 Years After Graduation.* Rutgers State U of New Jersey, 1984. 45/08A.

274   **Neums, Helen Patricia.** *The Relationship of Self-Esteem and Open-Mindedness to Women's Adjustment in Retirement.* New York U, 1985. 46/04B.

275   **Rhodes, Carol Louise.** *Women in Transition from Dependency to Autonomy: A Study in Self-Development.* Union for Experimenting Colleges and Universities, 1986. 48/02B.

276   **Schmalz, Mary Beth.** *Self-Actualization in Women and Its Relationship to Motherhood, Educational Background, Employment Status, and Present Age.* Indiana U, 1983. 45/09A.

277   **Steinem, Gloria,** 1935–   . *Revolution from Within: A Book of Self-Esteem.* Boston: Little, Brown, 1992.

At 57, American feminist Steinem devotes this book to the subject of self-respect. Chapter 5, "Bodies of Knowledge," considers "age" a "blessing."

278   **Thomas, Beryl L.** *Self-Esteem and Life Satisfaction in Noninstitutionalized Elderly Black Females: Effects of Meditation/Relaxation Training.* Temple U, 1987. 48/04B.

279   **Troll, Lillian E.** *Achievement Orientation in Middle-Aged and Older Women.* ERIC, August 1981. ED #210615. 13 pages.

280   **Whittington-Clark, Linda Enid.** *Stress and Self-Esteem of Female and Male Graduate Students.* U of Toledo, 1985. 46/06B.

Sexuality; Sex Role; Gender
See also Chapter 3: Love and Sexuality; Lesbian Relationships (441–475).

281   **Berman, Phyllis W., and Estelle R. Ramey, eds.** *Women: A Developmental Perspective.* ERIC, April 1982. ED #223862. 395 pages.

Sexuality and sex role were major considerations of the presenters of twenty-six papers delivered at a government-sponsored conference devoted to research on the health and development of women. They include Ramey's "The Natural Capacity for Health in Women," Pepper Schwartz's "Research on Adult Female Sexuality: The Next Decade," and Matilda White Riley's "Implications for the Middle and Later Years."

282   **Butler, Robert Neil, M.D.,** 1927– , **and Myrna L. Lewis.** *Love and Sex After 40: A Guide for Men and Women for Their Mid and Later Years.* New York: Harper & Row, 1986. bib, il, index.

This title is sometimes referred to as *Sexuality and Aging.* It is an updated and expanded version of their landmark *Sex After 60* (1976). Lewis is a psychotherapist, social worker, and gerontologist concerned with social and health issues of mid-life and older women.

283   **Depaul, Elizabeth Mae.** *How Divorcees and Widows Sanction Sexual Relations After the Termination of Marriage.* Florida Institute of Technology, 1982. 43/11B.

284   **Erdwins, Carol J., et al.** "A Comparison of Sex Role and Related Personality Traits in Young, Middle-Aged, and Older Women." *International J of Aging and Human Development* 1983 17(2): 451–452.

285   **Hagstad, Anita.** "Gynecology and Sexuality—Middle-Aged Women." *Women & Health* 1988 13(3–4): 57–80.

286   **Johnson, Beverly Karen.** *The Sexual Interest, Participation, and Satisfaction of Older Men and Women.* U of Texas at Austin, 1986. 47/12B.

287   **Kirkpatrick, Martha, ed.** *Women's Sexual Development: Explorations of Inner Space* and companion volume, *Women's Sexual Experience: Explorations of the Dark Continent.* New York: Plenum, 1980 and 1982. bib, index.

Women's Sexual Development is not a textbook or an encyclopedia but rather a collection reporting the variety of points of view held by women and men, including Chapter 4, "Physiological Aspects of Female Sexual Development: Gestation, Lactation,

Menopause, and Erotic Physiology," by Cori Baill and John Money. *Women's Sexual Experience* includes "Sex and Sexuality: Women at Midlife" by Lillian B. Rubin and "In Praise of Older Women" by B. Genevay.

288   **Leiblum, Sandra Risa.** "Sexuality and the Midlife Woman." *Psychology of Women Q* December 1990 14(4): 495–508. *See also* Ellen Cole and Esther Rothblum's "Commentary . . . ": 509–512.

289   **Levine, Barbara Jo.** *Intra- and Intergenerational Communication in Initial Dyadic Interchanges: The Effect of Age and Sex of Discloser and Target on Level of Self-Disclosure.* U of Wisconsin, Madison, 1980. 41/12B.

290   **Malatesta, Victor J.** "Sexuality and the Older Adult: An Overview with Guidelines for the Health Care Professional." *J of Women & Aging* 1989 1(4): 93–118.

291   **Mandel, Hilary.** *A Comparison of Differences in Gender Identity and Sex-Role Adoption Between Males and Females Younger than 25 and Older than 60.* Pacific Graduate School of Psychology, 1986. 47/09B.

292   **Meske, Richard Charles.** *Personal and Sociological Factors Influencing Sexual Activity in Late-Life Women.* Fielding Institute, 1983. 45/02A.

293   **Mooradian, Arshag D., and V. Greiff.** "Sexuality in Older Women." *Archives of Internal Medicine* May 1990 150(5): 1033–1038.

294   **Obler, Loraine K.** "Sex Differences in Aging: The Experimental Literature on the Psychology of Aging." *Resources for Feminist Research/Documentation sur la Recherche Féministe* July 1982 11(2): 209–210.

295   **Pomata, Agnes F.** *Attitudes Toward Sexual Problems in the Elderly: Helper-Bias in Determination of Treatment Planning.* Hofstra U, 1985. 47/02B.

296   **Porcino, Jane,** 1923– . "Growing Older Female with Love, Sex and Intimacy." *Generations: Q J of the Western Gerontological Society* Fall 1981 6(1): 8–9.
        The Summer 1990 issue, edited by Lou Glasse and John Hendricks, is a special "Gender & Aging" issue also published in book form by Baywood in 1992.

297   **Portonova, Marydonna, et al.** "Elderly Women's Attitudes Toward Sexual Activity Among Their Peers." *Health Care for Women International* 1984 5(5–6): 289–298.

298   **Ransohoff, Rita M.,** 1916– . *Venus After Forty: Sexual Myths, Men's Fantasies and Truths About Middle-Aged Women.* Far Hills: New Horizon Press/Macmillan, 1987. bib.
        Ransohoff's consideration of middle aged women's sexual behavior includes menopause.

299   **Rice, Susan.** "Sexuality and Intimacy for Aging Women: A Changing Perspective." *J of Women & Aging* 1989 1(1/2/3): 245–264.

300   **Schumacher, Dorin.** "Hidden Death: The Sexual Effects of Hysterectomy." *J of Women & Aging* 1990 2(2): 49–66.

301   **Turner, Barbara Formaniak, and Catherine G. Adams.** "The Sexuality of Older Women." In Elizabeth W. Markson, ed. *Older Women: Issues and Prospects.* Lexington: Heath, 1987. Chapter 4.

302   **Weg, Ruth B., ed.** *Sexuality in the Later Years: Roles and Behavior.* New York: Academic Press, 1983. bib, index.

Includes "A View from Other Countries," Florine B. Livson's "Gender Identity: A Life-Span View of Sex-Role Development," and Erika Landau and Benjamin Maoz's "Continuity of Self-Actualization: Womanhood in the Climacterium and Old Age."

3
Sociological Perspectives
on Women's Aging

The identification of women with reproduction has led the male world to wipe women of fifty years of age or older out of existence or deprive them of identity as women.

                                                    Jessie R. Bernard, 1903–   .

CARE; CAREGIVERS; CAREGIVER ROLE
See also Chapter 5: Nursing Homes; Adult Care Facilities (956–969).

303   **Abel, Emily K.** "Adult Daughters and Care for the Elderly." *Feminist Studies* Fall 1986 12(3): 479–497.

304   **Abel, Emily K.** "Family Care of the Frail Elderly: Framing an Agenda for Change." *Women's Studies Q* Spring/Summer 1989 17(1/2): 75–86.

305   **Abel, Emily K.** *Who Cares for the Elderly? Public Policy and the Experiences of Adult Daughters.* Philadelphia: Temple U Press, 1991. bib, index.
       The author's concern is with the interaction of caregivers and the formal service system. She combines historical analysis of family care in the United States since 1800 with a study of fifty-one women who are primary caregivers for one or more parents. Approximately one-quarter of persons aged 65 and older cannot care for themselves and their households without help. More than 4 million family members care

for disabled elderly at home. "Like other forms of domestic labor, care for the elderly continues to be allocated on the basis of gender." Chapter 6: "Mothers and Daughters"; Chapter 10: "An Agenda for Change."

306   **Allen, Susan Masterson.** *Dehospitalization and Spousal Caregiving: Are Wives at Risk?* Brown U, 1992. 63/11A.

307   **Archbold, Patricia G.,** 1943– . "An Analysis of Parentcaring by Women." *Home Health Care Services Q* Summer 1982 3(2): 5–26.

308   **Archbold, Patricia G.,** 1943– . *Impact of Parent-Caring on Women.* U of California, San Francisco, 1980. 41/08B.

309   **Aronson, Jane.** "Old Women's Experiences of Needing Care: Choice or Compulsion." *Canadian J on Aging* Autumn 1990 9(3): 234–247.

310   **Aronson, Jane.** "Women's Sense of Responsibility for the Care of Old People—'But Who Else Is Going to Do It?'" *Gender & Society* March 1992 6: 8–29.

311   **Bachmann, Gloria A.** "The Ideals of Optimal Care for Women at Midlife." In Marcha Flint, et al, eds. *Multidisciplinary Perspectives on Menopause: Annals of the New York Academy of Sciences* (Volume 592). New York: The Academy, 1990. 253–256.

312   **Bader, Jenane E.** "Respite Care: Temporary Relief for Caregivers." *Women & Health* 1985 10(2/3): 39–52.

313   **Bateson, Mary Catherine,** 1939– . "Caretaking." In her *Composing a Life.* New York: Atlantic Monthly Press, 1989. Chapter 8.

314   **Bowers, Barbara, and Barbara Liegel.** "Women as Health Care Providers: Family Caregivers of the Elderly [review essay]." In Carol J. Leppa, ed. *Women's Health Perspectives: An Annual Review,* Volume 3. Phoenix: Oryx Press, 1990. Chapter 14.

315   **Boyd, Sandra L., and Judith Treas.** "Family Care of the Frail Elderly: A New Look at Women in the Middle." *Women's Studies Q* Spring/Summer 1989 17(1/2): 66–74.

316   **Brody, Elaine M.** "Caregiving Daughters and Their Local Siblings: Perceptions, Strains, and Interactions." *Gerontologist* August 1989 29(4): 529–538.

317   **Brody, Elaine M.** "Women in the Middle and Family Help to Older People." *Gerontologist* 1981 21: 471–480.

318   **Brody, Elaine M.** *Women in the Middle: Their Parent-Care Years.* New York: Springer, 1990. bib, index.
        Well known as a specialist in this area, Brody here considers adult children and family relationships, including home care of aged parents in the United States.

319   **Brody, Elaine M., et al.** "What Should Adult Children Do for Elderly Parents: Opinions and Preferences of Three Generations of Women." *J of Gerontology* 1984 39: 736–746.

320   **Brody, Elaine M., et al.** "Women's Changing Roles and Help to Elderly Parents: Attitudes of Three Generations of Women." *J of Gerontology* 1983 28: 597–608.

321   **Cantor, Marjorie H., and Barbara Hirshorn.** "Intergenerational Transfers Within the Family Context—Motivating Factors and Their Implications for Caregiving." *Women & Health* 1988 14(3/4): 39–52.

322   Chichin, Eileen. "Community Care for the Frail Elderly: The Case of Non-Professional Home Care Workers." *Women & Health* 1988 14(3/4): 93–104.

323   Crossman, Linda, et al. "Older Women Caring for Disabled Spouses: A Model for Supportive Services." *Gerontologist* October 1981 21(5): 464–470.

324   Donovan, Rebecca. "'We Care for the Most Important People in Your Life': Home Care Workers in New York City." *Women's Studies Q* Spring/Summer 1989 17(1/2): 56–65.

325   Doress-Worters, Paula B. *The Effect of Caregiving Role Configuration on the Psychological Well-Being of Employed Middle-Aged Women.* Boston College, 1992. 53/09B.

326   England, Suzanne E., and Beatrice T. Naulleau. "Women, Work and Elder Care—The Family and Medical Leave Debates." *Women and Politics* 1991 11(2): 91–107.

327   Etaugh, Claire, and Maureen Spinner. "Perceptions of Caregivers of Elderly Parents by College Students: Effects of Caregiver Gender, Type of Care and Presence of Children." *J of Women & Aging* 1991 3(4): 37–52. Also available as ERIC, August 1991. ED #341942. 25 pages.

328   Etaugh, Claire, et al. "Perceiving Elder Caregivers: Effects of Gender, Employment and Caregiving Hours." ERIC, August 1992. ED #351658. 10 pages.

329   Feldblum, Chai R. "Home Health Care for the Elderly: Programs, Problems, and Potentials." *Harvard J on Legislation* Winter 1985 22(1): 193–254.

330   Feldman, Penny Hollander, et al. *Who Cares for Them? Workers in the Home-Care Industry.* New York: Greenwood Press, 1990. bib, index.
        Feldman, Alice M. Sapienza, and Nancy M. Kane recognize gender issues as factors to be included as they document working conditions in the service industry that provides home care for the elderly and the disabled in the United States. They use case studies of the industry in Milwaukee, New York, San Diego, and Syracuse. Part I considers the labor market, workforce, and industry conditions; Part II consists of case studies of workers; Part III is an overview of work life programs; Part IV provides recommendations and policy implications.

331   Finch, Janet, and Dulcie Groves. "By Women for Women: Caring for the Frail Elderly." *Women's Studies International Forum* 1982 5(5): 427–438.

332   Floyd, Maita. *Caretakers, the Forgotten People.* Phoenix: Eskualdun, 1988. il.
        Confused and overwhelmed by her husband's terminal illness, Floyd's autobiography revolves around how she coped with the crisis of cancer, death, and bereavement. Her poetry and sketches are included. One of a growing number of women's personal narratives of experience in the role of caretaker that "will give others courage and strength." Of related interest are books such as *Home Care: An Alternative to the Nursing Home* (Brethren Press, 1983), based on Florine Du Fresne's three-year "adventure in love" experience caring for her terminally ill husband in their home.

333   Gallagher, Dolores, et al. "Prevalence of Depression in Family Caregivers." In symposium, "Effectiveness of Caregiver Groups." *Gerontologist* August 1989 29(4): 449–456.

334   Gay, E. Greer, and Jennie J. Kronenfeld. "A Resource-Intensive Medicare Patient Effect of Profit Margin on Care." *J of Women & Aging* 1991 3(4): 53–77.

335   **Gibeau, Janice L.** *Breadwinners and Caregivers: Working Patterns of Women Working Full-Time and Caring for Dependent Elderly Family Members.* Brandeis U, 1988. 47/07A.

336   **Glasse, Lou.** "Caring for the Elderly: Undervalued Work." *Christian Science Monitor* December 18, 1989 82: 19.

337   **Graham, Hilary.** "Caring: A Labour of Love." In James Finch and Dulcie Groves, eds. *A Labour of Love: Women, Work and Caring.* London: Routledge & Kegan Paul, 1983. Chapter 1.

338   **Graves, Diane de.** "Women Caring for Women." Women as Elders issue. *Resources for Feminist Research/Documentation sur la Recherche Féministe.* July 1982 11(2): 212.

339   **Hamilton, Louise A., and Helen Carol Jones.** "The 'Unidentified Patient' in Home Health Care." ERIC, May 1986. ED #294075. 17 pages.

340   **Hooyman, Nancy R., and Rosemary Ryan.** "Women as Caregivers of the Elderly: Catch-22." In Josefina Figueira-McDonough and Rosemary Sarri, eds. *The Trapped Woman: Catch-22 in Deviance and Control.* Newbury Park: Sage, 1987. Chapter 6.

341   **Hooyman, Nancy R.** "Women as Caregivers of the Elderly: Implications for Social Welfare Policy and Practice." In David E. Biegel and Arthur Blum, eds. *Aging and Caregiving: Theory, Research, and Policy.* Newbury Park: Sage, 1990. Chapter 10.

342   **Horowitz, Amy.** *Adult Children as Caregivers to Elderly Parents: Correlates and Consequences.* Columbia U, 1982. 43/05A.

343   **Horowitz, Amy.** "Sons and Daughters as Caregivers to Older Parents: Differences in Role Performance and Consequences." *Gerontologist* December 1985 25(6): 612–617.

344   **Jamuna, D.** "Caring for Elderly Women: Perspectives of the Turn of the Century." *J of the Indian Academy of Applied Psychology* July 1990 16(2): 17–22.

345   **Johnsen, Pauline Joan Thorson.** *Women as Caregivers to the Elderly: The Filial Imperative in Anthropological Perspective.* Bryn Mawr College, 1988. 49/10A.

346   **Kaden, Joan, and Susan A. McDaniel.** "Caregiving and Care-Receiving: A Double Bind for Women in Canada's Aging Society." *J of Women & Aging* 1990 2(3): 3–26.

347   **Karon, Sarita Lynn.** *The Difference It Makes: Caregiver Gender and Access to Community-Based Long-Term Care Services in the Social/HMO.* Brandeis U, 1991. 52/05A.

348   **Kauffman, Janice King.** *The Caring Role of Middle-Aged Employed Women with Elderly Mothers: An Exploratory Study with Implications for Home Economics Educational Programming.* Michigan State U, 1982. 43/06A.

349   **Kayser-Jones, Jeanie Schmit.** *Old, Alone, and Neglected: Care of the Aged in Scotland and the United States.* Berkeley: U of California Press, 1981. bib, index.
        Case studies of so-called old age homes include anthropological analyses of Pacific Manor, a nursing home in California, and Scottsdale, a geriatric hospital in Scotland. In these two models of behavior isolation, the United States does not come off well. Only in Chapter 5, "Demographic Characteristics of the Residents," are women acknowledged and reasons for continuance of such formal "caregiving" identified.

350   Keith, Carolyn Cordy. *Caring for the Older Parent: Transformation of the Family into a Parentcare System.* U of Wisconsin, Milwaukee, 1991. 53/01A.

351   Kerson, Toba Schwaber. "Women and Aging: A Clinical Social Work Perspective." *J of Women & Aging* 1989 1 (1/2/3): 123–148.

352   Kohut, Jeraldine Joanne, and Sylvester Kohut, Jr., 1942– . *Hospice: Caring for the Terminally Ill.* Springfield: C. C. Thomas, 1984. bib, il, index.
    "Americans represent a death denial society." Hospice founder Jeraldine Kohut and professor Sylvester Kohut discuss and summarize the states of dying of Elisabeth Kubler-Ross, M.D., (1926–) and the work of nurse Dame Cicely M. Saunders (1918–) and St. Christopher's Hospital in London, England.

353   Lang, Abigail M., and Elaine M. Brody. "Characteristics of Middle-Aged Daughters and Help to Their Elderly Mothers." *J of Marriage and the Family* February 1983 45(1): 193–202.

354   Leppa, Carol J. "Women as Health Care Providers [review essay]." In Carol J. Leppa and Connie Miller, eds. *Women's Health Perspectives: An Annual Review,* Volume 1. Phoenix: Oryx, 1988. Chapter 10.

355   Leppa, Carol J. "Women as Health Care Providers [review essay]." In her *Women's Health Perspectives: An Annual Review,* Volume 2. Phoenix: Oryx, 1989. Chapter 10.

356   Levine, Laura E. *The Daughter's Dilemma: Psychological Aspects of Caring for an Elderly Mother.* Wright Institute, 1988. 49/08B.

357   Lewis, Jane E., and Barbara Meredith. *Daughters Who Care: Daughters Caring for Mothers at Home.* New York: Routledge, 1988. bib, index.
    The Equal Opportunities Commission found at least 1.25 million "carers" in Britain, of whom 35 percent were men. It stated that the family—in practice, women— must expect to provide the care of the future. Lewis and Meredith followed forty-one women who devoted most of their lives to caring for their mothers and who frequently noted physicians' lack of supportive understanding, incredible comments, etc. Christine Orton in her *New Statesman* (May 27, 1988 115: 36) review calls this "tough reading . . . not especially helpful to carers [but it should be read by] every professional."

358   Marsden, Dennis, and Sheila Abrams. "'Liberators,' 'Companions,' 'Intruders,' and 'Cuckoos in the Nest': A Sociology of Caring Relationships over the Life Cycle." In Patricia Allatt, et al, eds. *Women and the Life Cycle: Transitions and Turning Points.* New York: Macmillan, 1987. Chapter 14.

359   Marshall, Victor, et al. "Concerns About Parental Health." In Elizabeth W. Markson, ed. *Older Women: Issues and Prospects.* Lexington: Heath, 1987. Chapter 12.

360   McCrory, Audrey Mona. *The Impact of Caregiving on the Marital Need Satisfaction of Older Wives with Dependent Husbands.* U of North Carolina at Greensboro, 1984. 45/05A.

361   McCue, Maxine Marie. *The Caregiving Experience of the Elderly Female Caregiver of a Spouse Impaired by Stroke.* U of Alaska, Anchorage, 1990. M.S. thesis.

362   McDaniel, Susan A. "Women and Aging: A Sociological Perspective." *J of Women* 1989 1(1/2/3): 47–68.

363   **McGrew, Kathryn B.** *Daughters' Decision-Making About the Nature and Level of Their Participation in the Long-Term Care of Their Dependent Elderly Parents: A Qualitative Study.* Ohio State U, 1990. 51/12A.

364   **Meddaugh, Dorothy, et al.** "After-Effects of Alzheimer's Caregiving on Widows' Health and Financial Well-Being." *J of Women & Aging* 1991 3(2): 45–62.

365   **Mitchell, Margaret Lucretia.** *An Investigation of the Relationship Between Perceived Social Support, Support Satisfaction and Depression Among Working Female Caregivers.* Fordham U, 1991. 52/09A.

366   **Naysmith, Sheila M.** "Parental Care: Another Female Function?" *Canadian J of Social Work Education* 1981 7(2): 55–63.

367   **Norris, Jane, ed.** *Daughters of the Elderly: Building Partnerships in Caregiving.* Bloomington: Indiana U Press, 1988. bib.
     Daughters of aging parents are primary caregivers in homecare for the elderly. Norris attempts to offer them information about options. Winner of the 1990 Susan Koppelman Award, her book differs in approach from, for example, Nancy R. Hooyman and Wendy Lustbader's *Taking Care of Your Aging Family Members* (New York: Free Press, 1986), which devotes approximately five (of 322) pages to "women in the middle."

368   **Nygren, Richard Edwin.** *Empowering Widows to Become Care-Givers: A Process Designed to Empower and Train Widows to Become a Care-Giving Group, to Help Them Lament Their Loss and Then Through the Lament Process to Gain Significance for Their Life After the Death of Their Spouse.* Princeton Theological Seminary, 1981. The University Microfilms order number for the hard copy version of this Doctor of Ministry dissertation is AAC 8225553.

369   **Oberhofer Dane, Barbara T.** *The Differential Impact of Stress as It Relates to Gender Among Elderly Spouse Caregivers.* Fordham U, 1985. 47/06A.

370   **O'Bryant, Shirley L., et al.** "Contributions of the Caregiving Role to Women's Development." *Sex Roles* December 1990 23: 645–658.

371   **Orodenker, Sylvia Z.** *The Effects of Women's Labor Force Participation on Levels of Stress Associated with the Caregiving Experience.* Brandeis U, 1988. 49/10A.

372   **Peters, Laura Jean.** *Decision-Making Processes of Female Caregivers.* U of Utah, 1988. 49/06A.

373   **Pett, Marjorie A., et al.** "Intergenerational Conflict: Middle-Aged Women Caring for Demented Older Relatives." *American J of Orthopsychiatry* July 1988 58(3): 405–417.

374   **Phimister, Kathleen M.** *Easing the Stressful Passage: Women Caregivers in Hospice Home Care.* Bryn Mawr College, 1991. 52/04A.

375   **Pohl, Joanne Margaret.** *Mother-Daughter Relationships and Adult Daughters' Commitment to Caregiving for Their Aging Disabled Mothers.* U of Michigan, 1992. 53/12B.

376   **Premo, Terri L.** "A Blessing to Our Declining Years: Feminine Responses to Filial Duty in the New Republic." *International J of Aging and Human Development* 1984–1985 20(1): 59–74.

377   **Quinn-Mustrove, Sandra L.** "Extended Care-Giving: The Experience of Surviving Spouses." *J of Women & Aging* 1990 2(2): 93–107.

378   Randolph, Judy, et al. "Precipitants of Caregiver Stress: The Impact of Gender Roles and Filial Relationship on the Allocation of Provider and Personal Care Tasks." ERIC, November 1990. ED #348603. 8 pages.

379   Richman, Harold A., 1937– , and Matthew W. Stagner, 1959– . "The Family: Women and Grandparents as Kin-Keepers." In Alan J. Pifer, ed. *Our Aging Society*. New York: Norton, 1986. 141–160.

380   Robinson, Karen Meier. *Adjustment to Caregiving in Older Wives: Variations in Social Support, Health, and Past Marital Adjustment*. Indiana U, 1987. 49/07B.

381   Simon, Barbara Levy, 1949– . "Never-Married Women as Caregivers to Elderly Patients: Some Costs and Benefits." *Affilia* 1986 1(3): 29–42.

382   Skrzycki, Cindy. "Family Blessings, Burdens: [Women] Employees Struggle to Balance Work with Care of Aging Relatives as Well as Children." *Washington Post* December 24, 1989 113: H1.

383   Sommers, Tish, 1914–1985. "Caregiving: A Woman's Issue." *Generations* Fall 1985 10(1): 9–13.

384   Sommers, Tish, 1914–1985, and Laurie Shields, 1922–1989. *Women Take Care: The Consequences of Caregiving in Today's Society*. Gainesville: Triad, 1987. bib.
     Before she too died of cancer, Shields carried on the work to which these women were committed, completing *Women Take Care* with the Older Women's League Task Force on Caregivers and consulting-writer Judy MacLean. Sommers: "I stand firm on the danger of presuming that women will take on the caregiving role. . . . This problem of caregiving to the end of life belongs to our whole society. It belongs to women, to men, and certainly to the government."

385   Souder, J. Elaine. *A Comparison of High and Low General Levels of Reinforcement of Self-Reported Depression, Anger, and Somatic Symptoms in Female Spousal Caregivers of Alzheimer Patients and Spouses of Healthy Men*. Boston College, 1987. 49/11A.

386   Sptize, Glenna, and John Logan. "Gender Differences in Family Support: Is There a Payoff?" *Gerontologist* February 1989 29(1): 108–113.

387   Staight, Paula Rose. *Comparative and Descriptive Study of Elderly Women as Primary and Secondary Caregivers*. U of Oregon, 1987. M.S. thesis.

388   Stone, Robyn I. *Exploding the Myths: Caregiving in America: A Study by the . . . House Select Committee on Aging*. Publication 100-665. Washington: U.S. Government Printing Office, 1988. il.

389   Stueve, Charlotte Ann. *What's to Be Done About Mom and Dad? Daughters' Relations with Elderly Parents*. U of California, Berkeley, 1985. 47/03A.

390   Unks, Raymond Paul. *The Relative Influence of Social, Physical, and Psychological Factors on the Morale and Life Satisfaction of Elderly Wives of Stroke Patients: A Descriptive Exploratory Study*. U of Washington, 1983. 44/08A.

391   Walker, Alan. "Care for Elderly People: A Conflict Between Women and the State." In James Finch and Dulcie Groves, eds. *A Labour of Love: Women, Work and Caring*. London: Routledge & Kegan Paul, 1983. Chapter 6.

392   Walker, Ella Mae. *Influences on the Decision of Black Middle-Aged Career Women to Provide Care for Elderly Parents*. Texas Woman's U, 1987. 48/05A.

393   Walter, Carolyn Ambler. "Adult Daughters and Mothers: Stress in the Caregiving Relationship." *J of Women & Aging* 1991 3(3): 39–58.

394   Ward, Deborah Huntington. *The New Old Burden: Gender and Cost in Kin Care of Disabled Elderly.* Boston U, 1987. 49/03A.

395   Yancey, Philip. "Angel to the Dying: The Founder of the Modern Hospice Movement, Cicely Saunders [1918–   ], Has Made It Possible for Thousands to Die with Dignity." *Christianity Today* December 17, 1990 34(18): 22+.

CHILDLESSNESS
See also Chapter 6: Pregnancy and Childbirth (1187–1212).

396   Alexander, Baine B., et al. "A Path Not Taken: A Cultural Analysis of Regrets and Childlessness in the Lives of Older Women." *Gerontologist* October 1992 32(5): 618–626.

397   Beckman, Linda J. "The Consequences of Childlessness on the Social-Psychological Well-Being of Older Women." *J of Gerontology* March 1982 37(2): 243–250.

398   Bitting, Sylvia M. *The Consequences of Remaining Childless: Voluntary Childless Middle-Aged Women's Retrospective and Current Views, and Their Relationship to Life Satisfaction.* California School of Professional Psychology, Berkeley, 1988. 49/05B.

399   Goldberg, Gertrude S., et al. "Spouseless, Childless Elderly Women and Their Social Supports." *Social Work* March/April 1986 31: 104–112.

400   Houser, Betsy Bosak, et al. "The Relative Rewards and Costs of Childlessness for Older Women." *Psychology of Women Q* Summer 1984 8(4): 395–398.

401   Johnson, Colleen Leahy, and Donald J. Catalano. "Childless Elderly and Their Family Supports." *Gerontologist* December 1981 21(6): 610–619.

402   Johnson, Randell Bloom. *Psychodynamic and Developmental Considerations of Childless Older Women.* Northwestern U, 1981. 42/09B.

403   Myers, Jane E., et al. "To Have Not: The Childless Older Women." *J of Humanistic Education and Development* March 1984 22(3): 91–100.

404   Rice, Susan. "Single, Older, Childless Women: Differences Between Never-Married and Widowed Women in Life Satisfaction and Social Support." *J of Gerontological Social Work* 1989 13(3/4): 35–47. Adapted from part of her doctoral dissertation, *Single Older Childless Women: A Study of Social Support and Life Satisfaction.* U of California, Los Angeles, 1982. 43/04A.

DIVORCE
See also Chapter 4: Displaced Homemakers (723–737).

405   Atwood, Elizabeth Comer. *A Study of the Needs and Life Experiences of Former Wives of Retired Military Personnel.* Claremont Graduate School, 1984. 46/08B.

406   Byrd, Anne Justice. *The Decision to Remarry and the Ethic of Care: A Qualitative Study of Formerly Divorced Females.* U of North Carolina at Greensboro, 1986. 48/02A.

407   **Gander, Anita Moore.** "Economics and Well-Being of Older Divorced Persons." *J of Women & Aging* 1991 3(1): 37–57.

408   **Gander, Anita Moore.** "Reasons for Divorce: Age and Gender Differences." *J of Women & Aging* 1992 4(2): 47–60.

409   **Hagestad, Gunhild O.,** 1942– . "Sex and Gender in the Aging Society." In Alan J. Pifer and Lydia Bronte, eds. *Our Aging Society: Paradox and Promise.* New York: Norton, 1986. 111–140.

410   **Leonard, Frances.** "Divorce and Older Women [Older Women's League paper]." ERIC, 1988. ED #320060. 16 pages.

411   **Loew, Rebecca M.** *Determinants of Divorced Older Women's Labor Force Participation.* Brandeis U, 1992. 53/05A.

412   **Louis, Barbra Schantz.** *The Relationship of Learning to the Significant Life Events of Marital Separation and Divorce.* Rutgers State U of New Jersey, 1985. 46/09A.

413   **Norris, Amanda Malloy McPahil.** *From Divorce to a Stepfamily: The Woman's Psychological Experience.* Union for Experimenting Colleges and Universities, 1988. 49/04B.

414   **Taylor, Andrea Stuart.** *Divorce in Late Life: Case Studies of Urban Women.* Temple U, 1987. 48/04A.

415   **Weingarten, Helen R.** "Late Life Divorce and the Life Review." In Robert Disch, ed. *Twenty-Five Years of the Life Review: Theoretical and Practical Considerations.* Binghamton, New York: Haworth, 1988. 83–97.

FRIENDSHIP

416   **Armstrong, M. Jocelyn, and Karen S. Goldsteen.** "Friendship Support Patterns of Older American Women." *J of Aging Studies* Winter 1990 4(4): 391–404.

417   **Essex, Marilyn J., et al.** "Marital Status and Loneliness Among Older Women: The Differential Importance of Close Family and Friends." *J of Marriage and the Family* February 1987 49(1): 93–106.

418   **Greenberg, Reva M.** "Older Women: The Meaning of Involvement with Family and Friends." ERIC, November 25, 1980. ED #201938. 17 pages.

419   **Jacobs, Ruth Harriet.** "Friendships Among Old Women." *J of Women & Aging* 1990 2(2): 19–32.

420   **Lewittes, Hedva J.** "Just Being Friendly Means a Lot—Women, Friendship, and Aging." *Women & Health* 1988 14(3/4): 139–160.

421   **Martin, Sally S.** *Perceptions of Reciprocity and Relationship Quality Among Elderly Female Nonkin Peers.* Oregon State U, 1992. 53/08A.

422   **Newsome, Teresa Irene.** *The Therapeutic Functions of Friendship for Elderly Women: An Examination of Quality, Quantity, and Continuity.* U of Kentucky, 1985. 46/09B.

423   Reinhardt, Joann P. *Kinship Versus Friendship: Social Adaptation in Married and Widowed Elderly Women.* Fordham U, 1988. 49/04B.

424   Reinhardt, Joann P., and Celia B. Fisher. "Kinship Versus Friendship: Social Adaptation in Married and Widowed Elderly Women." *Women & Health* 1988 14(3/4): 191–212.

425   Roberto, Karen A., et al. "Friendship Patterns Among Older Women." *International J of Aging and Human Development* 1984–1985 19(1): 1–10.

426   Scott, Veronica Louise. *Elderly Women's Patterns of Friendship in a Recreation Organization.* U of Alberta, Canada, 1990. M.A. thesis.

427   Troll, Lillian E. "Old Age." In Carol Tavris, ed. *EveryWoman's Emotional Well-Being.* New York: Doubleday, 1986. Chapter 1.

428   Wright, Paul H. "Gender Differences in Adults' Same- and Cross-Gender Friendships." In Rebecca G. Adams and Rosemary Blieszner, eds. *Older Adult Friendship, Structure and Process.* Newbury Park: Sage, 1989. Chapter 9.

Homemakers; Housewife/Work Role
See also Chapter 4: Displaced Homemakers (723–737); Chapter 4: Work; Employment and Unemployment; "Women's Work"; "Working Mothers" (846–895); Chapter 6: Re-entry; Resuming Education and Employment (1269–1349).

429   Auman, Jane, and Robert Conroy. "An Evaluation of the Role, Theory, and Practice of the Occupation of Homemaker." *Home Health Care Services Q* Fall 1984/Winter 1984/85 5(3/4): 135–158.

430   Brubaker, Timothy H., and Charles B. Hennon. "Responsibility for Household Tasks: Comparing Dual-Earner and Dual-Retired Marriages." In Maximiliane Szinovacz, ed. *Women's Retirement: Policy Implications of Recent Research.* Beverly Hills: Sage, 1982. Chapter 14.

431   Henry, Mary E. "The Relationship of Life Satisfaction to Patterns of Past Employment and Homemaking Responsibility for Older Women." *J of Women & Aging* 1991 3(1): 5–21.

432   Keating, Norah C., and Priscilla Cole. "What Do I Do with Him 24 Hours a Day? Changes in the Housewife Role After Retirement." *Gerontologist* February 1980 20: 84–89.

433   Matthews, Glenna Christine, 1938– . *"Just a Housewife": The Rise and Fall of Domesticity in America.* New York: Oxford U Press, 1987. bib, index.
       The problem is finally identified in the final chapter, "Naming the Problem."

434   Skorupka, Patricia Conti. *A Study of Self-Esteem and Achievement Motivation in Middle-Aged Women in Student Versus Homemaker Roles.* U of Pittsburgh, 1988. 50/06B.

Leisure

435   Allen, Katherine R., and Victoria Chin-Sang. "A Lifetime of Work: The Context and Meanings of Leisure for Aging Black Women." *Gerontologist* December 1990 30(6): 734–740.

436   **Chamberlain, Letitia Anne.** *The Experience of Leisure, Time, and Meaning in Daily Life Among Retired Professional Women.* New York U, 1990. 52/03A.

437   **Chin-Sang, Victoria.** *Subjective Experiences of Leisure Among Older Black Women.* Texas Woman's U, 1989. 50/11A.

438   **Deem, Rosemary.** *All Work and No Play? The Sociology of Women and Leisure.* Milton Keynes: Open U Press, 1986. bib, index.
    Deem provides a wide-range analysis of women's leisure in Britain, treating activities and interests from competitive sport to sitting at home, emphasizing the complex relationships among leisure, class, age, and race. Chapter 1, "Do Women Have Leisure?" evidences feminist methodology; Chapter 7, "Leisure and Life Cycles," concerns age, middle age, and older women.

439   **Hupp, Sandra Lee.** *Satisfaction of Older Women in Leisure Programs: An Investigation of Contributing Factors.* U of Oregon, 1985. 46/11A.

440   **Myrvang, Vigdis Hegna.** "'Life Goes On as Usual': The 'Leisure' of Female Old-Age Pensioners [in Scandinavia]." *Ethnologia Scandinavica Lund* 1992 22: 83–94.

LOVE AND SEXUALITY; LESBIAN RELATIONSHIPS

See also Chapter 2: Sexuality; Sex Role; Gender (281–302); Chapter 7: Crones (1350–1356); #1920, #1921.

441   **Adelman, Marcy Robin.** *Adjustment to Aging and Styles of Being Gay: A Study of Elderly Gay Men and Lesbians.* Wright Institute, 1980. 41/02B.

442   **Adelman, Marcy Robin, ed.** *Long Time Passing: Lives of Older Lesbians.* Boston: Alyson, 1986.
    Dr. Adelman is a psychologist in the San Francisco Bay Area. In this collection of articles and interviews, referred to as case studies, lesbians ranging in age from 60 to 85 express their concerns about aging and changes in gay lifestyle as they discuss their past and present lives. Included, for example, is Faeth Reboin's "Lesbian Grandmother."

443   **Adelman, Marcy Robin.** "Stigma, Gay Lifestyles, and Adjustment to Aging: A Study of Later-Life Gay Men and Lesbians." *J of Homosexuality* 1990 20(3/4): 7–32.

444   **Almvig, Chris.** *The Invisible Minority: Aging and Lesbianism.* Utica, New York: Utica College of Syracuse U, 1982. bib, il. Originally presented as Almvig's thesis.

445   **Berger, Raymond M.** "Realities of Gay and Lesbian Aging." *Social Work* January-February 1984 29(1): 57–62.

446   **Berger, Raymond M.** "The Unseen Minority: Older Gays and Lesbians." *Social Work* May 1982 27(3): 236–242.

447   **Copper, Baba.** "The View from over the Hill: Notes on Ageism Between Lesbians." *Trivia* Summer 1985 7: 48–63. Reprinted in Jeffner Allen, ed. *Lesbian Philosophies and Cultures.* Albany: SUNY Press, 1990.

448   **Copper, Baba.** "Voices: On Becoming Old Women." In Jo Alexander, et al, eds. *Women and Aging: An Anthology by Women.* Corvallis: Calyx Books, 1986. 47–57.

449   **Cruikshank, Margaret.** "Lavender and Gray: A Brief Survey of Lesbian and Gay Aging Studies." *J of Homosexuality* 1990 20(3/4): 77–87.

450   **Curb, Rosemary Keefe,** 1940– , **and Nancy Manahan,** 1946– , eds. *Lesbian Nuns: Breaking Silence.* Tallahassee: Naiad Press, 1985. bib, il, index. (With the title *Breaking Silence: Lesbian Nuns on Convent Sexuality,* published without indexing in England by Columbus.)

A glossary of terms accompanies this biographical collection of fifty personal essays by lesbian nuns in the United States. Each writer's years in religious life are indicated (Curb 1958–1965, Manahan 1966–1967). Essays include "Gay and Celibate at Sixty-Five" by Sister Maria; "Life-Long Lovers" by Mary Mendola; "Mysticism: Love or Suffering" by Hannah Blue Herson; and "Recognizing Myself as a Lesbian" by Susan Weaver.

451   **Dorrell, Beth.** "Being There: A Support Network of Lesbian Women." *J of Homosexuality* 1990 20(3/4): 89–98.

452   **Douglas, Carol Anne.** "Passages: Lesbian Aging" and "Save Up Your Sunsets." *Off Our Backs [OOB]* April 1988 18(4): 16, 17.

453   **Friend, Richard** A. "Older Lesbian and Gay People: The Theory of Successful Aging." *J of Homosexuality* 1990 20(3/4): 99–118.

454   **Gervain, Edward James.** *A Comparative Analysis of Psychological Adaptation to Aging Between Gay Men and Gay Women.* U of Oregon, 1981. 42/08B.

455   **Goldberg, Sheryl.** "GLOE: A Model Social Services Program for Older Lesbians." *Catalyst: A Socialist J of the Social Services,* No. 21. 1987 6(1): 75–82.

456   **Gray, Diane Lee.** *Women's Sexuality from the Margin to the Center.* Georgia State U, 1987. 48/07A.

457   **Healey, Shevy.** "An Unbreakable Circle of Women—Can We Create It? Age-Segregation Privilege and the Politics of Inclusion." *Off Our Backs [OOB]* June 1991 21: 10+.

458   **Hite, Shere,** 1942– . *The Hite Report: Women and Love: A Cultural Revolution in Progress.* New York: Knopf, 1987. bib.

Hite's 1987 study considered the responses of 4,500 women to questions about their "inner emotional lives." Many in long-term marriages with men "finally gave up," and a large percentage of heterosexual women aged 40 and over indicated that they had left or were considering leaving their marriages—34 percent of lesbians 40 and over had previously been in heterosexual marriages. See pages 328–336 for the "No one wants an old woman" (and therefore females should marry) connection.

459   **Kehoe, Monika,** 1909– , **issue ed.** "Historical, Literary, and Erotic Aspects of Lesbianism [in the United States]." *J of Homosexuality* Spring/Summer 1986 12(3/4). Simultaneously published by Harrington Park Press in indexed-book form with bibliographies.

460   **Kehoe, Monika,** 1909– , **special issue compiler.** "Lesbians over 60 Speak for Themselves [in the United States]." *J of Homosexuality* 1988 16(3/4). Simultaneously published by Harrington Park Press in book form with bibliographies.

461   **Kehoe, Monika,** 1909– . "Lesbians over 65: A Triply Invisible Minority" and "A Portrait of the Older Lesbian." In her *Historical, Literary, and Erotic Aspects of Lesbianism.* New York: Haworth Press, 1986. 139–152, 157–161.

462   **Kirkpatrick, Martha.** "Middle Age and the Lesbian Experience." *J of Women & Aging* Spring/Summer 1989 17(1/2): 87–96.

463   **Lee, John Alan, issue ed.** "Gay Midlife and Maturity." *J of Homosexuality* 1990 20(3/4). Published in book form by Harrington Park Press in 1991. See Adelman (#441), Cruikshank (#449), Dorrell (#451), Friend (#453), and Winkler (#474).

464   **Neild, Suzanne, 1939– , and Rosalind Pearson, 1950– , eds.** *Women Like Us.* London: Women's Press, 1992.
　　　　This expansion of the British Channel 4 (comparable in some ways to American public television) documentary of the same title consists of the stories of nineteen middle-aged and aged British lesbians.

465   **Poor, Satile.** "Older Lesbians." In Margaret Cruikshank, ed. *Lesbian Studies, Present and Future.* Old Westbury: Feminist Press, 1982. 165–173.

466   **Raphael, Sharon M., and Mina K. Robinson.** "Lesbians and Gay Men in Later Life." *Generations* Fall 1981 6(1): 16–18.

467   **Raphael, Sharon M., and Mina K. Robinson.** "The Older Lesbian: Love Relationships and Friendship Patterns." *Alternative Lifestyles* May 1980 3(2): 207–229.

468   **Ruby, Jennie.** "Passages V: A Multicultural Conference on Aging and Ageism for All Lesbians" (held in Washington, D.C., on March 18, 1989). *Off Our Backs [OOB]* May 1989 19: 8.

469   **Sang, Barbara E., 1937– .** "Reflections of Midlife Lesbians on Their Adolescence." *J of Women & Aging* 1990 2(2): 111–117.

470   **Sang, Barbara E., 1937– , et al, eds.** *Lesbians at Midlife: The Creative Transition, an Anthology.* San Francisco: Spinsters Book Co., 1991. il.
　　　　Dr. Sang is a psychologist who has collected these first-person accounts of experiences. Sections include "Relating as Daughters, Relating as Mothers"; "Maintaining Our Equilibrium in Couples—Or Not"; "Our Changing Bodies"; "Preparing for Our Future," which includes legal protection and financial planning for retirement; and "Rediscovering Our Creativity and Spirituality," about crones.

471   **Stullman, Molly Eisner.** *Paths to Lesbian Identity Formation in Later Life: An Adult Developmental Study.* California School of Professional Psychology, Berkeley, 1985. 46/04B.

472   **Weitz, Rose.** "What Price Independence? Social Reactions to Lesbians, Spinsters, Widows and Nuns." In Jo Freeman, ed. *Women: A Feminist Perspective, 3d ed.* Palo Alto: Mayfield, 1984. 454–464.

473   **"West Coast Old Lesbian Conference and Celebration."** *Off Our Backs [OOB]* July 1987 7(17).

474   **Winkler, John J.** "Sappho and the Crack of Dawn (Fragment 58 L-P)." *J of Homosexuality* 1990 2(3/4): 227–233.

475   **Wolf, Deborah Goleman.** *The Lesbian Community: With an Afterword, 1980.* Berkeley: U of California Press, 1980. bib, il, index. Revision of the author's U of California, Berkeley 1977 thesis titled *Contemporary Amazons: A Study of a Feminist Community*, 38/08A.

Marriage and Remarriage; Family;
Other Relationships and Roles
See also this chapter: Motherhood; Adult Daughter; Mother/Daughter, Grandmother/Daughter, Stepmother/Children (497–545).

476   **Allen, Katherine Russell.** *A Life Course Study of Never-Married and Ever-Married Elderly Women from the 1910 Birth Cohort.* Syracuse U, 1984. 45/12A.

477   **Brown, Barbara Elizabeth.** *Married, Academic Women in Mid-Life Transition.* Temple U, 1982. 44/01A.

478   **Coleman, Lerita M., et al.** "Social Roles in the Lives of Middle-Aged and Older Black Women." *J of Marriage and the Family* November 1987 49(4): 761–771.

479   **Finch, Janet.** *Married to the Job: Wives' Incorporation into Men's Work.* Boston: Allen and Unwin, 1983. bib, index.
        Finch's interest in wives' effects on husbands' employment began with her doctoral thesis on wives of English clergy. Here she considers wives of spouses representing a variety of occupations, trades, and professions. Part 1, "Hedging Her In": how men's work structures their wives' lives. Part 2, "Drawing Her In": wives' contributions to their husbands' work. Part 3, "Married to the Job": foundations of wives' incorporation.

480   **Gafner, George, and Frank Uetz.** "Compulsive Gambling and the Aging Marital System." *Clinical Gerontologist* 1990 10(1): 45–47.

481   **Gibbs, Virginia Lee.** *The Relationship of the Quality of a Marital Relationship to Adjustment to Life Change Events Among Older Women.* California School of Professional Psychology, San Diego, 1991. 52/11B.

482   **Gilligan, Carol.** "Adult Development and Women's Development: Arrangements for a Marriage." In Janet Zollinger Giele, ed. *Women in the Middle Years: Current Knowledge and Future Directions for Research and Policy.* New York: Wiley, 1982. Chapter 3.

483   **Greenwood, Nancy Anne.** *Marriage and Self-Esteem Among the Elderly: Social Interaction as Opportunities for Self-Evaluations.* Washington State U, 1982. 43/09A.

484   **Guisinger, Shan.** *The First Years of the Second Marriage: Changing Parental and Couple Relations in the Remarriage Family.* U of California, Berkeley, 1984. 45/09B.

485   **Kaplan, Lori, and Linda Ade-Ridder.** "Impact on the Marriage When a Spouse Moves to a Nursing Home." *J of Women & Aging* 3(3): 81–101.

486   **Levine, David Harvey.** *Marital Adjustment Among Remarried Elderly Dyads.* Ohio State U, 1981. 42/10A.

487   **Longino, Charles F., Jr., and Aaron Lipman.** "The Married, the Formerly Married and the Never Married: Support System Differentials of Older Women in Planned Retirement Communities." *International J of Aging and Human Development* 1982 15(4): 285–297.

488   **Miles, Merle Yvonne.** *"Born and Bred" in Texas: Three Generations of Black Females: A Critique of Social Science Perceptions on the Black Female.* U of Texas at Austin, 1986. 47/05A.

489   **Morell, Marie, and Robin F. Apple.** "Affect Expression, Marital Satisfaction, and Stress Reactivity Among Premenopausal Women During a Conflictual Marital Discussion." *Psychology of Women Q* September 1990 14(3): 387–402.

490   **O'Keeffe, Janet Elizabeth.** *Starting a Second Family: The Effect of Children from a Husband's Prior Marriage and the Payment of Child Support on Birth Expectations in Women's First and Second Marriages.* U of California, Los Angeles, 1988. 49/07A.

491   Peters, Elizabeth. "Factors Affecting Remarriage." In Lois Banfill Shaw. *Midlife Women At Work: Fifteen-Year Perspective.* Lexington: Lexington, 1986. Chapter 7.

492   Preston, Deborah B., and Cheryl Dellasega. "Elderly Women and Stress: Does Marriage Make a Difference?" *J of Gerontological Nursing* April 1990 16(4): 26–32.

493   Reeves, Joy B., and Ray L. Darville. "Aging Couples in Dual-Career/Earner Families: Patterns of Role-Sharing." *J of Women & Aging* 1992 4(1): 39–55.

494   Siegel, Rachel Josefowitz. "Love and Work After 60: An Integration of Personal and Professional Growth Within a Long-Term Marriage." *J of Women & Aging* 1990 2(2): 69–79.

495   Steitz, Jean A., and Karen G. Welker. "Remarriage in Later Life: A Critique and Review of the Literature." *J of Women & Aging* 1990 2(4): 81–90.

496   Vartabedian, Laurel Cauthers Klinger. *The Influence of Age Difference in Marriage on Longevity.* U of Oklahoma, 1981. 42/07A.

MOTHERHOOD; ADULT DAUGHTER; MOTHER/DAUGHTER, GRANDMOTHER/DAUGHTER, STEPMOTHER/CHILDREN

See also this chapter: Care; Caregivers; Caregiver Role (303–395); Chapter 6: Pregnancy and Childbirth (1187–1212); #2025.

497   Abramowitz, Robert Howard. *Midlife Mothers and Adolescent Children: The Impact of Aspects of Mothers' Lives on the Mother-Child Relationship and Adolescent Adjustment.* Pennsylvania State U, 1985. 47/01B.

498   Abramson, Jane Beber. *Mothermania: A Psychological Study of Mother-Daughter Conflict.* Lexington: Lexington, 1987. bib, il, index.
    "Separation from the mother is scary business" declares Dr. Abramson in the preface to her book of case studies of American mothers' and daughters' interpersonal relationships and self-actualization.

499   Barranti, Chrystal Carol. *The Maternal Grandmother/Grandchild Relationship: Relationship Quality as Perceived by the Young Adult Grandchild.* U of Georgia, 1985. 46/05A.

500   Bassoff, Evelyn. *Mothers and Daughters: Loving and Letting Go.* New York: New American Library, 1988. bib, index.
    Psychologist Bassoff's 1988 book focuses on middle-aged women in the United States and the separation process experienced by them and their daughters.

501   Bromberg, Eleanor Mallach. "Mother-Daughter Relationships in Later Life: Negating the Myths." *Aging* Fall 1983 340: 15–20.

502   Bromberg, Eleanor Mallach. "Mother-Daughter Relationships in Later Life: The Effect of Quality of Relationship upon Mutual Aid." *J of Gerontological Social Work* September 1983 6: 75–91.

503   Brown, Judith Karen. *Stepmothering in Stepmother and Combination Families: The Strains and Satisfactions of Making the Role of Stepmother.* U of Texas at Austin, 1984. 45/07A.

504   Burton, Linda M., and Vern L. Bengston. "Black Grandmothers: Issues of Timing and Continuity of Roles." In Vern L. Bengtson and Joan F. Robertson, eds. *Grandparenthood.* Beverly Hills: Sage, 1985. Chapter 4.

505   **Cannon, Mildred Southern.** *Some Factors Influencing How Adult Daughters at Midlife Plan for Their Own Aging.* U of Maryland, College Park, 1988. 50/04A.

506   **Cochran, Maybelle M.** "The Mother-Daughter Dyad Throughout the Life Cycle." *Women & Therapy* Summer 1985 4(2): 3–8.

507   **Cohler, Bertram J., et al.** *Mothers, Grandmothers, and Daughters: Personality and Child Care in Three-Generation Families.* New York: Wiley, 1981. index.
Cohler, Henry U. Grunebaum, and Donna Moran Robbins present case studies of family relationships, the generation gap, socialization, and child care as they interrelate.

508   **DeLago, Louise R. Furia.** *Women at Mid-Life: Mothers at Home, Mothers at Work.* U of Pennsylvania, 1986. 47/07A.

509   **Downs, Delight.** *The Comparison of the 16 Personality Factors of Women, Retired or Retiring from the Motherhood Role.* U.S. International U, 1981. 42/02B.

510   **Eisenber, Ann R.** "Grandchildren's Perspectives on Relationships with Grandparents—The Influence of Gender Across Generations." *Sex Roles* August 1988 19(3–4): 205–217.

511   **Fischer, Lucy Rose.** *Linked Lives: Adult Daughters and Their Mothers.* New York: Harper and Row, 1986. bib, index.
This analysis of American mother-daughter relationships identifies two key turning points: when the daughter becomes a mother (Fischer assumes she does), and when the mother becomes frail. The mother's role in most families includes that of primary caregiver; that role is passed on from generation to generation.

512   **Gauchat, Juliet Valerie.** *Becoming a Mother-in-Law: A Complex Task in Parenting an Adult Daughter.* Boston U, 1989. 50/03A.

513   **Genevie, Louis, and Eva Margolies.** *The Motherhood Report: How Women Feel About Being Mothers.* New York: Macmillan, 1987. bib, index.
In 1985 the authors surveyed more than a thousand women aged 18–80 throughout the United States on a contract with National Family Opinion, Inc. Their purpose was to ascertain women's real feelings toward their children and about being mothers. The median age of 879 respondents was 44.7; a slightly larger percentage of the nonwhite women were willing to participate. Despite the authors' use of the unfortunate "working mother" term, their study is of interest.

514   **Gross, Zenith Henkin.** *And You Thought It Was All Over! Mothers and Their Adult Children.* New York: St. Martin's, 1985. bib, index.
Middle-aged women in the United States are often expected to fill dual roles of adult children and mothers.

515   **Jache, Ann Gail.** *The Adult Children of Elderly Widows: The Consequences of Being Part of a Support Network for Adult Children's Socialization for Their Own Old Age.* U of Notre Dame, 1986. 47/10A.

516   **Johnson, Elizabeth S.** "Older Mothers' Perceptions of Their Child's Divorce." *Gerontologist* August 1981 21: 395–401.

517   **Kahrl, Julia Gamble.** *Maternal Death as Experienced by Middle-Aged Daughters: Implications for Psychoeducational Interventions.* Ohio State U, 1988. 50/01A.

518   Lanter, Joyce Carolyn. *Relationship Satisfaction Between Elderly Mothers and Their Adult Children.* Virginia Polytechnic Institute and State U, 1986. 47/09A.

519   LaSorsa, Valeria A., and Iris G. Fodor. "Adolescent Daughter/Midlife Mother Dyad: A New Look at Separation and Self-Definition." *Psychology of Women Q* December 1990 14(4): 593–606.

520   Lee, Diane Maxine. *Providers and Recipients of Social Support: The Stressful Situation of the Young Grandmother.* U of Maryland, College Park, 1982. 44/10B.

521   Matthiesen, Valerie Jean. *Adult Daughters' Relationships with Their Institutionalized Mothers.* Rush U College of Nursing, 1986. 47/01B.

522   Merrill, Deborah, and Ann Dill. "Ethnic Differences in Older Mother-Daughter Co-Residence." *Ethnic Groups* 1990 8(3): 201–214.

523   Mink, Diane Leslie. *Early Grandmotherhood: An Exploratory Study.* California School of Professional Psychology, Los Angeles, 1987. 49/06B.

524   Payne, Karen, ed. *Between Ourselves: Letters Between Mothers and Daughters, 1750–1982.* Boston: Houghton, Mifflin, 1983. bib, index.
    "Matters of Life or Death" includes Constance Lytton (1869–1923) writing at age 40 to her mother, Edith, with whom she lived. Shortly after, she became committed to the English suffrage movement, ultimately imprisoned, forcibly fed, and invalided for life.

525   Popek, Paulene, and Andrew E. Scharlach. "Adult Daughters' Relationships with Their Mothers and Reactions to the Mothers' Deaths." *J of Women & Aging* 1991 3(4): 79–96.

526   Randell, Brooke Patterson. *Older Primiparous Women: The Evolution of Maternal Self-Perception Within the Context of Mother-Daughter and Spousal Relationships.* U of California, San Francisco, 1988. 49/04B.

527   Rice, Nancy Hall, and Ana Thacher. "Where's Mother?" *Heresies* 1988 6(3): 32–35. "Coming of Age" issue #23.

528   Robbins, Martha A. "Mourning the Myth of Mother/Hood: Reclaiming Our Mothers' Legacies." *Women & Therapy* 1990 10(1): 41–59.

529   Rosenberg, Angela Marie. *Identity Salience in the Midlife Woman's Relationship with Her Mother.* Washington U, 1988. 50/03B.

530   Rosebud-Harris, Mary Catherine. *A Description of the Interactional and Subjective Characteristics of the Relationships Between Black Grandmothers and Their Grandchildren Enrolled in the University of Louisville.* U of Iowa, 1982. 43/08A.

531   Rudenko, V. "Mothers and Daughters." (Appeared in Soviet weekly, about the complex attitudes of middle-aged women toward their aging mothers, translated by Emily Tall.) *Feminist Studies* September 1989 15: 119–124.

532   Samadani Fard, Mohammad. *The Perception of the Role of Daughters' Participation in Filial Responsibilities Toward Their Elderly Mothers.* Syracuse U, 1985. 47/02A.

533   Saunders, Martha J. "Mothers Are Our Sisters: Agencies, Responsibility and Community." (Discussion of Jeffner Allen's call for the "evacuation" of motherhood in *Lesbian Philosophy.*) *Resources for Feminist Research* September 1989 18: 47–50.

534   **Scharlach, Andrew Edmund.** *Filial Relationships Among Women and Their Elderly Mothers.* Stanford U, 1985. 46/08A.

535   **Sheehan, Susan.** *Kate Quinton's Days.* Boston: Houghton, Mifflin, 1984.
The material originally appeared in *New Yorker* magazine as a case study of home care, disabled senior women, and family relationships in New York City. Irish-American Kate Quinton, born in 1902, and her caregiver daughter, Claire—middle-aged, weight-fluctuating, under "a psychiatric therapist's treatment," drop-out nun—should be studied for the oppression conveyed.

536   **Siegel, Rachel Josefowitz.** "Old Women as Mother Figures." *Women & Therapy* 1990 10(1–2): 89–97. (Special "Motherhood: A Feminist Perspective" issue.)

537   **Silverstein, Sophie Muriel.** *The Transmission of Values Associated with the Independent Social Functioning of Young Children: A Comparison Between Value Orientation of Middle-Class Mothers and Maternal Grandmothers.* New York U, 1980. 41/06B.

538   **Sonnek, Ida Mae.** *The Maternal Grandmother Role in Families with Young Handicapped Children.* Indiana U, 1983. 44/10A.

539   **Steindel, Cheryl Debra.** *The Relationship of Self-Esteem and Life Satisfaction to Attachment Between Elderly Mothers and Their Middle-Aged Daughters.* Michigan State U, 1982. 43/02B.

540   **Stueve, Ann, and Lydia O'Donnell.** "The Daughter of Aging Parents." In Grace Kesterman Baruch and Jeanne Brooks-Gunn, eds. *Women in Midlife.* New York: Plenum Press, 1984. Chapter 8.

541   **Timberlake, Elizabeth M.** "The Value of Grandchildren to Grandmothers." *J of Gerontological Social Work* Fall 1980 3(1): 63–76.

542   **Uphold, Constance Rae.** *Contact, Socially Supportive Behaviors, and Positive Affect Between Adult, Working Women and Their Mothers and Mothers-in-Law.* U of Maryland at Baltimore, 1988. 49/08B.

543   **Uphold, Constance Rae.** "Positive Affect Between Adult Women and Their Mothers and Mothers-in-Law." *J of Women & Aging* 1991 3(4): 97–116.

544   **Walker, Alexis J., et al.** "Two Generations of Mothers and Daughters: Role Position and Interdependence." *Psychology of Women Q* June 1987 11(2): 195–208.

545   **Zeeb, Holly Cyrus.** *Languages of Mothering: A Psychological Study of Mothers of Sons and Mothers of Daughters at Mid-Life.* Harvard U, 1985. 46/08B.

Older Woman/Younger Man; Older Man/
Younger Woman
See also #1213; Chapter 8; #1916.

> *The acceptable May-December romances and popular "September Song"
> allude to an old man and a young woman. The practice of men seeking
> younger women as mates has origins in the economics of long ago, when
> women functioned as wives and mothers and sometimes as providers, and
> men were expected to function as providers. To locate serious consideration*

of the subject of a woman considerably older than the man in her life, one must search both periodicals and books. Some useful subject-headings are:

Age differences
Age groups—social aspects
Age (psychology)—social aspects
Conflict of generations
Couples
Interpersonal relations
Middle aged men—social aspects
Women—conduct of life
Young men

546   **Bove, Lucia A.** *Attitudes Toward Age Disparate Couples.* Hofstra U, 1985. 47/02B.

547   **Carley, Sylvia Marion.** *Of a Certain Age: Women and Age Discrepant Marriages.* U of Florida, 1988. 50/03A.

548   **Dereski, Arlene, and Sally B. Landsburg.** *The Age Taboo: Older Women—Younger Men Relationships.* Boston: Little, 1981. bib, index.
    By "older women," these therapists have in mind middle-aged women; "relationships" include cohabitation and marriage. They interviewed fifty couples committed to long-term relationships and with age differences ranging from six to twenty years.

549   **Gordon, Barbara, 1935– .** *Jennifer Fever: Older Men, Younger Women.* New York: Harper, 1988.
    Jennifer was the most popular name for girl babies for about fifteen years. Gordon interviewed people involved in what she refers to as the Jennifer Fever concept—older men, abandoned wives, and the young Jennifers—as well as psychologists, psychiatrists, and marriage counselors for her study of the motivations involved in traditional age disparity.

550   **Lovenheim, Barbara.** "Older Women, Younger Men." *New York* December 17, 1990 23(49): 47+.

551   **Massey, Veronica Jean.** *Older Women and Younger Men: The Initiation Narrative of the French Eighteenth Century.* Columbia U, 1983. 46/01A.

552   **Norment, Lynn.** "What's Behind the Older Woman–Younger Man Trend?" *Ebony* May 1992 47(7): 44+.

553   **Peterson, Sally H.** *The New Dyad: Older Women and Younger Men.* Fielding Institute, 1985. 45/10B.

554   **Randolph, Laura B.** "Older Women, Younger Men: A Relationship That Once Was Frowned Upon Is Becoming Very, Very Popular." *Ebony* May 1988 43(7): 156+.

555   **Sunila, Joyce.** *The New Lovers: Younger Men/Older Women.* New York: Fawcett, 1980.
    Sunila interviewed couples and concluded that younger males may be less prejudiced. Jack LaPatra and his spouse also interviewed "age-different" couples for *The Age Factor: Love, Sex, and Friendship Across the Generations* (Evans, 1980), although with greater age-spans, typically twenty years, and without gender focus.

Retirement

See also Chapter 5: Housing; Communal Arrangements; Retirement Places; "SRO" Single Room Occupancy (917–944); #2238; #2251.

> *The Women's Initiative of the American Association of Retired Persons makes available current publications related to women's retirement years, and the AARP itself sponsors with government agencies compilations such as* A Profile of Older Americans, 1990.

556   **Anson, Ofra, et al.** "Family, Gender, and Attitudes Toward Retirement." *Sex Roles* April 1989 20: 355–369.

557   **Atchley, Robert C.** "The Process of Retirement: Comparing Women and Men." In Maximiliane Szinovacz, ed. *Women's Retirement: Policy Implications of Recent Research.* Beverly Hills: Sage, 1982. Chapter 10.

558   **Barrett, Linda L.** *Older Workers' Attitude Toward Their Retirement.* (Sex-role identity. Gender. Occupation. Fishbein Model.) U of Missouri, Columbia, 1985. 47/04A.

559   **Batchelor, A. J.** "Senior Women Physicians: The Question of Retirement." *New York State J of Medicine* June 1990 90(6): 292–294.

560   **Beutner, Gloria Parks.** *Retirement: Differences in Attitudes and Preparatory Behavior Among Male and Female University Employees.* SUNY at Buffalo, 1980. 41/08A.

561   **Block, Marilyn R.** "Professional Women: Work Pattern as a Correlate of Retirement 'Satisfaction.'" In Maximiliane Szinovacz, ed. *Women's Retirement: Policy Implications of Recent Research.* Beverly Hills: Sage, 1982. Chapter 12.

562   **Cassidy, Margaret Louise.** *The Effects of Retirement on Emotional Well-Being: A Comparison of Men and Women.* Washington State U, 1982. 43/09A.

563   **Cavaghan, Peggy Jean Gibbons Todd.** *Social Adjustment of Women to Retirement.* U of California, Davis, 1981. 42/08A.

564   **Cavallaro, Marion Louise.** *Correlates of Perceived Job Deprivation and Life Satisfaction Among Retired Women of Different Occupational Groups.* Ohio State U, 1980. 41/04B.

565   **Chatman, Elfreda Annmary.** *The Information World of Retired Women.* New York: Greenwood Press, 1992. bib, index.
        Number 29 in the publisher's New Directions in Information Management series, this brief (150-page) work appears to be derived from Chatman's 1983 University of California, Berkeley library science work, *The Diffusion of Information Among the Working Poor.* With the goal of learning how retired women acquire their information, attitudes toward aged women retirees, and their social networks in the United States, fifty-five women, average age 82, in a Southeastern retirement community were studied. Although Chatman refers to use of network theory, there is little development of it.

566   **Cohen, Cynthia Fryer.** *Estimation and Analysis of Differentials in Expected Retirement Benefits Provided by the Private Pension System for Men and Women.* Georgia State U, 1980. 41/04A.

567   **Cook, Alicia Skinner.** "A Comparison of Leisure Patterns and Morale Between Retired Professional and Nonprofessional Women." *J of Women & Aging* 1991 3(3): 59–68.

568   Couchman, Glennis M. *Economics of Midlife Women: Employment and Retirement Issues.* Oklahoma State U, 1986. 47/08B.

569   Coyle, Jean M. "Retirement Planning and the Woman Business Owner." In Marilyn J. Bell, ed. *Women as Elders: Images, Visions, and Issues.* New York: Haworth Press, 1986. 55–58. (Also published as *Women & Politics* Summer 1986 6[2] issue and by Harrington Park Press with the subtitle, *The Feminist Politics of Aging.*)

570   Davis, Kathleen Dee. *Predicting Retirement Adjustment Problems in Women.* Texas A & M, 1983. 44/09B.

571   Delehanty, Mary Joan. *Women and Retirement: Gender Characteristics, Resources and Impairment.* SUNY at Albany, 1989. 50/02A.

572   Derr-Olmen, Diane Michele. *Personality and Social Support in Women and Adjustment to Change in Late Adulthood.* Catholic U of America, 1987. 47/12B.

573   Durrant, Anne Elizabeth. *The Effects of Preretirement Workshop Participation on Women's Retirement Knowledge, Anxiety Levels and Planning Behaviors.* Tennessee State U, 1985. 48/12A.

574   Erdner, Ruth A., and Rebecca F. Guy. "Career Identification and Women's Attitudes Toward Retirement." *International J of Aging & Human Development* 1990 30(2): 129–339.

575   Feuerbach, Eileen Johnstone. *Women's Retirement: The Influence of Work History on Retirement Attitudes and the Retirement Decision.* George Mason U, 1990. 51/04B.

576   Franks, Rosalie Horne. *Struggling to the Top: The Managerial Woman's View of Aging and Retirement.* Boston U, 1985. 48/08A.

577   Friedman, Roslyn, and Annette Nussbaum. *Coping with Your Husband's Retirement.* New York: Simon & Schuster, 1986.
       Interviews of seventy-five wives of retirees supplied guidance for couples whose men are living longer and retiring earlier and information on things to do together and separately.

578   Frye, Louise Meagher. *Adjustment to Retirement of Male and Female Professors.* U of Wisconsin, Madison, 1984. 45/02A.

579   Gardner, Marilyn. "The Gender Tilt to Retirement (Older Women's Retirement Prospects)." *Christian Science Monitor* May 18, 1990 82(121): 14.

580   Gigy, Lynn L. *Women's Adjustment to Retirement: Use of the Personal Past.* U of California, San Francisco, 1982. 43/03B.

581   Gitter, Robert J., et al. "Early Labor Market Withdrawal." In Lois Banfill Shaw. *Midlife Women at Work: Fifteen-Year Perspective.* Lexington, Massachusetts: Lexington, 1986. Chapter 6.

582   Harrison, Pauline Payne. *Morale Among Wives of Retired and Preretired Professors.* Oklahoma State U, 1983. 44/07A.

583   Hatch, Laurie Russell. "Gender Differences in Orientation Toward Retirement from Paid Labor." *Gender and Society* March 1992 6: 66–85.

584   Hatch, Laurie Russell. "Research on Men's and Women's Retirement Attitudes: Implications for Retirement Policy." In Edgar F. Borgatta and Rhonda J. V. Montgomery, eds. *Critical Issues in Aging Policy: Linking Research and Values.* Beverly Hills: Sage, 1987. Chapter 5.

585   Hatch, Laurie Russell. *A Structural Analysis of Men and Women in Retirement (Gender).* U of Washington, 1986. 47/12A.

586   Haug, Marie R., et al. "Partners' Health and Retirement Adaptation of Women and Their Husbands." *J of Women & Aging* 1992 4(3): 5–29.

587   Hayes, Christopher L., and Jane M. Deren, eds. *Pre-Retirement Planning For Women: Program Design and Research.* New York: Springer, 1990.
       The editors have created what one reviewer—Sandy K. Auburn in the *J of Women and Aging* 1992 4(1): 107–108—called "a nifty little book" for academics, practitioners, and others interested in aging issues for women. They present the central issues, program development, and research.

588   Jewson, Ruth Hathaway. "After Retirement: An Exploratory Study of the Professional Woman." In Maximiliane Szinovacz, ed. *Women's Retirement: Policy Implications of Recent Research.* Beverly Hills: Sage, 1982. Chapter 11.

589   Keith, Pat. "Working Women Versus Homemakers: Retirement Resources and Correlates of Well-Being." In Maximiliane Szinovacz, ed. *Women's Retirement: Policy Implications of Recent Research.* Beverly Hills: Sage, 1982. Chapter 5.

590   Kroeger, Naomi. "Preretirement Preparation: Sex Differences in Access, Sources, and Use." In Maximiliane E. Szinovacz, ed. *Women's Retirement: Policy Implications of Recent Research.* Beverly Hills: Sage, 1982. Chapter 6.

591   Levy, Sandra M. "The Adjustment of the Older Woman: Effects of Chronic Ill Health and Attitudes Toward Retirement." *International J of Aging and Human Development* 1980–1981 12(2): 93–110.

592   Ludwig-Beymer, Patti Ann. *A Descriptive Study of the Transition from Employment to Retirement for Women.* U of Utah, 1985. 48/06B.

593   MacFarlane, May. "Women and Retirement—Uncharted Territory." *Canadian Woman Studies/Les Cahiers de la Femme* Winter 1992 12: 55–57.

594   Madigan, Mary Frances. *Preparation for Prime Time: Three Business Women at Work and in Retirement.* Columbia U Teachers College, 1985. 46/09A.

595   Martin, Cora, et al. "Aging: A More Difficult Problem for Women than for Men?" In Harold J. Wershow, ed. *Controversial Issues in Gerontology.* New York: Springer, 1981. Chapter 7.

596   Martin, Kathryn. *A Question of Age: The Dorm and I.* Granthan: Thompson and Rutter, 1981.
       Martin's memoir is about the psychological aspects of her retirement from employment as a New England house mother and the conflict of generations.

597   Martindale, Judith A., 1947– , and Mary J. Moses, 1928– . *Creating Your Own Future: A Woman's Guide to Retirement Planning.* Naperville, Illinois: Sourcebooks, 1991.
       The emphases are on retirement guidance for American women at all ages and planning.

598   McKenna, Judy Sheaks. *Planning for Retirement Security: A Study of Women in the Middle Years.* Oklahoma State U, 1985. 47/03B.

599   McMahon, Betty Johnson. *Midlife Married Women's Perceptions of the Retirement Life Stage: An Exploratory Study with Implications for Preretirement Education and Home Economics/Human Ecology.* Michigan State U, 1988. 49/09B.

600   Mildenberger, Valerie I. *Retirement Age Policies and the Exclusion of Women.* Carleton U (Canada), 1990. Master's thesis.

601   Newman, Evelyn S., et al. "Retirement Expectations and Plans: A Comparison of Professional Men and Women." In Maximiliane E. Szinovacz, ed. *Women's Retirement: Policy Implications of Recent Research.* Beverly Hills: Sage, 1982. Chapter 7.

602   Ogle, Karen Marie. *Older Marriages in Retirement: A Study in Temperament, Intimacy and Marital Satisfaction.* Brigham Young U, 1985. 47/01B.

603   O'Rand, Angela M., and John C. Henretta. "Midlife Work History and Retirement Income." In Maximiliane E. Szinovacz, ed. *Women's Retirement: Policy Implications of Recent Research.* Beverly Hills: Sage, 1982. Chapter 2.

604   Pampel, Fred C. *Social Change and the Aged: Recent Trends in the United States.* Lexington: Lexington, 1981. bib, index.
        Dr. Pampel is a professor of sociology who reports that employment, income, senior women, and health generate the social and economic conditions of retirement. Chapter 3, "Compositional and Processual Effects on Changes in the Labor-Force Participation of Aged Males"; Chapter 4, "Cohort Change and Retirement Among Aged Females."

605   Perkins, Kathleen Patricia. *Blue-Collar Women and Retirement.* U of Pennsylvania, 1990. 52/03A.

606   Price-Bonham, Sharon, and Carolyn Kitchings Johnson. "Attitudes Toward Retirement: A Comparison of Professional and Nonprofessional Married Women." In Maximiliane E. Szinovacz, ed. *Women's Retirement: Policy Implications of Recent Research.* Beverly Hills: Sage, 1982. Chapter 8.

607   Reeves, Joy B. "Women in Dual-Career Families and the Challenge of Retirement." *J of Women & Aging* 1989 2(2): 119–132.

608   Reynolds, James Talmadge. *The Preretirement Educational Needs of Retired Black Women Who Were Domestic Workers in Dallas, Texas.* East Texas State U, 1981. 42/12A.

609   Ricardo-Campbell, Rita, and Edward P. Lazear, eds. *Issues in Contemporary Retirement.* Stanford: Stanford U Hoover Institution Press, 1988. index.
        The increase in labor force participation of middle-aged women 40 years and older has been extraordinary. Part 1, "Labor Force Activity," includes Chapter 3, "Women: Retirees and Widows" by Ricardo-Campbell, with discussion by John Shoven, who notes how little statistical information exists about women's retirement plans and even their actual retirement circumstances, and that public-use data tapes are both out-of-date and inadequate. Kingsley Davis (Chapter 7, "Retirement as a Dubious Paradise—Another Point of View") considers the Western Standard Retirement Path, "the ideal pursued by the United States and several other industrial countries," to have major problems. "Total retirement as a policy . . . consciously disregards the

singular contribution of women and therefore causes inequity and social disorganiza-tion." Women who have been in the labor market are entitled to retirement benefits, but many older women have either not been in the labor market or have been there only a short time.

610   **Richardson, Virginia.** "Gender Differences in Retirement Planning Among Edu-cators: Implications for Practice with Older Women." *J of Women & Aging* 1990 2(3): 27–40.

611   **Rosenthal, Lois Shapiro.** *Women's Retirement and Long Distance Relocation: A Comparative Study.* Union Institute, 1991. 52/02A.

612   **Rotman, Anita.** *Professional Women in Retirement.* U of Pittsburgh, 1981. 43/07A.

613   **Saxon, Sue V.** "Health Care and Midlife Women: Planning for Future Needs." In Christopher L. Hayes and Jane M. Deren, eds. *Pre-Retirement Planning for Women: Pro-gram Design and Research.* New York: Springer, 1990. 41–59.

614   **Skirboll, Esther, and Myrna Silverman.** "Women's Retirement: A Case Study Approach." *J of Women & Aging* 1992 4(1): 77–90.

615   **Solomon, Geetha Nalini.** *Attitude Towards Retirement: A Study of State-Employed Females of Iowa.* Iowa State U, 1981. 42/07A.

616   **Stone, Robyn Illene.** *The Effects of Retirement on the Health Status of Older Un-married Women.* San Francisco: U of California Aging Health Policy Center, 1984.
        Readers of this paper will also be interested in Dr. Stone's dissertation (#617). She found that retirement is associated with immediate and lagged decline in self-as-sessed health status.

617   **Stone, Robyn Illene.** *The Health Effects of Retirement for Older Unmarried Women.* U of California, Berkeley, 1985. 46/09B.

618   **Suh, Mary.** "When I'm 65." (Stress of six women in retirement or approaching "retirement age.") *Ms* November-December 1991 2: 58–62.

619   **Szinovacz, Maximiliane E.** "Beyond the Hearth: Older Women and Retire-ment." In Elizabeth W. Markson, ed. *Older Women: Issues and Prospects.* Lexington: Heath, 1987. Chapter 6.

620   **Szinovacz, Maximiliane E., ed.** *Women's Retirement: Policy Implications of Re-cent Research.* Beverly Hills: Sage, 1982. bib.
        "Obviously, if men and women experienced retirement in a similar fashion, special studies of women's retirement would be of little scientific or applied value. There is, however, good reason to believe that men's and women's retirement experi-ences and adjustment differ in substantial ways. . . . Not only does society place a dif-ferent value on . . . work in their occupational roles, but we may also expect that sex differences in socialization and other gender-based variations in men's and women's roles impact on their . . . retirement transition in particular" (pp. 9–10). Part I, "Em-ployment Status, Work History, and Life Situation of Older Women"; Part II, "Prepar-ing For Retirement: Attitudes and Plans"; Part III, "Adjusting to Retirement: The Fe-male Experience."

621   **Tremblay, Diane-Gabrielle, et al.** "Older Workers and Institutional Support in the Management of Human Resources/Les Travailleuses Vieillissantes et les Enjeux In-stitutionnels en Matiere de Gestion des Resources Humaines." *Canadian Woman Stud-ies/Les Cahiers de la Femme* Spring 1992 12: 40–45.

622   **U.S. Congress. House. Select Committee on Aging. Subcommittee on Retirement Income and Employment.** *How Will Today's Women Fare in Yesterday's Traditional Retirement System? Hearing Before the Subcommittee . . . 102nd Congress, Second Session, March 26, 1992.* Washington: For sale by the U.S. Government Printing Office, 1992. Govt. Doc. No.: Y 4.Ag 4/2:W 84/15. bib, il.

     The committee focused on discrimination experienced by aged women based on their sex as it relates to pensions and Social Security in particular. This 375-page book-like document is also available in most depository libraries in microfiche form.

623   **U.S. Congress. House. Select Committee on Aging. Subcommittee on Retirement Income and Employment.** *Women in Retirement: Are They Losing Out? Hearing Before the Subcommittee . . . 101st Congress, Second Session, May 22, 1990.* Washington: For sale by the U.S. Government Printing Office, 1990. Govt. Doc. No.: Y 4.Ag 4/2:W 84/11. il, bib.

     The committee heard testimony concerning retirement income, including old age pensions available to aged women and the economic conditions within which they must survive. This 172-page document is also available in most depository libraries in microfiche form.

624   **U.S. Department of Labor Women's Bureau.** *Retirement Equity Act of 1984: Its Impact on Women* and *Facts About the Joint and Survivor Benefits of the Retirement Equity Act (REA).* Washington: The Bureau, 1985.

625   **Urbas, Jeanette.** "The 'Golden Years.'" *Canadian Woman Studies/Les Cahiers de la Femme* Winter 1992 12: 51–53.

626   **Zietlow, Paul Harold.** *An Analysis of the Communication Behaviors, Understanding, Self-Disclosure, Sex Roles, and Marital Satisfaction of Elderly Couples and Couples in Earlier Life Stages.* Ohio State U, 1986. 47/07A.

SELF-DELIVERANCE; ASSISTED SUICIDE; RIGHT TO DIE

See also Chapter 2: Death and Dying (111–115); Chapter 5: Abuse; Coercion; Crime; Victimization; Violence; *Sati* (896–916); #960; #1559.

> *To locate serious consideration of this subject matter as it concerns women and particularly women in terms of their age, one must search both periodicals and books. Some useful descriptors are:*

> Assisted suicide
> Decision making
> Euthanasia
> Professional ethics
> Right to die
> Risk taking
> Suicide, assisted
> Treatment withholding
> Widow suicide

> *Most female suicides in the United States are in the 35–44 age range; most U.S. males who suicide are between 25 and 34. Internationally, the greatest*

rate of female suicide in 1990 was in Denmark; of male suicide in Austria
(*U.S. Bureau of the Census's* Statistical Abstract of the U.S. 1993, 113th
ed.). *A study released by the journal of the American Society of Law and
Medicine concluded that American courts usually reject turning off life-
support systems for* female *patients because women are considered more
emotional, immature, and in need of protection than men; "Dying," com-
mented Dr. Steven H. Miles, the study coauthor, "is not a gendered activity"*
(Newsweek *July 2, 1990 116: 6). The self-immolation of widows, labeled
"suicide" by some, is herein regarded as* violence *and considered in Chapter
5. The right to refuse medical treatment constitutes a chapter in Robert N.
Brown's* The Rights of Older Persons *(see #766).*

627   **Beck, Melinda.** "A Home Away from Home—Day Care Offers Self-Esteem to
the Elderly and Respite to the Family." *Newsweek* July 2, 1990 116(1): 56–58.

628   **David, Lester,** 1942– , **ed.** *Why Women Kill Themselves.* Springfield, Illinois:
C. C. Thomas, 1988. index.

Chapter 1, "Suicide in Women: An Overview," has data on age, occupation, nations, comparisons with men, etc. Contents include "Suicide and the Menstrual Cycle"
(menopause); "Virginia Woolf: The Life of a Completed Suicide"; "Dorothy Parker: The
Life of an Attempted Suicide."

629   **Kearney, Robert N.** "Women's Suicide in Sri Lanka." In Patricia Whelehan, ed.
Women and Health: Cross-Cultural Perspectives. Westport: Bergin & Garvey, 1988. Chapter 8.

630   **Logue, Barbara J.** "Taking Charge—Death Control as an Emergent Women's
Issue." *Women & Health* 1991 17(4): 97–121.

631   **Miles, Steven H., and Allison August.** "Courts, Gender and 'The Right to Die';
Second International Conference on Health Law and Ethics (1989, London, England)."
Law, Medicine & Health Care Spring-Summer 1990 18 (1–2): 85–95.

632   **Older Women's League.** *Taking Charge of the End of Your Life: Proceedings of a
Forum on Living Wills and Other Advance Directives, July 1985.* Washington: American
Bar Association's Commission on Legal Problems of the Elderly and The Older
Women's League, 1985. bib.

Although no longer in print, this 69-page document on American law and legislation regarding terminal care and the power-of-attorney and right to die is available
in many university and law libraries.

633   **Prado, C. G.** *The Last Choice: Preemptive Suicide in Advanced Age.* New York:
Greenwood, 1990. bib, index.

Philosophy professor Prado contends that "selective death in advanced age
must be recognized as a sensible alternative to demeaning deterioration and stultifying
dependency." His belief is "supported by good evidence that most of the recent increase
in elderly suicides is due to growing unwillingness by the old to endure the very mixed
benefits of medically and technologically lengthened life spans" (p. 5). He defends the
rationality of elective suicide in old age prior to affliction with terminal conditions.

634   **Rollin, Betty,** 1936– . *Last Wish.* New York: Simon and Schuster, 1985.

Last Wish is about the right to die and a health system ghastly for old women
even when money is not a concern. It has implications for the hospice movement. It also

conveys a feminine psychology that can add to old women's burdens—the good-little-girl/ladylike syndrome right to the agonizing end. Journalist Rollin discovered all this while caring for her mother, Ida Rollin (1908–1983). In her desperation, she remembered someone she had interviewed who claimed he had "helped his wife die and wrote a book about it." More up-to-date (1991) is *Final Exit: The Practicalities of Self-Deliverance and Assisted Suicide for the Dying* (Hemlock Society, POB 11830, Eugene, Oregon 97440), for which Rollin provided a foreword. Hemlock also published Ann Wickett's *Double Exit: When Aging Couples Commit Suicide Together* (1988).

635   **Sommers, Tish,** 1914–1985, **et al.** *Death and Dying: Staying in Control to the End of Our Lives.* (An Older Women's League "Gray Paper.") ERIC, August 1986. ED #320057. 25 pages.

636   **Tolchin, Martin.** "When Long Life Is Too Much: Suicide Rises Among [the] Elderly." *New York Times* July 19, 1989: 1, 10.

Single Women: Ever Single; Never Married; Unmarried
See also Chapter 5: Isolation and Loneliness (945–955); #1213.

637   **Allen, Katherine R.** *Single Women/Family Ties; Life Histories of Older Women.* Newbury Park: Sage, 1989. bib.
      Thirty American single women born in 1910 were studied from the life course perspective. The term *single* is used here to encompass unmarried, never-married, and widowed women. Of particular interest are Chapters 6, "The Middle Years: Taking Care of Families," and 7, "Growing Old as Single Women."

638   **Barresi, Charles M., and Kimberly Hunt.** "The Unmarried Elderly: Age, Sex, and Ethnicity." In Timothy H. Brubaker, ed. *Family Relationships in Later Life, 2d ed.* Newbury Park: Sage, 1990. Chapter 9.

639   **Braito, Rita, and Donna Anderson.** "The Ever-Single Elderly Woman." In Elizabeth W. Markson, ed. *Older Women: Issues and Prospects.* Lexington: Heath, 1987. Chapter 10.

640   **Cohen, Marilyn.** *Remaining Single into Midlife: An Investigation of Early Family Relationships, Traumatic Experiences, Idealism/Perfectionism, and Fear of Loss.* California School of Professional Psychology, 1987. 48/08B.

641   **Corby, Nan, and Judy Maes Zarit.** "Old and Alone: The Unmarried in Later Life." In Ruth B. Weg, ed. *Sexuality in the Later Years: Roles and Behavior.* New York: Academic Press, 1983. Chapter 6.

642   **Jensen, Roberta "Tobe."** *The Life Course of Independent Women: Career and Relationship Development of Mid-Life Single Women in Male-Dominated Professions.* Fielding Institute, 1989. 50/05A.

643   **Keith, Pat M.** "Postponement of Health Care by Unmarried Older Women." *Women & Health* Spring 1987 12: 47–60.

644   **Keith, Pat M.** *The Unmarried in Later Life.* New York: Praeger, 1989. bib, il, index.
      Ms. Keith's longitudinal study of the lives and well-being of old widowed and never-married women and men in the United States includes gender attitudes toward work and retirement. Tables include sex breakdowns.

645   **Kimmelman, Marilyn Irene.** *The Adult Years in the Life Cycles of Never-Married Professional Women.* Temple U, 1986. 47/03B.

646   **Lennon, Eugenia S.** *Autoperceptions of Aging by the Single Middle-Aged Woman: A Longitudinal Study.* Fielding Institute, 1990. 51/05A.

647   **Mahalski, Paulene A.** "The Value of Cat Ownership to Elderly Women Living Alone." *International J of Aging* 1988 27(4): 249–260.

648   **Olson, Carol.** "Socio-Economic Constraints on the 'Young-Elderly' Woman." *Free Inquiry in Creative Sociology* May 1980 8: 77–82.

649   **Peterson, Nancy Lee.** *The Ever-Single Woman: Life Without Marriage.* New York: Quill, 1982.

Originally titled *Our Lives for Ourselves: Women Who Have Never Married* (Putnam's, 1981), this is about American single women of all ages, into their seventies. Chapter 2: "The Age Thirty Crisis"; Chapter 3: "Into the Thirties and Early Midlife: Confronting the Biological Imperative"; Chapter 6: "Midlife: On Smoother Waters."

650   **Pratt, Clara C., et al.** "Autonomy and Decision Making Between Single Older Women and Their Caregiving Daughters." *Gerontologist* December 1989 29(6): 792–797.

651   **Simon, Barbara Levy,** 1949– . *Never-Married Women.* Philadelphia: Temple U Press, 1987. bib, il, index.

Here are autobiographical reflections of fifty American never-married women born between 1884 and 1918, from a variety of ethnic, occupational, and religious groups, who range in age from 65 to 105. In interviews conducted in the Greater New York–Philadelphia area from 1982–1984, nine refer to themselves as feminists. Chapter 1, "Being Marginal: The Single Woman as Caricature," points out that women writers are not exempt from prejudice. The novels of Barbara Pym, for example, "teem with highly idiosyncratic single women in middle and old age who have many of the negative characteristics of the 'old maid'" (p. 3). Chapter 6, "Aging and Retirement: A Study in Continuity," includes public policy issues. Other chapters consider being single, family, intimacy, and work. Simon is particularly concerned with "the discrepancy between popular images of 'old maids' and the actualities of single women's daily lives. . . . Minority groups in any culture occupy a vantage point that permits them, indeed, requires them, to inspect dominant norms and expectations with particular acuity." Her focus on their having often been judged but seldom studied leads to hope that research will increase. Of the four frequently referenced theories concerning the aging process—disengagement, activity, continuity, age stratification—disengagement and activity theories are most at odds with these women's experiences.

652   **Spector, Suzanne M.** *Realizing Their Prime: A Study of Single Women in Their Fifties.* Union Institute, 1991. 54/03B.

WIDOWS AND WIDOWHOOD

See also Chapter 2: Death and Dying (111–115); Chapter 2: Grief and Bereavement (153–174); Chapter 5: Abuse; Coercion; Crime; Victimization; Violence; *Sati* (896–916); #2251.

> Widow *is derived from Sanskrit, and means "empty." In modern usage,* widowed person *is considered preferable to the gendered* widow *and*

widower *to refer to the surviving spouse.* (Widower *is one of the few male words derived from the female-as-norm.) Because women typically live longer than men and are often younger than their spouses, widowhood is the experience of the majority.*

653   **Abzug, Bella Savitsky,** 1920– . "Martin, What Should I Do Now?" *Ms* July-August 1990 1: 95–96.

654   **Arens, Diana A.** "Widowhood and Well-Being: An Examination of Sex Differences Within a Causal Mode." *International Journal of Aging and Human Development* 1981–1983 15(1): 27–40.

655   **Aronson, Miriam Klausner.** *A Bio-Psycho-Social Survey of Community Elderly Widows: Implications for Comprehensive Care.* Columbia U Teachers College, 1980. 41/04B.

656   **Arsenault, Anne G.** *The Effect of Social Support Systems and Anticipatory Socialization on the Life Satisfaction of Widows.* Boston U, 1984. 44/10A.

657   **Avis, Nancy E., et al.** "The Effect of Widowhood on Health: A Prospective Analysis from the Massachusetts Women's Health Study." *Social Science & Medicine* 1991 33(9): 1063–1070.

658   **Bankoff, Elizabeth A.** "Aged Parents and Their Widowed Daughters: A Support Relationship." *J of Gerontology* 1983 38: 226–230.

659   **Bankoff, Elizabeth A.** "Social Support and Adaptation to Widowhood." *J of Marriage and the Family* November 1983 45(4): 827–839.

660   **Barrell, Lorna Mill.** *From Wife to Widow: The Transitional Process.* U of Illinois at Chicago, 1980. 41/10A.

661   **Bernikow, Louise.** *Alone in America: The Search for Companionship.* New York: Harper, 1986. (London: Faber & Faber, 1987 reprint.) index.
Bernikow addresses the 60+ million divorced, separated, unmarried, or widowed women and men in the United States, a significant number of whom are old women. "They cannot be friends to each other, this generation of widows, because they grew up in a world where women saw each other as competitors, threats, dangers" (Chapter 6, "Widows and Widowers"). Isolation and loneliness distress those who regard singleness as a social affliction and attempt to deal with it by putting their lives on hold. Her counsel (not how-to-find-someone advice, but how-to-thrive-without) contrasts with a more typical example such as Julia Grice's *How to Find Romance After 40* (M. Evans, 1985).

662   **Berrill, Naftali G.** *The Widow's Perception of Family as a Mediator of Complicated Bereavement.* Vanderbilt U, 1986. 47/08B.

663   **Bottar, Karen Rose.** *The Economic Well-Being and Social Adjustment of Mid-Life Widows.* Syracuse U, 1981. 42/10A.

664   **Burkhauser, Richard V., et al.** "Measuring the Well-Being of Older Women: The Transition from Wife to Widow." *Focus* Fall-Winter 1986 9(3): 1–27. Newsletter of the Institute for Research on Poverty, U of Wisconsin, 1180 Observatory Drive, 3412 Social Science Building, Madison, WI 53706.

665   **Castleman, Karen O.** *The Effect of Kin and Friend Support Systems on the Subjective Well-Being of Elderly Widows.* U of South Florida, 1984. 45/09B.

666 **Caylor, Margaret Reed.** *Living the Experience of Widowhood and Coping Through Reminiscence.* Texas Woman's U, 1990. 52/02A.

667 **Clary, Freddie Mae.** *Life Satisfaction Among Elderly Widowed Women.* U of Minnesota, 1983. 44/11A.

668 **Digiulio, Robert Christopher.** *Identity Loss and Reformulation in Young, Middle-Aged, and Older Widowed Women.* U of Connecticut, 1984. 45/04A.

669 **Estrin, Harriet Rosenman.** *Life Satisfaction and Participation in Learning Activities Among Widows.* Syracuse U, 1985. 46/12A.

670 **Farra, Robert Ross.** *The Widow/Bureaucratic Linkage During the Transition to Widowhood: An Exploratory Study.* Florida State U, 1982. 43/02A.

671 **Ferraro, Kenneth F.** "The Effect of Widowhood on the Health Status of Older Persons." *International J of Aging and Human Development* 1985–1986 21(1): 9–25.

672 **Ferraro, Kenneth F.** "Widowhood and Social Participation in Later Life: Isolation or Compensation?" *Research on Aging* December 1984 6(4): 451–468.

673 **Friday, Patricia Pittman.** *Coping with Widowhood: A Study of Urban and Rural Widows.* U of Wisconsin, Madison, 1985. 46/08A.

674 **Gentry, Margaret.** *Expectations and Perceptions: An Examination of the Self-Perceptions of Widows in Help-Seeking Situations.* Washington U, 1982. 43/09B.

675 **Goidel, Jeffrey Howard.** *Social, Situational and Personality Factors of the Psychological Adjustment of Widows and Widowers.* California School of Professional Psychology, Los Angeles, 1984. 45/09B.

676 **Golberg, Evelyn L.** "Health Effects of Becoming Widowed." In Ellen B. Gold, ed. *The Changing Risk of Disease in Women: An Epidemiological Approach.* Lexington: Heath, 1984. Chapter 4.

677 **Heinemann, Gloria Deanna Pitzer.** *Determinants of Primary Support System Strength Among Urban, Widowed Women: Does Life Stage Make a Difference?* U of Illinois at Chicago, 1980. 41/01A.

678 **Heinemann, Gloria Deanna Pitzer.** "Why Study Widowed Women: A Rationale." *Women & Health* Summer 1982 7(2): 17–29.

679 **Heinemann, Gloria Deanna Pitzer, and Patricia Evans.** "Widowhood: Loss, Change, and Adaptation." In Timothy H. Brubaker, ed. *Family Relationships in Later Life, 2d ed.* Newbury Park: Sage, 1990. Chapter 8.

680 **Hirsch, Sondra Modell.** *An Exploratory Study of the Social Functioning of Widows: The Relationship Between the Presence or Absence of Forewarning, Family Life-Cycle Stage, and Locus of Control of the Widow.* Columbia U Teachers College, 1980. 41/04A.

681 **Hudson, Cathie Mayes.** *The Transition from Wife to Widow: Short-Term Changes in Economic Well-Being and Labor Force Behavior.* Duke U, 1984. 46/05A.

682 **Hunter, Lisa Katherine.** *After Bereavement: A Study of Change in Attitudes About Life Among Older Widows.* Fielding Institute, 1990. 51/07A.

683   **Keith, Judy Gay Bryant.** *The Relationships Between the Adjustment of the Widowed and Social Support, Self-Esteem, Grief Experience and Selected Demographic Variables.* U of Tennessee, 1982. 43/09A.

684   **Kirschenbaum, Jill.** "A Widow's View of War." *Ms* November-December 1991 2: 86–87.

685   **Kinderknecht, Cheryl H., and Laree Hodges.** "Facilitating Productive Bereavement of Widows: An Overview of the Efficacy of Widow's Support Groups." *J of Women & Aging* 1990 2(4): 39–54.

686   **Lesnoff-Caravaglia, Gari.** "Widowhood: The Last Stage in Wifedom." In her *The World of the Older Woman: Conflicts and Resolutions.* New York: Human Sciences Press, 1984. Chapter 8.

687   **Lopata, Helena Znaniecka,** 1925– . "Widowhood." In George L. Maddox, ed. *Encyclopedia of Aging.* New York: Springer, 1987. 693–696.

688   **Lopata, Helena Znaniecka,** 1925– . *Widows.* Volume 1: *The Middle East, Asia and the Pacific.* Volume 2: *North America.* Durham, North Carolina: Duke U Press, 1987. index.
       Lopata is a sociology professor whose research focus relates to women as widows, widowhood, support systems, and social change.

689   **Lopata, Helena Znaniecka,** 1925– , **and Henry P. Brehm.** *Widows and Dependent Wives: From Social Problem to Federal Program.* New York: Praeger, 1986. bib, index.
       The authors include criticism from women's perspectives of the Social Security Act of 1935.

690   **Lubben, James E.** "Gender Differences in the Relationship of Widowhood and Psychological Well-Being Among Low-Income Elderly." *Women & Health* 1988 14(3/4): 161–190. Also in Lois Grau and Ida Susser, eds. *Women in the Later Years: Health, Social and Cultural Perspectives.* New York: Harrington Park Press, 1989.

691   **Macdonald, Joanne Ruth.** *Widows De Facto and De Jure: AFDC and OASDI.* Yeshiva U, 1982. 43/04A.

692   **Malatesta, Victor J.** "On Making Love Last in a Marriage: Reflections of Sixty Widows." *Clinical Gerontologist* 1989 9(1): 64–67.

693   **Matthews, Anne Martin.** "Canadian Research on Women as Widows: A Comparative Analysis of the State of the Art [review essay]." *Resources for Feminist Research/Documentation sur la Recherche Féministe.* July 1982 11(2): 227–239.

694   **McGloshen, Thomas H., and Shirley L. O'Bryant.** "The Psychological Well-Being of Older, Recent Widows." *Psychology of Women Q* March 1988 12: 99–116.

695   **Mineau, Geraldine P.** "Utah Widowhood: A Demographic Profile." In Arlene Scadron, ed. *On Their Own: Widows and Widowhood in the American Southwest, 1848–1939.* Champaign: U of Illinois Press, 1988. Chapter 6.

696   **Morgan, David L.** "Adjusting to Widowhood: Do Social Networks Really Make It Easier?" *Gerontologist* February 1989 29(1): 101–107.

697   **Nagesh, P. S. Nair, and A. P. Katti, eds.** *Widowhood in India.* Dharwad, Karnataka: Janata Shikshana Samiti, 1988. bib.

These papers of the National Seminar on Widowhood in India (1987), organized jointly under the auspices of Sri Dharmasthala Manjunatheshware Educational Trust, Ujire and Janata Shikshana Samiti, are in university libraries' collections and can be obtained from Dharwad, Karnataka. Part I: "Profiles of Widowhood"; Part II: "Issues and Perspectives"; Part III: "Policies and Programmes."

698   **Nagy, Mary Christine.** *Attributional Differences in Health Status and Life Satisfactions of Older Women: A Comparison Between Widows and Non-Widows.* U of Oregon, 1982. 43/12A.

699   **Neale, Anne Victoria.** *Social and Psychological Well-Being in Widowhood.* Wayne State U, 1981. 42/12B.

700   **Nocera, Doris Patterson.** *Neighborhood Satisfaction of Older Homeowning Widows.* Ohio State U, 1984. 45/06B.

701   **O'Bryant, Shirley L.** "Self-Differentiated Assistance in Older Widows' Support Systems." *Sex Roles* July 1988 19: 91–106.

702   **O'Bryant, Shirley L., and Leslie A. Morgan.** "Financial Experience and Well-Being Among Mature Widowed Women." *Gerontologist* April 1989 29(2): 245–251.

703   **Paul, Penelope Bradford.** *Adaptation in Widowhood Among Older Women.* U of Alabama, Birmingham, 1981. 43/02B.

704   **Porter, Eileen Jones.** *Older Widows' Experience of Living Alone at Home.* U of Wisconsin, Milwaukee. 52/08B.

705   **Ray, Robert Willard.** *Effects of Teaching Coping Skills to Widows in Groups.* U of Arizona, 1983. 44/03A.

706   **Rook, Karen Sue.** *Social Networks and Well-Being of Elderly Widowed Women.* U of California, Los Angeles, 1980. 41/08B.

707   **Scadron, Arlene, ed.** *On Their Own: Widows and Widowhood in the American Southwest, 1848–1939.* Champaign: U of Illinois Press, 1988. index.
Historian Scadron was interested in what it was like to be a widow in the America of the ninety years before 1940. The conclusion reached was that no typical widow existed.

708   **Silverman, Phyllis R.** *Widow-to-Widow.* New York: Springer, 1986. bib, index.
Three out of four women are widowed. The Widow-to-Widow Project at Harvard Medical School (1967–1973) is the main basis for Dr. Silverman's report on self-help groups for widows in the United States. She brings together current research on bereavement, the psychology of women, and mutual help interventions. She has also authored *Mutual Help Groups: Organization and Development* (Sage, 1980).

709   **Silverman, Phyllis R., and Adele Cooperband.** "Widow-to-Widow: The Elderly Widow and Mutual Help." In Gari Lesnoff-Caravaglia, ed. *The World of the Older Woman: Conflicts and Resolutions.* New York: Human Sciences Press, 1984. Chapter 9.

710   **Stein, Mary Kaufman.** *The Relationship of Psychological and Physical Symptomatology and Conditions Relating to Widowhood.* Kent State U, 1982. 44/01A.

711   **Sternberg, Malka B.** *The Long-Term Adaptations of Young and Middle-Aged Widows to the Loss of a Spouse.* Columbia U Teachers College, 1982. 43/10A.

712   **Stoll, Margaret Leslie.** *Predictors of Middle-Aged Widows' Psychological Adjustment.* California School of Professional Psychology, Los Angeles, 1981. 42/03B.

713   **Taich, Arlene Pitinsky.** *Reference Other Associations and Perceived Stress Among Older Widows.* Saint Louis U, 1980. 42/04A.

714   **Teaford, Margaret Hale.** *Predictors of Older Widows' Intentions to Move and Actual Relocation.* Ohio State U, 1992. 53/08A.

715   **Wambach, Julie Ann M.** *Widowhood as the Interruption and Reconstruction of Temporal Reality.* Arizona State U, 1983. 44/05A.

716   **Wegmann, Jo Ann.** *Hospice Home Death, Hospital Death, and Coping Abilities of Widows.* Claremont Graduate School, 1985. 46/08A.

717   **Whitted, Mabel Pollitt.** *An Exploratory Study: Life Satisfaction of Elderly Widows.* U of Michigan, 1983. 44/06A.

4

Economic Issues and Middle-Aged and Older Women

Forced to retire on inadequate income, robbed of identity and devoid of purpose, her spirit under siege, the elderly woman "exhibiting senile behavior" does not need drugs to "cure" her—what she needs is to be responded to, and be allowed to respond, as a human being.

Rhonda, "We Are All in This Together,"
Runes II (1977)

Consumerism; Credit: 718–722
Displaced Homemakers: 723–737
Income; Pension; Social Security; Alimony: 738–762
Policy; Law and Legislation; Political Economy: 763–811
Poverty; "Shopping Bag Ladies"; Homeless Women: 812–841
Volunteerism; Volunteers: 842–845
Work; Employment and Unemployment; "Women's Work"; "Working
    Mothers": 846–895

CONSUMERISM; CREDIT

See also Chapter 5: Housing; Communal Arrangements; Retirement Places; "SRO" Single Room Occupancy (917–944); Chapter 8: Media; Image; Stereotypes (1635–1679).

718   **Moore, Pat, and Charles P. Conn.** *Disguised.* Waco: Word Books, 1985. il.
    When American industrial designer Moore undertook her "experiment into her own future as an old woman," she was interested in old people as consumers, their environments in particular. Conn provided the gerontologist's perspective.

719   **Sherman, Elaine.** *Segmenting the Elderly Consumer Market: The Application of Age-Gender Categories Drawn from a Test of the Leveling Versus Double Jeopardy Hypotheses.* City U of New York, 1983. 44/05A.

720   **Tims, Mary K.** *Readability of Retail Printed Items and Shopping Behavior of Socially Active Older Women Shoppers of Apparel.* U of Tennessee, 1984. 46/02B.

721   **U.S. Congress. House. Select Committee on Aging. Subcommittee on Housing and Consumer Interests.** *Staying Healthy, Being Aware: Health Care After Forty: A Health Handbook for Women.* 102nd Congress, Second Session. Washington: For sale by the U.S. Government Printing Office, 1992. Govt. Doc. No.: Y 4.Ag 4/2:H 34/50. bib, il.
    Also available in most depository libraries in microfiche form.

722   **U.S. Congress. House. Select Committee on Aging. Subcommittee on Housing and Consumer Interests.** *Women at MidLife: Consumers of Second-Rate Health Care? Hearing . . . 102nd Congress, First Session, May 30, 1991.* Washington: For sale by the U.S. Government Printing Office, 1991. Govt. Doc. No.: Y 4.Ag 4/2:W 84/14. bib, il.
       Also available in most depository libraries in microfiche form.

Displaced Homemakers

> *The term* displaced homemaker *was coined by Tish Sommers in 1975 to describe the "middle-aged woman forcibly exiled" from her role as wife and mother and struggling to find a place in the job market. Later, it was broadened to encompass women in their middle years, generally 35–64, who have been deprived of their traditional role by the loss of spouse through separation, divorce, abandonment, or death. There are also many who have been unmarried, unpaid homemakers for parents, inlaws, and other women and who find themselves in this predicament.*

See also Chapter 3: Divorce (405–415); Chapter 3: Homemakers; Housewife/Work Role (429–434); this chapter: Poverty; "Shopping Bag Ladies"; Homeless Women (812–841); Chapter 6: Reentry; Resuming Education and Employment (1269–1349); #877.

723   **Andre, Rae.** *Homemakers: The Forgotten Workers.* Chicago: U of Chicago Press, 1981. bib, index.
       Although now more than ten years old, this important work by a professor of industrial administration underscores the domestic double standard. The concept of wages for housework is considered in Chapter 11.

724   **Baker, Nancy C.** *New Lives for Former Wives: Displaced Homemakers.* Garden City: Anchor Press/Doubleday, 1980. bib, index.
       Journalist Baker has been referred to as the "first person to deal with the problem of the displaced homemaker in book form."

725   **Benokraitis, Nijole.** "Older Women and Reentry Problems: The Case of Displaced Homemakers." *J of Gerontological Social Work* 1987 10(3/4): 75–92.

726   **Bracht, Dona Lansing.** "The Displaced Homemaker." In Naomi Gottlieb, ed. *Alternative Social Services for Women.* New York: Columbia U Press, 1980. Chapter 8.

727   **Chrisler, Miriam.** "Neither Employment Record nor Up-to-Date Skills." *E-SA: Engage/Social Action* March 1986 14(3): 32–35.

728   **Clark, Connie I.** *Middle-Aged Women Returning to the Work Force.* U of California, San Francisco, 1988. M.S. thesis.

729   **Crabtree, Jeanne L.** "The Displaced Homemaker: Middle-Aged, Alone, and Broke." *Aging* January-February 1980 303/304: 17–23.

730   **Gottlieb, Naomi,** 1925– , **ed.** *Alternative Social Services for Women.* New York: Columbia U Press, 1980. bib.
       By *alternative* the writers refer to such should-be nonsexist client groups as older women and displaced homemakers. Gottlieb's "Women and Mental Health: The Problem of Depression" (Chapter 1) includes issues in feminist therapy and therapeutic

aspects of consciousness-raising groups. Part 2, devoted to women in particular social statuses, includes Gottlieb's "The Older Woman"; Julie Campbell, et al's "Women in Midstream"; and Dona Lansing Bracht's "The Displaced Homemaker."

731   **Greenwood-Audant, Lois M.** "The Internalization of Powerlessness: A Case Study of the Displaced Homemaker." In Jo Freeman, ed. *Women: A Feminist Perspective, 3d ed.* Palo Alto: Mayfield, 1984. 264–281. Also appears as Chapter 14 in the 4th ed. (1989).

732   **Killpack, Ruth M.** *The Effectiveness of Two Educative/Therapeutic Programs for Single-Parent Women and Displaced Homemakers.* Brigham Young U, 1987. 48/09B.

733   **Meller, Jill.** "Displaced Homemakers in the Employment and Training System." In Sharon L. Harlan and Ronnie J. Steinberg, eds. *Job Training for Women: The Promise and the Limits of Public Policies.* Philadelphia: Temple U Press, 1989. Chapter 5.

734   **Nestel, Gilbert, et al.** "Economic Consequences of Midlife Change in Marital Status." In Lois Banfill Shaw, ed. *Unplanned Careers: The Working Lives of Middle-Aged Women.* Lexington: Lexington, 1983. 109–125.

735   **Obermiller, Janice.** *Displaced Homemakers: Vo-Tech Workshop Guide.* Newton, Massachusetts: WEEA Publishing Center, 1981.

The Women's Educational Equity Act Publishing Center (at 55 Chapel Street, #200, Newton 02158-1060; 1-800-225-3088) distributes this comprehensive curriculum guide to help women regain confidence and build decision-making, time management, and job-search skills, catalog #2231.

736   **Paladino, Kathryn Ann.** *A Case Study of the Psychological and Financial Issues of the Displaced Homemaker Who Has Become Independent After Divorce.* U of Pittsburgh, 1989. 50/06A.

737   **Roberts, Gloria Louise.** *A Study of Female Participants in Three Southern Mississippi Displaced Homemaker Centers.* U of Southern Mississippi, 1988. 49/10A.

INCOME; PENSION; SOCIAL SECURITY; ALIMONY
See also Chapter 3: Retirement (556–626); Chapter 8: Discrimination; Double Standards and Equity; Activist Responses; Sisterhood (1587–1634).

738   **Clark, Lynn.** *Financial Adjustment and Satisfaction with Level of Living: A Cross-Sectional View of Female Pensioners.* Florida State U, 1983. 44/07A.

739   **Douthitt, Robin Ann.** *Pension Information and the Retirement Decision of Married Women.* Cornell U, 1982. 43/04A.

740   **Finn, Judith B.** *The Treatment of Women Under Social Security: A Critique of the Proposed Reforms.* Washington: Free Congress Research & Education Foundation, 1981. bib.

This 63-page document is particularly concerned with employment of married women and Social Security. The Foundation address is 717 2nd St., N.E., Washington, D.C. 20002.

741   **Forman, Maxine.** "Social Security Is a Woman's Issue." *Social Policy* Summer 1983 14(1): 35–38.

742   Fowler, Elizabeth M. "Women Without Pensions." *New York Times* November 21, 1981: 12.

743   King, Gail Buchwalter. *The Changing Roles of Women and Their Implications for Social Security Policy*. Carnegie Mellon U, 1983. 44/03A.

744   Lingg, Barbara A. "Women Beneficiaries Aged 62 or Older, 1960–88." *Social Security Bulletin* July 1990 53(7): 2–12.

745   Miller, Dorothy C. *Women and Social Welfare: A Feminist Analysis*. New York: Praeger, 1990. bib.
       Women studies professor Miller uses the concept of "patriarchal necessity" to examine the treatment of women in the American social welfare system. Particularly relevant are Chapters 7, "Social Security and Women's Lives," and 8, "Pensions."

746   Moore, Libba Gate. *Mothers' Pensions: The Origins of the Relationship Between Women and the Welfare State*. U of Massachusetts, 1986. 47/07A.

747   Morgan, Leslie A. *After Marriage Ends: Economic Consequences for Midlife Women*. Newbury Park: Sage, 1991. bib, il, index.
       Published in cooperation with the National Council on Family Relations, this document considers both divorced women and widows in the United States.

748   Muller, Charlotte. "Income Supports for Older Women." *Social Policy* Fall 1983 14: 23–31.

749   Newton, Margaret W. "Women and Pension Coverage." In Sara E. Rix, ed. *The American Woman, 1988–1989: A Status Report*. Washington: Women's Education and Research Institute, 1988. 264–270.

750   Nusberg, Charlotte. "Pension and Long-Term Care Policies for Mid-Life and Older Women: A Perspective from the U.S. and Canada." *Ageing International* Winter 1986 13(5): 9–17.

751   O'Grady, Regina Ann. *Caring Work and Women's OASI Benefits: An Analysis of Proposed Changes in the Social Security Law*. Brandeis U, 1982. 43/05A.

752   Ozawa, Martha N. "The 1983 Amendments to the Social Security Act: The Issues of Intergenerational Equity." *Social Work* March-April 1982 29(2): 131–137.

753   Perlez, Jane. "Senate Approves Pension Measure to Benefit Women." *New York Times* August 7, 1984 I: 1.

754   Quadagno, Jill S. *The Transformation of Old Age Security: Class and Politics in the American Welfare State*. Chicago: U of Chicago Press, 1988. bib, index.
       Sociologist and gerontologist Quadagno's concerns here include widows and other women's access to private pensions, benefit levels, and public welfare. The title notwithstanding, old age pensions in both the United States and Europe are considered. The lengthy bibliography identifies books and articles from the pre–World War I—1980s decades.

755   Schofield, Rosalie Faulkner. *The Private Pension Coverage of Part-Time Workers*. Brandeis U, 1985. 46/03A.

756   Spector, William David. *The Adequacy of the Private Pension System for Women: A Look at Survivor Benefits and Vesting Provisions*. Brandeis U, 1981. 42/05A.

757   Uhlenberg, Peter, et al. "Change in Relative Income of Older Women, 1960–1980." *Gerontologist* April 1986 26(2): 164–170.

758   **U.S. Advisory Council on Social Security** (1989–1991). *Social Security and the Future Financial Security of Women: A Report of the Advisory Council on Social Security.* Washington: The Council, 1991. il.

759   **U.S. Congress. House. Select Committee on Aging. Subcommittee on Retirement Income and Employment.** *How Well Do Women Fare Under the Nation's Retirement Policies? A Report by the Ranking Republican . . . 102nd Congress, Second Session.* Washington: For sale by the U.S. Government Printing Office, 1992. Govt. Doc. No.: Y 4.Ag 4/2:W 84/17. bib, il.
       Also available in most depository libraries in microfiche form.

760   **U.S. Congress. House. Select Committee on Aging. Subcommittee on Retirement Income and Employment.** *Retirement Income for Women: Hearing . . . 101st Congress, Second Session.* Washington: For sale by the U.S. Government Printing Office, 1990. Govt. Doc. No.: Y 4.Ag 4/2:R 31/24. bib, il.
       Also available in most depository libraries in microfiche form.

761   **Wolf, Wendy A.** "Sex Discrimination in Pension Plans: The Problem of Incomplete Relief." *Harvard Women's Law J* Spring 1986 9: 83–103.

762   **Zedlewski, Sheila R.** "The Private Pension System to the Year 2020." In Henry J. Aaron and Gary T. Burtless, eds. *Retirement and Economic Behavior.* Washington: Brookings Institution, 1984. 315–344.

POLICY; LAW AND LEGISLATION; POLITICAL ECONOMY

See also Chapter 8: Discrimination (bias); Double Standards and Equity; Activist Responses; Sisterhood (1587–1634); this chapter: Income; Pension; Security; Alimony (738–762); this chapter: Poverty; "Shopping Bag Ladies"; Homeless Women (812–841).

763   **Abramovitz, Mimi.** *Regulating the Lives of Women: Social Welfare Policy from Colonial Times to the Present.* Boston: South End Press, 1988. bib, index.
       Abramovitz here focuses on public welfare policy as it has regulated the lives of poor women in the United States over the years. Chapters 1, "A Feminist Perspective of the Welfare State," and 2, "Old Age Insurance," are of particular interest.

764   **Block, Marilyn R., ed.** *The Direction of Federal Legislation Affecting Women over Forty.* College Park: National Policy Center on Women and Aging, 1982. bib. HE23.3002:W84.
       The Center, located at the University of Maryland, prepared this document related to the legal status of aged American women for the U.S. Administration on Aging.

765   **Brown, Diane Robinson.** *Employment and Health Among Older Black Women: Implications for Their Economic Status.* Wellesley College Center for Research on Women Working Paper No. 177. ERIC, 1988. ED #311112. 49 pages.

766   **Brown, Robert N., 1944–** . *The Rights of Older Persons, 2d ed., revised.* Carbondale: Southern Illinois U Press, 1989. bib.
       Brown considers medical care, "old age assistance," and the legal status of aged Americans, including a chapter, "The Right to Refuse Medical Treatment." Other titles

in the American Civil Liberties Union handbook series include Ross's *The Rights of Women* (#796), and James H. Stark and Howard Goldstein's *The Rights of Crime Victims* (Bantam, 1985). Other topics in ACLU's series concern the rights of tenants, mental and other patients, students, and the critically ill, as well as the right to government information.

767   **Cancian, Francesca M.** "Gender Politics: Love and Power in the Private and Public Spheres." In Alice S. Rossi, ed. *Gender and the Life Course.* New York: Aldine, 1985. Chapter 13.

768   **Carter, Helen S.** "Legal Aspects of Widowhood and Aging." In Arlene Scadron, ed. *On Their Own: Widows and Widowhood in the American Southwest, 1848–1939.* Urbana: U of Illinois Press, 1988. Chapter 11.

769   **Catchen, Harvey.** "Generational Equity: Issues of Gender and Race." *Women & Health* 1988 14(3/4): 21–38.

770   **Datan, Nancy,** 1941–1987. "Aging Women: The Silent Majority." *Women's Studies Q* Spring/Summer 1989 17(1/2): 12–19.

771   **Day, Alice Taylor, and Ann Harley.** "'I Hope That Something Will Come Out of This': Older Women and Government Policies for the Aged." *LaTrobe Working Papers in Sociology* May 1985, #72. LaTrobe University, Bundoora, Victoria, Australia.

772   **Eisler, Terri A.** "Older Women, Policy and Politics." In Marilyn J. Bell, ed. *Women as Elders: Images, Visions, and Issues.* New York: Haworth Press, 1986. 71–82. Also published as *Women & Politics* Summer 1986 6(2) issue and by Harrington Park Press with the subtitle *The Feminist Politics of Aging.*

773   **Estes, Carroll L.,** 1938– , et al. "Women and the Economics of Aging." *International J of Health Services* 1984 14(1): 55–68. Also published in Meredith Minkler and Carroll L. Estes, eds. *Readings in the Political Economy of Aging.* Amityville: Baywood, 1984. Chapter 13.

774   **Finch, Janet, and Dulcie Groves, eds.** *Labour of Love: Women, Work, and Caring.* Boston: Routledge, 1983. bib, index.
    The ten contributors' concern for the way society frequently views women as "natural carers" supplying domestic labor provides a political analysis of caregiving and the ways in which it fails to acknowledge the tensions between women's economic independence and any responsibility as caregivers. The bibliography accesses publications well into the 1980s decade, including international, British, and American periodicals and government agencies' documents.

775   **Giele, Janet Zollinger, ed.** *Women in the Middle Years: Current Knowledge and Directions for Research and Policy.* New York: Wiley, 1982. bib, index.
    The Social Science Research Council sponsored this edited collection, particularly useful in coping with the great need for research and its relationship to public policy. It includes Giele's "Women in Adulthood: Unanswered Questions" (Chapter 1) and "Women's Work and Family Roles" (Chapter 4).

776   **Glasse, Lou, and Frances Leonard.** "Policy from the Older Woman's Perspective." *Generations* 1988 12(3): 57–59.

777   **Harlan, Sharon L., and Ronnie J. Steinberg,** 1947– , eds. *Job Training for Women: The Promise and the Limits of Public Policies.* Philadelphia: Temple U Press, 1989. bib, index.

This volume in the "Women in the Political Economy Series" edited by Steinberg consists of five sections, each introduced by the editors: "Federal Training Initiatives"; "Targeted Groups and Program Experiences"; "Training for Nontraditional Jobs"; "Welfare, Workforce, and Training"; and "Public Training for the Private Sector."

778   **Harris, Louis, & Associates.** *Aging in the Eighties: America in Transition: A Survey.* . . . Washington, D.C.: National Council on the Aging, 1981.

The most extensive and recent data about aging available at the time, this statistical resource was a landmark. Based on more than 3,400 interviews conducted throughout the United States, the report showed trends in the aging experience and public opinion regarding status and problems of older Americans. Conducted for the National Council on the Aging, it updated NCOA's 1974 report, *The Myth and Reality of Aging in America*, which had prompted Tish Sommer's "Implications for Women [of the Myth . . .]" because of the dearth of sex/gender breakouts.

779   **Hess, Beth B.** "Aging Policies and Old Women: The Hidden Agenda." In Alice S. Rossi, ed. *Gender and the Life Course.* New York: Aldine. Chapter 17.

780   **Hess, Beth B.** "Old Women: Problems: Political and Policy Implications." In Elizabeth W. Markson and G. R. Batra, eds. *Public Policies for an Aging Population.* Lexington: Lexington, 1980. 39–59.

781   **Hing, Esther, and Beulah K. Cypress.** "Use of Health Services by Women 65 Years of Age and Over: United States." *Vital and Health Statistics.* August 1981 Series 13, "Data from the National Health Survey," #59.

782   **Holden, Karen C.** "Economic Status of Older Women: A Summary of Selected Research Issues." In Anna Regula Herzog, et al, eds. *Health and Economic Status of Older Women.* Amityville: Baywood, 1989. Chapter 5.

783   **Jackson, Jacquelyne Johnson.** "Aging Black Women and Public Policies." *Black Scholar* May-June 1988 19(3): 31–43.

784   **Jorgensen, Lou Ann B.** "Women and Aging: Perspectives on Public and Social Policy." *J of Women & Aging* 1989 1(1/2/3): 291–316.

785   **Ikehara, Elizabeth Slack.** *A Comparison of Sociopolitical Attitudes of Older Urban Women: The 1910–1924 Cohorts.* Portland State U, 1991. 52/08A.

786   **King, Nancy R., et al.** "Issues, Policies and Programs for Midlife and Older Women." ERIC, 1982. ED #225055. 179 pages.

787   **Lipson, Debra J.** "Medicare: Are There Any Holes in the Security Blanket?" (New Medicare catastrophic health care legislation). *Ms.* March 1988 16: 65.

788   **Meyer, Madonna Harrington.** *Universalism Vs. Targeting as the Basis of Social Distribution: Gender, Race and Long-Term Care in the United States (Medicare).* Florida State U, 1991. 52/08A.

789   **Minkler, Meredith, and Carroll L. Estes, 1938– , eds.** *Readings in the Political Economy of Aging.* Amityville, New York: Baywood, 1984. bib.

Section IV, "Aging as a Women's Issue," includes "Why Is Women's Lib Ignoring Old Women?" by Myrna I. Lewis and Robert H. Butler (Chapter 12), an unfortunately titled classic from 1972; Chapter 13, "Women and the Economics of Aging," by Estes, et al from 1982; and Chapter 14, "The Sociopolitical Context of Retirement," by Robyn Stone and Minkler.

790   **Nathanson, Paul S.** "Legal Issues Affecting Older Women." In Gari Lesnoff-Caravaglia, ed. *The World of the Older Woman: Conflicts and Resolutions.* New York: Human Sciences Press, 1984. Chapter 5.

791   **National Organization for Women. Legal Defense and Education Fund.** *The State-By-State Guide to Women's Legal Rights.* New York: McGraw-Hill, 1987.

The 1987 NOW LDEF guide included consideration for *elderly women* (tucked away in "Home and Family") and *age discrimination* (under "Employment").

792   **Nickols, Sharon V., et al.** "Economic Security for Older Women." *J of Home Economics* Spring 1983 75(1): 22–25.

793   **Paludi, Michele A., et al.** "Mentoring and Being Mentored: Issues of Sex, Power, and Politics for Older Women." *J of Women & Aging* 1990 2(3): 81–92.

794   **Rathbone-McCuan, Eloise.** "Health Needs and Social Policy." *Women & Health* Summer/Fall 1985 10 (2/3): 17–27. Also published in Sharon Golub and Rita Jackaway, eds. *Health Needs of Women as They Age.* New York: Haworth, 1985. 17–28.

795   **Rix, Sara E., and Anne J. Stone.** (Women's Research Institute, 1700 18 St., N.W. #400, Washington, D.C. 20009.) "Policy Options for Older Women." *Older Women: The Economics of Aging* January 1981: 27–33.

796   **Ross, Susan Deller, and Ann Barcher.** *The Rights of Women: The Basic ACLU Guide to a Woman's Rights. 2d ed.* New York: Bantam, 1983. bib.

This is a proactive guide, providing information about the law as well as areas of potential problems. *See also* Robert N. Brown's *The Rights of Older Persons, 2d ed., revised* (#766).

797   **Rossi, Alice S.,** 1922– . "Sex and Gender in an Aging Society." *Daedalus* Winter 1985 115(1): 141–169.

798   **Schlesinger, Joseph A., and Mildred Schlesinger.** "Aging and Opportunities for Elective Office." In Sara B. Kiesler, et al, eds. *Aging, Social Change.* New York: Academic Press, 1981. Chapter 9.

799   **Schuchardt, Jane Menninga.** *Objective Measures of Elderly Women's Economic Well-Being.* Iowa State U, 1985. 46/09A.

800   **Schuster, Michael R., et al.** *The Age Discrimination in Employment Act: An Evaluation of Federal and State Enforcement, Employer Compliance and Employee Characteristics: A Final Report of the NRTA-AARP Andrus Foundation.* Syracuse: Syracuse U School of Management, 1987. bib.

Of related interest is the U.S. Senate Special Committee on Aging's *Twenty Years of the Age Discrimination in Employment Act: Success or Failure?* hearings document Y 4.Ag 4:A.hrg.100-669 (1988), which considered the record of the Equal Employment Opportunity Commission (EEOC). Lawrence Meir Friedman's *Your Time Will Come: The Law of Age Discrimination and Mandatory Retirement* (Sage/Basic, 1984) considers federal and state laws, and is typical in its failure to recognize women as a special population in this context.

801   **Snyder, Eloise Colleen,** 1928– , ed. *Women, Work, and Age: Policy Challenges.* Ann Arbor: U of Michigan Institute of Gerontology, 1984. bib.

The proceedings of a conference sponsored by a Michigan coalition of educational and research institutions, government agencies, and advocacy organizations constitute this brief document.

802 **Sofaer, Shoshanna, and E. Abel.** "Older Women's Health and Financial Vulnerability: Implications of the Medicare Benefit Structure." *Women & Health* 1990 16(304): 47–67.

803 **Steinhauer, Marcia B., and Stefanie S. Auslander.** "Policy Directions and Program Design: Issues and Implications in Services for the Older Woman." In Gari Lesnoff-Caravaglia, ed. *The World of the Older Woman: Conflicts and Resolutions.* New York: Human Sciences Press, 1984. Chapter 11.

804 **Stewart, Abigail J., and Sharon Gold-Steinberg.** "Midlife Women's Political Consciousness: Case Studies of Psychosocial Development and Political Commitment." *Psychology of Women Q* December 1990 14(4): 543–566.

805 **Troll, Lillian E.** "Issues in the Study of Older Women: 1970–1985." In A. Regula Herzog, et al, eds. *Health and Economic Status of Older Women.* Amityville: Baywood, 1989. Chapter 2.

806 **Ungerson, Clare.** *Policy Is Personal: Sex, Gender and Informal Care.* New York: Tavistock, 1987. bib, index.

Ungerson's focus is on motivational and linguistic differences among female and male English "carers" of aged relatives in their own homes and without pay. Despite her labor-of-love philosophy, she cannot ignore the assigned gender-related role of women as the unpaid caregivers of the aged.

807 **Urquhart, Patria K.** *Senior Women and Public Services: A Comparative Analysis of Needs and Issues.* Golden Gate U, 1987. 49/03A.

808 **Vickers, Jill McCalla,** 1942– , ed. *Taking Sex into Account: The Policy Consequences of Sexist Research.* Ottawa: Carleton University Press/Oxford University Press, 1984. bib, index.

Proceedings of a 1982 conference sponsored by the Canadian Research Institute for the Advancement of Women have been made available in this compilation that considers aging, older women, and menopause in relationship to social science research, sexism, and public policy.

809 **Wagar, Linda.** "Saying No to Grandma: The Political Clout of the Elderly." *State Government News* March 1989 32(3): 10–14.

810 **Westlander, Gunnela,** 1930– , **and Jeanne Mager Stellman,** 1947– , eds. *Government Policy and Women's Health Care, the Swedish Alternative.* New York: Haworth, 1988. Also published as *Women & Health* 1989 13(3/4).

Here is a picture of Swedish women's health and well-being. In 1984, nearly 81 percent between ages 20 and 64 were employed for wages outside the home. The book has also been distributed with the title *Living Longer and Better: Ideals and Ideas from Swedish Health Care.*

811 **Williamson, John B., et al.** *The Politics of Aging: Power and Policy.* Springfield: C. C. Thomas, 1982. bib, il.

The aim of this monograph is to present "an empirically based analysis . . . of theoretical issues that define the emerging field of political gerontology . . . [and] the study of power as it involves the elderly" (pp. ix, 3). Ageism, gerontophobia, and sex differences receive some consideration in relationship to American political activity and government policy. Caretakers and gerontologists are seen as agents of social control. *See also* "Aging and Opportunities for Elective Office" by Schlesinger (#798).

POVERTY; "SHOPPING BAG LADIES"; HOMELESS WOMEN
See also this chapter: Displaced Homemakers (723–737); #77.

> *The terms* shopping bag lady *and* bag woman *are often confused. A shopping bag lady may be viewed as an eccentric going about collecting discarded objects and taking them home in shopping bags; Lisa Zeidner's novel,* Customs, *refers to a wealthy bag lady. But in reality she is likely to be homeless and elderly, living in public places and carrying her possessions in shopping bags. Diana K. Harris more accurately describes impoverished elderly women in urban areas who carry all of their possessions in shopping bags* (Dictionary of Gerontology. *Greenwood, 1988). Notably, information about them is too often cataloged under the heading "deviance."*

812   **Burwell, Elinor J.** "The Handwriting Is on the Wall: Older Women in the Future." *Resources for Feminist Research/Documentation sur la Recherche Féministe* July 1982 11(2): 208–209.

813   **Buss, Fran Leeper,** 1942– , **compiler.** *Dignity: Lower Income Tell of Their Lives and Struggles: Oral Histories.* Ann Arbor: U of Michigan Press, 1985.
These case studies are oral histories of ten working-class American women aged 33–72. Four are white; the others are black, native American, and of Japanese ancestry. Their lives have included homelessness.

814   **Butler, Sandra S., and Richard A. Weatherley.** "Poor Women at Midlife and Categories of Neglect." *Social Work* November 1992 37(6): 510–515.

815   **Clark, William F., et al.** *Old and Poor: A Critical Assessment of the Low-Income Elderly.* Lexington: Lexington, 1988. bib, index.
Clark and his fellow researchers, Anabel O. Pelham and Marleen L. Clark, made a quantitative study of poverty among a portion of America's elderly—California people aged 65 and over. Chapter 8 reports their 1980–1983 study of widows, using the California Senior Survey of Medicaid recipients; consideration of single old persons does not appear.

816   **Coston, Charisse Tia Maria.** *An Explanation of the Fear of Crime Among Shopping-Bag Ladies in New York City.* Rutgers State U of New Jersey, 1988. 49/06A.

817   **Day, Alice Taylor, et al.** *Older Women and Social Support: A Follow-Up Study.* Washington: The Urban Institute, 1988. bib.
The final report of an institute project was submitted to the National Institute on Aging.

818   **Ferraro, Geraldine A.** "Older Women and Poverty." *USA Today* July 1982 111(2446): 22–24.

819   **Grau, Lois.** "Illness—Engendered Poverty Among the Elderly." *Women & Health* 1987 12(3/4): 103–118.

820   Hand, Jennifer. "Shopping Bag Women: Aging Deviants in the City." In Elizabeth Markson, ed. *Older Women: Issues and Prospects.* Lexington: Heath, 1987. Chapter 8.

821   Jackson, Jacquelyne Johnson. "Poverty and Minority Status." In Marie R. Haug, et al, eds. *The Physical and Mental Health of Aged Women.* New York: Springer, 1985. Chapter 12.

822   Kates, Brian. *The Murder of a Shopping Bag Lady.* New York: Harcourt, Brace, Jovanovich, 1985.
        Phyllis Iannotta was a 67-year-old, mentally ill, homeless woman out on "rotation" from an overcrowded New York City shelter when she was murdered. Kates reconstructs her tragedy, without solving the crime or the age- and gender-related problems.

823   Malveaux, Julianne. *The Economic Predicament of Low-Income Elderly Women.* Southport: Southport Institute for Policy Analysis, 1992. bib.
        The Institute's Project on Women and Population Aging has sponsored this 55-page document in its Impact of Population Aging on Women series. Included is consideration of Social Security.

824   Minkler, Meredith, and Robyn Stone. "The Feminization of Poverty and Older Women." *Gerontologist* 1985 25: 351–357.

825   Moon, Marilyn. *Poverty Among Elderly Women and Minorities.* Washington: Urban Institute, 1985. bib.
        This brief (24 pages) discussion paper in the institute's Changing Domestic Priorities series is a revision of a paper delivered at the November 1984 Gerontological Society meetings.

826   National Advisory Council on Economic Opportunity. "No, Poverty Has Not Disappeared." *Social Policy* January/February 1981 11(4): 25–28.

827   O'Connor, A. Jamie. *Self-Concept and Epistemic Knowledge in Homeless Older Women.* Michigan Institute of Health Professions, 1989. Master's thesis.

828   Porcino, Jane, 1923– . "The Feminization of Poverty for Midlife and Older Women and Its Effects on Their Health." ERIC, November 1985. ED #264505. 8 pages.

829   Regina University (Saskatchewan). Seniors Education Centre. "Older Women and Poverty." ERIC, June 1992. ED #366739. 9 pages.

830   Rich, Spencer. "Many Elderly Women Face Privation." *Washington Post* May 5, 1988 111: A14.

831   Sarri, Rosemary C. "Federal Policy Changes and the Feminization of Poverty." In Ira Christopher Colby, ed. *Social Welfare Policy: Perspectives, Patterns, and Insights.* Chicago: Dorsey Press, 1989. 248–260.

832   Shields, Laurie, 1922–1989. "Who Will Need Me . . . Who Will Feed Me . . . When I'm 64?" *New Directions for Women* (newspaper) January/February 1988 17(1): 12–13.

833   Sidel, Ruth. "The Special Plight of Older Women." In her *Women and Children Last: The Plight of Poor Women in Affluent America.* New York: Viking, 1986. Chapter 8.

834   Smith, Milo. "An Older Woman Looks at Women's Poverty." *Christian Society* January-February 1986 76(3): 42–44.

835   Stone, Robyn I. "The Feminization of Poverty Among the Elderly." *Women's Studies* Q Spring/Summer 1989 17(1,2): 20–34.
        An earlier version of this paper was presented at the American Public Health Association's 1985 meeting; a 15-page, in-house U.S. Department of Health and Human Services Public Health Services update was made available through the National Technical Information Service in 1987. (HE 20.6514/2:P 86.)

836   "Study Finds Elderly Women More Susceptible to Poverty." *New York Times* September 24, 1984 Section I: 17.

837   Sullivan, Martha Adams. "The Homeless Older Woman in Context: Alienation, Cutoff and Reconnection." *J of Women & Aging* 1991 3(2): 3–24.

838   U.S. Congress. House. Select Committee on Aging. Subcommittee on Retirement Income and Employment. *Living in the Shadows: Older Women and the Roots of Poverty: Hearing . . . 102nd Congress, Second Session, May 15, 1992.* Washington: For sale by the U.S. Government Printing Office, 1992. Govt. Doc. No.: Y 4.Ag 4/2:W 84/16. bib, il. Also available in most depository libraries in microfiche form.

839   Warlick, Jennifer L. "Aged Women in Poverty: A Problem Without a Solution?" In William P. Brown and Laura Katz Olson, eds. *Aging and Public Policy: The Politics of Growing Old in America.* Westport: Greenwood, 1983. Chapter 3.

840   Warlick, Jennifer L. "Why Is Poverty After 65 a Women's Problem?" *J of Gerontology* 1985 40: 751–757.

841   Wilson-Ford, Vanessa. "Poverty Among Black Elderly Women." *J of Women & Aging* 1990 2(4): 5–20.

VOLUNTEERISM; VOLUNTEERS

Volunteerism is the tradition that encourages unpaid community and church service as the most acceptable activity for women away from home.

842   Fischer, Karla, et al. "Gender and Work History in the Placement and Perceptions of Elder Community Volunteers." *Psychology of Women* Q June 1991 15: 261–279.

843   Ishii-Kuntz, Masako. "Formal Activities for Elderly Women: Determinants of Participation in Voluntary and Senior Center Activities." *J of Women & Aging* 1990 2(1): 79–97.

844   Jusenius, Carol L. "Retirement and Older Americans' Participation in Volunteer Activities. Research Report Series, RR-83-01." ERIC, June 1983. ED #242943. 39 pages.

845   LaRossa, Ralph, and James J. Dowd. "Aging in a Women's Club: The Voluntary Association as a Social Support System." *Alternative Lifestyles* May 1980 3(2): 185–206.

WORK; EMPLOYMENT AND UNEMPLOYMENT; "WOMEN'S WORK"; "WORKING MOTHERS"

See also this chapter: Displaced Homemakers (723–737); Chapter 6: Pregnancy and Childbirth (1187–1212).

846   **Aber, Cynthia Sousa.** *Health of Widows: Paid-Work as a Critical Variable.* Boston U, 1989. 50/03A.

847   **Ackerman, Rosalie J.** "Career Developments and Transitions of Middle-Aged Women." *Psychology of Women Q* December 1990 14(4): 513–530.

848   **Adelmann, Pamela K., et al.** "A Causal Analysis of Employment and Health in Midlife Women." *Women & Health* 1990 16(1): 5–20.

849   **Baron, James M., and William T. Bielby.** "Organizational Barriers to Gender Equality: Sex Segregation of Jobs and Opportunities." In Alice S. Rossi, ed. *Gender and the Life Course.* New York: Aldine. Chapter 12.

850   **Basler, Barbara.** "Putting a Career on Hold." *New York Times Magazine* December 7, 1986 6(1): 152–160.

851   **Brody, Elaine M., and Claire B. Schoonover.** "Patterns of Parent-Care When Adult Daughters Work and When They Do Not." *Gerontologist* August 1986 26(4): 372–381.

852   **D'Amico, Ronald.** "Authority in the Workplace: Differences Among Mature Women." In Lois Banfill Shaw. *Midlife Women at Work: Fifteen-Year Perspective.* Lexington: Lexington, 1986. Chapter 4.

853   **Depner, Charlene, and Berit Ingersoll.** "Employment Status and Social Support: The Experience of the Mature Woman." In Maximiliane E. Szinovacz, ed. *Women's Retirement: Policy Implications of Recent Research.* Beverly Hills, California: Sage, 1982. Chapter 4.

854   **Frankel, David.** *Senior Citizens' Perceptions of Working Versus Nonworking Male and Female Seniors: A Semantic Differential Study.* Fordham U, 1986. 47/10A.

855   **Giele, Janet Zollinger.** "Women's Work and Family Roles." In Janet Zollinger Giele, ed. *Women in the Middle Years: Current Knowledge and Directions for Research and Policy.* New York: Wiley, 1982. 115–150.

856   **Gordon, Elizabeth Boltson.** *The Relationship of Work to Attitude Toward Retirement: A Study of Women in Late Middle Age.* U of Pittsburgh, 1985. 47/05A.

857   **Gottlieb, Naomi.** "Families, Work, and the Lives of Older Women." *J of Women & Aging* 1989 1(1/2/3): 217–244.

858   **Greenberg, Lisa Rae.** *Subjective Experiences of Elderly Women as a Function of Employment History and Experience of the Past.* Adelphi U, 1982. 43/03B.

859   **Groneman, Carol, and Mary Beth Norton, eds.** *"To Toil the Livelong Day": America's Women at Work, 1780–1980.* Ithaca: Cornell U Press, 1987. index.
    These papers were presented at the 6th Berkshire Conference on the History of Women in 1984; there is no bibliography, however. See Chapter 3, Carole Turbin's "Beyond Conventional Wisdom: Women's Wage Work, Household Economic Contribution, and Labor Activism in a Mid-19th-Century Working-Class Community."

860   **Haignere, Lois.** "Nontraditional Training for Women: Effective Programs, Structural Barriers and Political Hurdles." In Sharon L. Harlan and Ronnie J. Steinberg, eds. *Job Training for Women: The Promise and the Limits of Public Policies.* Philadelphia: Temple U Press, 1989. Chapter 14.

861   **Hale, Noreen,** 1943– . "Aging: A Women's Issue." In her *The Older Worker: Effective Strategies for Management and Human Resource Development.* San Francisco: Jossey-Bass, 1990. Chapter 9.

862   **Hatalla, Josephine Frances.** *A Descriptive Analysis of Chance and Contingency Factors in the Development of Middle-Aged College-Educated Women's Career Patterns.* U of Pittsburgh, 1987. 49/04A.

863   **Haurin, Donald R.** "Women's Labor Market Reactions to Family Disruptions, Husband's Unemployment, and Husband's Disability." In Lois Banfill Shaw. *Midlife Women at Work: Fifteen-Year Perspective.* Lexington: Lexington, 1986. Chapter 5.

864   **Henderson, Joanna, and Betty Lou Marple.** "When Older Women Work for Younger Women." In Lynda L. Moore, ed. *Not as Far as You Think: The Realities of Working Women.* Lexington: Lexington, 1986. Chapter 7.

865   **Herz, Diane E.** "Employment Characteristics of Older Women, 1987." *Monthly Labor Review* September 1988 111(9): 3–12.

866   **Hollenshead, Carol.** "Older Women at Work." *Educational Horizons* Summer 1982 60(4): 137–140, 195–196.

867   **Iams, Howard M.** "Employment of Retired-Worker Women." *Social Security Bulletin* March 1986 49(3): 5–13.

868   **James, Jacquelyn Boone.** *Women's Employment Patterns, Occupational Attitudes and Midlife Well-Being.* Boston U, 1989. 49/11B.

869   **Kahne, Hilda.** *Reconceiving Part-Time Work: New Perspectives for Older Workers and Women.* Totowa: Rowman & Allanheld, 1985. bib, index.
    "Although much has been written about occupational segregation and wage differentiation between women and men generally, little attention has been paid to the distinctive and often advantageous labor market experience of older women in relation to that of older men" (Chapter 4, "The Special Case of Women Workers: Distinctive Work Patterns and Needs"). Female part-time hourly earnings—about 75 percent of full-time hourly earnings—reflect the low economic status of such jobs. This academic but readable book consists of seventeen chapters written by different women and covering several areas, including multiple roles of mid-life women, motherhood at mid-life, and being a daughter of aging parents.

870   **Kaplan, Barbara Bayer.** *Women 65 and Over: Factors Associated with Their Decision to Work.* Brandeis U, 1985. 46/03A.

871   **Keating, Norah C., and Barbara Jeffrey.** "Work Careers of Ever-Married and Never-Married Retired Women." *Gerontologist* August 1983 23(4): 416–424.

872   **Keating, Nora C.** "Farm Women, Farm Work." *Sex Roles* August 1988 19(3–4): 155–168.

873   **Keeley, Suzanne L.** *Maternal Adaptation of Younger and Older Employed and Unemployed, First-Time Mothers.* U of Miami, 1985. 47/02B.

874   **Kratzer, Constance Young.** *Perceived Economic Well-Being of Three Cohorts of Rural Female Household Financial Managers.* Michigan State U, 1991. 52/10B.

875   **Lacy, Patricia Anne.** *The Impact of Selected Experiences on Women During Mid-Life Transition: A Retrospective Study (Career Change).* Oregon State U, 1986. 47/10A.

876   **Michigan Women's Commission. Task Force on Older Women's Issues.** *Older Women's Issues: A Report to the Legislature.* Lansing: Michigan Women's Commission, 1986. bib.

The commission's mailing address is P.O. Box 30026, Lansing, MI 48909. This 96-page document considers age and sex discrimination in employment of middle-aged and aged Michigan women, including the areas of old-age pensions and health insurance.

877   **Minton, Michael H., and Jean Libman Block.** *What Is a Wife Worth?* New York: Morrow, 1983. bib, index.

The concept of wages for housework and housewives has generally been rejected. This prominent divorce attorney "places a high dollar value on homemaking." Chapter 19, "The Displaced Homemaker," is of particular interest.

878   **Montgomery, Patricia Daum.** *The Experience of a Critical Event Leading to Dramatic Midlife Career Change for Women: A Phenomenological Investigation.* California Institute of Integral Studies, 1988. 49/07B.

879   **Moore, Lynda L., ed.** *Not as Far as You Think: The Realities of Working Women.* Lexington: Lexington, 1986. bib.

Despite the title's unfortunate use of "working women" (too often misused to refer to women employed outside the home for wages), the editor of this collection of articles has included significant consideration of older women and situations closely related to them, e.g., "Mentoring or Networking? Strong and Weak Ties in Career Development"; "Women as Bosses: Helping with the Transition"; "When Older Women Work for Younger Women" (see #864); and the often-overlooked women employed in the professions.

880   **Morgan, Leslie A.** "Work in Widowhood: A Viable Option?" *Gerontologist* 1980 20(5): 581–587.

881   **Mott, Frank L., and Lois B. Shaw.** "The Employment Consequences of Different Fertility Behaviors." In Lois Banfill Shaw. *Midlife Women at Work: Fifteen-Year Perspective.* Lexington: Lexington, 1986. Chapter 2.

882   **Olesen, Virginia.** "Self-Assessment and Change in One's Profession: Notes on the Phenomenology of Aging Among Mid-Life Women." *J of Women & Aging* 1990 2(4): 69–79.

883   **Pope, Jean.** *Voluntary Career Change Among Executive Women in Mid-Life.* U of Pittsburgh, 1988. 49/08A.

884   **Rich-McCoy, Lois, 1941– .** *Late Bloomer: Profiles of Women Who Found Their True Calling.* New York: Harper and Row, 1980.

These "profiles" are case studies of middle-aged American executive, professional, and self-employed women.

885   **Rife, John C.** "A Group Practice Strategy for Helping Unemployed Older Women Find Employment." *J of Women & Aging* 1992 4(1): 25–38.

886   **Rife, John C., et al.** "Older Women's Adjustment to Unemployment." *Affilia* Fall 1989 4: 65–77.

887   **Rosen, Ellen.** "Beyond the Sweatshop: Older Women in Blue-Collar Jobs." In Elizabeth Markson, ed. *Older Women: Issues and Prospects.* Lexington: Heath, 1987. Chapter 5.

888   Rosenthal, Carolyn J. "Family Responsibilities and Concerns: A Perspective on the Lives of Middle-Aged Women." *Resources for Feminist Research/Documentation sur la Recherche Féministe.* July 1982 11(2): 211.

889   **Shaw, Lois Banfill,** 1924– . *Midlife Women at Work: Fifteen-Year Perspective.* Lexington: Lexington, 1986. bib, il, index.
        Economist Shaw based her report on data from the National Longitudinal Surveys of Labor Market Experience of Mature [American] Women, begun in 1967 by the Ohio State University Center for Human Resource Research. Chapters 1 and 8 provide an introduction and overview to the report. These data have been utilized by other economists; query catalogs using the descriptor "Women workers—U.S.—longitudinal studies" and National Longitudinal Surveys of Labor Market Experience. Shaw's 16-page "Older Women at Work" (distributed in 1985 by the Women's Research and Education Institute of the Congressional Caucus for Women's Issues) also concerns middle-aged women in the United States and sex discrimination in employment experienced by them.

890   **Shaw, Lois Banfill,** 1924– , ed. *Unplanned Careers: The Working Lives of Middle-Aged Women.* Lexington: Lexington, 1983. bib, il, index.
        Basing her book on interviews made for the National Longitudinal Surveys of Labor Market Experience during 1967–1977, Dr. Shaw considers problems of labor-market reentry, causes of irregular employment patterns, attitudes toward women working for wages, and the economic consequences of poor health in mature women and of mid-life change in marital status.

891   **Stanley, Jo.,** ed. *To Make Ends Meet: Life Histories Collected by the Older Women's Project.* London: The Project, 1990.
        The Older Women's Project can be reached at the Older Women's Pensioners Link, 405–407 Holloway Road, London, England N7 6HJ. Women from the Caribbean, Britain, Burma, India, and the United States write about their attitudes toward paid employment—what it was like for them working in the 1920s and up to the present; job choices that were available to them; situations they faced at work; similarities and differences created by their backgrounds and cultures; and how they coped with caring for their homes and families while employed.

892   **Stentzel, Cathy, et al.** "Women, Work and Age: A Report on Older Women and Employment." (From the National Commission on Working Women.) ERIC, 1987. ED #284039. 49 pages.

893   **Treas, Judith.** "Women's Employment and Its Implications for the Status of the Elderly in the Future." In Sara B. Kiesler, et al, eds. *Aging, Social Change.* New York: Academic Press, 1981. Chapter 21.

894   **U.S. Congress. Joint Economic Committee.** *The Role of Older Women in the Work Force: Hearing . . . 98th Congress, Second Session.* ERIC, June 6, 1984. ED #260317. 121 pages.

895   **Wingrove, C. Ray, and Kathleen F. Slevin.** "A Sample of Professional and Managerial Women: Success in Work and Retirement." *J of Women & Aging* 1991 3(2): 95–117.

5
Living Arrangements

One of the traditions of the American social system is to keep its "un-desirables" out of sight.

Myrna L. Lewis and Robert Neil Butler, M.D.

ABUSE; COERCION; CRIME; VICTIMIZATION; VIOLENCE; *SATI*

As the United Nations has noted, girls are discriminated against throughout the world, often even before birth in cultures where more value is placed on boys. Sati *(a Sanskrit word meaning "virtuous woman" or "faithful and devoted wife") refers to the still-practiced Hindu rite of the widow sacrificing herself on her husband's funeral pyre; labeled suicide by some,* sati *should be labeled* violence. *(Accounts of the burning of widow Roop Kanwar in 1987 in India include "Trial by Fire: A Report on Roop Kanwar's Death," by the Women and Media Committee of the Bombay Union of Journalists). Information on this topic is often confounded by references to* suttee *and claims that the custom is no longer practiced.*

See also Chapter 3: Self-Deliverance; Assisted Suicide; Right to Die (627–636); Chapter 3: Widows and Widowhood (653–717).

896   **Baig, Tara Ali.** "Sati, Women's Status and Religious Fundamentalism." *Social Action* 1988 38(1): 78–83.

897   **Dewing, Bette.** "Intergenerational Gospel." (About violent crime and old women.) *New Directions for Women* (newspaper) September/October 1985 14(5): 22.

898   **Duberstein, Helen.** "Olive Distressed." *Heresies* ("Coming of Age" issue) 1988 6(3): 87–89.

899   **Fuller, Mary.** "Fear Sucks." *Heresies* ("Coming of Age" issue) 1988 6(3): 21.

900   Galbraith, Michael Wayne. *A Profile of Elder Abuse of Reported Cases from the Oklahoma Coalition on Domestic Violence and Sexual Assault.* Oklahoma State U, 1984. 45/09A.

901   Georgeson, Hanne. "Representations of Hindu Women Through Some of the Rewritings on Widow-Burning." *Australian J of Anthropology* (Sydney) 1992 3(3): 150–174.

902   Gordon, Margaret T., 1939– , and Stephanie Riger. *The Female Fear.* New York: Free Press, 1989. bib, index.
        The authors examine the social and psychological costs of the fear of rape among women in the United States, the country with the highest rate of rape in the world. "Female fear feeds on misinformation about rape. . . . Some of the common myths are: victims are young, careless, beautiful women who invite rape" (p. 6). From Chapter 2, "The Pervasiveness of Female Fear": "Race, marital status, and age are all related to women's sense of safety. . . . Those widowed, separated, or divorced feel less safe than the never or currently married; and older people report feeling less safe than younger people." Chapter 8 considers "Coping Strategies."

903   Guthman, Christine A. *The Effect of Age, Ethnicity, and Socioeconomic Status on the Treatment of Female Rape Victims.* New York U, 1987. 49/03A.

904   Hirst, Sandra P., and Jean Miller. "Aged Maltreatment: An Unexpected Outcome of Caring." *Canadian Woman Studies/Les Cahiers de al Femme* Winter 1992 12: 35–37.

905   Kercher, Kyle. "Causes and Correlates of Crime Committed by the Elderly: A Review of the Literature." In Edgar F. Borgatta and Rhonda J. V. Montgomery, eds. *Critical Issues in Aging Policy: Linking Research and Values.* Newbury Park, California: Sage, 1987. Chapter 10.

906   Mani, Lata. "Multiple Mediations: Feminist Scholarship in the Age of Multinational Reception." (On the practice of *sutee,* widow burning, in India.) *Feminist Review* Summer 1990 35: 24–42.
        Also "Multiple Mediations—Feminist Scholarship in the Age of Multinational Reception." (*Sati.* Roop Kanwar burned on husband's funeral pyre in Rajasthan on September 22, 1987.) *Women & Language* Fall 1990 13: 56–58. Also in the Group for the Critical Study of Colonial Discourse and the Center for Cultural Studies, University of California, Santa Cruz's *Inscriptions* 1989 5: 1–23.

907   McNeely, R. L. "Race, Sex, and Victimization of the Elderly." In McNeely and John L. Colen, eds. *Aging in Minority Groups.* Newbury Park, California: Sage, 1983. Chapter 11.

908   O'Connor, Frank, ed. "'Granny-Bashing': Abuse of the Elderly." In Nancy Hutchings, ed. *The Violent Family: Victimization of Women, Children and Elders.* New York: Human Sciences Press, 1988. Chapter 7.

909   Podnieka, Elizabeth. "The Lived Experience of Abused Older Women." *Canadian Woman Studies/Les Cahiers de la Femme* Winter 1992 12: 38–44.

910   Quinn, Mary Joy, and Susan K. Tomita. *Elder Abuse and Neglect: Causes, Diagnosis, and Intervention Strategies.* New York: Springer, 1986. bib, index.
        Registered nurse and social worker consider the whys of sexism and ageism within chapter 4, "Why Elder Abuse and Neglect Occur."

911   **Rathbone-McCuan, Eloise.** "The Abused Older Woman: A Discussion of Abuses and Rape." In Gari Lesnoff-Caravaglia, ed. *The World of the Older Woman: Conflicts and Resolutions.* New York: Human Sciences Press, 1984. Chapter 4.

912   **Romero, Joseph J.** *A Situational Analysis of Sexual Assault Among Four Age-Groups of Female Victims.* Temple U, 1986. 47/03A.

913   **Sakuntala Narashimhan,** 1940– . *Sati: Widow Burning in India.* New York: Doubleday, 1992. bib, il, index.

When Roop Kanwar burned to death on the pyre of her husband in 1987, the controversy about the legality of widow-burning and whether the government has the right to ban this "religious ritual" was renewed. The debate encompasses the much larger issue of the role of women in Indian society. Although *sati* was officially outlawed in 1829, its persistence indicates that the traditional position of women has changed little. Journalist Sakuntala Narashimhan outlines the reasons—education, role, economic compulsion, male chauvinism, and the devaluation of women—why women choose to become or can be forced to become *sati* and what this reveals about society as a whole.

914   **Sengstock, Mary C.** "Sex and Gender Implications in Cases of Elder Abuse." *J of Women & Aging* 1991 3(2): 25–43.

915   **Vinton, Linda.** "Abused Older Women: Battered Women or Abused Elders?" *J of Women & Aging* 1991 3(3): 5–19.

916   **Yang, Anand A.** "Whose Sati? Widow Burning in Early 19th-Century India." *J of Women's History* Fall 1989 1: 8–33.

Housing; Communal Arrangements; Retirement Places; "SRO" Single Room Occupancy

917   **Cantilena, Mary Ann.** *An Exploratory Study of the Factors Which Contribute to the Living Arrangements of Elderly Widows: Age-Segregated Vs. Age-Mixed Housing.* Rutgers SUNY of New Jersey, 1990. 51/11A.

918   **Dolbeare, Cushing N., and Anne J. Stone.** "Women and Affordable Housing." In Sara E. Rix, ed., for the Women's Research & Education Institute. *The American Woman, 1990–91: A Status Report.* New York: Norton, 1990. Chapter 2.

919   **Doyle, Cassie, and Janet McClain.** "Women, the Forgotten Housing Consumers." In Jill McCalla Vickers, ed. *Taking Sex into Account: The Policy Consequences of Sexist Research.* Ottawa: Carleton U Press/Oxford U Press, 1984. 219–242.

920   **Engler, May, and Roberta R. Spohn.** "The Elderly in New York City: Demographic Characteristics." In Eugenie Ladner Birch, ed. *The Unsheltered Woman: Women and Housing in the 80s.* New Brunswick: Center for Urban Policy Research/Transaction. Chapter 4.

921   **Fletcher, Susan, et al.** "The Living Arrangements of Older Women." *Essence: Issues in the Study of Ageing, Dying, and Death* 1980 4(3): 115–123.

922   **Gratton, Brian.** "Labor Markets and Old Ladies' Homes." In Elizabeth Markson, ed. *Older Women: Issues and Prospects.* Lexington: Heath, 1987. Chapter 7.

923   Janelli, Linda Marie. *Comparisons of Body Image Perception Among Older Women Residing in Long-Term Care Facilities, Intermediate Care Facilities, and Within the Community Attending Adult Day Care.* U of Rochester, 1987. 48/07A.

924   Jorgesen, Lou Ann B. "Women Residents in Public Housing: [Middle-Aged] Victims of Self-Sufficiency Programs." *J of Applied Social Sciences* Fall-Winter 1986–87 11(1): 48–64.

925   Kahana, Eva, and Boaz Kahana. "Institutionalization of the Aged Woman: Bane or Blessing?" In Marie R. Haug, et al, eds. *The Physical and Mental Health of Aged Women.* New York: Springer, 1985. Chapter 16.

926   Kalymun, Mary. *Factors Influencing Elderly Women's Decisions Concerning Their Living-Room Possessions During Relocation.* Pennsylvania State U, 1982. 43/01A.

927   Katsura, Harold M., et al. *Housing for Elderly in 2010: Projections and Policy Options.* Washington: Urban Institute Press, 1989. il.
        Appendix C, "Population and Household Projections to 2010," includes American females; note the demographic assumptions made in interpreting census data.

928   Kinderknecht, Cheryl H. "Aging Women and Long-Term Care: Truth and Consequences." *J of Women & Aging* 1989 1(4): 71–92.

929   Knapp, Nancy Mayer. "Institutionalized Women: Some Classic Types, Some Common Problems, and Some Partial Solutions." In Gari Lesnoff-Caravaglia, ed. *The World of the Older Woman: Conflicts and Resolutions.* New York: Human Sciences Press, 1984. Chapter 6.

930   Longino, Charles F., Jr., et al. "The Married, the Formerly Married and the Never Married: Support System Differentials of Older Women in Planned Retirement Communities." *International J of Aging and Human Development* 1982 15(4): 285–297.

931   Marten, Marie Lucille Cherry. *The Relationship of Level of Depression to Perceived Decision-Making Capabilities of Institutionalized Elderly Women.* Catholic U of America, 1982. 43/09B.

932   Netting, F. Ellen. "Older Women in Continuing Care Retirement Communities." *J of Women & Aging* 1991 3(1): 23–35.

933   Newsom-Clark, Sandra Kay. *A Study of the Communicative Efficiency in Institutionalized and Non-Institutionalized Aged Females.* U of Tennessee, 1980. 41/08B.

934   Obear, Mary E. Nursall. *The Nutritional Status of a Group of Elderly Institutionalized Women: Relationships to Stress and Social Support.* SUNY at Buffalo, 1985. 46/12A.

935   Paton, Helen, and Fiona Cram. "Personal Possessions and Environmental Control: The Experience of Elderly Women in Three Residential Settings." *J of Women & Aging* 1992 4(2): 61–78.

936   Sellers, Judith Bunnell. *The Influence of a Confidant on the Morale of Institutionalized Elderly Women.* Boston U, 1986. 47/04B.

937   Smith, Marsha Yaggie. *The Impact of Age and Environment on Gender Roles Among SRO (Single Room Occupancy) Elderly.* Purdue U, 1981. 42/11A.

938   Smithers, Janice A., 1931– . *Determined Survivors: Community Life Among the Urban Elderly.* New Brunswick: Rutgers U Press, 1985. bib, index.

Case studies of aged single people in Los Angeles retirement communities are included in Chapter 3, "The Gender Gap." Men outnumber women three to one in urban SROs (single room occupancy). Smithers's U of California, Los Angeles sociology Ph.D. thesis (1981) was titled *Determined Survivors: Coping Strategies Among the Urban Elderly.*

939   **Steiger, Thelma-Rose Barbara.** *Antecedents to Successful Senescence: A Study of Institutionalized Aged Women.* Bryn Mawr College, 1981. 42/08B.

940   **Thomas, Kausar, et al.** "Living Arrangements of Older Women: The Ethnic Dimension." *J of Marriage and the Family* May 1984 46(2): 301–311.

941   **Watson, Sophie, and Helen Austerberry.** *Housing and Homelessness: A Feminist Perspective.* Boston and London: Routledge & Kegan Paul, 1986. bib, index.
Homeless and other poor women in Great Britain are considered, age and aging specifically. A shift in focus to analysis of wider societal and economic structures and away from the sexual division of labor and dominant family model is advocated.

942   **Wenstein, Estelle (Stellye).** *The Sexual Attitudes, Interests and Activities of Senior Adults Residing in Age-Integrated and Age-Segregated Communities.* Hofstra U, 1983. 45/02A.

943   **West, Sheree L.** *Sharing and Privacy in Shared Housing for Older People.* City U of New York, 1985. 46/05A.

944   **Wyckoff, Shelley Ann Rice.** *The Effects of Housing and Race upon Depression and Life Satisfaction of Elderly Females.* George Peabody College for Teachers of Vanderbilt U, 1983. 45/06A.

ISOLATION AND LONELINESS

In 1992 12 percent of Americans lived alone—16 percent of men and 42 percent of women 65 years of age and over; 25 percent of American households consisted of one person. If one accepts the assumption that isolation and loneliness of women are related to living alone, then these census figures have great significance.

945   **Austin, Adriana Giardina.** *The Relationship of Social Support and Creative Potential to Loneliness in Older Women.* New York U, 1984. 45/07B.

946   **Beck, Cornelia M.** "Predictors of Loneliness in Older Women and Men." *J of Women & Aging* 1990 2(1): 3–31.

947   **Collins, Janet Martha.** *Functional Health, Social Support, and Morale of Older Women Living Alone in Appalachia.* U of Alabama at Birmingham, 1992. 53/04B. *See also* this title by Dr. Collins in the *J of Women & Aging* 1994 6(3): 39–52.

948   **Hornung, Karen L.** *Loneliness Among Older Urban Widows.* U of Nebraska, Lincoln, 1980. 41/07A.

949   **Kohen, Janet A.** "Old but Not Alone: Informal Social Supports Among the Elderly by Marital Status and Sex." *Gerontologist* February 1983 23: 57–63.

950   **Magaziner, Jay, and Doris A. Cadigan.** "Community Care of Older Women Living Alone." *Women & Health* 1988 14(3/4): 121–138. Also published in Lois Grau and

Ida Susser, eds. *Women in the Later Years: Health, Social and Cultural Perspectives.* Binghamton, New York: Harrington Park Press, 1989.

951   **Minkler, Meredith.** "Building Support Networks from Social Isolation." *Generations* Summer 1986 10(4): 46–49.

952   **Roybal, Edward Ross,** 1916– . *The Quality of Life for Older Women: Older Women Living Alone; A Report by the Chairman of the Select Committee on Aging.* ERIC, August 1989. ED #307513. 17 pages.
      Also available with the same title is the hearing before the U.S. Congress. House, Select Committee on Aging, Second Session, September 17, 1988. Washington: For sale by the U.S. Government Printing Office, 1989. Govt. Doc. No.: Y 4.Ag 4/2:L 62/3. bib, il. Available in most depository libraries in microfiche form.

953   **Seskin, Jane.** *Alone—Not Lonely: Independent Living for Women over Fifty.* Glenview: Scott Foresman, 1985. bib, index.
      The American Association of Retired Persons sponsored this publication, a life skills guide for and about single women and widows, in its Independent Living for Seniors series.

954   **Somerville, Barbara Levy,** 1949– . "Women Alone." *The Post* (newspaper of West Palm Beach, Florida) September 21, 1981: B1, B4.

955   **Thompson, Mark G., and Kenneth Heller.** "Facets of Support Related to Well-Being: Quantitative Social Isolation and Perceived Family Support in a Sample of Elderly Women." *Psychology & Aging* December 1990 5(4): 535–544.

Nursing Homes; Adult Care Facilities

956   **Beaton, Sarah Reese.** *Styles of Reminiscence and Levels of Ego Development of Older Women Who Reside in Long-Term Care Settings.* New York U, 1986. 47/12A. Also *International J of Aging and Human Development* 1991 32(1): 53–63.

957   **Brody, Claire M.** "Women in a Nursing Home: Living with Hope and Meaning." *Psychology of Women Q* December 1990 14(4): 579–592. Special "Women at Midlife and Beyond" issue.

958   **Carlson, Sylvia.** *The Relationship Among Institutionalized and Non-Institutionalized Ambulatory Older Women, Field Dependence-Independence and Crystallized Intelligence.* New York U, 1984. 46/06B.

959   **Foland, Kay L.** *Indices of Attachment in Elderly [65 and over] Women Who Are Not Mentally Compromised Residing in Nursing Homes.* U of Texas, Austin, 1990. 50/09A.

960   **Gray, Ruth Howard,** 1894– . *Survival of the Spirit: My Detour Through a Retirement Home.* Louisville: Westminster/John Knox Press, 1985.
      This "retirement home" is actually a nursing home; Gray writes about survival of the spirit within such an environment.

961   **Horner, Joyce Mary,** 1903–1980. *That Time of Year: A Chronicle of Life in a Nursing Home.* Amherst: U of Massachusetts Press, 1982.
      Horner taught English at Mt. Holyoke [women's] College until her retirement in 1969. She was an unmarried person who suffered greatly from arthritis and wrote

published poems and novels. She entered a nursing home voluntarily. Her journal covers the years 1975–1977; she wrote in her diary, "Everyone wants to go home. Perhaps that says too much. Everyone 'wants out.' Or there may be some who are beyond wanting as much as that."

962   **Johnston, Roxie Ann.** *The Relationship Between Locus of Control and Psychological Well-Being in Elderly Female Nursing Home Residents.* U of Maryland at Baltimore, 1981. 42/07A.

963   **Landsmark, Sarah T.** *Perceptions of Psychopathology by Elderly Female Nursing Home Residents: An Exploratory Study.* Columbia U, 1982. 43/12B.

964   **Lee-Hostetler, Jeri.** *Seasons of Change: Meeting the Challenge of a Nursing Home.* Elgin: Brethren Press, 1988.
        The author's great-grandmother, Louisa Basinger, died at age 106. This is a fictionalized account of her struggle to adapt to the inhabitants and regime of the nursing home where she waited out her life when she could no longer live independently.

965   **McHugh, Alice Rene.** *Strong-Campbell Interest Inventory Occupational Scales for Male and Female Nursing Home Administrators.* U of Missouri, Columbia, 1984. 45/08A.

966   **Miller, Dulcy B.** "Women and Long Term Nursing Care." *Women & Health* Summer/Fall 1985 10(2/3): 29–38. Also in Sharon Golub and Rita Jackaway Freedman, eds. *Health Needs of Women as They Age.* Binghamton, New York: Harrington Park Press, 1985.

967   **Vladeck, Bruce.** *Unloving Care: The Nursing Home Tragedy.* New York: Basic Books, 1980. bib, index.
        One must search diligently for equitable concern for women in many studies, government publications, and scholarly works. Vladeck's public policy Twentieth Century Fund study describes the typical nursing home resident as 80 years old, a "white widow or spinster" of relatively limited means suffering from three or four chronic ailments. Also of interest are Chapter 9, "The Staffing of Nursing Homes," in Colleen Leahy Johnson and Leslie A. Grant's *The Nursing Home in American Society* (Baltimore: Johns Hopkins U Press, 1985) and Esther Hing's *Use of Nursing Homes by the Elderly: Preliminary Data from the 1985 National Nursing Home Survey* DHHS Publication No. 135, PHS 87-1250 (Washington: Vital and Health Statistics, 1987).

968   **Zandi, Taker, and Naomi McCormick.** "Psychological Adjustment of Elderly Women: An Ecological Model and Comparison of Nursing Home and Community Residents." *J of Women & Aging* 1991 3(4): 3–21.

969   **Ziolkowski, Irene H.** *Happiness and Its Relationship to Rhythmic Patterns of Physiological Processes in the Elderly Females Residing in Adult Care Facilities.* D'Youville College, 1989. M.S. thesis.

Rural, Suburban, and Urban Environments

970   **Cape, Elizabeth.** "Aging Women in Rural Society: Out of Sight and Out of Mind." *Resources for Feminist Research/Documentation sur la Recherche Féministe* July 1982 11(2): 214–215.

971   **Dietz, Mariah.** *Sources of Stress Among Older Rural Women in North Dakota.* Catholic U of America, 1986. 47/04B.

972   **Hooyman, Nancy R.** "Mutual Help Organizations for Rural Older Women." *Educational Gerontology* October 1980 5(4): 429–447.

973   **Johnson, Elizabeth S.** "Suburban Older Women." In Elizabeth Markson, ed. *Older Women: Issues and Prospects.* Lexington: Heath, 1987. Chapter 9.

974   **Kivett, Vira R.** "Older Rural Women: Mythical, Forbearing, and Unsung." *J of Rural Community Psychology* 1990 11(1): 83–101.

975   **Leavitt, Jacqueline, and Mary Beth Welch.** "Older Women and the Suburbs: A Literature Review." *Women's Studies Q* Spring-Summer 1989 17(1, 2): 35–47.

976   **Markson, Elizabeth W., and Beth B. Hess.** "Older Women in the City." In Catharine R. Stimpson, et al, eds. *Women and the American City.* Chicago: U of Chicago Press, 1980. 124–139.

977   **Mouser, Nancy Fox.** *Social Networks of Older Widowers in Small Town and Rural Settings.* Iowa State U, 1983. 47/11A.

978   **Muir, M. S., and C. Brayne.** "A Longitudinal Study in Progress: A 5-Year Follow-Up of Women Aged 70–79 Years Living in a Rural Community." *Neuroepidemiology* 1992 11(1): 67–70.

979   **Peterson, Steven A.** "Elderly Women and Program Encounters: A Rural Study." *J of Women & Aging* 1989 1(4): 41–56.

980   **Salber, Eva J., M.D.** *Don't Send Me Flowers When I'm Dead: Voices of Rural Elderly.* Durham, North Carolina: Duke U Press, 1983. bib, il.
    "I want them *now*," declared 71-year-old Annie Lane. Salber's purpose in her book of interviews and black-and-white photographs of rural North Carolina elders was "to provide a channel through which this small group of elderly men and women transmit their feelings." Nine women make up the "Displaced" section.

981   **Scholl, Kathleen K.** "Marital Property Reforms: Implications for Older Farm Women." ERIC, March 22, 1988. ED #295091. 22 pages.

982   **Shenk, Dena.** "Someone to Lend a Helping Hand: Older Rural Women as Recipients and Providers of Care." ERIC, November 19, 1990. ED #329826. 31 pages.

983   **Walters, Judith Klass Hoekzema.** *Life Satisfaction Among Urban and Rural Elderly Widows.* Michigan State U, 1983. 44/09A.

984   **Weishaar, Katherine Ruth.** *Older Rural Women: An Experiential Analysis.* Union Institute, 1989. 51/04B.

6

Mid-Life and Women

Few women, I fear, have had such reason as I have had to think the long sad years of youth were worth living for the sake of middle age.
George Eliot (Marian Evans), 1819–1880, letter at age 38

Middle age is a relatively recent development in the life course, related to the increase of life expectancy.

CLIMACTERIC; MENOPAUSE

The climacteric *is the gradual transition from reproductive years of regular ovulation to the postmenopausal years when the ovaries cease functioning; it spans the ages between the late 30s and mid-50s.* Menopause *is the cessation of menstrual periods, defined as the passage of an entire year without menses in absence of any pathologic state that causes that cessation (Ada P. Kahn.* Midlife Health: Every Woman's Guide to Feeling Good. *New York: Facts On File, 1987. 237, 242). The Western medical system has tended to define menopause in terms of a disease paradigm. (It is indexed in the* International Classification of Diseases.) *Feminists contend that menopause should be viewed as a natural part of aging, a natural event in a woman's life. The menopause chapters of* Ourselves, Growing Older *and the* New Ourselves, Growing Older *provide a readable background. Briefly, menopause is permanent cessation of menstruation and reproductive capacity for women; it occurs during the climacteric, usually between ages 45 and 55.* Climacteric *is the ten- to fifteen-year period of change surrounding menopause, and, as a critical stage, the term can apply to both women and men. Paula Weideger has written that "Most women become sexually invisible after menopause, not because of any mysterious or well-known physical upheaval but because the culture expects them to"* (Menstruation and Menopause. *New York:*

Knopf, 1976). In using the literature, note that menopause is often presented in association with the menstrual cycle, e.g., #986, and Culture, Society, and Menstruation, *edited by Virginia L. Olesen and Nancy Fugate Woods (Washington: Hemisphere, 1986). Two topical periodicals are* Hot Flash: A Newsletter for Midlife and Older Women, *from the National Action Forum for Midlife and Older Women, and* Maturitas, *published in collaboration with the International Menopause Society.* See also *#2251.*

985   **Archer, David F.** "Biochemical Findings and Medical Management." In Ann Mae Voda, et al, eds. *Changing Perspectives on Menopause.* Austin: U of Texas Press, 1982. Chapter 3.

986   **Asso, Doreen.** *The Real Menstrual Cycle.* New York: Wiley, 1983. bib, index.
       Psychologist Asso presents menopause as part of the normal biological cycle.

987   **Avis, Nancy E., and Sonja M. McKinlay.** "Health Care Utilization Among Mid-Aged Women." In Marcha Flint, et al, eds. *Multidisciplinary Perspectives on Menopause: Annals of the New York Academy of Sciences* (Volume 592). New York: The Academy, 1990. 228–238.

988   **Bachmann, Gloria A.** "Sexual Issues at Menopause." In Marcha Flint, et al, eds. *Multidisciplinary Perspectives on Menopause: Annals of the New York Academy of Sciences* (Volume 592). New York: The Academy, 1990. 87–94.

989   **Bareford, Connie Gleim.** *An Investigation of the Nature of the Menopausal Experience: Attitude Toward the Menopause, Recent Life Change, Coping Method, and Number and Frequency of Symptoms in Menopausal Women.* New York U, 1988. 49/07B.

990   **Barnett, Elyse Ann.** "La Edad Crítica: The Positive Experience of Menopause in a Small Peruvian Town." In Patricia Whelehan. *Women and Health: Cross-Cultural Perspectives.* Westport: Bergin & Garvey, 1988. Chapter 3.

991   **Barrett-Connor, Elizabeth.** "Postmenopause Estrogen, Cancer and Other Considerations." *Women & Health* Fall/Winter 1986 11: 179–195.

992   **Bates, G. William, M.D.** "On the Nature of the Hot Flash." *Clinical Obstetrics and Gynecology* 1981 24(1): 231–241.

993   **Bell, Susan E.** "Sociological Perspectives on the Medicalization of Menopause." In Marcha Flint, et al, eds. *Multidisciplinary Perspectives on Menopause: Annals of the New York Academy of Sciences* (Volume 592). New York: The Academy, 1990. 173–177.

994   **Beyene, Yewoubdar.** "Cultural Significance and Physiological Manifestations of Menopause: A Biocultural Analysis." *Culture, Medicine and Psychiatry* 1986 10(1): 47–71.

995   **Beyene, Yewoubdar.** *From Menarche to Menopause: Reproductive Lives of Peasant Women in Two Cultures.* Albany: SUNY Press, 1989. bib.
       Beyene's doctoral dissertation (*see* Chapter 9 herein) and this book provide comparative studies of the reproductive histories of Mayan women in the village of Chichimila in Mexico's Yucatan region and of Greek women in the village of Evia. They focus on cultural variations in the physiological and psychological experience of menopause. Both the Mayan and Greek women view menopause as a natural phenomenon

rather than a disease needing medical intervention. Two factors with striking differences in these cultures were diet and fertility patterns, which could affect the production of estrogen. Beyene's proposal of a biocultural model of factors affecting menopause is supported by the fact that women throughout the world do not experience similar symptoms.

996   **Birnbaum, Davi.** "Self-Help for Menopause: A Feminist Approach." In Marcha Flint, et al, eds. *Multidisciplinary Perspectives on Menopause: Annals of the New York Academy of Sciences* (Volume 592). New York: The Academy, 1990. 250–252.

997   **Blask, David E.** "Potential Role of the Pineal Gland in the Human Menstrual Cycle." In Ann Mae Voda, et al, eds. *Changing Perspectives on Menopause.* Austin: U of Texas Press, 1982. Chapter 9.

998   **Bowles, Cheryl L.** *Measure of Attitude Toward Menopause Using the Semantic Differential Model.* Northern Illinois U, 1985. 45/09A. Also *Nursing Research* March-April 1986 35(2): 81–85.

999   **Bowles, Cheryl L.** "The Menopausal Experience: Sociocultural Influences and Theoretical Models." In Ruth Formanek, ed. *The Meanings of Menopause: Historical Medical and Clinical Perspectives.* Hillsdale: Analytic Press, 1990. 157–175.

1000   **Brinton, Louise A.** "Menopause and the Risk of Breast Cancer." In Marcha Flint, et al, eds. *Multidisciplinary Perspectives on Menopause: Annals of the New York Academy of Sciences* (Volume 592). New York: The Academy, 1990. 357–362.

1001   **Brooks-Gunn, Jeanne.** "A Sociocultural Approach" (to methods and models of menstrual-cycle research). In Ann Mae Voda, et al, eds. *Changing Perspectives on Menopause.* Austin: U of Texas Press, 1982. Chapter 14.

1002   **Buchsbaum, Herbert J.,** 1934– , ed. *The Menopause.* New York: Springer-Verlag, 1983. bib, il, index.
     Devoted entirely to the subject of menopause, this 225-page book is in the publisher's Clinical Perspectives in Obstetrics and Gynecology series. Buchsbaum is well known for his definitive publications in the field of gynecology, particularly gynecologic oncology.

1003   **Budoff, Penny Wise.** *No More Hot Flashes, and Other Good News.* New York: Putnams, 1983. il.
     Among the related concerns are "No More Scare Stories About Menopausal Therapy," "No More Unwanted Pregnancy at Age 40," and "No More Unnecessary Hysterectomies."

1004   **Cassells, Holly Beth.** *Health Beliefs and Osteoporosis Prevention by Menopausal Women.* U of Texas at Austin, 1988. 49/06B.

1005   **Cate, Mary Ann, and David E. Corbin.** "Age Differences in Knowledge and Attitudes Toward Menopause." *J of Women & Aging* 1992 4(2): 33–46.

1006   **Cobb, Janine O'Leary.** "Do Midlife Women Receive Second-Rate Health Care? A Friend Indeed Goes to Washington." *Canadian Woman Studies/Les Cahiers de la Femme* Winter 1992 12: 14–16.

1007   **Colditz, Graham, et al.** "Menopause and the Risk of Coronary Heart Disease in Women." *New England J of Medicine* April 30, 1987 316: 1105–1110.

1008   Cole, Ellen. "Sex at Menopause: Each in Her Own Way." *Women & Therapy* 1988 7(5): 159–168.

1009   Costlow, Judy, et al. *Menopause: A Self-Care Manual, rev. ed.* Santa Fe: Santa Fe Health Education Project, 1989. il. (POB 577, Santa Fe, NM 87504–0577.)
         Available in English and Spanish, this booklet considers misconceptions, progesterone replacement therapy, and natural remedies; the out-of-date birth control information may now be updated.

1010   Cramer, Daniel W. "Epidemiologic Aspects of Early Menopause and Ovarian Cancer." In Marcha Flint, et al, eds. *Multidisciplinary Perspectives on Menopause: Annals of the New York Academy of Sciences* (Volume 592). New York: The Academy, 1990. 363–375.

1011   Cutler, Winnifred Berg, et al. *Menopause: A Guide for Women and the Men Who Love Them.* New York: Norton, 1983. bib, il, index.
         Celso-Ramon Garcia and David A. Edwards participated in this guide's authorship; a preface for men is provided.

1012   Dan, Alice J. "The Interdisciplinary Society for Menstrual Cycle Research: Creating Knowledge from Our Experience." In Ann Mae Voda, et al, eds. *Changing Perspectives on Menopause.* Austin: U of Texas Press, 1982. Chapter 26.

1013   Davis, Dona Lee, 1948– . *Blood and Nerves: An Ethnographic Focus on Menopause.* St. John's: Institute of Social and Economic Research, Memorial U of Newfoundland, 1983. bib.
         This is #28 in the institute's *Social and Economic Studies* series. Davis's doctoral dissertation was titled *Women's Experience of Menopause in a Newfoundland Fishing Village* (U of North Carolina at Chapel Hill, 1980. 41/04A).

1014   Dege, Kristi, and Jacqueline Gretzinger. "Attitudes of Families Toward Menopause." In Ann Mae Voda, et al, eds. *Changing Perspectives on Menopause.* Austin: U of Texas Press, 1982. Chapter 5.

1015   Denicola, Louise Geraldine. *An Investigation of the Relationship of Life Change Stress, Nonspecific Sympathetic Activity, and Climacteric Symptoms in Women 40 to 55 Years Old.* New York U, 1987. 49/01B.

1016   Dickson, Geri L. "A Feminist Poststructuralist Analysis of the Knowledge of Menopause." *Advances in Nursing Science* 1990 12(3): 15–31.

1017   Doan, Helen. *Every Woman: Adapting to Mid-Life Change.* Toronto: Stoddart, 1987. bib, il, index.
         The title-word "change" refers to menopause. Stoddart Publishing Co., Ltd., is located at 34 Lesmill, Toronto, Canada.

1018   Doss, Juanita King. *The Women's Experience of Menopause.* Union for Experimenting Colleges and Universities, 1987. 49/04B.

1019   Downing, Christine, 1931– . *Journey Through Menopause: A Personal Rite of Passage.* New York: Crossroad, 1989. bib, il.
         Downing's biographical personal account of her experience of menopause encompasses health, psychological, and social aspects. At 50, she felt unprepared for menopause. Her account of the three-year "journey" is presented as a rite of passage—

preparation, transition, and return—consisting of a trip around the world and her "discovery that I was done with the hormone quest, the acceptance of weakness and vulnerability, the recognition of my dependence on other women, the revelation that I am loved enough."

1020   **DuToit, Brian M.,** 1935– . *Aging and Menopause Among Indian South African Women.* Albany: SUNY Press, 1990. index.

Anthropologist DuToit examines the lives and experiences of pre- and postmenopausal Hindu and Muslim Indian women living in a community west of Pretoria, South Africa.

1021   **Dyer, Ruth, and Linda C. McKeever.** "Menopause: A Closer Look for Nurses." In Diane K. Kjervik and Ida M. Martinson. *Women in Health and Illness: Life Experiences and Crises.* Philadelphia: Saunders, 1986. Chapter 20.

1022   **Dryenfurth, Inge.** "Endocrine Functions in the Woman's Second Half of Life." In Ann Mae Voda, et al, eds. *Changing Perspectives on Menopause.* Austin: U of Texas Press, 1982. Chapter 22.

1023   **Engle, Nancy Sharts.** "Menopausal Stage, Current Life Change, Attitude Toward Women's Roles, and Perceived Health Status." *Nursing Research* 1987 36(6): 353–357.

1024   **Feldman, B., et al.** "The Prevalence of Hot Flash and Associated Variables Among Perimenopausal Women." *Research in Nursing and Health* 1985 8: 261–268.

1025   **Flint, Marcha.** "Male and Female Menopause: A Cultural Put-On." In Ann Mae Voda, et al, eds. *Changing Perspectives on Menopause.* Austin: U of Texas Press, 1982. Chapter 25.

1026   **Flint, Marcha, and Ratna Suprapti Samil.** "Cultural and Subcultural Meanings of the Menopause." In Marcha Flint, et al, eds. *Multidisciplinary Perspectives on Menopause: Annals of the New York Academy of Sciences* (Volume 592). New York: The Academy, 1990. 134–148.

1027   **Flint, Marcha, et al, eds.** *Multidisciplinary Perspectives on Menopause: Annals of the New York Academy of Sciences,* (Volume 592). New York: The Academy, 1990. il.

A conference sponsored by the academy and the North American Menopause Society in September 1989 and funded by pharmaceuticals companies, the National Institute on Aging, and other agencies considered current research, societal impact on menopause, and preventive medicine. Many nations were represented among the contributors of reports (analyzed herein) and poster papers.

1028   **Formanek, Ruth, ed.** *The Meanings of Menopause: Historical, Medical, and Clinical Perspectives.* Hillsdale: Analytic Press, 1990. bib, index.

Myths and stereotypes associated with menopause are analyzed by the writers collected here. They question its medicalization, viewing it as a physiological event with socially constructed responses.

1029   **Frey, Karen A.** "Middle-Aged Women's Experience and Perceptions of Menopause." *Women & Health* 1982 6(1/2): 25–35.

1030   **Friederich, Mary Anna.** "Aging, Menopause, and Estrogens: The Clinician's Dilemma." In Ann Mae Voda, et al, eds. *Changing Perspectives on Menopause.* Austin: U of Texas Press, 1982. Chapter 23.

1031   **Fromer, Margot Joan,** 1939– . *Menopause: What It Is, Why It Happens, How You Can Deal with It.* Liberty: Pinnacle Books, 1985. bib.

Fromer considers estrogen replacement therapy and osteoporosis (as do most popular books on menopause) as well as cancer.

1032   **Gannon, Linda R.** *Menstrual Disorders and Menopause: Biological, Psychological, and Cultural Research.* New York: Praeger, 1985. bib, il, index.

This unique and important book consists of an extensive review of biological, psychological, and cultural research on these interrelated subjects, as well as analyses and comparisons of each. Tables summarize; there are fifty pages of annotated research studies.

1033   **Gannon, Linda.** "The Potential Role of Exercise in the Alleviation of Menstrual Disorders and Menopausal Symptoms: A Theoretical Synthesis of Recent Research." *Women & Health* 1988 14(2): 105–127.

1034   **George, Theresa.** *There Is a Time for Everything: A Study of Menopausal/Climacteric Experiences of Sikh Women in Canada.* U of Utah, 1985. 46/12B.

1035   **Gerson, Miryam, and Rosemary Byrne-Hunter.** *A Book About Menopause.* Montreal: Montreal Health, 1988.

The publisher of this self-help guide that utilizes a nonmedicalized approach, Montreal Health Press, Inc., is located at 3575 St. Laurent, Montreal, Canada.

1036   **Gognalons-Nicolet, Maryvonne.** "The Crossroads of Menopause: A Chance and a Risk for the Aging Process of Women." In Elizabeth Markson, ed. *Older Women: Issues and Prospects.* Lexington: Heath, 1987. Chapter 2.

1037   **Golub, Sharon, ed.** *Lifting the Curse of Menstruation: A Feminist Appraisal of the Influence of Menstruation on Women's Lives.* Binghamton, New York: Harrington Park Press, 1985.

This monograph has also been published as *Women & Health* Summer/Fall 1983 8(2/3). It includes "The Relationship Between Psychopathology and the Menstrual Cycle" and "Menopause: The Closure of Menstrual Life."

1038   **Goodman, Madeleine J.** "A Critique of Menopause Research." In Ann Mae Voda, et al, eds. *Changing Perspectives on Menopause.* Austin: U of Texas Press, 1982. Chapter 20.

1039   **Goodman, Madeleine.** "Toward a Biology of Menopause [review essay]." *Signs* Summer 1980 5(4): 739–753.

1040   **Goulding, A.** "Smoking, the Menopause and Biochemical Parameters of Bone Loss and Bone Turnover." *New Zealand J of Medicine* April 14, 1982 95(705): 218–220.

1041   **Greene, John Gerald,** 1942– . *The Social and Psychological Origins of the Climacteric Syndrome.* Brookfield: Gower, 1984. bib, il, index.

Also published in England by Aldershot, Greene's book is a standard in education-psychology as well as biomedicine libraries.

1042   **Greenwood, Sadja, M.D.,** 1930– . "Menopause Counselors Needed: Informed, Empathetic, Nonpartisan." In Marcha Flint, et al, eds. *Multidisciplinary Perspectives on Menopause: Annals of the New York Academy of Sciences* (Volume 592). New York: The Academy, 1990. 376–378.

1043   Greenwood, Sadja, M.D., 1930– . *Menopause Naturally: Preparing for the Second Half of Life, rev. ed.* San Francisco: Volcano Press, 1989. bib, il.

The original 1984 *Menopause Naturally* guide was praised for its emphases on nutrition and exercise as important factors in relieving menopausal symptoms and for its self-rating scale. This edition includes updated information on breast cancer, estrogens, osteoporosis, and uterine fibroids.

1044   Greer, Germaine, 1939– . *The Change: Women, Aging, and the Menopause.* London: Hamish Hamilton; New York: Knopf, 1991.

Born in Australia and educated there and at Cambridge, Greer's first book, *The Female Eunuch* (1970), was an instant best-seller. "There are many books written now for aging women which argue that there need be no change, that the middle-aged woman can continue being what she always was, an attractive and responsive lover, a dutiful wife, an efficient employee. These books never consider the possibility that a woman could actually be tired of being all these things, or that she might be conscious of having led an unexamined life. Such books assume that what the middle-aged woman is afraid of, that there is no point in a woman's life if she is not functioning as lover, wife and employee, is actually true. You are not reading one of those books. This book argues instead that women are whole people with a right to exist and a contribution to make in and as themselves" (pp. 40–41).

1045   Guillebaud, John. "Contraception for Women over 35." *Healthright* August 1990 9: 17–21.

1046   Griffen, Joyce. "Cultural Models for Coping with Menopause." In Ann Mae Voda, et al, eds. *Changing Perspectives on Menopause.* Austin: U of Texas Press, 1982. Chapter 18.

1047   Hamburger, Sonia, and Evelyn R. Anderson. "The Value of Education and Social-Psychological Support in a Menopause Clinic." In Marcha Flint, et al, eds. *Multidisciplinary Perspectives on Menopause: Annals of the New York Academy of Sciences* (Volume 592). New York: The Academy, 1990. 242–249.

1048   Heide, Wilma Scott, 1921–1985. "Now for the Feminist Menopause That Refreshes." In Gari Lesnoff-Caravaglia, ed. *The World of the Older Woman: Conflicts and Resolutions.* New York: Human Sciences Press, 1984. Chapter 10.

1049   Henrik, Elizabeth. "Neuroendocrine Mechanisms of Reproductive Aging in Women and Female Rats." In Ann Mae Voda, et al, eds. *Changing Perspectives on Menopause.* Austin: U of Texas Press, 1982. Chapter 8.

1050   Hill, Judith. "Smoking, Alcohol, and Body Mass Relationships to Early Menopause: Implications for Risk of Cardiovascular Disease." In Ann Mae Voda, et al, eds. *Changing Perspectives on Menopause.* Austin: U of Texas Press, 1982. Chapter 11.

1051   Huddleston, Donna Sue Tolley, and Beverly J. McElmurry. "The Natural Menopause [review essay]." In Carol J. Leppa, ed. *Women's Health Perspectives: An Annual Review,* Volume 3. Phoenix, Arizona: Oryx, 1990. Chapter 12.

1052   Josephson, Rose Lee. *The Mediating Effects of Social Support and Hardiness of Personality on the Life Change Events and Menopausal Symptoms of Midlife Women.* California School of Professional Psychology, Los Angeles, 1988. 49/10B.

1053   Kaufert, Patricia. "The Menopausal Woman and Her Use of Health Services." *Maturitas* 1980 2: 191–206.

1054   **Kaufert, Patricia.** "Menopause as Process or Event: The Creation of Definitions in Biomedicine." In Margaret Lock and Deborah R. Gordon, eds. *Biomedicine Examined.* Norwell: Kluwer, 1988. 331–339.

1055   **Kaufert, Patricia.** "Menstruation and Menstrual Change: Women in Midlife." In Virginia L. Olesen and Nancy Fugate Woods, eds. *Culture, Society, and Menstruation.* Washington: Hemisphere, 1986. 63–76.

1056   **Kaufert, Patricia.** "Methodological Issues in Menopause Research." In Marcha Flint, et al, eds. *Multidisciplinary Perspectives on Menopause: Annals of the New York Academy of Sciences* (Volume 592). New York: The Academy, 1990. 114–122.

1057   **Kaufert, Patricia.** "Myth and the Menopause." *Sociology of Health & Illness* July 1982 4(2): 141–166.

1058   **Kaufert, Patricia, and Penny Gilbert.** "The Context of Menopause: Psychotropic Drug Use and Menopausal Status." *Social Science & Medicine* 1986 23(8): 747–755.

1059   **Kaufert, Patricia, and Penny Gilbert.** "Women, Menopause, and Medicalization." *Culture, Medicine & Psychiatry* March 1986 10(1): 7–21. Special issue: "Anthropological Approaches to Menopause."

1060   **Kaufert, Patricia, and J. Syrotuik.** "Symptom Reporting at the Menopause." *Social Science and Medicine* 1981 15dE: 173–184.

1061   **Kay, Margarita, et al.** "Ethnography of the Menopause-Related Hot Flash." *Maturitas* 1982 4: 217–227.

1062   **Kincaid-Ehlers, Elizabeth.** "Bad Maps for an Unknown Region: Menopause from a Literary Perspective." In Ann Mae Voda, et al, eds. *Changing Perspectives on Menopause.* Austin: U of Texas Press, 1982. Chapter 2.

1063   **Koeske, Randi Daimon.** "Beyond Oppositional Analysis: Concluding Remarks." In Ann Mae Voda, et al, eds. *Changing Perspectives on Menopause.* Austin: U of Texas Press, 1982. Chapter 27.

1064   **Koeske, Randi Daimon.** "Toward a Biosocial Paradigm for Menopause Research: Lessons and Contributions from the Behavioral Sciences." In Ann Mae Voda, et al, eds. *Changing Perspectives on Menopause.* Austin: U of Texas Press, 1982. Chapter 1.

1065   **Kronenberg, Fredi.** "Hot Flashes: Epidemiology and Physiology." In Marcha Flint, et al, eds. *Multidisciplinary Perspectives on Menopause: Annals of the New York Academy of Sciences* (Volume 592). New York: The Academy, 1990. 52–86.

1066   **Lancaster, Jane B., and Barbara J. King.** "An Evolutionary Perspective on Menopause." In Virginia Kerns and Judith K. Brown, eds. *In Her Prime: New Views of Middle-Aged Women, 2d ed.* Urbana: U of Illinois Press, 1992 (also Brown and Kerns's *In Her Prime: A New View of Middle-Aged Women*, 1985). Chapters 1, 2.

1067   **Lance, Larrie Lynn.** *Reproduction and Breast Disease: An Intergenerational Study.* U of California, Los Angeles, 1981. 42/01B.

1068   **Landau, Erika, and Benjamin Maoz.** "Continuity of Self-Actualization: Womanhood in the Climacterium and Old Age." In Ruth B. Weg, ed. *Sexuality in the Later Years: Roles and Behavior.* New York: Academic Press, 1983. Chapter 12.

1069   LaRocco, Susan A., and Denise F. Polit. "Women's Knowledge About the Menopause." *Nursing Research* 1980 29(1): 10–11.

1070   Laws, Sophie. *Issues of Blood: The Politics of Menstruation*. London: Macmillan, 1990. bib, index.

Laws's feminist activism is apparent in her writing and research interest in women's health. She is Research Worker/Coordinator for Physical Disability Services for West Lambeth Health Authority in England. The term menstruation is often used to encompass menopause, both issues of blood. This substantial work focuses on social aspects as seen through public opinion. Men's attitudes toward menstruation are impossible to separate from how they perceive women generally. Ideas about women's "natural" inferiority, and concern that women's needs and problems may inconvenience men are common themes. If women fail to observe the etiquette of silence, they meet with angry hostility. Laws shows how an understanding of what women are up against may be needed to bring release from the negative messages of patriarchal cultures. Inevitably, menopause and women past menopause are considerations in this. The largest group of nonmenstruating women consists of women who have passed the menopause. A woman typically will menstruate for only half of her lifetime. "However, as long as the ability to bear children is held to be the 'purpose' of womankind, women who do not menstruate can be regarded by some as not fully female" (p. 4).

1071   Leidy, Lynette E. *The Timing of Menopause in Biological and Sociocultural Context: A Lifespan Approach [age scales]*. SUNY at Albany, 1991. 52/03A.

1072   Lennon, Mary Clare, 1948– . "Is Menopause Depressing? An Investigation of Three Perspectives." *Sex Roles* July 1987 17: 1–16.

1073   Lennon, Mary Clare, 1948– . "The Psychological Consequences of Menopause: The Importance of Timing as a Life Stage Event." *J of Health and Social Behavior* December 1982 23(4): 353–366.

1074   Lennon, Mary Clare, 1948– . *Psychological Reactions to Menopause: A Sociological Study*. Columbia U, 1980. 41/09A.

1075   Lincoln, Nancy Lynn. *Women's Attitudes Toward Menopause as Related to Self-Esteem*. U of Michigan, 1980. 41/09B.

1076   Lock, Margaret. "Models and Practice in Medicine: Menopause as Syndrome or Life Transition?" *Culture, Medicine and Psychiatry* 1982 6(3): 261–280.

1077   Logothetis, Mary Lou. "Our Legacy: Medical Views of the Menopausal Woman." In Dena Taylor and Amber Cloverdale Sumrall, eds. *Women of the 14th Moon: Writings on Menopause*. Freedom: Crossing, 1991. 40–46.

1078   MacPherson, Kathleen Isabelle. *Feminist Praxis in the Making: The Menopause Collective*. Brandeis U, 1986. 47/05A.

1079   MacPherson, Kathleen Isabelle. "Menopause as Disease: The Social Construction of a Metaphor." *Advances in Nursing Science* 1981 3(2): 95–113.

1080   MacPherson, Kathleen Isabelle. "Nurse-Researchers Respond to the Medicalization of Menopause." In Marcha Flint, et al, eds. *Multidisciplinary Perspectives on Menopause: Annals of the New York Academy of Sciences* (Volume 592). New York: The Academy, 1990. 180–184.

1081   **Mankowitz, Ann,** 1924– . *Change of Life: A Psychological Study of Dreams and the Menopause.* Studies in Jungian Psychology by Jungian Analysts, #16. Toronto: Inner City Books, 1984. bib, index.

The Jungian approach to knowing one's inner self confronts fears to find hidden sources of healing and renewal.

1082   **Martin, Emily.** "Medical Metaphors of Women's Bodies: Menstruation and Menopause." In her *The Woman in the Body: A Cultural Analysis of Reproduction.* Boston: Beacon, 1987. Chapter 3.

1083   **Martin, Emily.** "Menopause, Power and Heat." In her *The Woman in the Body: A Cultural Analysis of Reproduction.* Boston: Beacon, 1987. Chapter 10.

1084   **McCrea, Frances B.** "The Politics of Menopause: The 'Discovery' of a Deficiency Disease." *Social Problems* 1983 31(1): 111–123.

1085   **McKeever, Linda Crockett.** *Menopause: An Uncertain Passage: An Interpretive Study.* U of California, San Francisco, 1988. 49/09B.

1086   **McKinlay, John, et al.** "Health Status and Utilization Behavior Associated with Menopause." *American J of Epidemiology* 1987 125(1): 110–121.

1087   **McKinlay, Sonja, and John McKinlay.** "The Impact of Menopause and Social Factors on Health." *Progress in Clinical and Biological Research* 1989 320: 137–161. Also in Charles B. Hammond, et al, eds. *Menopause: Evaluation, Treatment, and Health Concerns: Proceedings of a National Institutes of Health Symposium . . . 1988.* New York: Liss, 1989.

1088   **Millette, Brenda McNamara.** "Menopause: A Survey of Attitudes and Knowledge." *Issues in Health Care of Women* 1981 3: 263–276.

1089   **Millette, Brenda McNamara, et al.** *Women and the Menopause.* Reston: Reston Publishing, 1983. bib, il, index.

With Joellen Beck Watson Hawkins, Mary Kurien, and Rachel R. Schiffman, Millette created a book for and about women and the climacteric.

1090   **Mitteness, Linda S.** "Historical Changes in Public Information About the Menopause." *Urban Anthropology* 1983 12(2): 161–179.

1091   **Moore, B.** "Climacteric Symptoms in an African Community." *Maturitas* March 1981 3(1): 25–29.

1092   **Moran, Jan, and Norah C. Keating.** "Making Sense Out of Feeling Different— The Experience of Menopause." *Canadian Woman Studies/Les Cahiers de la Femme* Winter 1992 12: 17–20.

1093   **Morokoff, Patricia J.** "Sexuality in Perimenopausal and Postmenopausal Women." *Psychology of Women Q* December 1988 12: 489–511.

1094   **Nachtigall, Lila E.** "The Medicalization of the Menopause." In Marcha Flint, et al, eds. *Multidisciplinary Perspectives on Menopause: Annals of the New York Academy of Sciences* (Volume 592). New York: The Academy, 1990. 179.

1095   **Notelovitz, Morris.** "Exercise and Health Maintenance in Menopausal Women." In Marcha Flint, et al, eds. *Multidisciplinary Perspectives on Menopause: Annals of the New York Academy of Sciences* (Volume 592). New York: The Academy, 1990. 204–220.

1096   Notelovitz, Morris. "Is There Need for Menopause Clinics?" In Marcha Flint, et al, eds. *Multidisciplinary Perspectives on Menopause: Annals of the New York Academy of Sciences* (Volume 592). New York: The Academy, 1990. 239–241.

1097   Notman, Malkah Tolpin. "Menopause and Adult Development." In Marcha Flint, et al, eds. *Multidisciplinary Perspectives on Menopause: Annals of the New York Academy of Sciences* (Volume 592). New York: The Academy, 1990. 149–155.

1098   Ojeda, Linda. *Menopause Without Medicine: Feel Healthy, Look Younger, Live Longer.* San Bernardino: Borgo Press; Claremont: Hunter House, 1989. bib, il.

Dr. Ojeda is a writer and lecturer on nutrition. Here she provides guidelines on the use of diet, exercise, and specific nutrients effective in treating and preventing such menopausal complaints as insomnia, hot flashes, and mood swings. Topics considered in menopause handbooks usually include estrogen therapy, exercise, osteoporosis, and sexuality. Other examples of this type of book include Susan Flamholtz Trien's *Change of Life: The Menopause Handbook* (New York: Fawcett Columbine, 1986) and Dr. Ann Mae Voda's fine *Menopause, Me and You: A Personal Handbook for Women* (Salt Lake City: U of Utah College of Nursing, 1984).

1099   Parlee, Mary Brown. "Integrating Biological and Social Scientific Research on Menopause." In Marcha Flint, et al, eds. *Multidisciplinary Perspectives on Menopause: Annals of the New York Academy of Sciences* (Volume 592). New York: The Academy, 1990. 379–389.

1100   Parlee, Mary Brown. "Reproductive Issues, Including Menopause." In Grace Kesterman Baruch and Jeanne Brooks-Gunn, eds. *Women in Midlife.* New York: Plenum Press, 1984. 303–313.

1101   Payne, Shelley Lynn. *Predicting Adjustment to the Female Menopause.* U of Miami, 1981. 42/12B.

1102   Perlmutter, Ellen Susan. *Women's Views of Menopause: An Experimental Attributional Approach.* Northwestern U, 1981. 42/05B.

1103   Perlmutter, Ellen Susan, and Pauline B. Bart. "Changing View of 'The Change': A Critical Review." In Ann Mae Voda, et al, eds. *Changing Perspectives on Menopause.* Austin: U of Texas Press, 1982. Chapter 13.

1104   Polit, Denise F., and Susan A. LaRocco. "Social and Psychological Correlates of Menopausal Symptoms." *Psychosomatic Medicine* May 1980 42(3): 335–345.

1105   Quinn, Agatha Anne. *Integrating a Changing Me: A Grounded Theory of the Process of Menopause for Perimenopausal Women.* U of Colorado Health Sciences Center, 1988. 50/01B.

1106   Rajangam, Sayee, and I. M. Thomas. "Menarche and Menopause—Tamil Brahmins of India." *Man in India* 1987 67(3): 264–275.

1107   Rankin, Marlene K. *Effect of Sound Wave Repatterning on Symptoms of Menopausal Women.* Texas Woman's U, 1984. 46/03B.

1108   Reitz, Rosetta. *Menopause: A Positive Approach.* New York: Penguin Books, 1983. bib, index.

Reitz includes consideration of the male climacteric.

1109   Ruble, Diane N., and Jeanne Brooks-Gunn. "Expectations Regarding Menstrual Symptoms: Effects on Evaluation and Behavior of Women." In Ann Mae Voda, et al, eds. *Changing Perspectives on Menopause.* Austin: U of Texas Press, 1982. Chapter 15.

1110   Sarrel, Philip M., et al. "Ovarian Steroids and the Capacity to Function at Home and in the Workplace." In Marcha Flint, et al, eds. *Multidisciplinary Perspectives on Menopause: Annals of the New York Academy of Sciences* (Volume 592). New York: The Academy, 1990. 156–161.

1111   Severne, Liesbeth. "Psychological Aspects of the Menopause." In Ann Mae Voda, et al, eds. *Changing Perspectives on Menopause*. Austin: U of Texas Press, 1982. Chapter 17.

1112   Seymour, Sandra Elizabeth Fields. *Attitudes Toward Menopause in Midlife Women*. Florida State U, 1986. 47/10A.

1113   Sharma, Vinod K. "The Construction and Development of a Menopausal Symptom Checklist." *Indian J of Clinical Psychology* March 1983 10(1): 63–70.

1114   Sharma, Vinod K., and M. S. L. Saxena. "Climacteric Symptoms: A Study in the Indian Context." *Maturitas* 1981 3: 11–20.

1115   Sheehy, Gail. "The Silent Passage: Menopause." *Vanity Fair* October 1991 54: 222–227, 252, 254, 256, 258, 260–263.

1116   Smith, Linda Kay. *Biological and Cultural Effects of Obesity on Women During Menopause*. Wayne State U, 1987. 48/04A.

1117   Stampfer, Meir J., et al. "Menopause and Heart Disease: A Review." In Marcha Flint, et al, eds. *Multidisciplinary Perspectives on Menopause: Annals of the New York Academy of Sciences* (Volume 592). New York: The Academy, 1990. 193–203.

1118   Strickland, Bonnie Ruth, M.D., 1936– . "Menopause." In Elaine A. Blechman and Kelly D. Brownell, eds. *Handbook of Behavioral Medicine for Women*. Elmsford: Pergamon, 1988. 41–47.

1119   Suggs, David N. *Climacteric Among the "New" Women of Mochudi, Botswana*. U of Florida, 1986. 48/04A.

1120   Taylor, Dena. "Menopause: Last Blood." In her *Red Flower: Rethinking Menstruation*. Freedom: Crossing Press, 1988. 92–106.

1121   Townsend, John Marshall, and Cynthia Carbone. "Menopausal Syndrome: Illness or Social Role—a Transcultural Analysis. *Culture, Medicine & Psychiatry* September 1980 4(3): 229–248.

1122   Treloar, Alan E. "Predicting the Close of Menstrual Life." In Ann Mae Voda, et al, eds. *Changing Perspectives on Menopause*. Austin: U of Texas Press, 1982. Chapter 21.

1123   Uphold, Constance R., and E. J. Susman. "Self-Reported Climacteric Symptoms." *Nursing Research* 1981 30(2): 84–88.

1124   Utian, Wulf H., M.D., 1939– . *Menopause in Modern Perspective: A Guide to Clinical Practice*. New York: Appleton-Century-Crofts, 1980. bib, il, index.
        A comparison of this clinical guide with Utian's popular book, *Your Middle Years: A Doctor's Guide for Today's Woman,* can be productive. Both were published in 1980 by Appleton.

1125   Utian, Wulf H., M.D., 1939– . "The Menopause in Perspective: From Potions to Patches." In Marcha Flint, et al, eds. *Multidisciplinary Perspectives on Menopause:*

Annals of the New York Academy of Sciences (Volume 592). New York: The Academy, 1990. 1–7.

1126   **Voda, Ann Mae,** 1930– . "Menopausal Hot Flash." In Ann Mae Voda, et al, eds. *Changing Perspectives on Menopause.* Austin: U of Texas Press, 1982. Chapter 10.

1127   **Voda, Ann Mae,** 1930– , et al. "Body Composition Changes in Menopausal Women." *Women & Therapy* 1991 11(2): 71–96.

1128   **Voda, Ann Mae,** 1930– , et al. *Changing Perspectives on Menopause.* Austin: U of Texas Press, 1982. bib, il, index.
        Part 1, "Interdisciplinary Perspectives on Menopause"; Part 2, "Anthropology, Biology/Physiology, and Psychology Research"; Part 3, "Methods and Models of Menstrual-Cycle Research"; Part 4, "Menopausal Facts, Fallacies, and Myths"; Part 5, "Aging and Estrogens"; Part 6, "Male and Female Menopause"; Part 7, "New Directions for Menopausal Research." These are professional papers. Dr. Voda's contribution is Chapter 10, "Menopausal Hot Flash." Contents are analyzed in *Women and Aging: A Guide to the Literature.*

1129   **Walsh, Brian, and Isaac Schiff.** "Vasomotor Flushes." In Marcha Flint, et al, eds. *Multidisciplinary Perspectives on Menopause: Annals of the New York Academy of Sciences* (Volume 592). New York: The Academy, 1990. 346–356.

1130   **Weg, Ruth B.** "Beyond Babies and Orgasm." *Educational Horizons* Summer 1982 60(4): 161–170+.

1131   **Weigle, Marta.** "Moon, Menstruation, Menopause: Myth and Ritual." In her *Spiders and Spinsters: Women and Mythology.* Albuquerque: U of New Mexico Press, 1982. Chapter 5.

1132   **White, Nancy E., and Judith M. Richter.** "Attitude Toward Menopause and the Impact of the Menopausal Event on Adult Women with Diabetes Mellitus." *J of Women & Aging* 1990 2(4): 21–38.

1133   **Wilbush, Joel.** "Climacteric Expression and Social Context." *Maturitas* 1982 4: 195–205.

1134   **Wilbush, Joel.** "Menopause and Menorrhagia: A Historical Exploration." *Maturitas* 1989 10: 83–108.

1135   **Wilbush, Joel.** "Menorrhagia and Menopause: A Historical Review." *Maturitas* 1988 10: 5–26.

1136   **Wilbush, Joel.** "What's in a Name? Some Linguistic Aspects of the Climacteric." *Maturitas* 1981 3: 1–9.

1137   **Wilheim, Beatrice Verdes.** *A Study of the Relationship Between Attitude Toward Menopause, Reported Symptoms and Role Involvements of Middle-Aged Women.* Temple U, 1988. 49/12A.

1138   **Woods, Nancy Fugate.** "Menopausal Distress: A Model for Epidemiologic Investigation." In Ann Mae Voda, et al, eds. *Changing Perspectives on Menopause.* Austin: U of Texas Press, 1982. Chapter 16.

1139   **World Health Organization. Scientific Group on Research on the Menopause.** *Research on the Menopause: Report of a WHO Scientific Group.* Technical Report Series,

#670. Geneva: WHO, 1986. bib. (WHO Publications Centre, 49 Sheridan Avenue, Albany, NY, USA 12210.)

The Proceedings of the International Congress on the Menopause are also of interest. Those of the fifth, held in Sorrento, Italy in 1987, were titled *The Climacteric and Beyond.* Those of the fourth, held in Lake Buena Vista, Florida in 1984, were titled *The Climacteric in Perspective* and edited by Morris Notelovitz and Peter A. VanKeep (MTP Press, 1986).

1140 **Wren, Barry G.** "Management of the Menopause." *Healthright* November 1989 9: 35–37.

1141 **Yeandle, Susan.** "Married Women at Midlife—Past Experience and Change." In Patricia Allatt, et al, eds. *Women and the Life Cycle: Transitions and Turning Points.* New York: Macmillan, 1987. Chapter 9.

EMPTY NEST SYNDROME

See also this chapter: Reentry; Resuming Education and Employment (1269–1349, especially #1278).

> *The term* empty nest syndrome *is used to refer to the post-parental period in the family life cycle after the children have left home. Although many agree that "women generally look forward to having their children launched," it has also been pointed out that "the concept of the 'empty nest' in contemporary society has itself been challenged" (Robert C. Atchley.* Social Forces and Aging, *4th ed. Wadsworth, 1985, p. 96; Terri L. Premo.* Winter Friends: Women Growing Old in the New Republic, 1785–1835, *rev. and enl. Urbana: U of Illinois Press, 1990, p. 81). In the 1990s, the term has received an additional meaning. The* never-empty nest *is associated with adult children who were not taught to be independent or who are leaving home later or returning home to parents in times of economic crisis.*

1142 **Adelmann, Pamela K., et al.** "Empty Nest, Cohort, and Employment in the Well-Being of Midlife Women." *Sex Roles* February 1989(3/4) 20: 173–189.

1143 **Borland, Dolores Cabic.** "A Cohort Analysis Approach to the Empty-Nest Syndrome Among Three Ethnic Groups of Women: A Theoretical Position." *J of Marriage and the Family* February 1982 44(1): 117–129.

1144 **Cooper, Kathryn Louise.** *Gender Identity and Ego Mastery Style in Forty-Three- to Fifty-One-Year-Old, Pre- and Post-Empty Nest Women.* Northwestern U, 1986. 47/06B.

1145 **Cooper, Kathryn Louise, and David L. Gutmann.** "Gender Identity and Ego Mastery Style in Middle-Aged, Pre- and Post-Empty Nest Women." *Gerontologist* 1987 27(3): 347–352.

1146 **DeVries, Helen M.** *Launching the Children: Gender Differences in Parents' Appraisals of a Family Transition.* Virginia Commonwealth U, 1991. 52/06B.

1147 **French, Lona M.** *The Relationship Between Life Satisfaction and Individuation in Homemakers in the Empty Nest Stage: Developmental Opportunities in the Second Half of Life.* Wright Institute, 1992. 53/06B.

1148   Gonzalez, Pamela C. *Ego Development and Ego Identity in Mothers at Mid-Life.* U of Pittsburgh, 1990. 51/05B.

1149   Lewis, Constance. *The Empty Nest Revisited.* Fielding Institute, 1986. 47/11A.

1150   Lewis, Robert A. "Empty Nest Syndrome Hits Fathers, Too." *USA Today* January 1990 118(2536): 10+.

1151   Raup, Jana L., and Jane E. Myers. "The Empty Nest Syndrome: Myth or Reality?" *J of Counseling and Development* November-December 1989 68(2): 180–183.

1152   Schoenholz, Dawne Rowena. *Life Style Selection and Personal Satisfaction Among Empty Nest Women.* U of Southern California, 1981. 41/11A.

1153   Small, Marguerite. *The Process of Leaving Home: Mothers' Perspectives on their Children's Emancipation.* California School of Professional Psychology, Berkeley/Alameda, 1991. 52/06B.

HEALTH AND HEALTH CARE

D E S

> *D E S stands for Diethylstilbestrol, a synthetic form of estrogen which was marketed under many brand names. Although linked with cancer by 1970, it had been prescribed to millions of women from 1940 into the 1970s to control miscarriage and prevent pregnancy complications, and for other conditions. Until 1979, other uses included as a fattening agent for beef cattle. Current scientific opinion indicates significantly higher health risks to children born to these women, including greater susceptibility to cancer and fertility problems, hence the terms* D E S Mother *and* D E S Daughter. *It is known that D E S causes cancer, and that it has caused abnormalities in D E S-affected offspring. D E S Mothers, many of whom were middle-aged at the time they were prescribed D E S, are now middle-aged and old women; D E S Daughters are typically now middle-aged. For further information perform online title-word searches; contact D E S Action at 1615 Broadway, #510, Oakland, CA 94612, and Long Island Jewish Hospital, New Hyde Park, NY 11040. Useful subject-headings include:*

Diethylstilbestrol—adverse effects
Fetus—effect of drugs on
Genital neoplasms, female—chemically induced
Iatrogenic diseases
Prenatal exposure delayed effects
Trust (psychology)
Vagina—cancer

1154   Apfel, Roberta J., 1938– , M.D., and Susan M. Fisher, 1937– , M.D. *To Do No Harm: D E S and the Dilemmas of Modern Medicine.* New Haven: Yale U Press, 1984. bib, index.

D E S was linked to cancer as early as 1940. Millions of American women received prescriptions from physicians for D E S or were exposed to it in the forty years prior to these psychiatrists' book, which considers a medical system that could permit such health care. Case histories and a glossary are provided.

1155   Bell, Susan E. "The Meaning of Risk, Choice, and Responsibility for a D E S Daughter." In Kathryn Strother Ratcliff, et al. *Healing Technology: Feminist Perspectives.* Ann Arbor: U of Michigan Press, 1989. 245–262.

1156   Edelman, David A. *D E S/Diethylstilbestrol: New Perspectives.* Lancaster, Lancashire, and Boston: MTP Press, 1986. bib, index.
    This is a technical book covering D E S toxicology, effect of such drugs on the fetus (production of human abnormalities), and such other adverse effects as female genital neoplasms.

1157   Fenichell, Stephen, and Lawrence S. Charfoos. *Daughters at Risk: A Personal D E S History.* New York: Doubleday, 1981.
    Daughters of women prescribed D E S have also been prone to cancer. Anne Needham, who as a young woman had a hysterectomy for cancer, sued White Laboratories, makers of a D E S drug. Charfoos (an attorney in the litigation) and Fenichell detail the case and provide a history of D E S development, research linking it early to cancer, the FDA's approval, the pharmaceutical company promotion, and the medical community's involvement.

1158   Gutterman, Elane M., et al. "Long-Term Distress Subsequent to Pregnancy Drug Administration: Women with In Utero Diethylstilbestrol (D E S) Exposed Daughters." *J of Psychosomatic Obstetrics & Gynaecology* March 1986 5(1): 51–63.

1159   Gutterman, Elane M., et al. "Vulnerability to Stress Among Women with In Utero Diethylstilbestrol (D E S) Exposed Daughters." *J of Human Stress* Fall 1985 11(3): 103–110.

1160   Hebert, Patricia Robertson. *Reproductive Performance in the D E S-Exposed Daughters.* U of Texas Health Sciences Center at Houston, 1984. 46/06B.

1161   Herbst, Arthur L., and Howard Alan Bern, 1920– , eds. *Developmental Effects of Diethylstilbestrol (D E S) in Pregnancy.* New York: Thieme-Stratton, 1981. bib, il, index.
    The effect of drugs such as D E S on the fetus and as a cancer-inducing drug upon generative organs is considered. Herbst also edited the "Symposium on D E S" 1977 Proceedings.

1162   Hines, Melissa Marie. *Prenatal Diethylstilbestrol (D E S) Exposure, Human Sexually Dimorphic Behavior and Cerebral Lateralization.* U of California, Los Angeles, 1981. 42/01B.

1163   Lish, Jenifer D., et al. "Prenatal Exposure to Diethylstilbestrol (D E S): Childhood Play Behavior and Adult Gender-Role Behavior in Women." *Archives of Sexual Behavior* October 1992 21(5): 423–441.

1164   Meyers, Robert. *D.E.S.: The Bitter Pill.* New York: Seaview/Putnam, 1983. bib, index.
    Although published more than a decade ago, this D E S book continues to be informative, for such considerations as use of D E S as a "morning-after" pill, D E S in our food, the D E S Registry and organizations, and recognition that it did (and could) happen to anyone, for example, Patsy Mink.

1165   Newman, Beth Melanie. *An Epidemiologic Study of Prenatal D E S Exposure and Immune Dysfunction in Women.* U of California, Berkeley, 1987. 48/09B.

1166   Orenberg, Cynthia. *D E S: The Complete Story.* New York: St. Martin's Press, 1981. il.

Orenberg's book differs from many trade-books in that the author, a D E S Mother, reassures D E S-exposed mothers and children and provides information on legal implications.

1167   **Saunders, Edward J.** "Physical and Psychological Problems Associated with Exposure to Diethylstilbestrol (D E S)." *Hospital & Community Psychiatry* January 1988 39(1): 73–77.

1168   **Schwartzman, Ellen Jean.** *The Relationship of the D E S Daughter to Her Mother: Psychological Impact of a Teratogen (Diethylstilbestrol).* California School of Professional Psychology, Berkeley, 1986. 47/04B.

1169   **Weiss, Kay.** "Vaginal Cancer: An Iatrogenic Disease?" In Elizabeth Fee, ed. *Women and Health: The Politics of Sex in Medicine.* Farmingdale: Baywood, 1983. Chapter 3.

1170   **Wilcox, Allen J., et al.** "Prenatal Diethylstilbestrol Exposure and Performance on College Entrance Examinations." *Hormones & Behavior* September 1992 26(3): 433–439.

1171   **Winchell, Donna Mae.** *An Examination of the Psychological Well-Being of D E S Daughters and Their Mothers.* Pennsylvania State U, 1988. 49/12A.

Estrogens; E.R.T.; hormone replacement therapy
See also this chapter: Climacteric; Menopause (985–1141); Chapter 1: Health and Health Care: Osteoarthritis; Osteoporosis (20–39).

> *Estrogens are female hormones responsible for female characteristics (e.g., breast development) and functions (e.g., menstruation). Estrone is the estrogen that is predominant after menopause. Estrogen replacement therapy ("E.R.T.") consists of the administration of a synthetic estrogen product to relieve symptoms experienced by some menopausal women. It is also advocated by some physicians for use by some postmenopausal women to reduce the risk of osteoporosis.*

1172   **Ballinger, Susan.** "Stress as a Factor in Lower Estrogen Levels in the Early Postmenopause." In Marcha Flint, et al, eds. *Multidisciplinary Perspectives on Menopause: Annals of the New York Academy of Sciences* (Volume 592). New York: The Academy, 1990. 95–113.

1173   **Gavaler, Judith S.** *The Determinants of Estrogen Levels in Postmenopausal Women.* U of Pittsburgh, 1986. 47/10B.

1174   **Kaufert, Patricia A., and Sonja M. McKinlay.** "Estrogen Replacement Therapy: The Production of Medical Knowledge and the Emergence of Policy." In their *Women and Healing: Toward a New Perspective.* New York: Tavistock, 1985. Chapter 5.

1175   **Kiel, Douglas, et al.** "Hip Fracture and the Use of Estrogens in Postmenopausal Women: The Framingham Study." *New England J of Medicine* November 5, 1987 317: 1169–1174.

1176   **Lobo, Rogerio A.** "Estrogen in Cardiovascular Disease." In Marcha Flint, et al, eds. *Multidisciplinary Perspectives on Menopause: Annals of the New York Academy of Sciences* (Volume 592). New York: The Academy, 1990. 286–294.

1177   **Logothetis, Mary Lou.** *Differences in Climacteric Women's Use of Estrogen Replacement Therapy Using Health Belief Constructs and Philosophical Orientation to Menopause.* Indiana U School of Nursing, 1988. 49/10B. Logothetis's "Women's Decisions About Estrogen Replacement Therapy" appeared in the *Western J of Nursing Research* August 1991 13(4): 458–474.

1178   **Myers, Linda Susan.** *Physiological and Subjective Sexual Arousal of Pre- and Postmenopausal Women and Postmenopausal Women Taking Estrogen Therapy.* Uniformed Services U of the Health Sciences, 1985. 49/05B.

1179   **Nachtigall, Lila E., M.D., and Joan Rattner Heilman.** *Estrogen: The Facts Can Change Your Life: The Latest Word on What the New, Safe Estrogen Therapy Can Do for Great Sex, Strong Bones, Good Looks, Longer Life, Preventing Hot Flashes.* New York: Harper & Row, 1986. bib.
    Endocrinologist Nachtigall and Heilman believe that osteoporosis is significantly curtailed by estrogen use, and in fact, that safe estrogen replacement therapy can contribute to numerous good things! Material on the transdermal patch is included.

1180   **National Women's Health Network.** *Taking Hormones and Women's Health: Choices, Risks and Benefits.* Washington: Women's Health Network, 1989.
    The National Women's Health Network, located at 514 10th St. N.W. #400, Washington, D.C. 20004, has produced this self-help guide for menopause, utilizing a nonmedicalized perspective.

1181   **Novak, Patricia J.** *Symptomatology of Menopause as a Function of Estrogen Replacement Therapy and Sex Role.* Oklahoma State U, 1980. 41/06B.

1182   **Olesen, Virgina.** "Sociological Observations on Ethical Issues Implicated in Estrogen Replacement Therapy at Menopause." In Ann Mae Voda, et al, eds. *Changing Perspectives on Menopause.* Austin: U of Texas Press, 1982. Chapter 24.

1183   **Padwick, Malcolm L., et al.** "A Simple Method for Determining the Optimal Dosage of Progestin in Postmenopausal Women Receiving Estrogens." *New England J of Medicine* October 9, 1986 315: 930–934.

1184   **St. Hillier, Donna Jones.** *Menopausal Women Receiving and Not Receiving Hormone Replacement Therapy: Generalized Contentment, Marital Satisfaction, Sexual Satisfaction, Health, Locus of Control, and Sex Role Identity Self-Reports.* Florida State U, 1989. 50/05A.

1185   **Weinstein, Milton C., and Anna N. A. Tosteson.** "Cost-Effectiveness of Hormone Replacement." In Marcha Flint, et al, eds. *Multidisciplinary Perspectives on Menopause: Annals of the New York Academy of Sciences* (Volume 592). New York: The Academy, 1990. 162–172.

1186   **Wilson, Jeanie.** "Estrogen After Menopause: Are the Rewards Worth the Risk?" *Town and Country* October 1990 44: 223–226, 297, 298.

Pregnancy and Childbirth
See also this chapter: Climacteric; Menopause (985–1141); #1003.

    Useful subject-headings for locating documents and information include:

    Childbirth after thirty-five
    Childbirth in middle age
    Maternal age

Pregnancy in middle age
Pregnancy in middle age complications

1187   **Anderson, Mary Margaret,** 1932– . *Pregnancy After Thirty.* London and Boston: Faber & Faber, 1984. bib, il, index.
  There were many popular guidebooks published in the 1980s on this subject. Two others published in both the United States and Britain are *Birth Over Thirty* by Sheila Kitzinger and edited for the United States by Penny Simkin (Sheldon Press, 1982; Penguin, 1985) and Penny Blackie's *Becoming a Mother After Thirty* (Oxford and New York: Blackwell, 1986).

1188   **Bowen, Sheila McCormick.** *Intimacy and Generativity in On-Time and Delayed Childbearing Women.* U of Tennessee, 1988. 50/04A.

1189   **Broms, Wynne E.** *The Effects of Age and Childbearing Intentions on Life Happiness and Inner-Directedness Among Childless Women, 20 to 39 Years of Age.* United States International U, 1989. 50/05B.

1190   **Caplan, Ronald M.** *The Doctor's Guide to Pregnancy After 30.* New York: Macmillan, 1986. il, index.
  Extensively illustrated, this popular work emphasizes prenatal care.

1191   **Coady, Susan Stickel,** 1939– . *Delayed Childbearing: Correlates of Maternal Satisfaction at One Year Postpartum.* Ohio State U, 1982. 43/10B.

1192   **Cobb, Judith Helen.** *Factors Influencing Childbearing Decisions in Women Who Have Deferred Childbearing Until Their Thirties.* New York U, 1986. 47/10A.

1193   **Cohen, Judith Blackfield.** *Parenthood After 30?* Lexington: Lexington, 1985. bib, il, index.
  Dr. Cohen's guide emphasizes personal choice. She has authored with Richard S. Lazarus a chapter, "Theory and Method in the Study of Stress and Coping in Ageing Individuals." In Lennart Levi, ed. *Society, Stress, and Disease.* Volume 5: *Old Age.* Oxford: Oxford U Press, 1987.

1194   **Fay, Francesca C., and Kathy Sammis Smith.** *Childbearing After 35: The Risks and the Rewards.* New York: Balsam Press/Rutledge Books, 1985. il, index.
  Nurse-practitioner Fay has experienced pregnancy after age 35. This comprehensive guide covers potential problems as well as advantages of becoming a parent at this time of life.

1195   **Fuller, Elizabeth,** 1946– . *Having Your First Baby After Thirty: A Personal Journey from Infertility to Childbirth.* New York: Dodd, Mead, 1983. bib, index.
  Fuller's focus is on female infertility patients.

1196   **Gillespie, Clark, M.D.** *Primelife Pregnancy: All You Need to Know About Pregnancy After 35.* New York: Harper, 1987. il, index.
  Gillespie provides obstetrical information: why infertility increases with age, principles of amniocentesis, ultrasound, and coping with diabetes and other conditions.

1197   **Gluck, Ann Judith.** *Women in Their Thirties and the Childbearing Choice: Developmental Perspectives.* Hahnemann U, 1988. 49/10B.

1198   **Hewitt, Maria Elizabeth.** *An Analysis of the Determinants of Amniocentesis Utilization Among Women Age 35 and Older at a New York City Hospital Using Validated Birth Certificate Data.* U of California, Los Angeles, 1985. 46/04B.

1199   **Logan, Constance Adams.** *Voluntary Childlessness: Psychosocial Factors Related to Childbearing Choice in Career Women over Thirty.* U of Cincinnati, 1987. 48/08B.

1200   **Mansfield, Phyllis Kernoff.** *Advanced Maternal Age and Pregnancy Outcome: A Critical Appraisal of the Scientific Literature.* Pennsylvania State U, 1983. 44/05A.

Also available in microfiche form from Microform Publications, College of Human Development and Performance, University of Oregon, Eugene, OR 97403. *See also* her *Pregnancy for Older Women: Assessing the Medical Risks* (New York: Praeger, 1986).

1201   **McKaughan, Molly.** *The Biological Clock: Reconciling Careers and Motherhood in the 1980s.* New York: Doubleday, 1987. bib.

McKaughan's concerns include so-called working mothers in the United States and choice.

1202   **Mercer, Ramona Thieme.** *First-Time Motherhood: Experiences from Teens to Forties.* New York: Springer, 1986. bib, index.

Here is a formal research report of the maternal role during the first year of motherhood. Mercer studied three age groups: 15–19, 20–29, and 30–42.

1203   **Morris, Monica B.,** 1928– . *Last-Chance Children: Growing Up with Older Parents.* New York: Columbia U Press, 1988. bib.

Morris includes consideration of aging American parents and family relationships, as well as children of parents who are older than typical parents.

1204   **Nord, Christine Winquist.** *Delayed Childbearing in the United States: An Exploration of the Implications for Women's and Children's Lives.* U of Pennsylvania, 1988. 49/09A.

1205   **Robrecht, Linda Clair,** 1944– . *The Mature Gravida's Orchestration of Pregnancy from Conceiving to Birthing.* U of California, San Francisco, 1991. 52/03B.

1206   **Rosin, Adolfo.** *Levels of Stress Between Married and Unmarried Maternity Patients as Affected by Wanted and Unwanted Pregnancy, Age, and Number of Children.* Texas Southern U, 1984. 46/04A.

1207   **Sanderson, Elizabeth Apfel.** *Late Childbearing Among Baby Boom Cohorts: An Exploratory Study of Delayed Motherhood Within a Developmental and Social Framework.* Fordham U, 1989. 50/05B.

1208   **Sapienza, Barbara Gail.** *Reproductive Choice and Ego Development in Women 35 to 50.* Pacific Graduate School of Psychology, 1987. 48/09B.

1209   **Schrotenboer, Kathryn, M.D., and Joan Solomon Weiss.** *The Doctor's Guide to Pregnancy over 35.* New York: Ballantine, Random, 1985. il.

Obstetrician-gynecologist and medical writer consider age-related genetic disorders, public prejudice, and career interruptions.

1210   **Scott, Lucy,** 1928– , **and Meredith Joan Angwin.** *Time Out for Motherhood: A Guide for Today's Working Woman to the Financial, Emotional, and Career Aspects of Having a Baby.* New York: J. P. Tarcher/St. Martin's Press, 1986. bib, index.

These writers consider the economic aspects of childbirth in middle age today in the United States. They emphasize choice.

1211   **Van de Kamp, Jacqueline.** *Pregnancy in the Older Woman: January 1983 Through December 1987: 327 Citations.* Bethesda, Maryland: National Library of Medicine, 1988.

This is a brief (15-page) bibliography of pregnancy in middle-aged women in the United States, #88-1 in the National Institutes of Health "Current Bibliographies in Medicine" series. HE 20.3615/2:88-1.

1212   Ventura, Stephanie J. *Trends and Variations in First Births to Older Women, 1970–86.* Hyattsville, Maryland: National Center for Health Statistics, 1989. bib. "Vital and Health Statistics. Series 21, Data from the National Vital Statistics System; #47." HE 20.6209:21/47.

The Prime Time Phenomenon

1213   Cohen, Joan Z., et al. *Hitting Our Stride: Good News About Women in Their Middle Years.* New York: Delacorte Press, 1980. bib, index.
    The authors of this contribution to the genre known as *life skills guides* use "middle age" to refer to the broad span of time when one is no longer struggling with the issues and tasks of youth and not yet dealing with the realities of old age. They point out that "criteria" could be chronological age, physical condition, roles, or attitudes (p. 260). They surveyed women in their middle years (over 800 responded—the questionnaire and report are appended) and found that 70 percent would feel comfortable about having a relationship with a younger man ("Older Women/Younger Men," Chapter 12). "On Our Own" (Chapter 11) considers single women.

1214   Fodor, Iris G., and Violet Franks. "Women in Midlife and Beyond: The New Prime of Life." *Psychology of Women Q* December 1990 14(4): 445–449.

1215   Franks, Helen. *Prime Time: The Mid-Life Woman in Focus.* London: Pan Books, 1981. bib, index. (Pan Books, Ltd., Cavaye Place, London, England SW 10 9PG.)
    How much the British and Americans have in common in their views of midlife women comes through in this book's indexing, sources quoted, and assumptions: Pauline Bart, Simone de Beauvoir, Shere Hite, Doris Lessing, Alison Lurie, Ann Oakley, Gail Sheehy, and Mary Wollstonecraft; alcoholism, ambition, anorexia nervosa, calcium, depression, graying hair, housework, menopause, oestrogen (estrogen), osteoporosis, reentry schemes, traditional voluntary work. Frank says mid-life is mid-30s to mid-50s. Her chapter on "Life Without Marriage" refers to after divorce.

1216   Mitchell, Valory, and Ravenna Helson. "Women's Prime of Life: Is It the 50s?" *Psychology of Women Q* December 1990 14(4): 451–470.

1217   Spodnik, Jean Perry, and David P. Cogan, M.D. *The 35-Plus Good Health Guide for Women: The Prime of Life Program for Women over 35.* New York: Harper & Row, 1989. il, index. The shorter, 1987 version was subtitled *The Breakthrough Metabolism Diet Developed at Kaiser Permanente for Women over 35.*

1218   Rice, Natalie. *Prime Time: A Study of the Experience of Women Who Perceive Themselves to Be Entering Middle Age.* Union for Experimenting Colleges and Universities, 1987. 48/08B.

1219   Tacha, Athena. "Reaching 50 (The Process of Aging II)." *Heresies* 1988 6(3): 4–6.

Psychosocial Perspectives

1220   Ascher, Barbara Lazear. *The Habit of Loving.* New York: Random House, 1989.
    This collection of essays by the author of *Playing After Dark* (Doubleday, 1986) includes such life change events as motherhood, middle age, pain, death, and American women at work. (Not to be confused with Doris Lessing's fiction of the same title.)

1221   Barth, Patricia A. *A Study of the Individuation Process in Women at the Midlife Transition.* Fielding Institute, 1987. 49/08B.

1222   Black, Sionag M., et al. "The Psychological Well-Being of Women in Their Middle Years." *Psychology of Women Q* Spring 1984 8(3): 282–292.

1223   Brooks-Gunn, Jeanne, and Barbara Kirsh. "Life Events and the Boundaries of Midlife Women." In Grace Kesterman Baruch and Jeanne Brooks-Gunn, eds. *Women in Midlife.* New York: Plenum Press, 1984. Chapter 1.

1224   Corl, Nancy Sonneland. *Mid-Life Distress in Women: Psychosocial Factors.* California School of Professional Psychology, Berkeley, 1980. 41/12B.

1225   Cox, Caral Beth. *Illness Behavior in Mid-Life Women.* U of Maryland, Baltimore, 1980. 41/07A.

1226   Dannenbaum, Dorothy Katzenberg. *Mid-Life Women and Achievement Patterns Associated with Role-Change.* Temple U, 1981. 42/05B.

1227   DeLorey, Catherine. "Women at Midlife: Women's Perceptions, Physicians' Perceptions." *J of Women & Aging* 1989 1(4): 57–69.

1228   Droege, Ruth. *A Psychosocial Study of the Formation of the Middle Adult Life Structure in Women.* California School of Professional Psychology, Berkeley, 1982. 43/05B.

1229   Erdwins, Carl J., et al. "Personality Traits of Mature Women in Student Versus Homemaker Roles." *J of Psychology* 1980 105: 189–195.

1230   Etaugh, Claire, et al. "Attitudes Toward Women: Comparsion of Traditional-Aged and Older College Students." *J of College Student Development* January 1989 30(1): 41–46.

1231   Fodor, Iris G., and Violet Franks, eds. "Women at Midlife and Beyond" issue. *Psychology of Women Q* December 1990 14(4).

1232   Frank, Susan J., et al. "The Effects of Sex-Role Traits on Three Aspects of Psychological Well-Being in a Sample of Middle-Aged Women." *Sex Roles* 1985 12(9/10): 1073–1087.

1233   Garver, Joan Menkin. *Multiple Role Behavior and Perception of Ambiguous Pictures in Middle-Aged Women: Satisfaction, Flexibility, and Control.* City U of New York, 1981. 42/04B.

1234   Herring, Kennise McKinzie. *An Examination of the Role of Object Relations in Female Mid-Life Adjustment.* Northwestern U, 1986. 47/06B.

1235   Jacobson, Joan M. "Midlife 'Baby Boom' Women Compared to Their Older Counterparts in Midlife." ERIC, November 1991. ED #350499. 25 pages.

1236   Lake, Geraldine Stirling. *An Application of Concepts from the Cobb Model to Female Coping with Mid-Life Events.* U of Maryland, 1984. 46/05A.

1237   Loewenstein, Sophie Freud. "Toward Choice and Differentiation in the Midlife Crises of Women." In Carol Landau Heckerman, ed. *The Evolving Female: Women in Psychosocial Context.* New York: Human Sciences Press, 1980. Chapter 6.

1238   Lucas, Donna Jean. *Change and Opportunity: A Life Transition Group for Women in Middle Adulthood.* Antioch U/New England Graduate School, 1988. 49/04B.

1239   Marcus, Suzanne. *The Effects of Maternal Employment and Family Life Cycle Stage on Women's Psychological Well-Being.* North Texas State U, 1984. 45/07B.

1240   **Miller, Cheryl Allyn.** *The Life Course Patterns of Chicago-Area Women: A Cohort Analysis of the Sequencing and Timing of Related Roles Through the Middle Years.* Loyola U of Chicago, 1982. 41/12A.

1241   **Millner, Nancy Bost.** *A Study of the Process of Feminine Mid-Life Renewal.* Union for Experimenting Colleges and Universities, 1988. 49/05B.

1242   **Moore, Ethie Lee.** *Apparel Purchasing Problems of the Middle-Aged Woman.* Texas Woman's U, 1982. 43/09A.

1243   **Nathanson, Constance A., and Gerda Lorenz.** "Women and Health: The Social Dimensions of Biomedical Data." In Janet Zollinger Giele, ed. *Women in the Middle Years: Current Knowledge and Directions for Research and Policy.* New York: Wiley, 1982. Chapter 2.

1244   **Nolen, William Anthony, M.D.,** 1928– . *Crisis Time! Love, Marriage and the Male at Mid-Life.* New York: Dodd, Mead, 1984. index.
        Nolen is a married parent of six, a surgeon who is also a women's magazine columnist. Here he writes about psychological aspects of middle age and men.

1245   **Notman, Malkah Tolpin, M.D.** "Changing Roles for Women at Mid-Life." In William H. Norman and Thomas J. Scaramella, M.D., eds. *Mid-Life: Developmental and Clinical Issues.* New York: Brunner/Mazel, 1980. Chapter 6.

1246   **Ohashi, Julianne Prichard.** *The Relationship of Maternal Role Expectation, Surprise, and Value Attainment to Role Satisfaction in Midlife Mothers of Teenagers.* U of Texas at Austin, 1986. 47/12B.

1247   **Picano, James John.** *Ego Development and Adaptation in Middle-Aged Women.* California School of Professional Psychology, Berkeley, 1984. 46/02B.

1248   **Porcino, Jane,** 1923– . *Growing Older, Getting Better: A Handbook for Women in the Second Half of Life.* Reading: Addison Wesley, 1983. bib, il, index.
        The author of this life skills guide, mother of seven, began her doctoral work at age 55. Porcino is the founder of *Hot Flash* newsletter and codirector of the National Action Forum for Midlife and Older Women.

1249   **Price, Jean G.** "Great Expectations: Hallmark of the Midlife Woman Learner." *Educational Gerontology* March-April 1991 17(2): 167–174.

1250   **Rockloff, Diane J.** *A Psychosocial Study of Dual-Career Women Entering Middle Adulthood.* California School of Professional Psychology, Berkeley, 1988. 49/07B.

1251   **Rogers, Judith Lawrence.** *Women in Middle Age: An Examination of the Interaction of Life Stage, Social Roles, and Locus of Control.* Ohio State U, 1980. 41/07B.

1252   **Rosewell-Jackson, Susan Louise.** *A Research Model Designed to Assess Women's Developmental Issues and Tasks: A Focus on Women in Early Midlife.* U of Colorado at Boulder, 1987. 48/08A.

1253   **Rountree, Cathleen.** *Coming into Our Fullness: On Women Turning Forty.* Freedom: Crossing Press, 1991. il.
        Rountree's interviews and photographs are of diverse, middle-aged American women: Frances Moore Lappe, Judy Chicago, Ina Lea Meibach, Elena Featherston, Susan Griffin, Barbara Boxer, Arisika Razak, Gabrielle Roth, Mayumi Oda, Barbara Hammer, Betsy Damon, Judy Phillips, Brooke Medicine Eagle, Cokie Roberts, Deena Metzger, Maxine Hong Kingston, Natalie Goldberg, and Linda Leonard.

1254   Sands, Roberta G., and Virginia Richardson. "Clinical Practice with Women in Their Middle Years." *Social Work* (United States) January-February 1986 31(1): 36–43.

1255   Schlossberg, Nancy. "Mid-Life." In Carol Tavris and Dianne L. Chambless, eds. *Everywoman's Emotional Well-Being.* New York: Doubleday, 1986. Chapter 12.

1256   Slate, Susan Harper. *Women During the Midlife Transition: The Relationship Between Lifestyles and Aging Experiences.* California School of Professional Psychology, Los Angeles, 1983. 44/06B.

1257   Slive, Zoya Sandomirsky. *Mid-Life Transiton: A Study of the Psychosocial Development of Married Women in Middle Adulthood.* Boston U, 1986. 46/12B.

1258   Spurlock, Jeanne. "Black Women in the Middle Years." In Grace Kesterman Baruch and Jeanne Brooks-Gunn, eds. *Women in Midlife.* New York: Plenum Press, 1984. Chapter 10.

1259   Theobald, Clarabelle. *Prose Memory of Middle-Aged Women: An Exploratory Study.* Arizona State U, 1982. 43/06B.

1260   Thomas, Deborah Ann. *Intergroup Comparisons of Middle-Aged Women.* Ohio State U, 1981. 42/10B.

1261   Thomas, Sandra P. "Predictors of Health Status of Mid-Life Women: Implications for Later Adulthood." *J of Women & Aging* 1990 2(1): 49–77.

1262   Thompson, Ira Jo Ann. *A Tentative Model of the Life Structures of a Selected Sample of Women Ages Forty to Fifty.* U of Tennessee, 1982. 43/02A.

1263   Thompson, Martha Jane. *Identity Attainment in Mid-Life Females: An Assessment Scale.* U of Georgia, 1980. 41/04A.

1264   Wegnild, Gail, et al. "Hardiness Among Elderly Women." ERIC, November 1988. ED #305529. 12 pages.

1265   Williams, Juanita H., 1922– . *Psychology of Women: Behavior in a Biosocial Context, 3d ed.* New York: Norton, 1987. bib, index.
        Chapter 13, "Middle Age and Aging," is of interest here. Another psychologist's concern for mid-life women is Jean Baker Miller, M.D.'s *Toward a New Psychology of Women, 2d ed.* (Beacon, 1986), in which she critiques sexual inequality; *see especially* Chapters 5, "Doing Good and Feeling Bad," and 6, "Serving Others' Needs—Doing for Others."

1266   Yates, Rebecca Riegler. "The Effects of Aging and Priming on Naming Latencies in Adult Women." U of Oklahoma, 1987. 48/03B.

1267   Zacks, Hanna. *The Self-Concept of College-Graduate Women in Midlife.* Case Western Reserve U, 1982. 43/06A.

1268   Zubrod, Louise Ann Casey. *A Study of the Psychosocial Development of Women: Transition into Middle Adulthood.* Boston U, 1980. 41/05B.

REENTRY; RESUMING EDUCATION AND EMPLOYMENT
See also Chapter 4: Displaced Homemakers (723–737); Chapter 10: Education (1820–1844).

> *It has become increasingly difficult to find information and documents supporting the reentry of women into life after caregiving, homemaking, and*

sometimes abandonment. The concept of "reentry women" is anathema to many persons, or at best, something from the past. Information and programs have been provided in terms of reentry persons, usually reentry to employment, ignoring many women's great need to resume both education and thereby, employment. "Reentry" now tends to be a physics-associated term. Some colleges refer to these mostly mid-life women as "resuming students." ERIC provides citations in two sources: (1) Resources in Education, *covering documents (e.g., #1235, #1264, #1278), and (2)* Current Index to Journals in Education, *covering approximately 750 journals and other serial publications. All ERIC citations include abstracts. Academic and some public libraries have the ERIC printed indexes and thesaurus, microfiche and hard copy documents, and online access. For greatest efficiency, consult the latest edition of the ERIC thesaurus, which identifies, for example,* Reentry students *and* Reentry workers. *Useful Library of Congress–established subject headings include:*

High school dropouts
College dropouts
Women
Employment
Reentry

1269   **Alders, Johnyce Ogee.** *The Reentry Community College Female Student: Identity Status, Life Events, and Family/Social Support.* U of Texas at Austin, 1985. 47/02A.

1270   **Atlas, Shirley S.** *Re-Entry Women Students: Variables Involved in the Decision to Return to School.* City U of New York, 1986. 47/03B.

1271   **Bach, Susan Abrams.** *An Assessment of Need-Press Relations in Programs for Returning Women Students in General and Special College Environments.* New York U, 1985. 56/08A.

1272   **Barr, Faye Tanner.** *Role of Reentry Women.* U of Tennessee, 1984. 46/01A.

1273   **Bird, Elizabeth, and Jackie West.** "Interrupted Lives: A Study of Women Returners." In Patricia Allatt, et al, eds. *Women and the Life Cycle: Transitions and Turning Points.* New York: Macmillan, 1987. Chapter 13.

1274   **Broach, Tommie Jean.** *Concerns of Black Women and White Women Returning to School.* U of Florida, 1984. 46/03A.

1275   **Brod, Harry.** "A Better Class of Men: Comment on Husbands Educational Attainment and Support for Wives' Return to School." (With "The Importance of Emotional Support in the Face of Stressful Status Transitions: A Response to Brod" by J. Jill Suitor [pp. 254–257].) *Gender & Society* June 1990 4: 251–253.

1276   **Campaniello, Jean Ann.** *When Women Return to School: A Study of Role-Conflict and Well-Being in Multiple-Role Women.* U of Massachusetts, 1987. 48/02A.

1277   **Christman, Jolley Bruce.** *Making Both Count: An Ethnographic Study of Family and Work in the Lives of Returning Women Graduate Students.* U of Pennsylvania, 1987. 48/03A.

1278   **Coad, Cynthia P.** *Your Full Future . . . After the Empty Nest.* Muncie, Indiana: Accelerated Development, Inc., 1989. (Accelerated Development, Inc., 3400 Kilgore Avenue, Muncie, IN 47304–4896.)

This book designed for women who want to react to the empty nest syndrome with a new career is also available as ERIC fiche document ED #345167 (118 pages). It functions as a guide that can be used in the classroom and includes activities.

1279   **Coats, Margaret A. M.** *Women Returners: A Study of Mature Undergraduates and Their Educational Histories.* U of Technology, Loughborough, U.K., 1988. 49/08A.

1280   **Corvin, Sue Ann.** *Analyses of Differences in Support Between Two Groups of Women Returning to College.* U of Oklahoma, 1985. 46/11A.

1281   **Creech, Jeanne Williams.** *The Re-Entry Women Students in a Metropolitan Multi-Campus Community College: Their Internal and External Needs.* Georgia State U, 1984. 45/08A.

1282   **Cronin, Noreen Nappo.** *Reentry Women: Degree Completion After Interruption.* SUNY Buffalo, 1987. 48/10A.

1283   **D'Acunto, Mary.** *Reentering Women Graduate Students: Levels of Leadership and Self-Esteem with Respect to Selected Variables.* Fordham U, 1985. 46/11A.

1284   **Diness, Phyllis Allegretto.** *Reschooling for Careers: A Sociological Analysis of the Education and Career Attainment of Older Reentry Women Students, 1970–1975.* American U, 1981. 42/03A.

1285   **Firestein, Naomi Low.** *The Relationship of Family Supportiveness to Perceived Ease of College Re-Entry for Mature Women.* U of Pennsylvania, 1984. 45/07A.

1286   **Fisher, Jerilyn.** "Returning Women in the Feminist Classroom." *Women's Studies Q* Fall/Winter 1987 15(3/4): 90–95.

1287   **Gellert, Jane C.** *An Evaluation of the Effectiveness of Two Career/Life Development Programs for Reentry Women.* SUNY Albany, 1986. 47/04A.

1288   **Gibbard, Suzanne Downing.** *Programming Practices for Reentry Women in Institutions of Higher Education in Four Southwestern States.* U of Mississippi, 1987. 48/12A.

1289   **Greenwood, Claudia Mignon.** *Factors Which Influence Reentry Women in College Composition Classes: A Descriptive Study.* Indiana U of Pennsylvania, 1987. 48/12A.

1290   **Grubb, Kevin.** "Women Who Wow!" *Dance Magazine* August 1984 58: 40–47.

1291   **Hammer-Higgins, Paula Nell.** *Situational, Institutional and Dispositional Predictors of Personal Strain in Reentry Women.* U of Kentucky, 1987. 49/02A.

1292   **Harwell, Sharon H.** *Ego Development, Self-Concept, Anxiety, and Role-Conflict Coping Preference Styles in Reentry and Traditional Age Women Students.* George Peabody College for Teachers of Vanderbilt U, 1986. 48/04A.

1293   **Hendry, Mildred Dalton.** "Black Reentry Females: Their Concerns and Needs." *J of the National Association for Women Deans, Administrators, and Counselors* Summer 1985 48(4): 5–10 (now the National Association for Women in Education).

1294   **Henson, Donna Smith.** *An Investigation of Selected Characteristics of Women in Two Reentry Workshops.* East Texas State U, 1988. 49/10A.

1295   **Hoehlein, Jill Lossee.** *A Descriptive Study of the Relationship Among Sex-Role, Self-Confidence, and Career Selection in Women Returning to College.* Michigan State U, 1985. 47/02A.

1296   **Hottenstein, Eleanor Mary.** *The Female Mid-Life Student: A Case Study of Three Mid-Life Women at the Luzerne County Community College (Pennsylvania).* U of Pennsylvania, 1986. 47/05A.

1297   **Jacobi, Maryann.** *A Contextual Analysis of Stress and Health Among Reentry Women to College.* U of California, Irvine, 1984. 45/09A.

1298   **Jaffe, Elizabeth Latimer.** *Management Women's Life Transitions: New Opportunities for Adult Learning.* Columbia U Teachers College, 1985. 56/03A.

1299   **Kane, John Charles.** *Two Essays on the Return to Education for Females.* SUNY Stony Brook, 1986. 47/05A.

1300   **Kaplan, Susan Romer.** *Reentry of Women over 30 into Professional Schools.* U of California, Berkeley, 1980. 41/07A.

1301   **Kirk, Cynthia Formanek, et al.** "Satisfaction and Role Strain Among Middle-Age and Older Reentry Women Students." *Educational Gerontology* January-February 1983 9(1): 15–29.

1302   **Laing, Diane Lee Arnold.** *An Analysis and Comparison of the Concerns of Three Age Groups of Women Students Enrolled in Office Information Systems Courses at Oakland [Michigan] Community College.* Michigan State U, 1985. 47/02A.

1303   **Lane, Carol Felt.** *The Meanings of Returning to Work for Women at Midlife.* New York U, 1988. 49/08A.

1304   **Lenick, Mary Ann Anderson.** *An Assessment of the Motivations of Nontraditional Women Students in Postsecondary Education.* U of South Dakota, 1985. 46/08A.

1305   **Lewis, Linda H., ed.** *Addressing the Needs of Returning Women.* San Francisco: Jossey-Bass, 1988. index.
    These case studies of women 35 years of age and over may show program administrators, counselors, and instructors how the educational needs and concerns of women who resume their postsecondary education differ from those of other persons. To meet the continuing education and adult education requirements of this segment of the population as they attempt to return to employment and/or education is also addressed.

1306   **Mastrocola, Katherine.** *Where Are They Now? Follow Up Case Study of Twelve Returning Graduate Women from the 1960s–80s: Their Hopes, Expectations, and Realizations.* U of Pittsburgh, 1985. 46/06A.

1307   **McBride, Virginia Howell.** *Social Networks Among Returning Women Students Enrolled in an Urban Community College Nursing Program.* U of Michigan, 1985. 56/07A.

1308   **Mendelsohn, Pamela, 1944– .** *Happier by Degrees: A College Reentry Guide for Women, new rev. ed.* Berkeley: Ten Speed Press, 1986. bib, index.
    This "guide for women returning to school" consists mainly of fourteen case histories of women who resumed their education after age 25 for career purposes. Considered are such basics (for any woman) as types of schools and degrees offered, admissions, financial aids, study methods, and "hints," as well as aspects that are of particular interest, e.g., child care.

1309   **Menger, Geraldine Hickey.** *A Comparative Study of Transitional Role Strain in Reentry Women Students.* Texas Tech U, 1988. 48/09A.

1310   Meyer, Susan. *An Investigation of Self-Concept Change in Black Reentry Women.* Columbia U Teachers College, 1986. 47/03A.

1311   Moen, Phyllis, et al. "Labor-Force Reentry Among U.S. Homemakers in Midlife: A Life-Course Analysis." *Gender and Society* June 1990 4(2): 2130–2143.

1312   Moore, Wanda Young Cadman. *Barriers Nontraditional-Age Freshmen Women Encounter as They Seek Entrance to Four-Year Colleges and Universities.* U of Oregon, 1985. 46/11A.

1313   Morgan, Margaret Irene. *Women Returning to Community College: A Response to Life Changes and a Desire for a Revised Identity (A Case Study of Paul D. Camp Community College)[Franklin, Virginia].* College of William and Mary, 1987. 48/04A.

1314   Morgan, William R. "Returning to School at Midlife: Mature Women with Educational Careers." In Lois Banfill Shaw. *Midlife Women at Work: Fifteen-Year Perspective.* Lexington: Lexington, 1986. Chapter 4.

1315   Muench, Karen Elizabeth. *The Relationship Between the Return to Higher Education of the Adult Female Learner and the Reworking of Identity.* U of Wisconsin, Madison, 1985. 46/10A.

1316   Mulliken, Elizabeth Y., et al. *The Rewarding Challenge: Welcoming Re-Entry Women Students to the Small College.* Newton: EDC, 1986. (Education Development Center, 55 Chapel Street, Newton, MA 02160.)
    This 64-page guide to designing a program for women who are reentering college after an interval of child rearing or outside employment was based on a program at Midland Lutheran College (Fremont, Nebraska). It is an example of the many products enabled by the Women's Educational Equity Act Program (WEEAP), this for college administrators and faculty; *see also* #1336.

1317   Neikirk, Mary Margaret. *Characteristics of Reentry Women Students and Their Purposes for Participating in Movement Activities.* U of Georgia, 1985. 46/07A.

1318   Nordenberg, Nikki Pirillo. *A Descriptive Analysis of the Presence, Characteristics and Influence of Mentoring in the Development of Reentry Women.* U of Pittsburgh, 1988. 49/07A.

1319   Osorio Trujillo, Josina. *Self-Concept and Career Decidedness: Two Salient Elements in the Career Development of Reentry Women.* Washington State U, 1985. 56/06A.

1320   Pickering, Glenn Scott. *An Empirical Study of a Sample of Reentry Women.* U of Minnesota, 1985. 46/12B.

1321   Pirnot, Karen Hutchins. *Reentry Women: A Follow-Up Study of Women Who Enter College at a Nontraditional Age.* U of Iowa, 1986. 47/08A.

1322   Porter, Karen Louise. *The Scheduling of Life Course Events, Economic Adaptations, and Marital History: An Analysis of Economic Survival After Separation and Divorce for a Cohort of Midlife Women.* Syracuse U, 1985. 46/08A.

1323   Price, Barbara Neff. *The Working-Class, Midlife Woman in Community College: The Factors That Influenced Her Career Decision.* U of Pennsylvania, 1985. 46/12A.

1324   Roehl, Janet E., and Morris A. Okun. "Life Events and the Use of Social Support Systems Among Reentry Women." *J of the National Association for Women Deans,*

Administrators, and Counselors Summer 1985 48(4): 12–30 (now the National Association for Women in Education).

1325   **Ross, Jovita Martin.** *Undergraduate Reentry Women: Developmental Forces Influencing the Decision to Return to School.* U of Georgia, 1985. 56/09A.

1326   **Rucki, Sheila Quinn.** *An Analysis of Selected Variables That Predict Persistence of Re-Entry Women in an External Degree Baccalaureate Nursing Program.* U of Connecticut, 1988. 49/11B.

1327   **Russell, Seena Ann.** *The Reentry Adult Woman at Long Island University: A Three Center Study.* Yeshiva U, 1984. 46/02A.

1328   **Sangster, Ella W.** *Older Women Graduate Students: Coping Patterns in a Large University (Michigan).* U of Michigan, 1984. 45/12A.

1329   **Sather, Ruth Bromert.** *Comparison of Ancillary Support Services and Family Support Systems and Academic Persistence or Non-Persistence of Nontraditional-Aged College Women.* U of Nebraska, 1984. 45/07A.

1330   **Schatzkamer, Mary Bray.** *Returning Women Students in the Community College: A Feminist Perspective.* U of Massachusetts, 1986. 47/09A.

1331   **Schuman, Nancy, and William Lewis,** 1946– . *Back to Work: How to Reenter the Working World.* Hauppauge: Barron, 1985. bib.
    This is a very typical example of vocational guidance books catering to the 1980s market about reentry to the "working world." Presumably the authors refer to employment for wages, usually outside the home; their focus here is "the business world." Included are descriptions of automated equipment a woman might encounter and job-hunting.

1332   **Scott, Doris J.** *Traditional and Reentry Women Nursing Majors: Motivational Factors, Vocational Personalities, Barriers and Enablers to Participation.* Ball State U, 1989. 50/05A.

1333   **Segalla, Rosemary Anastasio.** *Departure from Traditional Roles: Mid-Life Women Break the Daisy Chains.* Ann Arbor, Michigan: UMI Research Press, 1982. bib, index.
    This revision of Segalla's thesis focuses on college-educated women aged 35–45. "Alternate lifestyles" that traditional married women have been able to choose after childrearing years have decreased; "options" Segalla sees are volunteer work, full and part-time employment, and study.

1334   **Shea, Beverly.** "Late Bloomers: They Got Their First Jobs at 50." *Ms. Magazine* November 1985 14: 51+.

1335   **Silva, Adelina Solis.** *Stressful Life Experiences and Career Choices of Reentry Women in Community Colleges.* U of Texas at Austin, 1988. 49/06A.

1336   **Simmons, Michelle Daniels.** *A Survey of Programming Practices for Reentry Women in Pennsylvania Two Year and Four Year Colleges (WEEA Program).* U of Pittsburgh, 1984. 46/03A. *See also #1316.*

1337   **Singer, Nancy Goldstone.** *An Exploratory Study of the Early and Midlife Adult Development of Women Following a Reentry Life Pattern.* U of Pittsburgh, 1981. 43/01A.

1338   **Smalarz, Mary.** *Returning to School Women: An Examination of the Relationships Among Learning Style, Locus-of-Control, Age and Major.* Boston U, 1988. 49/08A.

1339   Speer, Lenora J., et al. "The Outcomes of Reentry Education: Personal and Professional Development in Middle-Aged and Older Women Graduates." *Educational Gerontology* 1986 12(3): 253–265.

1340   Sturges, Phyllis, et al. "Social Work Education and the Older Woman Student." *J of Women & Aging* 1989 1(4): 119–131.

1341   Suitor, Jaclynn Jill. *Families and Social Networks in Transition: Married Mothers Return to School.* SUNY at Stony Brook, 1985. 47/02A.

1342   Thacker, Charlene, et al. "Student Role Supports for Younger and Older Middle-Aged Women: Applications of a Life-Event Model." *Canadian J of Higher Education* 1991 21(1): 13–36.

1343   Thompson, Irene, and Audrey Roberts, eds. *The Road Retaken: Women Reenter the Academy.* New York: LMA America, 1985. bib.
        The "academy" is higher education—women as graduate students and college and university teacher-employees. Mainline women studies people will recognize such names as Pauline Bart, Barbara Hillyer Davis, Ellen Messer-Davidow, Nancy Zumwalt, and others. The lives of twenty-five career and family "balancers" (women who interrupted their education for more than five years) are explored in terms of the problems they encountered in returning to graduate-level degree programs and getting academic appointments (employment) in the United States. There is need to challenge the depreciatory attitudes toward reentry women.

1344   Van Tour, Darlene. *Career Maturity Attitudes and Selected Characteristics of Adult Women Students Returning to College.* Texas Woman's U, 1987. 48/04A.

1345   Vitols, Roberta McGraw. *Learning Style Preferences of Traditional Age Versus Re-Entry-Age Female Undergraduates.* Claremont Graduate School, 1985. 46/09A.

1346   Westoff, Leslie Aldridge. *Breaking Out of the Middle-Age Trap.* New York: New American Library, 1980.
        Based on interviews of more than one hundred middle-aged (40–65) women in a variety of fields, Westoff urges them to strive beyond tradition to reenter education and employment they merit. "Nervous breakdowns" and breakups along the way may require self-help psychology.

1347   Wiesner, Paula L. *Re-Entry Women's Perceived Attributions for Success and Failure: The Effects of Personal Situational and Institutional Barriers on Persistence in Post-Secondary Education.* U of Texas at Austin, 1984. 46/04A.

1348   Wood, Dorothy Anne. *Educated Women over 45 Who Have Completed the Mid-Life Transition from the Traditional Role to a Career in the World of Work.* Fielding Institute, 1986. 48/03B.

1349   Yohalem, Alice M., et al. *Women Returning to Work.* Lanham, Maryland: Allanheld Osmun, 1980. bib, index.
        Job-reentry data relative to advanced industrial nations—Federal Republic of Germany, France, Sweden, United Kingdom, United States—are provided by the contributors.

7
Old Age and Women

Being seventy is not a sin.
Golda Myerson Meir, 1899–1978

Crones: 1350–1356
Elderly; Old Old: 1357–1399
Health and Health Care: 1400–1503
Psychosocial Perspectives: 1504–1568

CRONES

Mary Daly (1928–) believes that "The Great Hags of history, when their lives have not been prematurely terminated, have lived to be crones . . . , the survivors of the perpetual witch-craze of patriarchy. . . . " "As for 'old,' ageism is a feature of phallic society. For women who have transvaluated this, a Crone is one who should be an example of strength, courage and wisdom" (Gyn/Ecology: The Metaethics of Radical Feminism. *Boston: Beacon, 1978. 16). Although* Broomstick *magazine is defunct, issues can be found in the collections of many libraries and campus women's centers; it carried many articles about crones. See, for example, May/June 1988 10(3) and November/December 1988 10(6).*

See also Chapter 3: Love and Sexuality; Lesbian Relationships (441–475); this chapter: Elderly; Old Old (1357–1399); Chapter 10: Religion; Spirituality; Theology (1877–1909).

1350   **Bell, Marilyn J.** "Feminist Spirituality: Bags, Hags and Crones." *Resources for Feminist Research/Documentation sur la Recherche Féministe.* July 1982 11(2): 223–224.

1351   **Breeze, Nancy.** "Crones Nest: The Vision." In Marilyn J. Bell, ed. *Women as Elders: Images, Visions, and Issues.* New York: Haworth Press, 1986. 71–82. Also published as *Women & Politics* Summer 1986 6(2) issue and by Harrington Park Press with the subtitle, *The Feminist Politics of Aging.*

1352   **Chalmer, Judith, and Fran Solin.** "Turning 12: A Menarche Ceremony [and] Becoming a Crone: Ceremony at 60 . . . " *Lilith* Fall 1988 21: 17–18.

1353   **Gentry, Jacquelyne, and Faye Seifert.** "A Joyous Passage: Becoming a Crone." In Barbara Sang, et al, eds. *Lesbians at Midlife: The Creative Transition, An Anthology.* San Francisco: Spinsters Book Co., 1991. 225–233.

1354   **Levine, Helen, 1924– .** "The Crones of Ottawa." *Resources for Feminist Research/Documentation sur la Recherche Féministe.* July 1982 11(2): 222–223.

1355   Walker, Barbara G. *The Crone: Woman of Age, Wisdom, and Power.* New York: Harper, 1985. bib.

      The history of "the key issues of the grass roots movement of elder women and the women's spirituality movement" and the historic role of female elders until their displacement by patriarchal religion are traced. The transition from ancient goddess to witch has led to the archetypal elder woman—invisible or superfluous. But she also represents wisdom, teaching, and healing. Walker presents myths from many cultures, documents past roles of female elders, and includes consideration of the prepatriarchal goddess, religious aspects of matriarchy and patriarchy, and a final chapter, "The Future Crone."

1356   Ward, Edna M., 1928– , ed. *Celebrating Ourselves: A Crone Ritual Book.* Portland: Astarte Shell Press, 1992. bib, il.

      Sylvia Sims has illustrated this book of rituals for the religious life of aged women.

Elderly; Old Old
See also this chapter: Crones (1350–1356).

> *Persons over age 75 used to be called "old old," but the term now refers to those over 85, because the group from 75 to 84 stays healthier and lives more independently than previously. (The term* old old *is also used by some to refer only to persons who are ill or disabled.)*

1357   Abraham, Ivo L., et al. "Effects of Cognitive Group Interventions on Depression and Cognition Among Elderly Women in Long-Term Care." *J of Women & Aging* 1992 4(1): 5–24.

1358   Anderson, Trudy Bohrer. *Primary Resources of Elderly Women.* U of Nebraska, Lincoln, 1981. 42/11A.

1359   Azzaro, Beverly Z. Hummel. *The Effects of Recreation Activities and Social Visitation on the Cognitive Functioning of Elderly Females.* West Virginia U, 1987. 49/05B.

1360   Babchuk, Nicholas, et al. "Older Widows and Married Women: Their Intimates and Confidants." *International J of Aging and Human Development* 1989 28(1): 21–35.

1361   Bell, Marilyn J., ed. *Women as Elders: Images, Visions, and Issues.* New York: Haworth Press, 1986. bib. Also published as *Women & Politics* Summer 1986 6(2) issue and by Harrington Park Press with the subtitle, *The Feminist Politics of Aging.*

1362   Berry, Bernita C. *The Global Well-Being of the Older Black Woman.* Kent State U, 1988. 50/03A.

1363   Berry, Jane Marie. *Memory Complaint and Performance in Older Women: A Self-Efficacy and Causal Attribution Model.* Washington U, 1986. 47/10B.

1364   Choskey, Linda Leon. *Elderly Women of Achievement: A Phenomenological Study of Professional Eminence.* U of Michigan, 1980. 41/05A.

1365   Downey, Nancy Racine. *The Effect of Process and Outcome Instructions on the Experience of Control and the Level of Mindfulness Among Elderly Women.* Boston College, 1987. 49/02A.

1366   **Dudley, Anne.** "Relationships and Male and Female Elders." *Smith College Studies in Social Work* June 1983 53(3): 177–187.

1367   **Faulkner, Audrey Olson, and Margaret Micchelli.** "The Aging, the Aged, and the Very Old: Women the Policy Makers Forgot." *Women & Health* 1988 14(3/4): 5–20. Also in Lois Grau and Ida Susser, eds. *Women in the Later Years: Health, Social and Cultural Perspectives.* New York: Harrington Park Press, 1989.

1368   **Ford, Janet, 1944– , and Ruth Sinclair.** *Sixty Years On: Women Talk About Old Age.* London: Women's Press, 1987.
          The Women's Press, Ltd. is located at 34 Great Sutton Street, London EC1V 0DX. Sociologist Ford and researcher Sinclair report that more than 10 million women are of pensionable age in Britain, and that they greatly outnumber pensionable-age men. Although not indexed and without bibliographic support, two pages of notes are provided. Chapter 1 is about ageism and older women; other chapters are interviews of a variety of individual women aged 60–90. Statistics of the elderly in Britain are appended. Particularly useful in social welfare.

1369   **Gottlieb, Naomi, 1925– .** "The Older Woman." In her *Alternative Social Services for Women.* New York: Columbia U Press, 1980. Chapter 7.

1370   **Greenblatt, Robert B., M.D., et al.** "The Endocrine and Reproductive System of Aged Women." In Marie R. Haug, et al, eds. *The Physical and Mental Health of Aged Women.* New York: Springer, 1985. Chapter 6.

1371   **Hagestad, Gunhild O.** "Older Women in Intergenerational Relations." In Marie R. Haug, et al, eds. *The Physical and Mental Health of Aged Women.* New York: Springer, 1985. Chapter 10.

1372   **Hartranft, Linda Bussard.** *The Ninth Decade: Six Central Ohio Women.* Ohio State U, 1992. 53/08A.

1373   **Holden, Constance.** "Why Do Women Live Longer than Men?" *Science* October 9, 1987 238: 158–160.

1374   **James, Alexander Robertson, Jr.** *Unfinished as a Person: The Course of Attachment in the Life of an Eighty-Year-Old Woman.* U of Massachusetts, 1983. 44/04B.

1375   **Karras, Christa Karina.** "Letter to a Friend." *Canadian Woman Studies/Les Cahiers de la Femme* Winter 1992 12: 59–61.

1376   **Kerzner, Lawrence J.** "Physical Changes After Menopause." In Elizabeth Markson, ed. *Older Women: Issues and Prospects.* Lexington: Heath, 1987. Chapter 14.

1377   **Linville, Sue Ellen.** *Acoustic Characteristics of Adult Women's Voices with Advancing Age: A Production and Perception Study.* Northwestern U, 1981. 42/06B.

1378   **Linville, Sue Ellen.** "Maximal Phonational Frequency Range Capabilities of Women's Voices with Advancing Age." *Folia Phoniatrica: International J of Phoniatrics, Speech Therapy and Communication Pathology* November-December 1987 39(6): 297–301.

1379   **MacKeracher, Dorothy Margaret.** *A Study of the Experience of Aging from the Perspective of Older Women.* U of Toronto, 1982. 43/12A.

1380   **Macpherson, Kay, and Vi Thompson.** "Thoughts on Getting Old." *Canadian Woman Studies/Les Cahiers de la Femme* 1991 12: 95–98.

1381   **Martyn, Ann Henderson.** *Rehearsal for Survivorship: A Qualitative Analysis of Later Life Husbands and Wives.* Virginia Polytechnic Institute and State U, 1980. 51/07A.

1382   **Norman, Suzanne Marie.** *Adult Development Life Patterns of Older Women.* U of Kansas, 1991. 54/04B.

1383   **O'Rand, Angela M.** "Women." In Erdman Ballagh Palmore, ed. *Handbook on the Aged in the United States.* Westport: Greenwood, 1984. Chapter 8.

1384   **Patterson, Carol A.** *Selected Body Measurements of Women Aged Sixty-Five and Older.* Florida State U, 1981. 42/10A.

1385   **Reid, Margaret.** "Aging: One Woman's Pattern." *Canadian Woman Studies/Les Cahiers de la Femme* Winter 1992 12: 11–13.

1386   **Replogle, Mary Anna.** *Explorations into the Life of a Nonagenarian Woman: A New Age Study of Aging.* Union for Experimenting Colleges, 1984. 46/01A.

1387   **Siegel, Rachel Josefowitz.** "We Are Not Your Mothers: Report on Two Groups for Women Over Sixty." *J of Women & Aging* 1990 2(2): 81–89.

1388   **Smart, Anne.** "Representing Older Women in Saskatchewan." *Canadian Woman Studies/Les Cahiers de la Femme* Winter 1992 12: 6–9. "Growing into Age" special issue guest edited by Mary Sue McCarthy, et al.

1389   **Soldo, Beth J., et al.** "Family, Households, and Care Arrangements of Frail Older Women: A Structural Analysis." *Journals of Gerontology* November 1990 45(6): S238–S249.

1390   **Sommers, Tish,** 1914–1985, **guest ed.** "Women and Aging" issue. *Generations* August 1980 4(4): 1–40.

1391   **Soniat, Barbara Ann.** *Older Women: An Analysis of the Influences of Race, Health Status, and Social Network Involvement on Use of Community Services.* U of Maryland at Baltimore, 1992. 53/07A.

1392   **Todoroff, Milana.** "'Life Has a Sense': An Interview with Anna." *Canadian Woman Studies/Les Cahiers de la Femme* Winter 1992 12: 99–100.

1393   **Troll, Lillian E.** "Poor, Dumb, and Ugly: The Older Woman in Contemporary Society." ERIC, August 1984. ED #250615. 20 pages.

1394   **Van Zandt, P. L.** *The Invisible Woman: Women over Age 85 in Today's Society.* U of Nebraska, Lincoln, 1988. 50/03A.

1395   **Walker, Corinne Theresa.** *Educational Gerontology: Health Behavior of Elderly African-American Women.* U of Illinois at Urbana-Champaign, 1989. 50/11A.

1396   **West, Gale Ellen, and Ronald L. Simons.** "Sex Differences in Stress, Coping Resources, and Illness Among the Elderly." *Research on Aging* June 1983 5(2): 235–268.

1397   **Willis, Sherry L., and K. Warner Schaie.** "Gender Differences in Spatial Ability in Old Age: Longitudinal and Intervention Findings." *Sex Roles* February 1988 18: 189–203.

1398   **Wolanin, Mary Opan.** "The Aging Woman and Confusion." In Marie R. Haug, et al, eds. *The Physical and Mental Health of Aged Women.* New York: Springer, 1985. Chapter 9.

1399   **Wright, Bonnie Mclean.** *Sex Differences in Psychomotor Reminiscence and Per-formance in Elderly Subjects.* U of Georgia, 1983. 44/11B.

HEALTH AND HEALTH CARE

1400   **Abdellah, Faye G.** "The Aged Woman and the Future of Health Care Delivery." In Marie R. Haug, et al, eds. *The Physical and Mental Health of Aged Women.* New York: Springer, 1985. Chapter 18.

1401   **Abernethy, Marilyn Medaugh.** *Food Intake as a Function of Food Attitudes for a Population of Older Women.* U of North Carolina at Chapel Hill, 1984. 46/02B.

1402   **Aker, Charles Randall.** *A Study of the Effects of Aging, Stimulus Characteristics, and Response Format on Adult Females' Performance on a Diotic Listening Task.* Florida State U, 1981. 42/10B.

1403   **Arendell, Teresa Jayne, and Carroll Lynn Estes,** 1938– . "Unsettled Future: Older Women—Economics and Health." *Feminist Issues* Spring 1987 7(1): 3–27.

1404   **Bajart, Ann M., M.D.** "Common Eye Problems in the Older Woman." *Women & Health* 1985 10(2/3): 85–114.

1405   **Baker, Judith A.** "Breast Self-Examination and the Older Woman: Field Testing an Educational Approach." *Gerontologist* June 1989 29(3): 405–407.

1406   **Baulch, Yvonne Suzanne,** 1962– . *The Relationship Between Visual Acuity, Tactile Sensation, and Mobility of the Upper Extremities and Proficient Breast Self-Examination in Women 65 and Older.* U of California, San Francisco, 1991. M.S. thesis.

1407   **Belgrave, Linda Liska.** *The Experience of Chronic Disease in the Everyday Lives of Elderly Women.* Case Western Reserve U, 1985. 46/09A.

1408   **Belgrave, Linda Liska.** "The Relevance of Chronic Illness in the Everyday Lives of Elderly Women." *J of Aging & Health* November 1990 2(4): 475–500.

1409   **Benton, Donna** Marie. *An Exploratory Study of Factors Associated with Black Aged Females' Willingness to Seek Professional Psychological Help.* California School of Professional Psychology, Los Angeles, 1983. 44/11B.

1410   **Breen, James L., ed.,** 1926– . *The Gynecologist and the Older Patient.* Rockville: Aspen, 1988. bib, il, index.
        Breen preceded his book with "The Gynecologist and the Aging Patient" (*Clinical Therapeutics* 1986 8[5]: 462–466). The geriatric gynecologist is a specialist whose subspecialty is diseases of aged women; a geriatrician is another physician, whose primary specialty is usually internal medicine.

1411   **Browne, Colette V.** *The Relationship of Gender Role to Health Practices in Later Life.* U of Hawaii, 1990. 52/04B.

1412   **Burd, Stephen.** "NIH Awards Research Center $140 Million to Coordinate Study of [Postmenopausal] Women's Health." *Chronicle of Higher Education* October 14, 1992 39(8): A27. And "NIH Failed to Warn Women of Side Effects in Breast-Cancer Study [of Postmenopausal Women.]" October 28, 1992 39(10): A32.

1413   Bush, Trudy L. "The Epidemiology of Cardiovascular Disease in Post-menopausal Women." In Marcha Flint, et al, eds. *Multidisciplinary Perspectives on Menopause: Annals of the New York Academy of Sciences* (Volume 592). New York: The Academy, 1990. 263–271.

1414   Butler, Frieda Roxanne. *Factors Related to Compliance with a Treatment Regimen in Black Elderly Diabetic Women.* U of Maryland, College Park, 1980. 42/02B.

1415   Byyny, Richard L., and Leon Speroff. *A Clinical Guide for the Care of Older Women.* Baltimore: Williams & Wilkins, 1990. bib, index.
        Byyny's special interest is hypertension and the elderly.

1416   Champion, Victoria L. "Breast Self-Examination in Women 35 and Older: A Prospective Study." *J of Behavioral Medicine* December 1990 13(6): 523–538.

1417   Cimons, Marlene. "Cervical Cancer Deaths Said Highest for Elderly." *Los Angeles Times* Wednesday, February 7, 1990: A4, column 1.

1418   Clark, K., et al. "The Accuracy of Self-Reported Hearing Loss in Women Aged 60–85 Years." *American J of Epidemiology* October 1, 1991 134(7): 704–798.

1419   Clark, M. A., et al. "Cervical Cancer: Women Aged 35 and Younger Compared to Women Aged 36 and Older." *American J of Clinical Oncology—Cancer Clinical Trials* August 1991 14(4): 352–356.

1420   Coleman, Elizabeth Ann Griffith. *Efficacy of Breast Self-Examination Teaching Methods Among the Aging.* U of Texas at Austin, 1989. 50/07B.

1421   Cox, Janine Ann. *Self-Perceived Health and Aging of Older Females in Prison: An Exploratory Age-Group Case Study.* Southern Illinois U at Carbondale, 1982. 43/05A.

1422   Dickason, Elizabeth Louise. *Use of the Health Belief Model in Determining Mammography Screening Practice in Older Women.* Temple U, 1991. 52/10A.

1423   Doress, Paula Brown, et al. "Women Growing Older." In Boston Women's Health Book Collective. *The New Our Bodies, Ourselves: A Book by and for Women, Updated and Expanded for the 1990s.* New York: Simon & Schuster, 1992. Chapter 23. *See also* #12.

1424   Eardley, Anne, and A. Elkind. "Breast Screening Among Women Aged 65 and Over—What Do They Think of It." *J of Public Health Medicine* August 1991 13(3): 172–177.

1425   Edmonds, Mary McKinney. "The Health of the Black Aged Female." In Zev Harel, et al, eds. *Black Aged: Understanding Diversity and Service Needs.* Newbury Park: Sage, 1990. 205–220.

1426   Edmonds, Mary McKinney. *Social Class and the Functional Health Status of the Aged Black Female.* Case Western Reserve U, 1982. 32/06A.

1427   Egginton, Mary, et al. *An Older Woman's Health Guide.* New York: McGraw-Hill, 1984. bib, index.
        Joan Mintz was director of the Older Woman's Health Project. This guide includes appendices with addresses (current in 1984) and information about organizations providing health, as well as other services. Considered are mental health goals for older women, social relationships, alternative approaches to health care, and nutrition.

1428   Eisenhandler, Susan A. "The Social Value of 'Physiological Autonomy': Urinary Incontinence and Continence in a Sample of Older Women." *J of Women & Aging* 1992 4(3): 45–58.

1429   Engle, Veronica F., et al. "Self-Assessed and Functional Health of Older Women." *International J of Aging and Human Development* 1985–1986 22(4): 301–313.

1430   Evers, Helen. "Care or Custody? The Experience of Women Patients in Long-Stay Geriatric Wards." In Bridget Hutter, ed. *Controlling Women: The Normal and the Deviant*. London: Croom Helm, 1981. Chapter 5.

1431   Evers, Helen. "The Frail Elderly Woman: Emergent Questions in Aging and Women's Health." In Ellen Lewin and Virginia Olesen, eds. *Women, Health and Healing: Toward a New Perspective*. New York: Tavistock, 1985. Chapter 4.

1432   Fincham, Jack E. "Adverse Drug Reaction Occurrence in Elderly Women." *J of Women & Aging* 1991 3(2): 85–94.

1433   Friedan, Betty Goldstein, 1921– . "Us Not Them: Breaking Through Denial of Age." In Shulamit Reinharz and Graham D. Rowles, eds. *Qualitative Gerontology*. New York: Springer, 1988. 311–314.

1434   George, Julie, and Shah Ebrahim, eds. *Health Care for Older Women*. New York: Oxford U Press, 1992. bib, il, index.
    Ebrahim's medical specialization is stroke. Deborah T. Gold has favorably reviewed this geriatrics guide in the *J of Women & Aging* 1993 5(1): 115–117.

1435   Grady, Kathleen E. "Older Women and the Practice of Breast Self-Examination." *Psychology of Women Q* December 1988 12(4): 473–487.

1436   Haley, Ella, and Ann Hauprich Canodion. "Elderly and Able?" *Healthsharing* December 1987 9(1): 24–28.

1437   Hammond, Doris B. "Health Care for Older Women: Curing the Disease." (Consists of: "The Problem," "Women's Health Activism," "Health Problems," "Political Activism as a Solution.") In Marilyn J. Bell, ed. *Women as Elders: Images, Visions, and Issues*. New York: Haworth Press, 1986. 59–69.

1438   Hardin, Sonya Renae. *Let the Circle Be Unbroken: Health of Elderly Southern Appalachian Widows*. U of Colorado Health Sciences Center, 1990. 51/10B.

1439   Harper, Doreen Connor. *The Effect of a Medication Self-Care Program on Knowledge of Medication, Health Locus of Control and Self-Care Behavior Among Black Elderly Hypertensive Women*. U of Maryland, College Park, 1980. 41/08A.

1440   Hatfield, Denise Webb. *Effect of Dietary Protein (Mixed, Defatted Beef or Cottonseed) on the Amino Acid Status of Healthy Elderly Women*. Texas Woman's U, 1982. 44/01B.

1441   Haug, Marie R., et al, eds. *The Physical and Mental Health of Aged Women*. New York: Springer, 1985. bib, index.
    Behavioral and medical approaches to the physical and mental health, care, and services provided aged American women are considered by health care practitioners, service providers, family members, and aged women themselves. Drs. Haug, Amas B. Ford, and Marian S. Sheafor provide eighteen chapters and an epilogue in which they

"have selected three major questions to summarize the need for more intensive investigation in this field": Why do women live longer than men? Why are all elderly surviving longer? What will be the impact of the changing character of the family and the changing role of women?" The contents are analyzed by authors and subjects in *Women and Aging: A Guide to the Literature.*

1442   **Hazelden Foundation.** (Center City, Minnesota. Sponsor: Minnesota State Department of Human Services, St. Paul. Chemical Dependency Program Division.) "Chemical Abuse Among Older Women, Older Adults and Disabled People. Final Grant Report." ERIC, June 30, 1989. ED #330159. 196 pages.

1443   **Heidrich, Susan M.** *Health Status and Psychological Well-Being of Elderly Women: The Self-System as Mediator.* U of Wisconsin, Madison, 1990. 51/02B.

1444   **Herman, Carla J.** *Action for Health: Older Women's Project.* Cleveland: Fairhill Institute for the Elderly, 1992. bib, il.
    Herman was principal investigator and Nancy Wadsworth, co-principal investigator and director of this project funded by the U.S. Administration on Aging and the American Cancer Society's Cuyahoga Unit through Case Western Reserve University School of Medicine, Geriatric C.A.R.E. Center. The Institute is located at 12200 Fairhill Road, Cleveland, OH 44120. Govt. Doc. #HE 1.1002:H 34/2.

1445   **Herzog, Anna Regula,** 1941– , et al, eds. *Health and Economic Status of Older Women.* Amityville: Baywood, 1989. bib, index.
    Based on presentations made at a 1984 research conference, this collection is formatted in eight chapters, with subject and author indexes. Part 4, by Mildred M. Seltzer, provides a conclusion; Appendix A, by Nancy A. Fultz, consists of useful "Descriptions of Survey Data Sets." Ageism is recognized as a concept.

1446   **Hofmeister, Frederick J., ed.** *Care of the Postmenopausal Patient.* Philadelphia: G. F. Stickley, 1985. bib, il, index.
    Hofmeister's medical specialization is surgical gynecology.

1447   **Hoppel, Charles L., M.D.** "The Uses and Misuses of Pharmacology." In Marie R. Haug, et al, eds. *The Physical and Mental Health of Aged Women.* New York: Springer, 1985. Chapter 15.

1448   **Howze, Elizabeth H.** "Social Support and Health Maintenance Among Older Married Women." ERIC, November 21, 1986. ED #277962. 12 pages.

1449   **Hummel, James Franklin.** *Related Factors in Self-Actualization and Susceptibility to Nutrition Quackery Among Adult Women 65 Years of Age and Older.* Texas Woman's U, 1985. 46/06B.

1450   **Jacobsen, S. J., et al.** "Regional Variation in the Incidence of Hip Fracture— United States White Women Aged 65 Years and Older." *JAMA—J of the American Medical Association* July 15, 1990 264(4): 500–502.

1451   **Jenest, Helen Catherine.** *Factors Related to Breast Self-Examination in Older Women.* MGH Institute of Health Professions, 1991. M.S. thesis.

1452   **Kannel, William B.,** 1923– , **and Frederick N. Brand.** "Cardiovascular Risk Factors in the Elderly Woman." In Elizabeth Markson, ed. *Older Women: Issues and Prospects.* Lexington: Heath, 1987. Chapter 15.

1453   Khaw, Kay-Tee, et al. "Cigarette Smoking and Levels of Andrenal Androgens in Postmenopausal Women." *New England J of Medicine* June 30, 1988 318: 1705–1709.

1454   Koren, Mary Elaine. *The Practice of Self-Breast Exam Among Elderly Women.* Rush U College of Nursing, 1991. 52/12A.

1455   Krakoff, Lawrence R., M.D. "Hypertension in Women." *Women & Health* Summer/Fall 1985 10(2/3): 75–83.

1456   Lemke, Diane Lorraine. *Body Fat and Hot Flash Frequency in Postmenopausal Women.* U of Minnesota, 1988. 49/06B.

1457   Lewis, Myrna. "Older Women and Health: An Overview." In Sharon Golub and Rita Jackaway Freedman, eds. *Health Needs of Women as They Age.* New York: Haworth, 1985. 1–15.

1458   Luggen, Ann Schmidt. *The Pain Experience of Ten Selected Elderly Women.* U of Cincinnati, 1985. 47/03A.

1459   Mahoney, Diane Feeney. "Gender and Role as Issues in Ambulatory Health Service Utilization by Older Women." ERIC, November 18, 1984. ED #155797. 11 pages.

1460   Malinoff, Rochelle Lee. *Effects of the Normal Aging Process and Sex Differences on the Evaluation of Audiologic Brainstem Response.* City U of New York, 1985. 46/11B.

1461   Mann, William J., M.D. "Reproductive Cancer." *Women & Health* Summer/Fall 1985 10(2/3): 63–73.

1462   Manzella, Diane S. *Activity Patterns of Hearing Impaired Elderly Women.* U of California, Los Angeles, 1982. 43/10A.

1463   Markides, Kyriakos S. "Aging, Gender, Race/Ethnicity, Class, and Health." In his *Aging and Health: Perspectives on Gender, Race, Ethnicity, and Class.* Newbury Park: Sage, 1989. Chapter 1.

1464   McElmurry, Beverly J., and Emily C. Zabrocki. "The Health of Older Women [review essay]." In Carol J. Leppa, ed. *Women's Health Perspectives: An Annual Review 2.* Phoenix: Oryx, 1989. Chapter 7.

1465   McKeever, Linda, and Ida Martinson. "Older Women's Health Care." In Diane K. Kjervik and Ida M. Martinson. *Women in Health and Illness: Life Experiences and Crises.* Philadelphia: Saunders, 1986. Chapter 4.

1466   Melnick, Mary Evans, and James N. Logue. "The Effect of Disaster on the Health and Well-Being of Older Women." *International J of Aging and Human Development* 1985–1986 21(1): 27–38.

1467   Mitchell, Carol O. "Nutrition as Prevention and Treatment in the Elderly." In Marie R. Haug, et al, eds. *The Physical and Mental Health of Aged Women.* New York: Springer, 1985. Chapter 13.

1468   Muller, Charlotte, 1921– , et al. *Costs and Effectiveness of Cervical Cancer Screening in Elderly Women.* Washington: U.S. Congress, Office of Technology Assessment, 1990. bib. Govt. Doc. No. Y 3.T 22/2:2 C 33. "Preventive Health Services Under Medicare Paper #4."

1469   National Center for Women and Retirement Research. (Supported by the U.S. Administration on Aging.) "Taking Control of Your Health and Fitness." Southampton: The Center, 1989. bib. Govt. Doc. No. HE 23.3002:W 84/5.

1470   National Institute on Aging. *Health Resources for Older Women, rev.* Rockville: U.S. Dept. of Health and Human Services, Public Health Service, National Institutes of Health, 1988. Govt. Doc. No. HE 20.3852.H 34/988. bib.
        The U.S. Task Force on Women's Health Issues included *senior women* in its *Women's Health: Report of the Public Health Service Task Force on Women's Health Issues* (Washington: U.S. Public Health Service, 1985). *See also* #1488. Also of interest are "Use of Health Services by Women 65 Years of Age and Over in the United States," data from the National Health Survey, Series 13, #29, published in 1981; the National Institute on Aging's "The Older Woman: Continuities and Discontinuities" in 1980; and "The Aging Woman" and "Answers About the Aging Woman" in 1987.

1471   Nickel, Jennie Tallent. *Functional Disability and the Use of Health Services by Elderly Women with Coronary Heart Disease.* Ohio State U, 1986. 47/10B.

1472   Older Women's League. "The Picture of Health for Midlife and Older Women in America." *Women & Health* 1988 14(3/4): 53–74.

1473   Pearson, Barbara P., and Cornelia M. Beck. "Physical Health of Elderly Women." *J of Women & Aging* 1989 1(1/2/3): 149–174.

1474   Perry, Charlotte Marie. *The Relationship of Social Support Networks and Support Network Function to the Health Status of Older Widowed Black Females.* U of North Carolina at Greensboro, 1991. 52/08A.

1475   Riley, Matilda White, 1911– . "The Changing Older Woman: A Cohort Perspective." In Marie R. Haug, et al, eds. *The Physical and Mental Health of Aged Women.* New York: Springer, 1985. Chapter 1.

1476   Roberto, Karen A. "Elderly Women with Hip Fractures: Functional and Psychosocial Correlates of Recovery." *J of Women & Aging* 1992 4(20): 3–20.

1477   Rodgers, A. "Breast Screening in Women Aged 65–79 [a letter]." *British Medical J* February 16, 1991 302(6773): 411.

1478   Rudolph, Mary Alice. *Breast Cancer Early Detection: An Exploratory Study of Knowledge, Attitudes, and Practices of Women Attending Senior Centers.* Southern Illinois U at Carbondale, 1987. 48/10A.

1479   Satariano, William A., et al. "Aging and Breast Cancer: A Case-Control Comparison of Instrumental Functioning." *J of Aging & Health* May 1989 1(2): 209–233.

1480   Satariano, William A., et al. "Difficulties in Physical Functioning Reported by Middle-Aged and Elderly Women with Breast Cancer—A Case-Control Comparison." *Journals of Gerontology* January 1990 45(1): M3–M11.

1481   Scarinzi, Ann Marie Elizabeth. *Effects of Aging on Some Perceptual and Acoustic Features of the Adult Female Voice.* U of Oklahoma Health Sciences Center, 1981. 42/07B.

1482   Shingleton, Hugh M., and W. Glenn Hurt, 1938– , eds. *Postreproductive Gynecology.* New York: Churchill Livingstone, 1990. bib, index.
        The authors consider genital diseases of middle-aged and elderly females. Shingleton's specialization is gynecological oncology.

1483   Smith, Margaret M., et al. "Designing a Self-Directed Health Promotion/Wellness Program for Older Women." ERIC, April 1984. ED #151770. 37 pages.

1484   Stein, Lindsay M. *Acquired Hearing Impairment Among Older Females With Psychopathology.* U of Cincinnati, 1990. 50/11A.

1485   Stenchever, Morton A., and George Aagaard, ed. *Caring for the Older Woman.* New York: Elsevier, 1991. bib, il, index. The publisher markets this 230-page book in its Current Topics in Obstetrics and Gynecology series.

1486   Swenson, Norma, et al. "Women, Health, and Aging." In Mary Feeley, ed. *The Women's Annual, Number 5 1984–1985.* Boston: G. K. Hall, 1985. 22–42.

1487   Trippet, Susan E. "Being Aware: The Relationship Between Health and Social Support Among Older Women." *J of Women & Aging* 1991 3(3): 69–80.

1488   U.S. Congress. House. Task Force on Social Security and Women. *Older Women's Health: Hearing Before the Task Force . . . 99th Congress, Second Session, February 5, 1986.* Washington: For sale by the U.S. Government Printing Office, 1986. Govt. Doc. No.: Y 4.Ag 4/2:W 84/10. il, bib. *See also* #1470.

1489   U.S. Congress. Senate. Special Committee on Aging. *Challenges for Women: Taking Charge, Taking Care: Hearing Before the Special Committee . . . 99th Congress, First Session, Cincinnati, Ohio, November 18, 1985.* Washington: For Sale by the U.S. Government Printing Office, 1986. Govt. Doc. No.: Y 4.Ag 4:S. hrg. 99–629.

1490   U.S. Congress. Senate. Special Committee on Aging. *Prospects for Better Health for Older Women: Hearing Before the Special Committee . . . 99th Congress, First Session, Toledo, Ohio.* ERIC, April 15, 1985. ED #167365. 74 pages.

1491   Vallbona, Carlos, M.D., and Susan Beggs Baker. "Prospects for Rehabilitation for the Aged Woman." In Marie R. Haug, et al, eds. *The Physical and Mental Health of Aged Women.* New York: Springer, 1985. Chapter 17.

1492   Verbrugge, Lois M. "An Epidemiological Profile of Older Women." In Marie R. Haug, et al, eds. *The Physical and Mental Health of Aged Women.* New York: Springer, 1985. Chapter 4.

1493   Verbrugge, Lois M. "Gender, Aging, and Health." In Kyriakos S. Markides, ed. *Aging and Health: Perspectives on Gender, Race, Ethnicity, and Class.* Newbury Park: Sage, 1989. Chapter 2.

1494   Verbrugge, Lois M. "A Health Profile of Older Women with Comparisons to Older Men." *Research on Aging* September 1984 6(3): 291–322.

1495   Verbrugge, Lois M. "Women and Men: Mortality and Health of Older People." In Matilda White Riley, et al, eds. *Aging in Society: Selected Reviews of Recent Research.* Hillsdale: Erlbaum, 1983. 139–174.

1496   Welch, Claude E., M.D. "Surgery and Aged Women: Indications and Contraindications." In Marie R. Haug, et al, eds. *The Physical and Mental Health of Aged Women.* New York: Springer, 1985. Chapter 14.

1497   West, Gale Ellen. *The Impact of Coping Resources and Strategies upon Health: An Analysis of Age and Sex Differences.* Iowa State U, 1987. 48/06A.

1498   Wheeler, David L. "Johns Hopkins Study Aims to Examine Health of More Than 1,000 Elderly Women." *Chronicle of Higher Education* June 16, 1993 39(41): A9–A10.

1499   Wilke, Darline Julia. *Knowledge and Utilization of Knowledge of Cardiovascular Risk Factors in Women over Age Sixty.* Loyola U of Chicago, 1987. 47/11A.

1500   Wisocki, Patricia A., and Nancy K. Keuthen. "Later Life." In Elaine A. Blechman and Kelly D. Brownell, eds. *Handbook of Behavioral Medicine for Women.* New York: Pergamon Press, 1988. 48–58.

1501   Wylie, Charles M., M.D. "Contrasts in the Health of Elderly Men and Women: An Analysis of Recent Data for Whites in the U.S." *J of the American Geriatrics Society* September 1984 32(9): 670–676.

1502   Zabrocki, Emily C., and Beverly J. McElmurry. "The Health of Older Women [review essay]." In Carol J. Leppa, ed. *Women's Health Perspectives: An Annual Review 2.* Phoenix: Oryx, 1989. Chapter 7.

1503   Zabrocki, Emily C., and Beverly J. McElmurry. "Omega Women: The Health of Older Women [review essay]." In Carol J. Leppa, ed. *Women's Health Perspectives: An Annual Review 3.* Phoenix: Oryx, 1990. Chapter 13.

Psychosocial Perspectives

1504   Angle, Marilyn Ditzen. *The Relationship of Perceived Competence to Subjective Well-Being, Fear of Aging, and Sex-Role Orientation in Older Women.* U of Minnesota, 1988. 50/02A.

1505   Backer, Jane Hubbs. *Testing a Model for Coping Effectiveness in Older Adult Women.* Indiana U, 52/08A.

1506   Baker, Laverne Lucille. *Speech and Voice Characteristics of Aging Afro-American Female and Male Speakers Based on Listener-Perceived Age Estimates.* Wichita State U, 1981. 42/07B.

1507   Beckman, Linda J. "Effects of Social Interaction and Children's Relative Inputs on Older Women's Psychological Well-Being." *J of Personality and Social Psychology* December 1981 41(6): 1075–1086.

1508   Bowman, Thomas Eugene. *Electrocortical and Behavioral Aspects of Visuospatial Processing and Cognitive Orientation in Young, Middle-Aged and Elderly Females.* U of Southern California, 1981. 41/12B.

1509   Bush, Melissa Lynn. *Sleep Patterns and Bedtime Routines of Elderly Women.* Michigan Institute of Health Professions, 1991. M.S. thesis.

1510   Connidis, Ingrid. "The Relationship of Work History to Self-Definition of Employment Status Among Older Women." *Work and Occupations: An International Sociological J* August 1986 13(3): 348–358.

1511   Davis, Donna Lee, 1948– . "Belligerent Legends: Bickering and Feuding Among Outport Octogenarians." *Aging and Society* December 1985 5(4): 431–448.

1512   Day, Alice Taylor. *Remarkable Survivors: Insights into Successful Aging Among Women.* Washington: Urban Institute Press, 1991. bib, il.

Day uses the social survey approach to identifying success among women in the United States. *See also* her "'I Hope That Something Will Come Out of This': Older Women and Government Policies for the Aged" (#771) and *Older Women and Social Support: A Follow-Up Study: Final Report* (#817).

1513   **DeVore, Irven, and C. Owen Lovejoy.** "The Natural Superiority of Women." In Marie R. Haug, et al, eds. *The Physical and Mental Health of Aged Women.* New York: Springer, 1985. Chapter 3.

1514   **Dolinsky, Elaine H.** *The Relationships of Perceived Social Support and Self-Disclosure to the Morale of Older Women.* New York U, 1987. 48/03B.

1515   **Dunkle, Ruth E., et al.** "An Examination of Coping Resources. Very Old Men and Women: Their Association to the Relationship Between Stress, Hassles and Function." *J of Women & Aging* 1992 4(3): 79–104.

1516   **Echenhofer, Frank Geibel.** *EEG Filtration Analysis Relationships to Reaction Time Performance in Young and Elderly Males and Females.* Temple U, 1985. 46/03B.

1517   **Engelman, Marge.** "The Response of Older Women to a Creative Problem-Solving Program." *Educational Gerontology* March 1981 6(2): 165–173.

1518   **Engle, Veronica Frances.** *A Study of the Relationship Between Self-Assessment of Health, Function, Personal Tempo and Time Perception in Elderly Women.* Wayne State U, 1981. 42/02B.

1519   **Farris, Martha, and John W. Gibson.** "The Older Woman Sexually Abused as a Child: Untold Stories and Unanswered Questions." *J of Women & Aging* 1992 4(3): 31–44.

1520   **Fennell, Graham, et al.** "Women and Old Age." In their *The Sociology of Old Age.* Milton Keynes (England) and Philadelphia: Open U Press, 1988. Chapter 6.

1521   **Fooken, Insa.** "Old and Female: Psychosocial Concomitants of the Aging Process in a Group of Older Women." In Joep M. A. Munnichs, et al, eds. *Lifespan and Change in a Gerontological Perspective.* Orlando: Academic Press, 1985. 77–101.

1522   **Giesen, Carol Boellhoff.** *Perceptions of Aging: Women's Views of Their Change over Time.* West Virginia U, 1980. 41/12B.

1523   **Goodman, Sara F.** *Women in Their Later Years: A Study of the Psychosocial Development of Women Between 45–60.* Boston U, 1980. 41/05B.

1524   **Gove, Water R.** "The Effect of Age and Gender on Deviant Behavior: A Biopsychosocial Perspective." In Alice S. Rossi, ed. *Gender and the Life Course.* New York: Aldine, 1985. Chapter 7.

1525   **Grambs, Jean Dresden,** 1919– . *Women over Forty: Visions and Realities, rev. ed.* New York: Springer, 1989. bib, index.

In 1981 Marilyn R. Block, et al's *Women over Forty: Visions and Realities* was published. (It had appeared in 1978 as *Uncharted Territory: Issues and Concerns of Women over Forty.*) In chapters on demographics, images, menopause, life situations, family relationships, employment and retirement, and ethnic and racial variations of old women, research considerations related to each were identified. Creation of policies based on research studies has been needed ongoingly to inspire both policies and the related programs. The 1989, revised edition is #4 in Springer's Focus on Aging series and provides an update and review of normal aging as revealed in recent research. Rosalind C. Barnett of the Wellesley College Center for Research on Women reviewed the 1989 book and found its treatment of some issues "troubling" (*Psychology of Women Q* December 1990 14[4]: 618–619).

1526   **Harrison, Carolyn A.** "Older Women in Our Society: America's Silent, Invisible Majority." *Educational Gerontology* March-April 1991 17(2): 111–121.

1527   **Heller, Kenneth, and William E. Mansbach.** "The Multifaceted Nature of Social Support in a Community Sample of Elderly Women." *J of Social Issues* Winter 1984 40(4): 99–112.

1528   **Irvin, Yvonne F.** *The Relationship of Age and Adjustment to the Subjective Well-Being of Older Black Women.* U of Pittsburgh, 1982. 43/09B.

1529   **Jacoby, Susan.** "An Age-Old Question [women in old age]." ("Hers" column.) *New York Times Magazine* October 21, 1990 140: 28, column 3.

1530   **Jamison, Cheryl Charisse.** *Concerns and Morale of the Female Aged.* Institute of Advanced Psychological Studies, 1983. 44/03B.

1531   **Janata, Jeffrey Ward.** *Psychological Factors Affecting Physical Self-Perception in Postmenopausal Women.* Case Western Reserve U, 1984. 46/02B.

1532   **Janesh, Patricia A.** *Anger Expression Styles, Loneliness, and Selected Personality Determinants in Women 60–70 Years of Age.* United States International U, 1989. 50/02B.

1533   **Kinderknecht, Cheryl H.** "What's Out There and How to Get It: A Practical Resource Guide for the Helpers of Older Women." *J of Women & Aging* 1989 1(1/2/3): 363–396.

1534   **Klooz, Nancy Ann.** *Lateralization of Function in Aging Men and Women.* Wayne State U, 1987. 48/04B.

1535   **Kossowsky, Hanita.** *The Relationship Among Ego Development, Hardiness and Adjustment in a Group of Active Elderly Men and Women.* U of Pittsburgh, 1986. 47/06B.

1536   **Lasser, Sylvia.** *Adjustment to Cardiac Illness: The Effects of Age, Gender and Socioeconomic Status.* St. John's U, 1984. 45/11A.

1537   **Lemmon, Janet Ann.** *Family Relationships and the Psychological Well-Being of Elderly Women.* U of Colorado at Boulder, 1983. 44/09B.

1538   **MacRae, Hazel.** "Older Women and Identity Maintenance in Later Life." *Canadian J on Aging* Fall 1990 9(3): 248–267.

1539   **Marshall, Doris,** 1911– . *Silver Threads: Critical Reflections on Growing Old.* Toronto: Between the Lines, 1987. bib, il.
    Many years of social work with aging women and men in Canada provided Marshall with the background to critique society's attitudes and practices.

1540   **McNaughton, Mary E., et al.** "Stress, Social Support, Coping Resources, and Immune Status in Elderly Women." *J of Nervous and Mental Disease* July 1990 178(7): 460–461.

1541   **Mendes, Dinah Merkin.** *Social and Psychological Predictors of Quality of Life in Older Women.* Yeshiva U, 1985. 46/12B.

1542   **Miller, Melody, and Dan Lago.** "The Well-Being of Older Women: The Importance of Pet and Human Relations." *Anthrozoos* Spring 1990 3(4): 245–252.

1543   **Moore, Alinde M.** *Life Moves On: An Exploration of Motivation in Elderly Women.* U of Illinois, Urbana-Champaign, 1990. 50/11B.

1544   **More, Rebecca Sue.** *The Relationship of Locus of Control and Perceived Situational Constraint Among Elderly Women.* Indiana U, 1983. 44/10B.

1545   **Morris, Beverly Rettig.** *Leaving the Goods Life: Elderly Women and Their Cherished Personal Possessions.* U of Kentucky, 1989. 50/05A.

1546   **Morris, Beverly Rettig.** "Reducing Inventory: Divestiture of Personal Possessions." *J of Women & Aging* 1992 4(2): 79–92.

1547   **Mrotek, Diana Defeo.** *Women 62–82: A Contextual Analysis in an Adult Developmental Framework.* Northwestern U, 1982. 43/07A.

1548   **Norris, Joan E.** "The Social Adjustment of Single and Widowed Older Women." *Essence: Issues in the Study of Ageing, Dying, and Death* 1980 4(3): 135–144.

1549   **Preston, Deborah Bray.** *The Effects of Marital Status, Sex Roles, Stress, Coping, and Social Support on the Health of the Elderly.* Pennsylvania State U, 1984. 46/01B.

1550   **Primas, Marion.** *Friendship Intimacy, Financial Security, and Morale Among Elderly Women.* U of Maryland, 1984. 46/02A.

1551   **Rae, Hazel M.** "Older Women and Identity Maintenance in Later Life." *Canadian J on Aging* Fall 1990 9(3): 148–167.

1552   **Raymond, Patricia Mary.** *The Effect of Age Vs. Life Expectancy on the Higher Cortical Functions of Middle-Aged and Older Women.* U of Rhode Island, 1982. 43/11B.

1553   **Rich, Cynthia,** 1933– . *Desert Years: Undreaming the American Dream.* San Francisco: Spinsters/Aunt Lute, 1989. il.
         Karen Sjoholm provided the cover and interior illustrations for this biographical book about aged women in the California desert. The jacket assigns it to "Ecology. Aging," while cataloging refers to "Psychology." Earlier, Rich coauthored *Look Me in the Eye: Old Women, Aging and Ageism* (#1580). Here she describes experiences living in the desert for six years in a trailer community of old people, mostly women.

1554   **Rodeheaver, Dean, and Joanne Stohs.** "The Adaptive Misperception of Age in Older Women: Sociocultural Images and Psychological Mechanisms of Control." *Educational Gerontology* March-April 1991 17(2): 141–156.

1555   **Rosenbloom, Sandra.** "The Travel Patterns of Elderly Women Alone: A Research Note." *Specialized Transportation Planning and Practice* 1989 3: 195–309.

1556   **Sabatello, Eitan F., and Dorith Tal.** "Women's Health, Work Experience, and Social Roles at Older Ages." *Genus Rome* 1990 46(3/4): 85–96.

1557   **Shack, Sybil.** "The Best Is Yet to Be? Challenging the Myths About Aging." Reprint. *Canadian Woman Studies/Les Cahiers de la Femme* Spring 1991 11: 34–35.

1558   **Stephens, Marlene Ruth.** *Social Support in Long-Term Customer Relationship Between Older Women and Their Hairdressers.* U of Toronto, 1990. M.S. thesis.

1559   **Stryker, Jeff.** "In Re: Conroy: History and Setting of the Case." In Joanne Lynn, ed. *No Extraordinary Means: The Choice to Forgo Life-Sustaining Food and Water.* Bloomington: Indiana U Press, 1986. 227–235.

1560   **Sundstrom, Gerdt.** "The Elderly, Women's Work and Social Costs." *Acta Sociologica* 1982 25(1): 21–38.

1561   **Trager, Natalie P.** "Social Class and the Older Family Member." In Gari Lesnoff-Caravaglia, ed. *The World of the Older Woman: Conflicts and Resolutions.* New York: Human Sciences Press, 1984. Chapter 3.

1562   **Trippet, Susan Elaine.** *Being Aware: The Meaning of the Relationship Between Social Support and Health Among Independent Older Women.* U of Alabama at Birmingham, 1988. 49/08B.

1563   **Troll, Lillian E.** "Gender Differences in Cross-Generation Networks." *Sex Roles* December 1987 17: 751–766.

1564   **Troll, Lillian E.** "The Psychosocial Problems of Older Women." In Gari Lesnoff-Caravaglia, ed. *The World of the Older Woman: Conflicts and Resolutions.* New York: Human Sciences Press, 1984. Chapter 2.

1565   **Troll, Lillian E., and E. M. Parron.** "Age Changes in Sex Roles and Changing Sex Roles: The Double Shift." In Carl Eisdorfer, ed. *Annual Review of Gerontology and Geriatrics* 1981 2: 118–143.

1566   **Wagnild, Gail, and H. M. Young.** "Resilience Among Older Women." *Image: The J of Nursing Scholarship* Winter 1990 22(4): 252–255.

1567   **Walker, Eleanor Ann Taylor.** *Perceptions, Race and Institutionalization: A Study of Older Women.* Catholic U of America, 1991. 52/01A.

1568   **Wonn, Marla, et al.** *Aging Is a Woman's Issue.* Albuquerque: The Commission, 1985. bib, il.

The final report on hearings cosponsored by the State Agency on Aging and the New Mexico Commission on the Status of Women, which was concerned about social and economic conditions and attitudes in their state. The commission's address is 129 Madeira Drive, S.E., Albuquerque, NM 87108.

8

Ageism/Sexism

Age discrimination in employment is well in place by age thirty for women in many occupations.

Lou Glasse

Ageism and Sexism: 1569–1586
Discrimination (bias); Double Standards and Equity; Activist Responses;
    Sisterhood: 1587–1634
Media; Image; Stereotypes: 1635–1679

The term ageism, *for gerontophobia, was coined by Robert Neil Butler, M.D., to refer to prejudices and stereotypes applied to older persons based solely on their age. Butler and Myrna I. Lewis have described ageism as a process of systematic stereotyping of and discrimination against people because they are old, just as racism and sexism are responses to skin color and gender. The AgeLine thesaurus states that "Negative or prejudicial image of aging held by society or by individuals may make age an influencing factor in situations where it is in fact inappropriate or irrelevant . . . related terms are age discrimination, age stereotypes, and labeling." A Feminist Dictionary more forthrightly declares that ageism "assumes that older people are not real people; not only are their needs fewer, and in some important areas such as sexuality, nonexistent, but it is considered that their experience is of little account and is to be avoided. Nobody knows what to do with older people, especially older women . . . " (Cheris Kramarae and Paula A. Treichler. London and Boston: Pandora Press, 1985). "Sexism is the belief that one sex is superior to another; a belief system that legitimizes male dominance and supports unequal treatment . . . regarding older women reflected in our language by such terms as* old maid, old hag, old girl, *and* old age" *(#2245, p. 61).*

AGEISM AND SEXISM
See also #2251.

1569   **Arber, Sara, 1949– , and Jay Ginn.** *Gender and Later Life: A Sociological Analysis of Resources and Constraints.* London (England) and Newbury Park: Sage, 1991. bib, index.

Social conditions that impose ageism on British women are the subject of Arber and Ginn's 1991 book. Their related publications include "Gender, Class and Income Inequalities in Later Life" (*British J of Sociology* September 1991 42[3]: 369–396) and a review article, "The Invisibility of Age: Gender and Class in Later Life" (*Sociological Review* May 1991 39[2]: 260–291).

1570   **Axinn, June.** "Women and Aging: Issues of Adequacy and Equity." *J of Women & Aging* 1989 1(1/2/3): 339–362.

1571   **Beeson, Diane, et al.** "Aging: A More Difficult Problem for Women than for Men?" In J. Harold Wershow. *Controversial Issues in Gerontology.* New York: Springer, 1981. Chapter 7.

1572   **Cohen, Leah,** 1945– . *Small Expectations: Society's Betrayal of Older Women.* Toronto: McClelland and Stewart, 1984. bib, il.

This is a compendium of facts and figures about women's old age and case histories of 250 women interviewed in Canada, England, and the United States. Cohen points to culturally induced self-hatred of women whose attractiveness is considered to terminate at age 30 and to the sexual disqualification resulting from the double standard of sexuality.

1573   **Copper, Baba.** *Over the Hill: Reflections on Ageism Between Women.* Freedom: Crossing Press, 1988. bib.

"Baba Copper is an old radical lesbian separatist obsessed by the capacity of ideas to unfetter us" (*Trivia* Summer 1985). Here, in more than twenty essays, she reflects on different aspects of being a woman over the age of 60 relating to women who are younger. Partial contents: "Mother-Blaming"; "Is This What Young Lesbians Really Want?"; "Do Lesbians Really Need Old Victims?"; "Youth Addiction"; "Witch Killing"; and "Anti-Ageist Work." Her 1987 16-page pamphlet, "Ageism in the Lesbian Community," was also published by Crossing Press.

1574   **Deri, Susan.** "The Aged and Women: Partners by Prejudice." *Psychoanalytic Review* Winter 1990 77(4): 519–523.

1575   **Gerike, Ann E.** "The Aging and Ageism Caucus"; and Ruth Heidelbach's "Aging and Ageism: Keeping or Losing Love?" "Aging and Ageism" section, *NWSAction* Winter 1988 1: 10–13.

1576   **Hale, Noreen,** 1943– . "Being Old: Seven Women, Seven Views." *J of Women & Aging* 1980 2(2): 7–17.

1577   **Hess, Beth B., and Joan Waring.** "Family Relationships of Older Women: A Women's Issue." In Elizabeth Markson, ed. *Older Women: Issues and Prospects.* Lexington: Heath, 1987. Chapter 11.

1578   **Jennings, Cheryl.** "Aging and Ageism Focus of Red Passages Question." *Off Our Backs (OOB)* December 1986 16: 17.

1579   **Macdonald, Barbara,** 1912– . "Outside the Sisterhood: Ageism in Women's Studies." *Women's Studies Q* Spring/Summer 1989 17(1/2): 6–11.

This speech delivered to the 1985 National Women's Studies Association conference also appeared in *Calyx J* Winter 1986 9(2/3): 20–25 and *Sojourner: The Women's Forum* August 1985.

1580   **Macdonald, Barbara,** 1912– , **and Cynthia Rich,** 1933– . *Look Me in the Eye: Old Women, Aging and Ageism.* San Francisco: Spinsters, Ink, 1983.

Essays reprinted with minor changes from *Broomstick, Equal Times, Gay Community News, New Women's Times, Sinister Wisdom, Sojourner,* and *Trivia* confront ageism in various areas, including as it is applied to women. Spinsters, Ink is an independent, women's publishing company now located at 32 East 1 Street, #330, Duluth, MN 55802.

1581   **McLaren, Arlene T.** "The Myth of Dependency." *Resources for Feminist Research/Documentation sur la Recherche Féministe* July 1982 11(2): 213.

1582   **Merriam, Eve.** "Women, Aging and Ageism [essay–book reviews]." *Ms. Magazine* March-April 1992 2(5): 58.

1583   **Miller, Camille Wright.** *Triple Jeopardy or Leveling? To Be Old, Black, and Female.* U of Virginia, 1987. 49/11A.

1584   **Rosenthal, Evelyn R., ed.** *Women, Aging, and Ageism.* New York: Haworth Press, 1990. bib, index. Also published as the 1990 2(2) issue of the *J of Women & Aging.*

Dr. Rosenthal begins with "Women and Varieties of Ageism." Analyzed by authors and subjects in *Women and Aging: A Guide to the Literature.*

1585   **Thone, Ruth Raymond.** *Women and Aging: Celebrating Ourselves.* New York: Haworth Press, 1992. bib, index.

Thone's celebration considers the psychology of aged American women and acknowledges ageism.

1586   **Woodward, Kathleen M.** *Aging and Its Discontents: Freud and Other Fictions.* Bloomington: Indiana U, 1991. bib, index.

Freudian psychoanalysis and twentieth-century literature are described as complicit in Western culture's negative view of aging. Woodward argues that, in the West, ageism, like sexism and racism, is rooted in physical differences and discrepancies in social power. Chapter 4: "The Look and the Gaze: Narcissism, Aggression, and Aging . . . Virginia Woolf's *The Years.*" Chapter 5: "Gender, Generational Identity, and Aging . . . Eva Figes' *Waking.*"

DISCRIMINATION (BIAS); DOUBLE STANDARDS AND EQUITY; ACTIVIST RESPONSES; SISTERHOOD

Many writers (Marilyn Block, Ruth Harriet Jacobs, Maggie Kuhn, Elissa Melamed, Jane Porcino, and Lillian Rubin are represented in Women and Aging: A Guide to the Literature*) have pointed out that ageism is much more frequently experienced by women because of what Susan Sontag referred to in 1972 as the* double standard of aging; *the double standards of aging phrase is now used to describe how aging takes different forms for men and women in our society. Two main examples: women become sexually ineligible earlier than men; a woman is criticized for marrying a younger man. See also Chapter 3: Older Woman/Younger Man; Older Man/Younger Woman (546–555); #1972; #2251; #2252.*

1587   **Alington, Diane E., and Lillian E. Troll.** "Social Change and Equality: The Roles of Women and Economics." In Grace Kesterman Baruch and Jeanne Brooks Gunn, eds. *Women in Midlife.* New York: Plenum Press, 1984. Chapter 7.

1588   **Brudney, Juliet F., and Hilda Scott,** 1915– . "Half a Loaf." In their *Forced Out: What Veteran Employees Can Do When Driven from Their Careers.* New York: Simon & Schuster, 1987. Chapter 8.

1589   Burwell, Elinor J. "Sexism in Social Science Research on Aging." In Jill McCalla Vickers, ed. *Taking Sex into Account: The Policy Consequences of Sexist Research.* New York: Oxford U Press, 1984.

1590   Chappell, Neena L., and Betty S. Haven. "Old and Female: Testing the Double Jeopardy Hypothesis." *Sociological Q* Spring 1980 21: 157–171.

1591   Ciano-Boyce, Claudia. *Psythotherapists' Perceptions of the Mental Health of Women and Men of Varying Ages.* U of Massachusetts, 1985. 46/12B.

1592   Finch, Janet, and Dulcie Groves. "Community Care and Family: A Case for Equal Opportunities?" *J of Social Policy* October 1980 9(4): 487–511.

1593   Friedman, Lawrence Meir, 1930– . "Your Time Will Come: The Law of Age Discrimination and Mandatory Retirement." In Russell Sage Foundation. *Social Research Perspectives: Occasional Reports on Current Topics, No. 10.* New York: Basic Books, 1984.

1594   Gergen, Mary M. "Finished at 40: Women's Development Within the Patriarchy." *Psychology of Women Q* December 1990 14(4): 471–493.

1595   Gerike, Ann E. "On Gray Hair and Oppressed Brains." *J of Women & Aging* 1990 2(2): 35–46.

1596   Greene, Roberta Rubin, 1940– . *Ageism and Death Anxiety as Related to Geriatric Social Work as a Career Choice.* U of Maryland at College Park, 1980. 42/02A.

1597   Healey, Shevy. "Growing to Be an Old Woman: Aging and Ageism." In Jo Alexander, et al, eds. *Women and Aging: An Anthology by Women.* Corvallis: Calyx Books, 1986. 58–62.

1598   Heen, Mary L. "Sex Discrimination in Pensions and Retirement Annuity Plans After *Arizona Governing Committee v. Norris*: Recognizing and Remedying Employer Noncompliance." *Women's Rights Law Reporter* Summer 1985 8(3): 155–176.

1599   Heen, Mary L. "Sex Discrimination, Mortality Tables, and Pensions: Improving the Economic Status of Older Women." *Women & Health* Spring 1986 11(1): 119–131.

1600   Hess, Beth B. "Antidiscrimination Policies Today and the Life Chances of Older Women Tomorrow"; and Paula Dressel's "An Overview of the Issues." *Gerontologist* April 1986 26(2): 132–135, 128–131. "Symposium—Civil Rights, Affirmative Action, and the Aged of the Future: Will Life Chances Be Different for Blacks, Hispanics and Women?" issue.

1601   Huckle, Patricia, 1937– . *Tish Sommers, Activist, and the Founding of the Older Women's League.* Knoxville: U of Tennessee Press, 1991. bib, il, index.
        Sommers (1914–1985) was a feminist concerned with the welfare of women as they age. It is generally recognized that she originated the *displaced homemaker* term and concept as well as the admonition, "Don't agonize, organize!" The lengthy bibliography of books and periodical articles is appropriate to this scholarly and readable book, enhanced by numerous photographs.

1602   Kahne, Hilda. "Not Yet Equal: Employment Experience of Older Women and Older Men." *International J of Aging and Human Development* 1985–1986 22(1): 1–13.

1603   Kautzer, Kathleen M. *Moving Against the Stream: An Organizational Study of the Older Women's League.* Brandeis U, 1988. 49/08A.

1604   Keith, Beverley Jean. *Is There a Double Standard of Aging? Sex Effects in Age Stereotyping.* New School for Social Research, 1984. 45/11B.

1605   Kelly, James J., and Susan Rice. "The Aged." In Harvey L. Sochros, et al, eds. *Helping the Sexually Oppressed.* New York: Prentice-Hall, 1986. Chapter 8.

1606   Klemesrud, Judy. "Conference on Aging Views Older Women." *New York Times* December 1, 1981: A28. "Older Women: No Longer 'Invisible.'" *New York Times* December 2, 1981: C1, C8–C9. "For Older Women, Parley Raises Hope." *New York Times* December 5, 1981 52: 5. "Problems of Older Women Focus of Parley." *New York Times* October 26, 1983 III(1): 2.

1607   leRiche, Pat, and Chloe Rowlings. "Feminist Group Work with Older Women: Emerging Issues and Future Possibilities." *International Social Work* April 1990 33(2): 121–136.

1608   Lesnoff-Caravaglia, Gari. "Double Stigmata: Female and Old". In her *The World of the Older Woman: Conflicts and Resolutions.* New York: Human Sciences Press, 1984. Chapter 1.

1609   Lewin, Tamar. "Change Is Urged in Social Security: Way of Determining Benefits Discriminates, Says Study by a Women's Group." (Older Women's League Report.) *New York Times* May 10, 1990 139: A22. "Group Says Older Women Are Earning Less than Men." (Older Women's League Report.) *New York Times* May 11, 1991 140: 7. "Income Gap Between Sexes Found to Widen in Retirement." (Study by Older Women's League.)

1610   Longino, Charles F. "Among the United States Elderly, Men Are Better Off than Women." *Los Angeles Times* December 12, 1987: 36.

1611   Lykes, M. Brinton. *Discrimination in the Lives of Older Black Women.* ERIC, April 1983. ED #244168. 13 pages.

1612   Macdonald, Barbara, 1912– . "Politics of Aging—I'm *Not* Your Mother." (The Neglect of Aging Women by Feminists.) *Ms Magazine* July-August 1990 1: 57–58.

1613   MacLean, Judy, ed. *Growing Numbers, Growing Force: A Report from the White House Mini-Conference on Older Women.* Oakland: Older Women's League Educational Fund; San Francisco: Western Gerontological Society, 1980.

Coordinated by Tish Sommers, with cartoons by Bulbul, this important document consists mainly of workshop reports and includes material on ensuring adequate income, health concerns, quality of life, impact of aging, minority women, and the Older Women's League (OWL). Failing to gain consideration of older women in plans for *the* White House Conference on Aging, these people organized the White House Mini-Conference on Older Women, attended by four hundred delegates. Two hundred stayed on to form OWL. In 1981, the United States Department of Health and Human Services published the *White House Conference on Aging: Reports; Background Papers* and *Final Report . . .*, said to be "A series of documents on special aging populations and issues that reviews progress and recurring problems since the 1971 White House Conference on Aging." The first had been held in 1961.

1614   Mason, Jennifer. "A Bed of Roses? Women, Marriage and Inequality in Later Life." In Patricia Allatt, et al, eds. *Women and the Life Cycle: Transitions and Turning Points.* New York: Macmillan, 1987. Chapter 7.

1615   **National Coalition on Older Women's Issues.** *Midlife and Older Women: A Resource Directory.* Washington, 1986.

It was possible in 1986 to identify over fifty organizations working on issues of concern to women in terms of their age. This 88-page reference work is in the collections of the National Council on Aging Library and other libraries.

1616   **Nuccio, Kathleen E.** "The Double Standard of Aging and Older Women's Employment." *J of Women & Aging* 1989 1(1/2/3): 317–338.

1617   **Older Women's League.** OWL is located in Washington, D.C., with chapters throughout the United States.

It was begun in 1980 by Tish Sommers and Laurie Shields, who recognized and defined the need for older women to organize nationally and become advocates for change in public policy. At present, it "is the only national membership organization dedicated exclusively to promoting social and economic equity for mid-life and older women." Its current publications and audiovisual materials are listed in an annual publications list; some are identified in *Women and Aging: A Guide to the Literature.* OWL's *Gray Paper* series included in-depth analyses. 1–6 were authored by Shields and Sommers:

1. "Older Women and Public Policy," 1979.
2. "Social Security: Adequacy and Equity for Older Women."
3. "Older Women and Health Care: Strategy for Survival," 1980.
4. "Older Women and Pensions: Catch 22."
5. "Welfare: End of the Line for Women," 1980.
6. "The Disillusionment of Divorce for Older Women," 1980.
7. "Till Death Do Us Part: Caregiving Wives of Severely Disabled Husbands," rev., 1986.
8. "'Not Even for Dogcatcher': Employment Discrimination and Older Women," by Frances Leonard, et al, 1982, reprinted 1986.
   "Death and Dying: Staying in Control to the End of Our Lives," 1986.
   "Health Care Financing and Midlife Women: A Sick System," 1986.
   "Divorce and Older Women," 1988.

OWL's *Mother's Day Reports* have included "Paying for Prejudice: A Report on Midlife and Older Women in America's Labor Force," by Christine L. Owens and Esther Koblenz, 1991; "Heading for Hardship: Retirement Income for American Women in the Next Century," 1990; "Employment Discrimination Against Older Women: A Handbook on Litigating Age and Sex Discrimination Cases," 1989; "Failing America's Caregivers: A Status Report on Women Who Care," 1989; "The Road to Poverty: A Report on the Economic Status of Midlife and Older Women," 1988; "The Picture of Health for Midlife and Older Women," 1987; and "Older Women and Job Discrimination: A Primer," 1984. *See also* Indexes under Older Women's League; Shields; and Sommers, #1603; #1609; #1613.

1618   **Ortmeyer, Linda Elizabeth.** *Ageism and Sexism: Elementary Public School Teachers' Attitudes Toward a 70- to 85-Year-Old Female, Male, and Person, and How Attitudes Relate to Knowledge.* U of Washington, 1981. 42/06A.

1619   **Paludi, Michele A., et al.** "Mentoring and Being Mentored: Issues of Sex, Power, and Politics for Older Women." *J of Women & Aging* 1990 2(3): 81–92.

1620 **Pell, Eve.** "Brokenhearted Me: Does a [Middle-Aged] Feminist Have the Right to Sing the Blues?" *Ms Magazine* June 1987 15: 80.

1621 **Porcino, Jane,** 1923– . "Psychological Aspects of Aging in Women." *Women & Health* 1985 10(2/3): 115–122.

1622 **Reinharz, Shulamit.** "Feminism and Anti-Ageism: Emergent Connections." In Anna Regula Herzog, et al, eds. *Health and Economic Status of Older Women.* Amityville: Baywood, 1989. Chapter 3.

1623 **Reinharz, Shulamit.** "Friends or Foes: Gerontological and Feminist Theory." *Women's Studies International Forum* 1986 9(5): 503–514. Also in Renate D. Klein and Deborah Lynn Steinberg, eds. *Radical Voices: A Decade of Feminist Resistance from "Women's Studies International Forum."* New York: Pergamon Press, 1989.

1624 **Russell, Cherry.** "Ageing as a Feminist Issue." *Women's Studies International Forum* 1987 10(2): 125–132.

1625 **Sancieri, Betty.** "Growing Older Feminist [editorial]." *Affilia* September 1987 2: 3–5.

1626 **Segrest, Mab.** "Barbara Deming: 1917–1984; Portrait of an Activist." *Southern Exposure* March-June 1985 13(2/3): 72–75.

1627 **Shaw, Lois Banfill.** *Older Women at Work.* Washington: Women's Research and Education Institute of the Congressional Caucus for Women's Issues, 1985. bib, il.

This 16-page document focuses on sex discrimination in employment of middle-aged women in the United States, i.e., discrimination based on both their age and sex/gender.

1628 **Snyder, Catherine J., and Gerald V. Barrett.** "The Age Discrimination in Employment Act: A Review of Court Decisions." *Experimental Aging Research* Spring 1988 14(1): 3–47.

1629 **Spender, Dale, ed.** *Feminist Theorists: Three Centuries of Key Women Thinkers.* New York: Pantheon, 1983. bib.

Originally published in Great Britain by The Women's Press, Ltd and reprinted with a new introduction. A significant number of these mostly English and also American women began their work at mid-life and later, and any notoriety has generally come in later years. For many, it has been a lifelong need and commitment. "It should not have escaped attention that all of these many books of feminist theory which have existed through the ages, themselves have no name, no category as a genre—another way in which their disappearance is facilitated" (p. 380 of Spender's essay about their reinvention of rebellion).

1630 **Spender, Dale, ed.** *Women of Ideas—and What Men Have Done to Them from Aphra Behn to Adrienne Rich.* London and Boston: Routledge & Kegan Paul, 1982. index.

Susan B. Anthony, Mary R. Beard, Aphra Behn, Matilda J. Gage, Elizabeth C. Stanton, Lucy Stone, Ray C. Strachey, and Rebecca West are some of the intellectuals whose ideas and lives were restricted by sexist ageism.

1631 **Stone, Robyn I., and Meredith Minkler.** "The Sociopolitical Context of Women's Retirement." In Meredith Minkler and Carol L. Estes, eds. *Readings in the Political Economy of Aging.* Amityville: Baywood, 1984. 225–238.

1632   Ticoll, Elsie. "One Woman's Life Journey [on the Older Women's Network]." *Canadian Woman Studies/Les Cahiers de la Femme*. Winter 1992 12: 49–50.

1633   Turner, Rebecca Anne. *Social Categorization by the Elderly and the Young: Examination of Intergroup Perceptions*. George Washington U, 1987. 47/12B.

1634   U.S. Congress. House. Select Committee on Aging. *Age Discrimination in the Workplace: A Continuing Problem for Older Workers: Hearing Before the . . . Committee . . . 102nd Congress, First Session, September 24, 1991*. Washington: For sale by the U.S. Government Printing Office, 1992. Govt. Doc. No.: Y 4.Ag 4/2:Ag 4/24. bib, il.

MEDIA; IMAGE; STEREOTYPES
See also Chapter 10: Humor (1868–1876).

1635   Allen, Jeanne Thomas, ed. *Now, Voyager*. Madison: U of Wisconsin Press, 1984.
        Allen's clever and insightful analysis of the production process of Hollywood's version of *Now, Voyager* has been published by the Wisconsin Center for Film and Theater Research in its Screenplay Series. Olive Higgins Prouty (1882–1974)'s 1941 novel (title from a Walt Whitman poem) was part of a trilogy that also included *Lisa Vale*, and was published when Prouty was 59. In the 1942 Warner Brothers film, Charlotte Vale, the "spinster" central character, was played by Bette Davis (1908–1989), then 34 years old. The devouring mother, played by Dame Gladys Cooper (1888–1971), perceived her daughter as servant, unpaid employee, guest, legal ward, "my little girl," "my ugly duckling." The "unwanted daughters" to whom Charlotte refers are herself and Tina, the leading man's daughter. Allen explores the evolution of the script and points out aspects of photography and script development related to the emergence of the character of Charlotte.

1636   Barton, Priscilla, et al, eds. "Editorials." *Heresies* 1988 6(3): 2–3. "Coming of Age" issue #23.

1637   Buchman, Patti. "Title VII Limits on Discrimination Against Television Anchorwomen on the Basis of Age-Related Appearance." *Columbia Law Review* January 1985 85(1): 190–215.

1638   Burke, Judith Lee. "Young Children's Attitudes and Perceptions of Older Adults." *International J of Aging and Human Development* 1981–1982 14(3): 205–222.

1639   Craft, Christine, 1944– . *Too Old, Too Ugly, and Not Deferential to Men: An Anchorwoman's Courageous Battle Against Sex Discrimination*. Rocklin: Prima Publishing and Communication, 1988.
        Originally published in 1986 by Ms. Craft and Capra Press, this edition includes a new introduction. In 1983, American broadcast journalist Craft sued under existing laws and statutes her former employer for age and sex discrimination. KMBC-TV in Kansas City had taken the advice of a Texas media consulting firm and fired Craft as news co-anchor based on her being too old, too ugly, and not deferential to men. Her response contrasted with the more usual compromise attitude, e.g., "Half a Loaf," Chapter 8 of Juliet F. Brudney and Hilda Scott's *Forced Out: What Veteran Employees Can Do When Driven from Their Careers* (Simon & Schuster, 1987).

1640   Dail, Paula W. "Prime-Time Television Portrayal of Older Adults in the Context of Family Life." *Gerontologist* October 1988 28(5): 700–706.

1641   Davidson, Tina, and the Older Feminist Network. "Age." In Kath Davies, et al, eds. *Out of Focus: Writings of Women and the Media*. London: The Women's Press, 1987. Part I: 14–37.

1642   Davis, Richard H. *Television and the Aging Audience*. Los Angeles: U of Southern California Andrus Gerontology Center, 1980. bib.
        Although television as used by programmers and advisers as well as its reception by older adults are crucial communications issues, recognition of the significance of sex/gender and age roles has been limited. Chapter 2, "The World of TV," includes models for sex and age roles; Chapter 4, "Program Issues," includes the image of aging women and men on camera.

1643   DeRenzo, Evan G., and Jim Malley. "Increasing Use of Ageist Language in Skin-Care Product Advertising: 1969 Through 1988." *J of Women & Aging* 1992 4(3): 105–126.

1644   Elliott, Joyce C. "The Daytime Television Portrayal of Older Adults." *Gerontologist* December 1984 24(60): 628–633.

1645   Elliott, Joyce C. *Images of Older Adult Characters on Daytime Television Serial Drama*. Columbia U Teachers College, 1981. 43/06A.

1646   Engle, Molly. "Little Old Ladies Are Much Maligned: Diversity Reconsidered." *Educational Gerontology* July-August 1990 16(4): 339–346.

1647   Faye, Alice, 1915– , with Dick Cleiner. *Growing Older, Staying Younger*. New York: Dutton, 1990.
        Faye has traveled the United States as Pfizer Pharmaceuticals' "Ambassador for Good Health," promoting steps for healthy living in later years. She downplays her arthritis as she urges seniors to "Keep on moving!" Born in New York's Hell's Kitchen, Fay went on to a film career and starring with Tyrone Power, Spencer Tracy, and other leading men. Her recent activities include a film shown on PBS, "We Still Are!"

1648   Fillmer, H. Thompson. "Sex Stereotyping for the Elderly by Children." *Educational Gerontology* 1982 8(1): 77–85.

1649   Franzen, Monika, and Nancy Ethiel, comps. *Make Way! 200 Years of American Women in Cartoons*. Chicago: Chicago Review Press, 1988. il.
        Most of these cartoons and caricatures are from Historical Pictures Service, Chicago, Illinois, archives, of which Dr. Franzen is part owner. "I hate looking at those old cartoons. I'm fascinated too . . . ," reports cartoonist Nicole Hollander in her introductory note.

1650   Fung, Victoria M. "Anchor Jobs Go to Young Women and Experienced Men." *WJR: Washington Journalism Review* October 1988 10(8): 20–24.

1651   Glospie, Walter Wallace. *A Comparison of the Aged Portrayed in Contemporary Realistic Fiction for Children, with United States Census Data*. Lehigh U, 1986. 47/08A.

1652   Harris, Julianne, and Charles M. Fiedler. "Preadolescent Attitudes Toward the Elderly: An Analysis of Race, Gender and Contact Variables." *Adolescence* Summer 1988 23: 335–340.

1653   Hollenshead, Carol, and Serit Ingeroll. "Middle-Aged and Older Women in Print Advertisements." *Educational Gerontology* January-February 1982 8(1): 25–41.

1654   **Isaacs, Leora W.** *The Development of Children's Attitudes Toward the Aged.* City U of New York, 1982. 42/12B.

1655   **Kahn, P. Lynne.** *A Cross-Sectional Multi-Method Study of Children's Views of Adulthood and Old Age.* Indiana U, 1981. 41/12B.

1656   **Kalau, Elisabeth (Betsy).** *Experience of Old Age as Reflected in U.S. and West German Children's Literature: A Comparative Study.* Southern Illinois U at Carbondale, 1980. 41/06B.

1657   **Lang, Martha Reeves.** *An Exploratory Study of Children's Perceptions of Grand-parent-Grandchild Relationships.* Columbia U Teachers College, 1980. 41/04A.

1658   **Lieberman, Devorah A., et al.** "Age-Related Differences in Nonverbal Decoding Ability." *Communication Q* Fall 1988 36(4): 290–297.

1659   **Nett, Emily M.** "Is There Life After Fifty? Images of Middle Age for Women in *Chatelaine* Magazine, 1984." *J of Women & Aging* 1991 3(10): 93–115.

1660   **Newman, Jacquelyn Gail.** *Perceptions of Aging in an Older Sample: Life Satisfaction, Evaluations of Old Age, and Responses to Cartoons About Old People.* U of Arizona, 1986. 47/07B.

1661   **O'Neill, Marylee Ritter.** *The Widow's Peak: Popular Images of Widowhood in America, 1920–1960.* Boston U, 1984. 45/06A.

1662   **Piggrem, Gary Wayne.** *Sixth, Ninth, and Twelfth Graders' Stereotypes and Knowledge of Elderly Persons.* Ohio State U, 1983. 44/04B.

1663   **Pool, Jonelle Elaine.** *A Comparison of the Imposition of Stereotypes in Young and Old Persons.* U of Georgia, 1980. 41/02A.

1664   **Quam, Jean, and Carol D. Austin.** "Coverage of Women's Issues in Eight Social Work Journals, 1970–81." *Social Work* (United States) July-August 1984 29(4): 360–365.

1665   **Rice-Erso, Harold Martin.** *The Impact of Midlife on the Stereotypically Gender-Linked Personality Traits for Female Lawyers and Female Nurses.* Northwestern U, 1985. 46/08B.

1666   **Rothbell, Gladys Weisberg.** *The Case of the Jewish M-Other: A Study in Stereotyping.* SUNY at Stony Brook, 1989. 54/03A.

1667   **Salisbury, Paul Allen.** *Aging and Communication: An Exploratory Study of Mass Media Uses and Gratifications in Late Life.* Columbia U, 1980. 41/02A.

1668   **Sanders, Marlene, 1931– , and Marcia Rock.** *Waiting for Prime Time: The Women of Television News.* Urbana: U of Illinois Press, 1988. il, index.

Sanders is a well-known American broadcast journalist whose years of capable work led to appointment in 1978 as producer of CBS News documentaries. But in 1987 she was asked to move to radio . . . she did not fit the profile of the A-Team TV correspondents of the 1980s. Middle age was no asset. This is, however, neither an autobiography nor an account of litigation-response to discrimination. It is about American women journalists, particularly in TV news, and a history that includes their reporting only seventy-six of 609 news stories appearing on all three networks (1986 survey), with less than 1 percent increase since 1975 in women reporting! Copious notes.

1669   Secunda, Victoria H. *By Youth Possessed: The Denial of Age in America.* New York: Bobbs, 1984. index.

American public opinion is indeed prejudiced against age, aging, and the aged. Chapters 4, "How the Media Define Age"; 5, "Working: When Experience Does, and Doesn't Count"; and 7, "The School: First and Last Chances," are particularly relevant to knowing about and understanding ageism's impact on females and gender considerations.

1670   Serra, Judith K., and Pose Lamb. "The Elderly in Basal Readers." *Reading Teacher* December 1984 38(3): 227–281.

1671   Spencer, Mickey, and Polly Taylor. "Journey on a Broom: Some Adventures of Two Over-40 Editing Feminists [editors of *Broomstick: By, For, and About Women over 40*]." *Frontiers* 1989 10(3): 14–15.

1672   Steenland, Sally. "Prime Time Women: An Analysis of Older Women on Entertainment Television." Washington: National Commission on Working Women, 1984. ERIC, 1984. ED #303148. 30 pages.

1673   Stoddard, Karen Marie. *The Image of the Aging Woman in American Popular Film, 1930–1980.* U of Maryland, College Park, 1980. 41/06A.

1674   Stoesel, Sue. "Women as TV Audience: A Marketing Perspective." In Helen Baehr and Gillian Dyer, eds. *Boxed In: Women and Television.* New York: Pandora Press, 1987. 107–116.

1675   U.S. Commission on Civil Rights. *Characters in Textbooks: A Review of the Literature.* Washington: The Commission, May 1980. bib.

Clearinghouse Publication No. 62 examined the findings of more than twenty scholarly studies investigating the treatment of racial minorities, women, and "the elderly" in textbooks used in elementary and secondary schools and colleges.

1676   Vernon, Joetta A., et al. "Media Stereotyping: A Comparison of the Way Elderly Women and Men Are Portrayed on Prime-Time Television." *J of Women & Aging* 1990 2(4): 44–68.

1677   Vraney, Mary W., and Carol J. Barrett. "Marital Status: Its Effects on the Portrayal of Older Characters in Children's Literature." *J of Reading* March 1981 24(6): 487–493.

1678   Walker, Nancy. *A Very Serious Thing: Women's Humor and American Culture.* Minneapolis: U of Minnesota Press, 1988. bib, index.

Walker's history of American women's humor is accompanied by a list of collections and individual works of humor by American women. Chapters are devoted to the female humorist; male tradition and female tradition (women tend to be story, rather than joke, tellers); humor, intellect, and femininity; feminist humor; the tradition and beyond; and contemporary women's humor and the canon of American literature.

1679   Wear, Delese, and Lois LaCivita Nixon. "Try Thinking About It This Way: Redescribing Women and Age." *J of Women & Aging* 1991 3(4): 117–125.

9

Cross-Cultural and International Perspectives on Women's Aging

The news from China has been confusing. . . . The Communists gave axes to the old ladies and said, "Go and kill yourself. You're useless."
Maxine Hong Kingston, 1940– , *The Woman Warrior: Memories of a Girlhood Among Ghosts* (1976)

Anthropology and Ethnography: 1680–1692
Cross-Cultural Perspectives: 1693–1763
International Perspectives: 1764–1804

ANTHROPOLOGY AND ETHNOGRAPHY

1680   **Beyene, Yewoubdar.** *An Ethnography of Menopause: Menopausal Experiences of Mayan Women in a Yucatan Village.* Case Western Reserve U, 1985. 46/03A.

1681   **Brown, Judith K.** "A Cross-Cultural Exploration of the End of the Childbearing Years." In Ann Mae Voda, et al, eds. *Changing Perspectives on Menopause.* Austin: U of Texas Press, 1982. Chapter 4.

1682   **Cohler, Bertram J.** "Stress or Support: Relations Between Older Women from Three European Ethnic Groups and Their Relatives." In Ron C. Manuel, ed. *Minority Aging: Sociological and Social Psychological Issues.* Westport: Greenwood, 1982. Chapter 12.

1683   **Counts, Dorothy Ayers.** "Tamparonga: 'The Big Women' of Kallai (Papua New Guinea)." In Virginia Kerns and Judith K. Brown, eds. *In Her Prime: New Views of Middle-Aged Women, 2d ed.* Urbana: U of Illinois Press, 1992. Chapter 6. *See also* Brown and Kerns's *In Her Prime: A New View of Middle-Aged Women,* 1985.

1684   **Flint, Marcha.** "Anthropological Perspectives on the Menopause and Middle Age." *Maturitas* 1982 4: 173–180.

1685   **Hrdy, Sarah Blaffer.** "'Nepotists' and 'Altruists': The Behavior of Old Females Among Macaques and Langur Monkeys." In Pamela T. Amoss and Stevan Harrell, eds. *Other Ways of Growing Old: Anthropological Perspectives.* Stanford: Stanford U Press, 1981. 59–76, 253–256.

1686   **Hungry Wolf, Beverly,** 1950– . *The Ways of My Grandmothers.* New York: Morrow, 1980. il, index.
    Hungry Wolf has provided a record of the Siksika Indian women, learning from them, their dances, myths, legends, and teachings. She hopes "that some of the

young women who read this book grow to become grandmothers, following ways that their grandchildren will one day consider valuable enough to record also" (p. 10).

1687   **Jacobs, Ruth Harriet,** 1924– . "Out of the Mikvah into the Sauna: A Study of Women's Health Clubs." In Elizabeth Markson, ed. *Older Women: Issues and Prospects.* Lexington: Heath, 1987. Chapter 3.

1688   **Kaufert, Patricia.** "Anthropology and the Menopause: The Development of a Theoretical Framework." *Maturitas* 1982 4: 181–193.

1689   **Kerns, Virginia,** 1948– . "Sexuality and Social Control Among the Garifuna (Belize)." In Virginia Kerns and Judith K. Brown, eds. *In Her Prime: New Views of Mid-dle-Aged Women, 2d ed.* Urbana: U of Illinois Press, 1992. Chapter 6. *See also* Brown and Kerns' *In Her Prime: A New View of Middle-Aged Women,* 1985.

1690   **Lock, Margaret, guest ed.** "Anthropological Approaches to Menopause: Questioning Received Knowledge." Special issue of *Culture, Medicine and Psychiatry* 1985 10(1).

1691   **Miller, Elvira Demesa.** *Elderly Females Living Alone: An Ethnographic Study.* Columbia U Teachers College, 1985. 46/03A.

1692   **Skultans, Vieda.** "Menstrual Symbolism in South Wales." In Thomas Buckley and Alma Gottlieb, eds. *Blood Magic: The Anthropology of Menstruation.* Berkeley: U of California Press, 1989. 137–160.

CROSS-CULTURAL PERSPECTIVES

1693   **Ashley, Laurel Maria.** *Self, Family and Community: The Social Process of Aging Among Urban Mexican-American Women (California).* U of California, Los Angeles, 1985. 47/10A.

1694   **Blackman, Margaret B.** *During My Time—Florence Edenshaw Davidson, a Haida Woman.* Seattle: U of Washington Press, 1982. bib, index.
        The Haida are Indians of the northwest coast of British Columbia, Canada. This is a " . . . partial accounting of the experiences and feelings of an elderly Haida woman" born in 1896. The " . . . never-ending labor and lack of time for self speak to a whole generation of North American rural women" (p. 153).

1695   **Boddy, Janice.** "Bucking the Agnatic System: Status and Strategies in Rural Northern Sudan." In Virginia Kerns and Judith K. Brown, eds. *In Her Prime: New Views of Middle-Aged Women, 2d ed.* Urbana: U of Illinois Press, 1992. Chapter 10. *See also* Brown and Kerns's *In Her Prime: A New View of Middle-Aged Women,* 1985.

1696   **Chambliss, Judith Ann.** *"Así Es la Vida" (Thus Is Life): Health and the Experience of Suffering Among Elderly Mexican-American Women.* California Institute of Integral Studies, 1990. M.A. thesis.

1697   **Chaney, Elisa M., ed.** *Empowering Older Women: Cross-Cultural Views.* Washington: American Association of Retired Persons, 1990. bib.
        This "booklet" (72 pages) is a teaching tool to spark dialog on how mid-life and older women become empowered. Included are transcripts of two "conversations" of groups of Latin American and American (i.e., U.S.) women, a background paper,

resources for leaders, and Third World demographic statistics on aging. The AARP with the Pan American Health Organization published *Midlife and Older Women in Latin America and the Caribbean*, edited by Lee Sennott-Miller (1989). With the International Federation on Ageing, *Older Women Around the World*, by Mary Jo Storey Gibson (1985), and *Coping with Social Change: Programs That Work* (for mid-life and old women in Latin America), edited by Irene Hoskins (1990).

1698   **Chang-Kon, Joyce Sau-Han.** *Selected Factors Influencing Decision-Making About Living Arrangements and Social Services Among Elderly Chinese Women.* Catholic U of America, 1993. 54/03A.

1699   **Coles, Catherine.** "The Older Woman in Hausa Society: Power and Authority in Urban Nigeria." In Jay Sokolovsky, ed. *The Cultural Context of Aging.* New York: Bergin & Garvey, 1990. Chapter 3.

1700   **Connors, Denise Donnell.** *"I've Always Had Everything I've Wanted—But I Never Wanted Very Much": An Experiential Analysis of Irish-American Working-Class Women in Their Nineties.* Brandeis U, 1986. 47/05A.

1701   **Counts, Dorothy Ayers.** "Aging, Health and Women in West New Britain." *J of Cross-Cultural Gerontology. Dordrecht* 1991 6(3): 277–285.

1702   **Counts, Dorothy Ayers, and David R. Counts, eds.** *Aging and Its Transformations: Moving Toward Death in Pacific Societies.* ASAD (Association for Social Anthropology in Oceania) Monograph #10. Lanham: U Press of America, 1985. bib, il, index.
Part I: "Aging and Gender" consists of Chapters 1, "Introduction: Linking Concepts Aging and Gender, Aging and Death; 2, "Koro and Kuia: Aging and Gender Among the Maori of New Zealand" by Karen P. Sinclair; 3, "Gender Complementarity, Aging and Reproduction Among New Zealand Pakeha Women" by Michele D. Domeny; and 4, "Kinship, Gender, and Aging on Pulap, Caroline Islands" by Juliana Flinn. Part II: "Aging, Gender, and Dying" includes Chapter 8, "Gender, Aging and Dying in an Egalitarian Society" by Maria Lepowsky.

1703   **Cruikshank, Julie, et al.** *Life Lived Like a Story: Life Stories of Three Yukon Native Elders.* Lincoln: U of Nebraska Press, 1990. bib.
The life histories of three women of Tutchone, Tagish, and Tlingit ancestry from Canada's Southern Yukon Territory are recounted, as they use their culture's oral traditions as a framework for their autobiographies.

1704   **Curtis-Boles, Harriet Ann.** *Life Satisfaction in the Later Years: A Cross-Cultural Investigation.* U of California, Berkeley, 1984. 45/09B.

1705   **Datan, Nancy, et al.** *A Time to Reap: The Middle Age of Women in Five Israeli Subcultures.* Baltimore: Johns Hopkins U Press, 1981. bib, index.
These case studies consider the human life cycle, focusing on the menopause.

1706   **Datan, Nancy, et al.** "Tradition, Modernity, and Transitions in Five Israeli Subcultures." In Virginia Kerns and Judith K. Brown, eds. *In Her Prime: New Views of Middle-Aged Women, 2d ed.* Urbana: U of Illinois Press, 1992. Chapter 13. *See also* Brown and Kerns's *In Her Prime: A New View of Middle-Aged Women,* 1985.

1707   **Davis, Dona Lee,** 1948– . *Women's Experience of Menopause in a Newfoundland Fishing Village.* U of North Carolina at Chapel Hill, 1980. 41/04A.

1708   **Davis, Dona Lee,** 1948– . "Women's Status and Experience of the Menopause in a Newfoundland Fishing Village." *Maturitas* 1982 4: 207–216.

1709   **Du Toit, Brian M.,** 1935– . *Aging and Menopause Among Indian South African Women.* Albany: SUNY Press, 1990. bib, il, index.
    Part of the SUNY Series in Medical Anthropology, this lengthy (343 page) work considers social aspects of menopause among Muslim and Hindu women of South Africa.

1710   **Facio, Linda.** *Constraints, Resources, and Self-Definition: A Case Study of Chicano Older Women.* U of California, Berkeley, 1988. 50/04A.

1711   **Foner, Nancy.** "Older Women in Nonindustrial Cultures: Consequences of Power and Privilege." *Women & Health* 1988 14(3/4): 227–238. Also in Lois Grau and Ida Susser, eds. "Women in the Later Years: Health, Social and Cultural Perspectives" (published as a book by Harrington Park Press in 1989).

1712   **Glugoski, Greta G.** *A Participatory Study of the Self-Concept of Elderly Hispanic Women: Díalogo con las Ancianas.* U of San Francisco, 1989. 51/02A.

1713   **Goodman, Catherine Chase.** "The Caregiving Roles of Asian American Women." *J of Women & Aging* 1990 2(1): 109–120.

1714   **Groessl, Patricia Ann.** *Depression and Anxiety in Postmenopausal Women: A Study of Black, White, and Hispanic Women.* Western Michigan U, 1987. 48/06A.

1715   **Heisel, Marsel A.** "Older Women in Developing Countries." *Women & Health* 1988 14(3/4): 253–272. "Women in the Later Years: Health, Social, and Cultural Perspectives" issue.

1716   **Hemmings, Susan, ed.** *A Wealth of Experience: The Lives of Older Women.* London and Boston: Pandora Press, 1985. bib.
    Journalist Hemmings founded the Older Feminist Network in 1981 in Britain. She provides case studies of eighteen middle-aged and older women, including politically involved, employed, black, immigrant, lesbian, and working-class women of various religions. "Women of 40 to 65 have received little positive attention" (p. 91).

1717   **Information on Women (Comunicación e Informacíon de la Mujer).** "Little Old Ladies." In special section, "Approaching Old Age," prepared by Information on Women journalists. *ISIS Latin American and Caribbean Women's Health J* April-June 1991 2: 33–37.

1718   **Ingstad, Benedicte, et al.** "Care for the Elderly, Care by the Elderly: The Role of Elderly Women in a Changing Tswana Society." *J of Cross-Cultural Gerontology. Dordrecht* 1992 7(40): 379–398.

1719   **Kaufert, Patricia, et al.** "[Problems in Cross-Cultural] Menopause Research: The Korpilampi Workshop. The Ninth International Conference: Social Sciences and Medicine (1985, Korpilampi, Finland)." *Social Science & Medicine* 1986 22(1): 1285–1289.

1720   **Kearns, Bessie Jean Ruley.** "Perceptions of Menopause by Papago Women." In Ann Mae Voda, et al, eds. *Changing Perspectives on Menopause.* Austin: U of Texas Press, 1982. Chapter 6.

1721   **Kerns, Virginia,** 1948– . "Female Control of Sexuality: Garifuna Women at Middle Age." In Kerns and Judith K. Brown, eds. *In Her Prime: New Views of Middle-*

Aged Women, 2d ed. Urbana: U of Illinois Press, 1992. Chapter 8. *See also* Brown and Kerns's *In Her Prime: A New View of Middle-Aged Women,* 1985.

1722   **Kerns, Virginia, 1948– , and Judith K. Brown, eds.** *In Her Prime: New Views of Middle-Aged Women, 2d ed.* Urbana: U of Illinois Press, 1992. bib, il, index.
    See also Brown and Kerns's 1985 *In Her Prime: A New View of Middle-Aged Women.* The contents of this book (both editions) are analyzed in *Women and Aging: A Guide to the Literature.* These professors of anthropology provide ethnographic data that can enable social scientists to assess the similarities and differences in the experiences of middle-aged women in a variety of societies. Their scholar-contributors document great need for a transcultural definition of "middle age."

1723   **Lambek, Michael.** "Motherhood and Other Careers in Mayotte (Comoro Islands)." In Virginia Kerns and Judith K. Brown, eds. *In Her Prime: New Views of Middle-Aged Women, 2d ed.* Urbana: U of Illinois Press, 1992. Chapter 7. *See also* Brown and Kerns's *In Her Prime: A New View of Middle-Aged Women,* 1985.

1724   **Lee, Richard B.** "Work, Sexuality, and Aging Among Kung Women." In Virginia Kerns and Judith K. Brown, eds. *In Her Prime: New Views of Middle-Aged Women, 2d ed.* Urbana: U of Illinois Press, 1992. Chapter 4. *See also* Brown and Kerns's *In Her Prime: A New View of Middle-Aged Women,* 1985.

1725   **Lesnoff-Caravaglia, Gari.** "The 'Babushka' or Older Woman in Soviet Society." In her *The World of the Older Woman: Conflicts and Resolutions.* New York: Human Sciences Press, 1984. 127–136.

1726   **Lesnoff-Caravaglia, Gari.** "The Black 'Granny' and the Soviet 'Babushka': Commonalities and Contrasts." In Ron C. Manuel, ed. *Minority Aging: Sociological and Social Psychological Issues.* Westport: Greenwood, 1982. Chapter 11.

1727   **Lock, Margaret.** "New Japanese Mythologies: Faltering Discipline and the Ailing Housewife." *American Ethnologist* 1988 15(1): 43–60. Special issue on medical anthropology.

1728   **Lock, Margaret.** "Cultural Construction of the Menopausal Syndrome: The Japanese." *Maturitas* 1988 10: 317–332.

1729   **Loustaunau, Amarhta Oehmke.** "Hispanic Widows and Their Support Systems in the Mesilla Valley of Southern New Mexico, 1910–1940." In Arlene Scadron, ed. *On Their Own: Widows and Widowhood in the American Southwest, 1848–1939.* Champaign: U of Illinois Press, 1988. Chapter 4.

1730   **Magashalala, Theophilus Ntobeko Vincent.** *An Analysis of Support Systems Among African Widows in the Tyhume Basin, Ciskei, South Africa.* U of Alabama, 1984. 46/04A.

1731   **Mason, Theresa Hope.** *Experience and Meaning: An Interpretive Study of Family and Gender Ideologies Among a Sample of Mexican-American Women of Two Generations.* U of Texas at Austin, 1987. 48/05A.

1732   **Miller, Jay, 1947– , ed.** *Mourning Dove: A Salishan Autobiography, 1888–1936.* Lincoln: U of Nebraska, 1990. bib, il, index.
    Mourning Dove, pen name of Christine Quintasket (1888–1936), "now best known as the first Native American woman to publish a novel [*Cogewea,* published in

1927, fifteen years after completion] . . . was a regional celebrity throughout the Inland Northwest during her lifetime" (p. xi). She worked as a seasonal laborer. On her burial marker, she was recorded as "Mrs. Fred Galler." This annotated edition of manuscript fragments of her unfinished autobiography includes Chapters 4, "The Dutiful Wife," and 7, "Widowhood." Miller has also written "Mourning Dove: The Author as Cultural Mediator," pp. 160–182 in *Being and Becoming Indian: Biographic Studies of Native American Frontiers*, published in 1989 by Dorsey.

1733   **Moller, Valerie.** "Black South African Women on Excursions: A Reflection on the Quality of Township Life for Seniors." *J of Cross-Cultural Gerontology. Dordrecht* 1992 7(40): 399–428.

1734   **Nelson, Sarah M.** "Widowhood and Autonomy in the Native-American Southwest." In Arlene Scadron, ed. *On Their Own: Widows and Widowhood in the American Southwest, 1848–1939.* Champaign: U of Illinois Press, 1988. Chapter 1.

1735   **Nielsen Allen, Corinne Akita.** *Factors Influencing Life Decisions and Attitudes Toward Life Decisions: An Intergenerational Study of Crucian Women (Virgin Islands).* Indiana U, 1983. 44/10A.

1736   **Olowo, Ojoade-J.** "The Older Woman as Seen Through African Proverbs: Fragmentary Remarks About African Society." *Folkore (Calcutta)* 1985 26(6): 110–114; 26(7): 139–140; 26(8): 152–157.

1737   **Padgett, Deborah.** "Aging Minority Women: Issues in Research and Health Policy." *Women & Health* 1988 14(3/4): 213–226.

1738   **Pang, Keum Young Chung.** "Hwabyung: The Construction of a Korean Popular Illness Among Korean Elderly Immigrant Women in the United States." *Culture, Medicine & Psychiatry* December 1990 14(4): 495–512.

1739   **Pang, Keum Young Chung.** *Korean Elderly Women in America: Everyday Life, Health, and Illness.* Immigrant Communities and Ethnic Minorities in the United States and Canada, #69. New York: AMS Press, 1991. bib, index.
        Pang's concern is for health of mind and body of aged Korean-American and immigrant women from Korea in the United States.

1740   **Peterson, Jane W.** "Age of Wisdom: Elderly Black Women in Family and Church." In Jay Sokolovsky, ed. *The Cultural Context of Aging: Worldwide Perspectives.* Westport: Bergin & Garvey, 1990. 213–227.

1741   **Rasmussen, Susan Jane.** *Gender and Curing in Ritual and Symbol: Women, Spirit Possession, and Aging Among the Kel Ewey Taureg (Niger, Africa).* Indiana U, 1986. 47/05A.

1742   **Raybeck, Douglas.** "A Diminished Dichotomy: Kelantan Malay and Traditional Chinese Perspectives." In Virginia Kerns and Judith K. Brown, eds. *In Her Prime: New Views of Middle-Aged Women, 2d ed.* Urbana: U of Illinois Press, 1992. Chapter 12. *See also* Brown and Kerns's *In Her Prime: A New View of Middle-Aged Women,* 1985.

1743   **Rosenberger, Nancy Ross.** *Middle-Aged Japanese Women and the Meanings of the Menopausal Transition.* U of Michigan, 1984. 45/07A.

1744   **Rosenberger, Nancy Ross.** "Productivity, Sexuality and Ideologies of Menopausal Problems in Japan." In Edward Norbeck and Margaret Lock, eds. *Health, Illness, and*

Medical Care in Japan: Cultural and Social Dimensions. Honolulu: U of Hawaii, 1987. 155–188.

1745   **Rosenman, Linda S., and Sharon Winocur.** "Australian Women and Income Security for Old Age: A Cohort Study." *J of Cross-Cultural Gerontology.* Dordrecht 1990 5(3).

1746   **Sanchez-Ayendez, Melba.** *Puerto Rican Elderly Women: Aging in an Ethnic Minority Group in the United States.* U of Massachusetts, 1984. 45/10A.

1747   **Sanchez-Ayendez, Melba.** "Puerto Rican Elderly Women: The Cultural Dimension of Social Support Networks." *Women & Health* 1988 14(3/4): 239–252.

1748   **Schlegel, Alice.** "Hopi Family Structure and Experience of Widowhood." In Arlene Scadron, ed. *On Their Own: Widows and Widowhood in the American Southwest, 1848–1939.* Champaign: U of Illinois Press, 1988. Chapter 2.

1749   **Seltzer, Joyce Pauline.** *Huasteca Widows [Potosi Huasteca, Mexico].* U of Texas at Austin, 1980. 41/04A.

1750   **Shomaker, Dianna.** "Health Care, Cultural Expectations and Frail Elderly Navajo Grandmothers." *J of Cross-Cultural Gerontology.* Dordrecht 1990 5(1): 21–34.

1751   **Sinclair, Karen P.** "A Study in Pride and Prejudice: Maori Women at Midlife." In Virginia Kerns and Judith K. Brown, eds. *In Her Prime: New Views of Middle-Aged Women, 2d ed.* Urbana: U of Illinois Press, 1992. Chapter 9. *See also* Brown and Kerns's *In Her Prime: A New View of Middle-Aged Women,* 1985.

1752   **Solway, Jacqueline S.** "Middle-Aged Women in Bakgalagadi Society (Botswana)." In Virginia Kerns and Judith K. Brown, eds. *In Her Prime: New Views of Middle-Aged Women, 2d ed.* Urbana: U of Illinois Press, 1992. Chapter 5. *See also* Brown and Kerns's *In Her Prime: A New View of Middle-Aged Women,* 1985.

1753   **Udvardy, Monica.** "Fertility of the Post-Fertile: Concepts of Gender, Aging and Reproductive Health Among the Giriama of Kenya." *J of Cross-Cultural Gerontology.* Dordrecht 1992 7(40): 289–306.

1754   **Udvardy, Monica, and Maria Cattell.** "Gender, Aging and Power in Sub-Saharan Africa: Challenges and Puzzles." *J of Cross-Cultural Gerontology.* Dordrecht 1992 7(40): 275–288.

1755   **Ugwu, Ferdinana Ogbuehe.** *The Impact of Rural-Urban Youth Migration on Their Elderly Mothers in Imo State of Nigeria.* Fordham U, 1983. 47/06A.

1756   **Vanderburgh, Rosamond M.** "Tradition and Transition in the Lives of Ojibwa Women." *Resources for Feminist Research/Documentation sur la Recherche Féministe* July 1982 11(2): 218–219.

1757   **Vatuk, Sylvia.** "Sexuality and the Middle-Aged Woman in South Asia." In Virginia Kerns and Judith K. Brown, eds. *In Her Prime: New Views of Middle-Aged Women, 2d ed.* Urbana: U of Illinois Press, 1992. Chapter 11. *See also* Brown and Kerns's *In Her Prime: A New View of Middle-Aged Women,* 1985.

1758   **Vatuk, Sylvia.** "South Asian Cultural Conceptions of Sexuality." In Virginia Kerns and Judith K. Brown, eds. *In Her Prime: New Views of Middle-Aged Women, 2d ed.* Urbana: U of Illinois Press, 1992. Chapter 9. *See also* Brown and Kerns's *In Her Prime: A New View of Middle-Aged Women,* 1985.

1759   Wilbush, Joel. "Surveys of Climacteric Semiology in Non-Western Populations: A Critique." *Maturitas* 1985 7: 289–296.

1760   Wright, Anne Lucille. *Cultural Variability in the Experience of Menopause: A Comparison of Navajo and Western Data.* U of Arizona, 1980. 40/11A.

1761   Wright, Anne Lucille. "Variation in Navajo Menopause: Toward an Explanation." In Ann Mae Voda, et al, eds. *Changing Perspectives on Menopause.* Austin: U of Texas Press, 1982. Chapter 7.

1762   Yassin, Z., and R. D. Terry. "Health Characteristics of Rural Elderly Malay Females in Selected Villages in Negeri Sembilan." *Medical J of Malasia* December 1990 45(4): 310–318.

1763   "Young and Old Women" issue. *Connexions: An International Women's Q* 1983 #7.

INTERNATIONAL PERSPECTIVES

See also Cross-cultural and international perspectives in Subject Index.

1764   Akiyama, Hiroko, et al. "Exchange and Reciprocity Among Two Generations of Japanese and American Women." In Jay Sokolovsky, ed. *Cultural Context of Aging: Worldwide Perspectives.* New York: Bergin & Garvey, 1990. Chapter 6.

1765   Ashkanani, Zubaydah Ali M. *Middle-Aged Women in Kuwait: "Victims of Change."* U of Durham (United Kingdom), 1988. 49/09A.

1766   Barnett, Elyse A. *Perceptions of Menopause: Importance of Role Satisfaction in a Peruvian Town.* Stanford U, 1986. 47/04A.

1767   Bloom, Thelma Ruth. *Dark Encounters: A Study of Midlife Transformation in the Life of the Archetype Jacob and Selected Women in Israeli Society.* Union for Experimenting Colleges and Universities, 1985. 47/01B.

1768   Bushell, Alma, ed. *Yesterday's Daughters: Stories of Our Past by Women over 70.* Melbourne: Nelson, 1986. il.
    Bushell has gathered and edited biographical material by and about aged Australian women.

1769   Cain, Mead T. "The Activities of the Elderly in Rural Bangladesh." *Population Studies* 1991 45(3).
    Summarized with the title "The Daily Life of Older Women in Rural Bangladesh" in *Network News*, a newsletter of the Global Link for Midlife and Older Women.

1770   Campbell, Ruth, and Elaine M. Brody. "Women's Changing Roles and Help to the Elderly: Attitudes of Women in the United States and Japan." *Gerontologist* December 1985 25(6): 584–592.

1771   Cattell, Maria G. "Praise the Lord and Say No to Men: Older Women Empowering Themselves in Samia, Kenya." *J of Cross-Cultural Gerontology.* Dordrecht 1992 7(4): 307–330.

1772   Coopmans, Marianne, et al. *The Social and Economic Situation of Older Women in Europe.* Luxembourg: Office for Official Publications of the European Communities, 1989. bib.

Social and economic conditions of aged women residing in European Economic Community countries are reported in this relatively brief (92-page) document.

1773   **Cordero, Dolores.** "Old and Female in Latin America." *ISIS: Latin American and Caribbean Women's Health J* April-June 1991 2: 42–45.

1774   **Ecklein, Joan L.** "Women in the German Democratic Republic: Impact of Culture and Social Policy." In Janet Zollinger Giele, ed. *Women in the Middle Years: Current Knowledge and Directions for Research and Policy*. New York: Wiley, 1982. Chapter 5.

1775   **Esseveld, Johanna.** *Beyond Silence: Middle-Aged Women in the 1970s*. Philadelphia: Coronet, 1988.
This 276-page doctoral thesis was completed in Sweden at Lund University's Department of Sociology.

1776   **Gibson, Mary Jo.** "Older Women: An Overlooked Resource in Development." *Ageing International* Winter 1985–1986 12(4): 12–15, 20.

1777   **Goist, Doris Francis.** *"Will You Still Need Me? Will You Still Feed Me? When I'm 84."* Case Western Reserve U, 1980. 41/03A.

1778   **Gray, Alison.** *Springs in My Heels: Stories About Women and Change*. Wellington: B. Williams, 1991. il.
Using case studies and biography, Gray considers the psychological aspects of New Zealand's middle-aged women and the "mid-life crisis" experienced with career changes. Ten years earlier Gray authored with Rosemary Eleanor Barrington *The Smith Women: 100 New Zealand Women Talk About Their Lives* (A. H. and A. W. Reed), and in 1987 her novel *Stepping Out* was published by Allen & Unwin/Port Nicholson Press.

1779   "How Do Older Women Fare in the European Community? Cross-National Study." *Ageing International* June 1990 17(1): 38–42.

1780   **Kadom, Wajeha Thabit.** *A Comparison of Influences That Motivate a Desire in Women Participants Age 15–45 from Rural and Urban Areas of Iraq to Continue Their Education After Completing People's School*. Kansas State U, 1984. 46/01A.

1781   **Karkal, Malini.** "Differentials in Mortality by Sex [in India]." *Economic and Political Weekly* August 8, 1987 32: 1343–1347.

1782   **Kaufert, Patricia.** "Midlife in the Midwest: Canadian Women in Manitoba." In Virginia Kerns and Judith K. Brown, eds. *In Her Prime: New Views of Middle-Aged Women, 2d ed.* Urbana: U of Illinois Press, 1992. Chapter 12. *See also* Brown and Kerns's *In Her Prime: A New View of Middle-Aged Women*, 1985.

1783   **Kaufert, Patricia, and Margaret Lock.** "'What Are Women For?': Cultural Constructions of Menopausal Women in Japan and Canada." In Virginia Kerns and Judith K. Brown, eds. *In Her Prime: New Views of Middle-Aged Women, 2d ed.* Urbana: U of Illinois Press, 1992. Chapter 14. *See also* Brown and Kerns's *In Her Prime: A New View of Middle-Aged Women*, 1985.

1784   **Kawashima, Yoko.** "The Place and Role of [Middle-Aged] Female Workers in the Japanese Labor Market." *U.S. International Forum* 1987 10(6): 599–611.

1785   **Manna, Samita, and Panchali Chakravorty.** "Aged Widows of Bengal." *Man and Life Calcutta* 1991 17(1–2): 1–20.

1786   **Mercer, Susan D., and J. Dianne Garner.** "An International Overview of Aged Women." *J of Women & Aging* 1989 (1/2/3): 13–46.

1787   **Nair, Sobha B.,** 1959– . *Social Security and the Weaker Sections: A Study of Old Women Agricultural Workers in Kerala.* Delhi: Renaissance Publishing House, 1990. bib.
         The Kerala is a state located in the extreme southwest of the Republic of India.

1788   **Novero, Evangelina Pegenia.** *Perceptions of Filial Responsibility by Elderly Filipino Widows and Their Primary Caregivers.* Kansas State U, 1985. 46/06A.

1789   **Peace, Sheila.** *An International Perspective on the Status of Older Women.* Washington: International Federation on Ageing, 1981. bib.
         This background paper was prepared for the United Nations "Decade for Women" World Conference held in July 1980 in Copenhagen, Denmark.

1790   **Plath, David W.** *Long Engagements: Maturity in Modern Japan.* Stanford U Press, 1980. index.
         Plath based this social science work on 1972 interviews of middle-class, middle-aged Japanese women and men in the mainly urban Osaka-Kobe region. Two of the four "characters" in the life histories he draws are women—a model housewife and a woman who is not. As in many other locales, she is perceived as combining motherhood with a full-time job ("career"). The men are a "businessman" and a "playboy."

1791   **Rhodes, Linda M.** "Women Aging: Address Before the United Nations NGO Committee on Aging at the Secretariat, New York, January 7, 1982." *Resources for Feminist Research/Documentation sur la Recherche Féministe* July 1982 11(2): 205–208.

1792   **Rix, Sara E.** "Older Women: Making a Difference in Development." *Ageing International* March 1992 19(10): 1–11.

1793   **Rozee, Patricia D., and Gretchen VanBoemel.** "The Psychological Effects of War Trauma and Abuse on Older Cambodian Refugee Women." *Women & Therapy* 1989 8(4): 23–50.

1794   **Rudkin-Miniot, Laura Louise.** *Gender Differences in Well-Being Among the Elderly of Java, Indonesia.* Princeton U, 1992. 53/01A.

1795   **Saraceno, Chiara.** "Changes in Life-Course Patterns and Behavior of Three Cohorts of Italian Women." *Signs* Spring 1991 16: 502–521.

1796   **Tanaka, Kazuko.** *Women, Work and Family in Japan: A Life Cycle Perspective.* U of Iowa, 1989. 49/04A.

1797   **Tanaka, Ukiko, ed.** *To Live and to Write: Selections by Japanese Women Writers, 1931–1938.* Seattle: Seal Press, 1987. il.
         Seal Press's Women in Translation Series includes these selections by nine twentieth-century Japanese literary women and introductory biographical essays by Dr. Tanaka. An earlier book had caused comments about a depressing picture for Japanese women. She wishes to reintroduce readers to Japanese women who are strong, independent individuals determined to shape their own futures, and has selected writers ranging from 1913: Tamura Toshiko (1884–1945), "A Woman Writer," to 1937: Okamoto Kanoko (1889–1939), "A Floral Pageant."

1798   **Taub, Beverly Ruth.** *Female Identity Through the Life Cycle in the Short Fiction of Katherine Mansfield, Maria Luisa Bombal, and Clarice Lispector. (New Zealand, Chile, Brazil).* U of Texas at Austin, 1987. 49/03A.

1799   Todd, Judith, et al. "Women Growing Stronger with Age: The Effect of Status in the United States and Kenya." *Psychology of Women Q* December 1990 14(4): 567–577.

1800   **"UN Examines Vulnerability Among Older Women."** *Network News* (of the Global Link for Midlife and Older Women) July 1991 6(1): 1–5.

1801   **Vatuk, Sylvia.** "The Aging Woman in India: Self-Perceptions and Changing Roles." In Alfred deSouza, ed. *Women in Contemporary India: Traditional Images and Changing Roles, 2d rev. ed.* New Delhi: Manohar, 1980. Chapter 12.

1802   **Vlassoff, Carol.** "The Value of Sons in an Indian Village: How Widows See It." *Population Studies* 1990 44. *See also* "The Role of Sons in Providing Economic Security in Old Age in India." *Network News* (a newsletter of the Global Link for Midlife and Older Women) July 1991 6(1): 15.

1803   **Wils, Anne Babette, and Douglas A. Wolf.** "Varieties of Independent Living: Older Women in the Netherlands." *Genus Rome* 1992 48(1/2): 183–197.

1804   **Yee, Barbara W. K.** *Control in British and Asian Elderly Women.* U of Denver, 1982. 43/03B.

10
Creativity and Productivity

The poor lady, having passed the prime of her years in gaiety and company . . . and having all this while been so over-careful of her body, that she had no time to improve her mind, which therefore affords her to safe retreat, now she meets with disappointments abroad, and growing every day more and more sensible that the respect which used to be paid her decays as fast as her beauty. . . .

Mary Astell, 1666–1731,
From "A Serious Proposal to the Ladies for the
Advancement of Their True and Greatest Interest" (1694)

The Arts: 1805–1814
Creativity: 1815–1819
Education: 1820–1844
History: 1845–1867
Humor: 1868–1876
Religion; Spirituality; Theology: 1877–1909

THE ARTS
See also this chapter: Creativity (1815–1819).

1805   **Apthorp, Elaine Sargent.** *The Artist at the Family Reunion: Visions of the Creative Life in the Narrative Technique of Willa Cather, Sarah Orne Jewett, Mary Wilkins Freeman, and Dorothy Canfield Fisher.* U of California, Berkeley, 1986. 47/07A.

1806   **Berman, Avis; photographs by Nancy Rica Scheff.** "When Artists Grow Old." *ARTnews* December 1983 82(10): 76–83.
        Includes Isabel Bishop, Alice Neel, Louise Nevelson.

1807   **Fadiman, Anne.** "American Dreamer: Elizabeth Layton [1900–]: Portrait of the Artist as an Old Woman." *Life* March 1987 10(3): 21–24.
        Other articles about Layton include "Reflections of Genius," *Saturday Review* January/February 1984 10: 22–25; "Sketches from Life . . . ," *American Artist* November 1983 47: 108; and "Grandma Layton's Drawings Don't Just Reflect a Big Talent—They've Cured Her 40-Year Depression," *People Weekly* February 24, 1986 25: 93–94. *See also* #71.

1808   **Hills, Patricia.** *Alice Neel.* New York: Abrams, 1983. bib, il, index.
        American artist Alice Hartley Neel lived from 1900–1984. She has been referred to as "quintessential Bohemian." She was a representational painter known for portraits and having had the first major exhibition in Moscow, in 1981.

1809   **Kallir, Jane.** *Grandma Moses: The Artist Behind the Myth.* New York: Clarkson Potter, 1982. bib, index.

American folk artist Anna Mary Robertson Moses (1860–1961) "always wanted to be independent." After bearing ten children, raising the five survivors, and working on the farm until she was 78, she had some time of her own to paint again. Chapter 5, "Artistic Growth," considers her continuing development and late style.

1810   **Lipman, Jean,** 1909– . *Nevelson's World.* New York: Hudson Hills Press, 1983. bib, il, index.

American sculptor Louise Berliawsky Nevelson (1899–1988) was born in Russia and emigrated to the United States. She has been called a "wood nymph and high priest of sculpture" (*Ms.* January/February 1989 17: 95). Her long wait for recognition began when she left her husband of eleven years and, at 32, apprenticed with painter Diego Rivera, taught art, and sculpted.

1811   **Noggle, Anne,** 1922– . *Silver Lining.* U of New Mexico Press, 1983.

The text for Noggle's photographs and an essay are provided by Janice Zita Grover. Clearly, Noggle is concerned with age, and many of these photographs are portraits of women members of her family and of herself. She is a pilot and photographer.

1812   **O'Bradovich, Donica.** "Artist [Doris Chase, 1923–] Creates New Video Style." *New Directions for Women* January-February 1987 16(1): 6.

1813   **Painter, Charlotte.** *Gifts of Age: Portraits and Essays of 32 Remarkable Women.* San Francisco: Chronicle Books, 1985. il, index.

Pamela Valois's photo-portraits of these California women—all over 65 and, at the time, living—are accompanied by Painter's comments. They include: Louise M. Davies, born in 1900, "Volunteer"; Margaret Murdock, born 1894, "Ringing Changes"; Julia Child, born 1912, "Marriage"; Monika Kehoe, born 1909, "The Company of Women"; Haruko Obata, born 1893, "The Way of the Flower"; Joan Bridges Baez, born 1913, "Children of War"; Tish Sommers, born 1914, "Care-Giving"; Frances Mary Albrier, born 1898, "Breaking Ground"; and Martha St. John, born 1918, "Healing."

1814   **Tate, Claudia, ed.** *Black Women Writers at Work.* New York: Continuum, 1983. Published in 1985 outside the United States by Oldcastle Books.

These African-American women writers are briefly introduced, with accompanying interviews and criticism. They include: Maya Angelou, born in 1928; Toni Cade Bambara, born 1931; Gwendolyn Brooks, born 1917, first black woman to receive a Pulitzer Prize for her poetry, "Annie Allen"; Alexis Deveaux, born 1948; Nikki Giovanni, born 1943; Kristin Hunter, born 1931; Gayl Jones, born 1949; Audre Lorde, born 1934; Toni Morrison, born 1931; Sonia Sanchez, born 1934; Ntozake Shange, born 1949; Alice Walker, born 1944; Dr. Margaret Abigail Walter, born 1915; and Shirley Anne Williams, born 1944.

CREATIVITY

See also Chapter 4: Work; Employment and Unemployment; "Women's Work"; "Working Mothers" (846–895); this chapter: History (1845–1867); Chapter 11.

1815   **Hoyt, Margaret Jenne.** *Language Production Skills of High-Functioning Elderly Women.* Boston U, 1989. 50/05A.

1816   **Lenz, Karen Chapman.** *Women Authors: Age-Related Changes in Productivity, Life Satisfaction, and Multiple Roles.* Claremont Graduate School, 1985. 46/09A.

1817   Mazo-Calif, Karyn, et al. *Among Us: A Collection of Writings.* Altadena: Peace Ventures Press, 1989.

The essays, poems, and short fiction collected here were written by five women (Mazo-Calif, Ann Melbye, Marilyn Reynolds, Anne Scott, and Frances B. White) who first met through a writers' program. All are "late bloomers" of varied experiences and consider themselves to be "common."

1818   Vaillant, George E., and Caroline O. Vaillant. "Determinants and Consequences of Creativity in a Cohort of Gifted Women." *Psychology of Women Q* December 1990 14(4): 607–616.

1819   Zeidenstein, Sondra, ed. *A Wider Giving: Women Writing After a Long Silence.* Goshen: Chicory Blue Press, 1988.

Dr. Zeidenstein's small literary press frequently publishes anthologies of mature women's works. These are middle-aged women, and their mostly reprinted poetry, fiction, and personal narratives are accompanied by autobiographical material.

EDUCATION

See also Chapter 6: Reentry; Resuming Education and Employment (1269–1349).

1820   Abel, Emily, guest ed. "Teaching About *Women and Aging*" issue. *Women's Studies Q* Spring/Summer 1989 17(1/2).

1821   Barnes, Carol Elizabeth M. *Faculty Attitudes Toward Older Adult Learners.* Miami U, 1981. 43/02A.

1822   Boegeman, Margaret. "Teaching Creative Writing to Older Women." *Women's Studies Q* Spring/Summer 1989 17 (1/2): 48–55.

1823   Cornwall, Katharine K. "Forgotten Students: Women's Experience in a Proprietary School." *Educational Gerontology* March-April 1991 17(2): 175–186.

1824   Davenport, Judith Ann. *Learning Style and Its Relationship to Sex, Age, and Educational Attainment Among Wyoming Elderhostel Participants.* U of Wyoming, 1985. 46/12A.

1825   Deaton, Anne Simonetti. *Work-Related Education Among Older Adults: Case Studies of Selected Older Women in Urban Areas.* Virginia Polytechnic Institute and State U, 1988. 49/04A.

1826   DeCosta, Sandra Bradford. "Head Start—Late Start: Retrieving Education and Identity." *Educational Gerontology* March-April 1991 17(2): 123–139.

1827   Gerlach, Jeanne, guest ed. "Women, Education, and Aging" issue. *Educational Gerontology* March-April 1991 17(2).

Contents are analyzed in *Women and Aging: A Guide to the Literature.*

1828   Harold, Sharon. "Education in Later Life: The Case of Older Women." *Educational Gerontology* July-August 1992 18(5): 511–527.

1829   Hart, Betty L. "Never Too Young, Never Too Old to Teach: Women, Writing, and Aging." *Educational Gerontology* March-April 1991 17(2): 187–201.

1830   Henshaw, Diana Monroe. *An Analysis of Barriers to Post-Secondary Educational Participation by Mature Women.* North Carolina State U at Raleigh, 1980. 41/03A.

1831   Hooyman, Nancy R. "Older Women and Social Work Curricula." In Diane S. Burden and Naomi Gottlieb, eds. *The Woman Client: Providing Human Services in a Changing World.* New York: Tavistock, 1987. Chapter 21.

1832   Hooyman, Nancy R., et al, eds. *Women Working Together: A Collection of Course Syllabi About Women from Schools of Social Work.* Batesville: Council on Social Work Education, 1988.

Thirteen women concerned about the potential of older women compiled these syllabi under the auspices of the Commission on the Role and Status of Women in Social Work Education. They deal with American social work practice, treatment, therapy, health care, and public policy. Other syllabi sources useful in preparation of relevant courses, units, workshops and seminars include:

- **Auger, Jeanette A.** "The Sociology of Aging." In *Resources for Feminist Research/Documentation sur la Recherche Féministe* July 1982 11(2): 244–246.
- **Connecticut U School of Social Work, Storrs.** "The Older Woman." In *Resources for Feminist Research/Documentation sur la Recherche Féministe* July 1982 11(2): 249–252.
- **Fisher, Joy.** "The Lesbian Novel." In Margaret Cruikshank, ed. *Lesbian Studies.* Old Westbury: Feminist Press, 1982. 222–225.
- **Jacobs, Ruth Harriet,** 1924– . *Older Women: Surviving and Thriving.* (Manual outlining twelve workshop sessions with exercises; developed under the sponsorship of the Gerontology Institute of the U of Massachusetts College of Public and Community Service, Boston.) 1986. (Family Service of America, 11700 West Lake Park Drive, Milwaukee, WI 53224.)
- **National Council on the Aging.** *Facing Our Future.* (Women's Programs, 600 Maryland Avenue, West Wing 100, S.W., Washington, D.C. 20024.)
- **Sorgman, Margo L., and Marilou Sorensen.** "Ageism: A Course of Study." *Theory into Practice* Spring 1984 23: 117–123.
- **Storrie, Kathleen, and John Thompson.** "The Sociology of Aging." In *Resources for Feminist Research/Documentation sur la Recherche Féministe* July 1982 11(2): 247–248.

1833   Iandoli, Ce Ce Claire. *Middle-Aged Women's Studies Professors: A Comparative Analysis of Fifteen Educators' Perceptions of Their Personal and Professional Changes.* Harvard U, 1984. 45/07A.

1834   Kanter, Sandra. "The Value of the College Degree for Older Women Graduates." *Innovative Higher Education* Spring-Summer 1989 13(2): 90–105.

1835   Papalia-Finlay, Diane, et al. "Attitudes of Older Women Toward Continuing Adult Education at the University Level: Implications for Program Curriculum Development." *Educational Gerontology* September-October 1981 7(2/3): 159–166.

1836   Rathbone-McCuan, Eloise. "Older Women, Mental Health and Social Work Education." *J of Education for Social Work* 1984 20: 33–41.

1837   Starks, Gretchen Ann. *Adult [Reentry] Female Student Retention in [Rural] Community Colleges: Findings from Exceptional Case Studies.* Syracuse U, 1989. 50/06A.

1838   Sullivan, Kathleen McCann. *Meeting Educational Needs of Women in Midlife Through Postsecondary Institutional Planning.* U of Mississippi, 1981. 42/02A.

1839   **Turner, Barbara Formanek, and Catherine G. Adams.** "Teaching About the Sexuality of Older Women." *Women's Studies Q* Winter 1984 12(4): 34–35.

1840   **Villarreal, Elias Esteban.** *The Motivational Factors of Senior Citizens Enrolled in Noncredit Avocational Continuing Education Courses in the Public Community Colleges in Texas.* East Texas State U, 1984. 45/08A.

1841   **Walker, Joanna.** "Older Women and Later Life Learning." *Adults Learning (England)* March 1991 2(7): 209–210.

1842   **Wheeler, Helen Rippier,** 1926– . "A Multidisciplinary Facts on Women's Aging Quiz to Enhance Awareness." *J of Women & Aging.* 1990 2(4): 91–107.

See also Chapter 13, "Researching." And for information about Professor Erdman Palmore's Facts on Aging Quiz, see his:

- "Facts on Aging: A Short Quiz." *Gerontologist* 1977 17: 315–320.
- "The Facts on Aging Quiz: A Review of Findings." *Gerontologist* 1981 21: 431–447.
- "What Do You Know About Aging?" In Harold J. Wershow, ed. *Controversial Issues in Gerontology.* New York: Springer, 1981. Chapter 1.
- "The Facts on Aging Quiz: A Handbook of Uses and Results." New York: Springer, 1988.

1843   **Whitefield, Patricia T.** *Patterns of Success in Non-Traditionally Prepared Mature Women Educational Leaders: Six Case Studies.* Brigham Young U, 1984. 46/01A.

1844   **Wood, Vivian.** "Older Women and Education." ERIC, 1980. ED #199576. 13 pages.

HISTORY
See also Chapter 11.

1845   **Baldwin, Deborah J.** "A Successful Search for Security: Arizona Pioneer Society Widows." In Arlene Scadron, ed. *On Their Own: Widows and Widowhood in the American Southwest, 1848–1939.* Champaign: U of Illinois Press, 1988. Chapter 9.

1846   **Bendremer, Jutta.** "Female Survivors of the Holocaust: Heroines All." *Educational Gerontology* March-April 1991 17(21): 83–95.

1847   **Bever, Edward.** "Old Age and Witchcraft in Early Modern Europe." In Peter N. Stearns. *Old Age in Preindustrial Society.* New York: Holmes & Meir, 1982. 150–190.

1848   **Conrad, Margaret.** "No Discharge in This War: A Note on the History of Women and Aging." In *Resources for Feminist Research/Documentation sur la Recherche Féministe.* July 1982 11(2): 216–217.

1849   **Feinson, Marjorie Chary.** "Where Are the Women in the History of Aging? [review essay]." *Social Science History* Fall 1985 9(4): 429–452.

1850   **Gonzalez, Deena J.** "The Widowed Women of Santa Fe: Assessment on the Lives of an Unmarried Population, 1850–1880." In Arlene Scadron, ed. *On Their Own: Widows and Widowhood in the American Southwest, 1848–1939.* Champaign: U of Illinois Press, 1988. Chapter 3.

1851   **Goodfriend, Joyce D.** "The Struggle for Survival: Widows in Denver, 1880–1912." In Arlene Scadron, ed. *On Their Own: Widows and Widowhood in the American Southwest, 1848–1939.* Champaign: U of Illinois Press, 1988. Chapter 7.

1852   **Guy, Donna J.** "The Economics of Widowhood in Arizona, 1890–1940." In Arlene Scadron, ed. *On Their Own: Widows and Widowhood in the American Southwest, 1848–1939.* Champaign: U of Illinois Press, 1988. Chapter 8.

1853   **Joyce, Rosemary Owsley.** *A Woman's Place: The Life History of a Rural Ohio Grandmother [Sarah Flynn Penfield].* Ohio State U, 1980. 41/04A.

1854   **Kehara, Elizabeth Slack.** *A Comparison of Sociopolitical Attitudes of Older Urban Women: The 1910–1924 Cohorts.* Portland State U, 1991. 52/08A.

1855   **Kennedy, Patricia Scileppi, and Gloria Hartmann O'Shields, eds.** *We Shall Be Heard: Women Speakers of America, 1828–Present.* Dubuque: Kendall/Hunt, 1983. bib, il, index.

 This anthology of public speeches and "significant" women orators consists of: nine early period pioneers (e.g., Frances Wright's July 4, 1828 address—she was 33 at the time); ten representatives from the Civil War to the turn of the century; and nine since World War I (e.g., Elisabeth Kubler-Ross's 1976 "Death Does Not Exist," when she was 50).

1856   **Luchetti, Cathy,** 1945– , **and Carol Olwell,** 1944– . *Women of the West.* St. George: Antelope Island Press, 1982. bib, il.

 Here are eleven women who ranged in age from 47 to 93 and whose lives spanned the nineteenth and twentieth centuries. Many photographs and their narratives and correspondence enhance the account of the American history they helped to make.

1857   **Maples, Donna Elaine.** *Building a Literary Heritage: A Study of Three Generations of Pioneer Women, 1880–1930.* U of Missouri, Columbia, 1988. 50/04A.

1858   **McNamara, Mary, and Katherine Burkett.** "Reviewing 1987 . . . the Laughter, Tears, and Triumphs!" *Ms. Magazine* January 1988 16(7): 34–37.

 ("New York's Oldest Undercover Operative Comes Out of the Shadows—81-Year-Old Muriel Clark . . . Hulda Crooks, 91, Reaches the Top of Mount Fuji . . . Runner Priscilla Welch Wins the Women's Division of the New York Marathon—Oldest Person Ever to Win . . . ")

1859   **Moore, Sandra Lynne Smith.** *Continuity and Change in Women: A Ten-Year Study of Forty-One Women Aged 35–65.* U of Kansas, 1988. 50/05A.

1860   **Myres, Sandra L., ed.** *Ho For California! Women's Overland Diaries from the Huntington Library.* San Marino: Huntington Library, 1980.

 Myres has edited and annotated some of the pioneer women's diaries in the collection of the Henry E. Huntington Library and Art Gallery (1151 Oxford Road, San Marino, California 91108). Included are: "The Isthmus of Panama, 1849: A Diary Kept by Mrs. Jane McDougal," who died in 1862. "The California Trail, 1850: A Journal of Mary Stuart Bailey, 1852," who lived from 1830 to 1890. "A Trip Across the Plains in an Ox Cart, 1857" by H. Carpenter—Helen McCowen Carpenter lived from 1838 to 1917. "The Southwestern Trails, 1869–1870 by H. Bunyard"—Harriet Bunyard, "a young single woman," lived from 1850 to 1900. "Diary of a Young Girl, 1869." And the 1870 "Journal" of M. Shrode—Maria Hargrave Shrode was a "middle-aged wife and mother."

1861   O'Connell, Agnes N., and Nancy Felipe Russo, 1943– , eds. *Models of Achievement: Reflections of Eminent Women in Psychology, Volume 2.* Hillsboro: Erlbaum, 1988. bib, index. The first volume of this title was published by Columbia U Press in 1983.

1862   **Premo, Terri L.** *Winter Friends: Women Growing Old in the New Republic, 1785–1835, rev. and enl. ed.* Urbana: U of Illinois Press, 1990. bib, il, index.

Originally titled *Women Growing Old in the New Republic: Personal Responses to Old Age, 1785–1835* and prepared as Premo's Ph.D. dissertation (U of Cincinnati, 1983. 44/06A). To establish the important link between women's history and the history of aging, Premo examined "records from the 50 years following the Revolution, a period traditionally acknowledged as critical in the development of early American society." Her study does not rely on data that imply a standard of power based on political office-holding or possession of property. "Kinship ties, friendships between women, and strong moral and spiritual beliefs comprise the dominant value system of the women studied here . . . historians can no longer be blind to the presence of women in the history of old age or of old women in feminist scholarship. From these personal documents, we learn the significance of continuity and connection in the lives of aging women . . . " (pp. 3–4).

1863   **Schilpp, Madelon Golden, and Sharon M. Murphy.** *Great Women of the Press.* Carbondale: Southern Illinois U Press, 1983. bib, index.

Many of these eighteen journalists from America's past lived unusually long lives and first achieved in mid-life. Some, like muckraker Ida Minerva Tarbell (1857–1944), are well known; others, like *Boston Transcript* editor Cornelia Walter (1813–1898), are less familiar names.

1864   **Somers, Anne R.** "Toward a Female Gerontocracy? Current Social Trends." In Marie R. Haug, et al, eds. *The Physical and Mental Health of Aged Women.* New York: Springer, 1985. Chapter 2.

1865   **Stanley, Autumn.** "Invention Begins at Forty: Older Women of the 19th Century as Inventors." *J of Women & Aging* 1990 2(2): 133–151.

1866   **Stearns, Peter N.** "Old Women: Some Historical Observations." *J of Family History* Spring 1980 5: 44–57.

1867   **Waciega, Lisa Wilson.** *Widowhood and Womanhood in Early America: The Experience of Women in Philadelphia and Chester Counties, 1750–1850 (Pennsylvania).* Temple U, 1986. 47/08A.

Humor

Humor *may refer here to supposedly humorous depiction of females in terms of their age and sex/gender, or to humor created by women—so-called women's humor, or to feminist humor about females in terms of their age. Some information can be found using the following descriptors and wordings in libraries' card and online catalogs and other data bases:*

American wit and humor, pictorial
Feminism—caricatures and cartoons
Sex customs—caricatures and cartoons
Women—caricatures and cartoons

Addition of certain subject subdivisions (in the manner of caricatures and cartoons, *above) can also be productive, e.g.:*

... —anecdotes
... —anecdotes, facetiae, satire, etc.
... —humor
... —personal narratives

See also Chapter 8: Media; Image; Stereotypes (1635–1679).

1868   **Barrick, Ann Louise J.** *Aging and Emotion: Ratings of Cartoons and the Survey of the Quality of Life of Adult Men and Women.* Ball State U, 1986. 47/06B.

1869   **Debord, Beverly Cardwell.** *The Widow in Restoration Comedy.* West Virginia U, 1983. 44/04A.

1870   **Diller, Phyllis Driver,** 1917– . *The Joys of Aging and How to Avoid Them: Can Sex Keep You Young?* New York: Doubleday, 1981. il.
    American commedian and actor Diller broke into comedy in mid-life, initially known for her outrageous appearance and stories about spouse "Fang." She is also a concert pianist, identified by *Who's Who of American Women* as "actress, authoress."

1871   **Hollander, Nicole.** *The Whole Enchilada: A Spicy Collection of Sylvia's Best.* New York: St. Martin's, 1986. il.
    Hollander is probably best known for her "Sylvia" comic strip. Sixteen pages of this feminist cartoon collection about middle-aged women are in color.

1872   **Scobey, Joan.** *I'm a Stranger Here Myself: The Panic (and Pleasure) of Middle Age.* New York: St. Martin's, 1984.
    The much-used title is derived from poet-humorist Ogden Nash via Sinclair Lewis. Publishers seem to prefer book titles that suggest a genderless middle-age. There is no hint from the table of contents that the book encompasses women's middle-aging or is a "basically serious investigation," as the publisher describes it. The assumption is that middle-aged women are married with kids. Scobey lives in suburban New York, writes for women's magazines, and has experienced mid-life as a woman.

1873   **Weaver, Frances.** *The Girls with the Grandmother Faces: Single and Sixty Is Not for Sissies.* Lake George: Century One Press, 1987.
    Century One Press's address is POB 129, Lake George, NY 12845. The "girls" are widows, whose lifestyles are conveyed as part of twentieth-century American biographical humor despite their positive and serious concerns with self-fulfillment.

1874   **White, Betty,** 1924?– . *Betty White in Person.* New York: Doubleday, 1987.
    White played Sue Ann Nivins on the "Mary Tyler Moore Show" from 1970 to 1977 and Rose Nyland on "Golden Girls" beginning in 1985. (Biography Almanac lists her as Mrs. Allen Ludden.) Her personal narrative may be marketed as humor, but this is a charming, intelligent person.

1875   **Wilt, Judith.** "The Laughter of Maidens, the Cackle of Matriarchs: Notes on the Collision Between Comedy and Feminism." In Janet Todd, ed. *Gender and Literary Voice.* New York: Holmes & Meier, 1980. 173–196.

1876   **Wyse, Lois.** *Funny, You Don't Look Like a Grandmother.* New York: Crown, 1990. il.

Also available in large type. "In the spirit of Erma Bombeck, advertising executive/grandmother Lois Wyse shares anecdotes about the joys of being a grandmother in the 90s," says her publisher.

RELIGION; SPIRITUALITY; THEOLOGY
See also Chapter 7: Crones (1350–1356).

1877   **Atkinson, Bruce Earl.** *Religious Maturity and Psychological Distress Among Older Christian Women.* Fuller Theological Seminary, 1986. 47/10B.

1878   **Beecher, Maureen Ursenbach, et al.** "Widowhood Among the Mormons: The Personal Accounts." In Arlene Scadron, ed. *On Their Own: Widows and Widowhood in the American Southwest, 1848–1939.* Champaign: U of Illinois Press, 1988. Chapter 4.

1879   **Bowman, Meg, and Diane Haywood, eds.** *Readings for Older Women: A Compilation of Wit and Wisdom.* San Jose: Hot Flash Press, 1984. il, index.
Hot Flash Press's address is POB 21506, San Jose, CA 95151. Sponsored by the Women and Religion Task Force, a committee of the Pacific Central District, Unitarian Universalist Association, this "compilation of wit and wisdom" consists of writings of women and men under the rubrics of ageism, growing old gracefully, happiness, humor, living and dying, rites and rituals, sisterhood, social change, and wisdom and serenity. Bowman is a member of the San Jose State University sociology faculty; she has also authored *Readings for Women's Programs: Memorial Services for Women.*

1880   **Buchanan, Constance H.** "The Fall of Icarus: Gender, Religion and the Aging Society." In Clarisa W. Atkinson, et al, eds. *Shaping New Vision: Gender and Values in American Culture.* Ann Arbor: UMI Research Press, 1987. 169–190.

1881   **Conway, James Floyd.** *Early Mid-Life Women: A Study of Self-Reported Mid-Life Crisis Among Evangelical Women Age 34–45 and Their Likelihood to Participate in Learning Experiences.* U of Illinois at Urbana-Champaign, 1987. 48/07A.

1882   **Curtis, Linda Laverne Kroamer.** *Life Satisfaction of Older Catholic Sisters: A Study of Four Communities.* Oklahoma State U, 1991. 52/11A.

1883   **Daniewicz, M. S. W.** "Change, Resources and Self-Esteem in a Community of Women Religious." *J of Women & Aging* 1991 3(1): 71–91.

1884   **Demetrakopoulos, Stephanie,** 1937– . *Listening to Our Bodies: The Rebirth of Feminine Wisdom.* Boston: Beacon Press, 1983. bib, index.
The concern here is with literature as an interdisciplinary vehicle for knowing about the human life cycle. Included are "Femininity as Entrapment: The Older Woman in Toni Morrison's *Song of Solomon*" (Chapter 7) and "The Older Woman as Matriarch" (Chapter 4, about mid-life crises).

1885   **Dobbie, Barbara Jean.** *The Spiritual Experience of Women in Midlife Transition Who Are Active Members of the United Church of Canada.* Union for Experimenting Colleges and Universities, 1988. 50/04B.

1886   **Downey, Dorothy Jean.** *Attitudes Toward Aging and Retirement of Retired and Non-Retired Women Religious in Four Midwestern States.* Ohio State U, 1981. 42/07A.

1887   **Fine, Irene.** *Midlife and Its Rite of Passage Ceremony.* San Diego: Women's Institute for Continuing Jewish Education, 1983. bib, il.
Included is a "Midlife Celebration" by Bonnie Feinman.

1888   **Fischbacher-McCrae, Elise.** *The Aging Process for Women: Focus on the Influence of Spirituality on Adaptation.* Union for Experimenting Colleges and Universities, 1988. 50/03A.

1889   **Herman, Shirley Jean.** *Enabling Relationships Between Female Preteenagers and Elderly Women in the Congregation.* Drew U, 1986. 47/10A.

1890   **Junkkari, Kaija.** *Investigation of Dialogical Model Betweeen Feminist Analytical Psychology and Feminist Theology with Women in Midlife Transition.* Pacific School of Religion, 1991. bib.
This 270-page doctoral project is in the collection of the Graduate Theological Union, Berkeley, California.

1891   **Loewen, Irene Leona.** *Widowhood: The Relationship Between Religious Orientation and Adjustment to the Loss of a Spouse.* California School of Professional Psychology, Fresno, 1985. 45/12B.

1892   **Lytle, Vanita Louise.** *Levels of Religiosity in Relationship to Death Anxiety in Elderly Black and White Females.* George Peabody College for Teachers of Vanderbilt U, 1986. 47/06A.

1893   **Magee, James Joseph.** *Selected Predictors of Life Satisfaction Among Retired Nuns.* Fordham U, 1984. 47/06A.

1894   **Margraff, Rita L.** "Aging: Religious Sisters Facing the Future." In Marilyn J. Bell, ed. *Women as Elders: Images, Visions, and Issues.* New York: Haworth Press, 1986. 35–49.

1895   **McCain, Marian Van Eyk.** *Blood into Wisdom: The Spiritual Significance of Menopause.* California Institute of Integral Studies, 1989. M.A. thesis.

1896   **McGloshen, Thomas Hilton.** *Factors Related to the Psychological Well-Being of Elderly Recent Widows.* Ohio State U, 1985. 46/06A.

1897   **Repka, Frances Marie.** *The Effects of an Experiential Group Treatment on the Life Satisfaction of Female Religious Retirees.* U of Cincinnati, 1987. 48/03A.

1898   **Rosik, Christopher Hastings.** *The Impact of Religious Orientation in Conjugal Bereavement Among the Elderly.* Fuller Theological Seminary, 1986. 47/08B.

1899   **Rozzano, Mary Janet.** *An Exploratory Study of Personal Spirituality and Its Importance in the Lives of Older Women.* San Jose State U, 1991. M.S. thesis.

1900   **Ruggeri, Marianne T.** *The Psychological Development of Women Religious Aged 45 to 55.* Antioch U New England Graduate School, 1988. 49/06B.

1901   **Sered, Susan Starr.** *Women as Ritual Experts: The Religious Lives of Elderly Jewish Women in Jerusalem.* New York: Oxford U Press, 1992. bib, index.
Sered is on the Department of Sociology and Anthropology faculty of Bar Ilan University in Israel. She considers the customs and practices of religious life of aged Kurdish Jewish women in Jerusalem.

1902   **Sered, Susan Starr.** "Women, Religion, and Modernization: Tradition and Transformation Among Elderly Jews in Israel." *American Anthropologist* June 1990 92(2): 306–318.

1903   Stevenson, Robert Thompson. *The Relationship Between Religiosity and Attitudes of Nurse's Aides Toward Sexual Expression by Older Adults in Nursing Homes.* U of Georgia, 1983. 44/06A.

1904   Thurston, Bonnie Bowman. *The Widows—a Women's Ministry in the Early Church.* Minneapolis: Fortress Press, 1989. bib.

The author, a West Virginia Jesuit College faculty member, examines the position of Christian widows from the time of Jesus to A.D. 325, aiming "to draw the modern church's attention to the high regard in which the widows of the early church were held and to the material help they received" (p. 7). She begins with 1983 magazine articles reporting elderly women the fastest growing poverty group and the reality she sees of "this very group of older women who were carrying the primary burden of service to and support of their congregations."

1905   Willems, Elizabeth L. *Ethics of Trust: Theological and Psychological Perspectives on Midlife Women.* Marquette U, 1986. 47/05A.

1906   Wolf, Mary Alice. "The Crisis of Legacy: Life Review Interviews with Elderly Women Religious." *J of Women & Aging* 1990 2(3): 67–79.

1907   Wolf, Mary Alice. "Growth and Development with Older Women Religious: An Exploration in Life Review." *Lifelong Learning* January 1986 9(4): 7–10.

1908   Yeager, Garry Lynn. *Developing a Manual for Ministering with a Congregation Having Widowed, Separated or Divorced Persons.* Drew U, 1982. 43/04A.

1909   Yeck, Marla Ann. *Effect of Career Status on the Retirement Needs of Women Religious.* Michigan State U, 1985. 46/12A.

11

Biography:
Diaries, Journals, Letters, Memoirs, Oral Histories and Testimonies, Personal Narratives

A sheltered life can be a daring life as well. For all serious daring starts from within.

Eudora Welty, 1909– . (1983)

Biography and Autobiography: 1910–1982
Oral History: 1983–1990
Uses and Critical Studies of Biography: 1991–2002

BIOGRAPHY AND AUTOBIOGRAPHY

Publications within this section are arranged alphabetically by the subjects' surnames, i.e., by the biographees' last names. See also subjects' names within Subject Index.

1910   **Deegan, Mary Jo,** 1948– . *Jane Addams and the Men of the Chicago School, 1892–1918.* New Brunswick: Transaction Books, 1988. bib, il, index.
American settlement founder and social reformer Jane Addams (1860–1935) was influential in the development of sociology at the University of Chicago. This scholarly work documents a dual, sex-stratified network in the field.

1911   **Angelou, Maya,** 1928– . *The Heart of a Woman.* New York: Bantam, 1981.
In her fourth autobiographical work, dedicated to her grandson, we see the mature Angelou, one of the few women members of the Directors Guild. *See also* #1814.

1912   **Cott, Nancy F., ed.** *A Woman Making History: Mary Ritter Beard Through Her Letters.* New Haven: Yale U Press, 1991. bib, index.
Mary Ritter Beard (1876–1958) is often cited as the founder of the modern field of women's history. This work attempts to restore her place in history through her private letters although against her own wishes. Beginning with the suffrage years, the first letter is dated January 1, 1912, when she was 36 years old; the last, January 26, 1955. In 1951 she records the Harvard University Librarian (i.e., the director) asking how many books she thinks the library would need to cover the history of women: Mr. Metcalf wonders whether 5,000 would be necessary! *See also* #1630.

1913   **Beauvoir, Simone de,** 1908–1986. *A Very Easy Death.* Translated from the French by Patrick O'Brian. New York: Pantheon, 1985.

Originally published in 1965, the day-by-day recounting of her mother's death is a translation of *Une Mort Tres Douce*. Beauvoir describes the final weeks and her own responses to death and the experience of dying.

1914   **Evans, Mary.** "Simone de Beauvoir: Dilemmas of a Feminist Radical." In Dale Spender, ed. *Feminist Theorists: Three Centuries of Key Women Thinkers.* New York: Pantheon, 1983. 348–365.

1915   **Schwarzer, Alice,** 1942– . *After "The Second Sex": Conversations with Simone de Beauvoir.* Translated from the French by Marianne Howarth. New York: Pantheon, 1984. il.

Originally published by Rowholt Verlag Gambh in the Federal Republic of Germany in 1983 as *Simone de Beauvoir Heute,* the first English edition was published in 1984 by Chatto & Windus. Schwarzer conducted these interviews from 1972–1982 (Beauvoir was 64–74 years old), while working together in the French Women's Movement. The last piece (pp. 105–120), "Being a Woman Is Not Enough," was written when Beauvoir was 74. Schwarzer's quote of Beauvoir, "Women are exploited—and they allow themselves to be exploited—in the name of love," was edited out of the French version. *See also* #2000, #2001, #2002.

1916   **Stutman, Suzanne, ed.** *My Other Loneliness: Letters of Thomas Wolfe and Alice Bernstein.* Chapel Hill: U of North Carolina Press, 1983.

Alice Frankau Bernstein (1881–1955) was of Jewish background, a stage and costume designer, spouse, parent. Her long love affair with novelist Thomas Wolfe (1900–1938), who was Christian and much younger, is reflected in these letters from 1925 to 1936.

1917   **Jones, Linda R. Wolf.** *Eveline M. Burns and the American Social Security System, 1935–1960: A Model of Professional Leadership.* Yeshiva U, 1985. 46/11A. (Eveline Mabel Burns, 1900–1985.)

1918   **Carpenter, Arie,** 1885–1978. *Aunt Arie: A Foxfire Portrait.* Linda Garland Page and Eliot Wigginton, eds. New York: Dutton, 1983.

Aunt Arie Carpenter lived in Macon County, North Carolina. Her "portrait" is based on autobiographical writings.

1919   **Carpenter, Elizabeth Sutherland,** 1920– . *Getting Better All the Time.* New York: Simon & Schuster, 1987.

Press secretary and staff director for Lady Bird Johnson from 1963 to 1969, Liz Carpenter recounts how she has "had a whale of a good time" on earth.

1920   **Lee, Hermoine.** *Willa Cather: Double Lives.* New York: Pantheon, 1989. bib, il, index.

Willa Sibert Cather (1873–1947) produced several of her best novels during her middle years. Her last published work was *Sapphira and the Slave Girl,* an "indirect autobiography . . . her own experience of the pain and handicap of old age, and her own desire to maintain a stoic dignity in the face of death." Lee's Chapter 9, "The Thing Not Named," may refer to menopause and to lesbianism. *See also* Sharon O'Brien's "'The Thing Not Named': Willa Cather as a Lesbian Writer." *Signs* Summer 1984 9(4): 576–599.

1921   **Poggi, S.** "Baba Copper, 69, Pioneer in Battle Against Ageism." *Gay Community News* September 25, 1988 16(11): 18.

1922   **Douglas, Marjory Stoneman,** 1890– . *Voice of the River: An Autobiography.* Berkeley: Pineapple Press, 1987. il.

Environmentalist Douglas wrote from Florida.

1923   **Fisk, Erma J.,** 1905– . *Parrots' Wood.* New York: Norton, 1985.

Also available in large print. Fisk spent the latter part of her life banding birds and in amateur ornithological research. This journal was written on a Belize plantation.

1924   **Flanner, Janet,** 1892–1978. *Darlinghissima: Letters to a Friend.* Edited and with commentary by Natalia Danesis Murray. New York: Random House, 1985. il, index.

American author, journalist, and lecturer, "Genet" wrote from France of twentieth-century intellectual life. She was well known as *New Yorker* magazine's Paris correspondent. *Darlinghissima* spans the years 1944–1975, when she was aged 52–83.

1925   **Gardiner, Muriel,** 1901–1985. *Code Name "Mary": Memoirs of an American Woman in the Austrian Underground.* New Haven: Yale U Press, 1983. il.

American Gardiner attended medical school in Vienna and was present in the early 1930s as fascism dominated pre-Nazi Austria. As 33-year-old "Mary," she became a member of the underground, and may have been Lillian Hellman's *Julia.*

1926   **Gidlow, Elsa,** 1898–1986. *Elsa: I Come with My Songs: The Autobiography of Elsa Gidlow.* San Francisco: Booklegger, 1986. il, index.

American lesbian feminist poet Gidlow's books and tapes are available from Booklegger. *See also* her "Memoirs" in *Feminist Studies* Spring 1980 6(1): 107–127.

1927   **Gingold, Hermione Ferdinana,** 1897–1987, **and Anne Clements Eyre.** *How to Grow Old Disgracefully: My Life.* New York: St. Martin's Press, 1988. il.

English actor Gingold's films included "Gigi." She won a Grammy for narration of "Peter and the Wolf." Although her friend, Lady Eyre (Anne Clements Eyre), assisted with organization of this autobiography, it bears none of the symptoms of assisted authorship.

1928   **Graham, Virginia Komiss,** 1912– . *Life After Harry: My Adventures in Widowhood.* New York: Simon & Schuster, 1988.

For many years Graham hosted a popular daytime TV talk show. She has also experienced cancer and widowhood. Her book includes: "Follow Your Heart," "Widow Beware!" "Family Traps," "Get in Gear," "Alone and Loving It," and "Living a Golden Life." This is an example of the many "name" personal narratives marketed as self-help materials for widows.

1929   **Kohfeldt, Mary Lou.** *Lady Gregory: The Woman Behind the Irish Renaissance.* New York: Atheneum, 1983. bib, index.

Irish Lady Isabella Augusta Gregory (1852–1932) began her successful career in mid-life, following her husband's death. She was an Abbey Theatre founder, playwright, writer of comedies, theater manager, and fund-raiser dedicated to restoring Irish culture and political independence.

1930   **Grenfell, Joyce Irene,** 1910–1970, **and Katharine Moore,** 1898– . *An Invisible Friendship: An Exchange of Letters, 1957–1979.* London: Macmillan, 1981.

Correspondence between Grenfell and novelist Moore (*see* #2123) from the years 1957 to 1979 and their invisible friendship are reprinted here. Grenfell retired from the stage in 1973 following a successful career as writer, stage actor, and TV performer. She was president of the Society of Women Broadcasters and Writers, probably best known in the United States for her one-woman show.

1931   **George, Emily.** *Martha Griffiths.* Washington: U Press of America, 1982. index.
Martha Wright Griffiths (1912–) is the American attorney and politician who, as a congressional representative in 1972 (at age 60), got the Equal Rights Amendment out of the House Judiciary Committee, where it had been bottled up for fifty years. Chapter 6, "Retirement." In 1982 she became Michigan lieutenant-governor, but *see also* "Throwing Martha Off the Train: Michigan's Governor [James J. Blanchard] Stirs a Storm by Dropping His Running Mate." *Time* September 17, 1990 135(12): 53. At age 78 she saw herself as "a warrior who takes no prisoners . . . I like that!"

1932   **Sicherman, Barbara.** *Alice Hamilton: A Life in Letters.* Cambridge: Harvard U Press, 1984.
These 131 letters were written between 1888 and 1965. Hamilton (1869–1970) was an unmarried physician and reformer who devoted her life to pioneer work in industrial toxicology. She was the first woman to hold the rank of professor at Harvard University, invited on condition that she promise not to use the Harvard Club, a male faculty stronghold. Her papers are at the Schlesinger Library on the History of Women in America (Radcliffe College, Cambridge, Massachusetts) and open to the public.

1933   **Hasselstrom, Linda M.,** 1943– . *Windbreak: A Woman Rancher on the Northern Plains.* Berkeley: Barn Owl, 1987.
A freelance writer, Hasselstrom has been a teacher and publisher. Her diary of life on a South Dakota ranch in the twentieth century was a Literary Guild Alternate selection.

1934   **Heard, Regie, and Bonnie Langenhahn.** *Reggie's Love: A Daughter of Former Slaves Recalls and Reflects.* Menomonie Falls: McCormick and Schilling, 1989. il. (POB 722, Menomonie Falls, WI 53051.)
This is an expanded, illustrated edition of Heard's autobiography, set in Milwaukee, where she was a nursing home patient.

1935   **Haney, Eleanor Humes.** *A Feminist Legacy: The Ethics of Wilma Scott Heide and Company.* Buffalo: Margaret Daughters, Inc., 1985. index.
Wilma Scott Heide (1921–1985) was an American feminist known for, among other accomplishments, her presidency of the National Organization for Women.

1936   **Faber, Doris,** 1924– . *Life of Lorena Hickok: E.R.'s Friend.* New York: Morrow, 1986. bib, il, index.
Lorena Alice Hickok (1893–1968) was an Associated Press reporter and friend of Anna Eleanor Roosevelt (1884–1962). Their letters from 1932 to 1962 have been examined by Faber to suggest a lesbian relationship that probably did not exist.

1937   **Hubbell, Sue.** *A Country Year: Living the Questions.* New York: Random, 1986. il.
"When I travel, people seldom notice or talk to me. I am unnoticeable in my ordinariness. If I were young and pretty, I might attract attention. But I am too old to be pretty, and rumpled besides, so I am invisible. . . . There are so many of us that it is tempting to think [of older women] as a class. We are past our reproductive years. Men don't want us. . . . It makes good biological sense for males to be attracted to females who are at an earlier part in their breeding years and who still want to build nests, and if that leaves us no longer able to lose ourselves in the pleasures and closeness of pairing, well, we have gained our selves" (pp. 195–196). Hubbell ventures from her Ozark Mountains country life to sell honey from her bee-agribusiness, which is now her living, part of her mid-life post-divorce "adjustment." She contributed an essay to the "Being

Alone" section of Nancy R. Newhouse's *Hers: Through Women's Eyes* (Villard, 1984). This is her complete and wonderful natural history of life in the Missouri countryside.

1938   **Jones, Anne H.** "The Centennial of Clementine Hunter." *Woman's Art J* Spring/Summer 1987 8(1): 23–27.

1939   **Hunter, Laura Russell, with Polly Hunter Memhard.** *The Rest of My Life*. Riverside: Growing Pains Press, 1981.
        An 80-year-old widow writes an astute and humorous account of her final years as a nursing home resident. It suggests caresharing conditions that encourage self-determination during aging, illness, and dying.

1940   **Jeazell, Ruth Bernhard, ed.** *The Death and Letters of Alice James: Selected Correspondence*. Berkeley: U of California Press, 1981. il, index.
        As invalid diarist Alice James (1848–1892) died at age 44 of cancer, she considered her death an achievement, for her life had passed in the shadow of her older, educated, accomplished, and respected brothers and her unvalidated illness. Jeazell has contributed a biographical essay to the collection, which is mostly from Alice James's final years.

1941   **Foner, Philip Sheldon,** 1910– , **ed.** *Mother Jones Speaks: Collected Writings and Speeches*. New York: Monad Press, 1983.
        Mary Harris Jones (1830–1930) came to socialism and began labor organizing in the United States at age 50. (Her chronology appears as pp. 51–59.) In an interview at age 83, she said, "I have no time to think about getting old; besides I have a lot to accomplish yet."

1942   **Kerfoot, Justine,** 1906– . *Woman of the Boundary Waters: Canoeing, Guiding, Mushing, and Surviving*. Grand Marais: Women's Times Publishing, 1986. il, index.
        Illustrated with black-and-white photographs, drawings, and end-paper map, and provided with a glossary and material on the Sunflint Trail, this personal narrative of wilderness living in Minnesota by a senior woman is history.

1943   **King, Florence,** 1936– . *Lump It or Leave It*. New York: St. Martin's Press, 1990.
        The first essay, "Fiftysomething," is of most interest here, although all of King's writings are relevant to women's reaching middle and old age. "*Lear's* is the brainchild of sixtyish Frances Lear, the former Mrs. Norman Lear, who decided to build the confidence of older women by giving them their own magazine and naming it after the man who paid her $112 million for divorcing him. . . . Writing for women's magazines is a matter of skirting their various taboos. Pedophobia at *Family Circle* and Lesbianism at *Cosmopolitan* make sense, but the great taboo at *Lear's*, according to one of their many former editors, is the word 'menopause.' . . . In the south of my childhood, no woman could weather the 'Change' completely unscathed; it was femininity's Appomattox and you had to milk it for every possible drop of theater" (pp. 1–2).

1944   **Kuzwayo, Ellen,** 1914– . *Call Me Woman*. San Francisco: Spinster's Ink, 1985. il.
        Originally published in 1985 in London by Women's Press, Ltd. Nadine Gordimer (1923–) provided a preface and Bessie Head (1937–1986) a foreword for this book mainly about social reformer Kuzwayo's career. Contents include "'Minors' Are Heroines" and rosters of South African black women medical doctors and lawyers.

1945   **Franklin, Penelope, ed.** *Private Pages: Diaries of American Women, 1830s-1970s*. New York: Ballantine, 1986.

Thirteen young, middle-aged, and old women's diaries are introduced and provided an afterword by Franklin. The contents lists diaries' dates, subjects' age ranges at the time, and their locations. The diaries are arranged from the youngest to oldest subjects. Deborah Norris Logan's excerpt covers her years in nineteenth-century Pennsylvania, when she was age 70–77 (pp. 449–491); Ethel Robertson Whiting was age 42–48 when she recorded her life in California during the 1924–1930 period.

1946   **Premo, Terri L.** "'Like a Being Who Does Not Belong': The Old Age of Deborah Norris Logan." *Pennsylvania Magazine of History and Biography* January 1983 107: 85–112.

In March 1980, the diary of Deborah Norris Logan (1761–1838) was transcribed and edited by Marleen S. Barr as her doctoral dissertation. *See also* #1945.

1947   **Smith, Bonnie G.,** 1940– . *Confessions of a Concierge: Madame Lucie's History of Twentieth-Century France.* New Haven: Yale U Press, 1985. index.

Smith first discusses the richness and humanity of fictional narratives: traditionally, historians have focused on the "who," whereas novelists base their claims on the "how." Mme. Lucie was born perhaps in 1890; *Confessions* spans 1900–1981. Homeless during World War II, she became a Paris concierge in 1943 to solve the family's housing problem. "Whatever [daughter] Colette decided, Mme. Lucie maintained that the legalization of abortion in 1974 was the greatest blessing women had received in her memory" (p. 106).

1948   **Maris, Cora,** 1868–1920, **and Faith Maris.** "Life at the Pebble Quarry, Nye County, Nevada, 1916–1919." *Nevada Historical Society Q* 1982 25: 53–64.

1949   **Bateson, Mary Catherine,** 1939– . *With a Daughter's Eye: A Memoir of Margaret Mead [1901–1978] and Gregory Bateson.* New York: Morrow, 1984. bib, il.

Chapter 14, "Steps to Death," of these cross-generational reflections on the author's parents is of particular interest. When, in 1978, both were diagnosed with cancer, "Margaret's" denial contrasted with her father's acceptance.

1950   **Meigs, Mary,** 1917– . "Memories of Age." *Trivia* Fall 1988 13: 57–65.

1951   **Millett, Katherine,** 1934– . *The Loony-Bin Trip.* New York: Simon & Schuster, 1990.

In 1970 Kate Millett's *Sexual Politics* was published and became a seminal work for the women's liberation movements in the United States and the United Kingdom. *Loony-Bin*, written when she was 56, followed Dr. Millett's experience as a psychotherapy patient in twentieth-century America. The "hardest thing now" is to function and "summon cheerfulness against the humiliation" of being expected to disguise the teacher, the artist, the writer that she has been and is.

1952   **Moore, Honor,** 1945– . "My Grandmother Who Painted." In Janet Sternburg, ed. *The Writer on Her Work.* New York: Norton, 1980. 45–70.

1953   **Nin, Anais,** 1903–1977. *The Diary of Anais Nin . . . Volume 7: 1966–1974.* Edited and prefaced by Gunther Stuhlmann. New York: Harcourt, 1980. index.

Born in Paris, American diarist and novelist Nin fluctuated among diary form, writer's notebook, and autobiography as she recorded her concerns for work and love. Volume 7 (she was aged 63–71) concluded the series. She died of cancer.

1954   Webb, Allie Bayne Windham, ed. *Mistress of Evergreen Plantation: Rachel O'Connor's Legacy of Letters, 1823–1845.* Albany: SUNY Press, 1983. il, index.

Twice widowed and having lost two sons, Rachel Swayze Bell O'Connor (1774–1846) centered her life around running her Louisiana cotton plantation. These letters to her family are from the last twenty-two years of her life, from age 49 to 79, and deal with her work and the need for dependence on male relatives in legal and financial matters, and finally, even in death.

1955   Meade, Dorothy, 1934– . *Dorothy Parker: What Fresh Hell Is This?* New York: Villard Books/Random, 1987.

American writer Dorothy Rothschild Parker (1893–1967) was known mainly for her snappy and witty comments, but her life can be considered tragic in many ways. Her poignant play, *The Ladies of the Corridor*, written with Arnaud d'Usseau (1916–) and premiered in 1953, is about the respectable, lonely older women who then resided in nice New York hotels. It is considered in Chapter 16, "Toad Time, 1948–1955."

1956   Willis, Jean L. "Alice Paul: The Quintessential Feminist." In Dale Spender, ed. *Feminist Theorists: Three Centuries of Key Women Thinkers.* New York: Random, 1983. 285–295. Alice Paul (1885–1977)'s Papers are in the collection of the Schlesinger Library on the History of Women in America.

1957   Holt, Hazel, 1928– . *A Lot to Ask: A Life of Barbara Pym.* New York: Macmillan, 1990. index.

Holt worked with Barbara Pym (1913–1980) at the International African Institute in London. As her literary executor, she edited the unpublished novels (*see* #2134, #2135, #2136) and, with Hilary Pym Walton, Pym's letters and diaries (*see* #1958). During the 1950s, Pym's novels (*Some Tame Gazelles*, 1950; *Excellent Women*, 1952; *A Glass of Blessings*, 1958) acquired a following, but she sometimes wrote about unfashionable, depressing parts of many people's experiences—gossip, loneliness, old age, retirement. *See* Janice Rossen's *Independent Women: The Functions of Gender in the Novels of Barbara Pym* (#2023). After *No Fond Return of Love* (1961), she was unable to get her writing past the gatekeepers of publishing and, of necessity, continued her income-producing office work. In 1977, the *Times Literary Supplement* published a list of the most "underrated writers of the century," on which her name appeared. With the "rediscovery" of her work, her books were reissued, and her fiction began to be published the same year: *Quartet in Autumn* and *The Sweet Dove Died.* A last novel, *A Few Green Leaves*, was published posthumously in 1980, and *An Unsuitable Attachment*—rejected in 1963—and edited by Holt, in 1982.

1958   Holt, Hazel, 1928– , and Hilary Pym Walton. *A Very Private Eye: An Autobiography in Diaries and Letters.* New York: Dutton, 1984. il, index.

Twentieth-century English novelist Barbara Pym (1913–1980) and her work, neglected for many years, enjoyed renewed interest during the final three years of her life until her death of cancer. *See also* #1957.

1959   Wyatt-Brown, Anne M., 1939– . *Barbara Pym: A Critical Biography.* Columbia: U of Missouri Press, 1992. bib, index.

Wyatt-Brown includes consideration of how the English writer's experience of aging and ill health influenced her work.

1960   Robey, Harriet Stevens, 1900– . *There's a Dance in the Old Dame Yet.* Boston: Little, Brown, 1982.

Robey inspiringly narrates her life from age 75 to 80, a period that included widowhood, retirement from psychiatric social work, blindness, and extreme pain.

1961   **Roseanne,** 1952– . *Roseanne: My Life as a Woman.* New York: Harper, 1989. il.
Here is middle-aged Roseanne, contemporary American comedic actor, producer, and writer.

1962   **Russell, Dora Winifred Black,** 1894–1986. *The Tamarisk Tree.* London: Virago, 1977, 1980, 1985. bib, il, index.
The first part of *The Tamarisk Tree,* published in 1977, "My Quest for Liberty and Love," had concluded with divorce from Bertrand Russell in 1935. The second is "My School and the Years of War," in which there remains for her the running of Beacon Hill School until World War II, when she is at the Ministry of Information. The third part, "Challenge to the Cold War," is also published by Virago.

1963   **Sarton, May,** 1912–1995. *After the Stroke: A Journal.* New York: Norton, 1988.
On February 20, 1986, American lesbian poet-novelist Sarton experienced a stroke. This diary-journal was written during the year that followed. "It has made me aware that it is men not women who have held my work in high regard. . . . I had somehow imagined when I came here [to coastal Maine], well-known as a writer—I was sixty then—that I would have occasionally been invited out. That has not happened. People come from outside the area to see me. . . . But the fact is I am always an outsider" (pp. 3, 112–113 of the large-print edition). Her experiences with the American health care system during her year's recovery are too familiar to old, alone women, although she conveys no recognition of any relationship between her status and the mistreatment that she receives. *See also* #1993.

1964   **Sarton, May,** 1912–1995. *At Seventy: A Journal.* New York: Norton, 1984. il.
This diary covers the period May 3, 1982—Sarton's 70th birthday—to May 2, 1983. " . . . I said, 'This is the best time of my life. I love being old.' At that point a voice from the audience asked loudly, 'Why is it good to be old?' I answered . . . 'Because I am more myself than I have ever been. There is less conflict. I am happier, more balanced, and (I heard myself rather aggressively) more powerful'" (p. 10).

1965   **Sarton, May,** 1912–1995. *Endgame: A Journal of the Seventy-Ninth Year.* New York: Norton, 1992.
The preface is dated June 3, 1991. She has published nineteen volumes of verse, nineteen novels, eleven journals, and two books for children. May 3, 1992 was her 80th birthday and she was at work on a new novel, another journal, and poetry. She struggles with frailty and illness, no longer able to work at the typewriter. Her publisher makes a big thing of her personal courage, but, in fact, she is in great and constant pain—the victim of uncaring and "wrong" doctors.

1966   **Scott-Maxwell, Florida Pier,** 1884– . "The Measure of My Days: Journal Entries." *Southern Exposure* March/June 1985 24(2/3): 19–20.

1967   **Folkart, Burt A.** "Laurie Shields [1922–1989], Formed Women's League." *Los Angeles Times* March 5, 1989 I: 40, column 4. *See also* "Laurie Shields, 67, Leader of Struggle for Older Women [obit]." *New York Times* March 4, 1989 138: 11, column 4.
The *Times* reports that "Mrs. Shields" died on March 3, 1989, and that her husband, actor Arthur Shields, died in 1970. It goes on to list her accomplishments: cofounder of the Alliance for Displaced Homemakers, organizer of White House Mini

Conference on Older Women in 1980, member of the Older Women's League board, and that she died of breast cancer.

1968 **Sweet, Ellen.** "Tish Sommers [1914–1985]: Organize—Don't Agonize!" *Ms.* January 1982 10(7): 61, 80.

1969 **Smith, Lynn.** "Older Women's Advocate Dies at 71: Tish Sommers [1914–1985] Was Co-Founder of 15,000–Member Group [obit]." *Los Angeles Times* October 19, 1985 104(4): 7, column 4.

1970 **Goodman, Charlotte Margolis,** 1934– . *Jean Stafford: The Savage Heart.* Austin: U of Texas Press, 1990. bib, index.

American author Jean Stafford (1915–1979) is well known for her novel, *The Catherine Wheel.* She dedicated her *Collected Stories* to the old woman who had played a major role in promoting her career as a writer of short fiction, *New Yorker* magazine fiction editor Katharine Whie (*see* Chapter 11, "Life Is No Abyss"). Chapter 12, "The End of a Career," "dramatizes the desperate and ultimately futile quest of an aging woman to preserve her beauty and her youthful appearance, [and] is an indictment both of the narcissistic woman and of a society that places a premium on feminine beauty and youthfulness."

1971 **Strong, Tracy B., and Helene Keyssar.** *Right in Her Soul: The Life of Anna Louise Strong.* New York: Random, 1983. bib, index.

American radical journalist Anna Louise Strong (1885–1970) was deeply involved in labor issues and developed a commitment to communism. Her great-nephew and his spouse prepared this biography. *See also #1863.*

1972 **Truitt, Anne,** 1921– . *Turn: The Journal of an Artist.* New York: Viking, 1986.

Truitt is an artist and sculptor. Her diary narrative covers her widowhood, family crises, recognition of her disparate University of Maryland salary as a full professor, a period at Yadoo artists' community, and the shock of what growing old is physically.

1973 **Urrutia, Virginia,** 1913– . *Two Wheels and a Taxi: A Slightly Daft Adventure in the Andes.* Seattle: Mountaineers, 1987. il.

"Two wheels" are this grandmother's bicycle. She was 70 years old at the time of the trip she describes in the Andes mountain range of South America.

1974 **Rooke, Patricia T.** "Public Figure, Private Woman: Same-Sex Support Structures in the Life of Charlotte Whitton [1896–1975]." *International J of Women's Studies* November-December 1983 6: 412–428.

1975 **Tribble, Edwin, ed.** *A President in Love: The Courtship Letters of Woodrow Wilson and Edith Bolling Galt.* Boston: Houghton Mifflin, 1981.

Edith Bolling Galt Wilson (1872–1961) was a well-to-do, middle-aged Washington, D.C., widow when the recently widowed American president courted her in their April-December 1915 letters. (Thomas Woodrow Wilson 1856–1924.)

1976 **Wilson, June P.** Untitled essay about her mother. In Nancy R. Newhouse, ed. *Hers: Through Women's Eyes.* New York: Villard, 1985. 150–153.

"In his fiftieth class reunion, he summed it up with typical diplomacy. 'My wife is an activist; I supply the wisdom'" (p. 153).

1977 **Wilson, Mary,** 1944– , **and Patricia Romanowski.** *Supreme Faith: Someday We'll Be Together.* New York: Harper, 1990. il, index.

The sequel to Wilson's *Dreamgirl: My Life as a Supreme* (St. Martin's, 1986) continues her life in the music business.

1978   **Winters, Shelley,** 1922– . *Shelley II: The Middle of My Century.* New York: Simon & Schuster, 1989. il, index.

Shirley Schrift (Shelley Winters) writes responsibly, "It was during those times that I finally escaped the cunning dumb blonde-bombshell images Universal and I had created and broke through the crippling sexual double standard that had been imposed on women throughout history. I hope I . . . became a woman who took responsibility for her actions and who helped fight for equality and dignity for herself and her sisters" (p. 12).

1979   "**Mary Dodge Woodward** [1826–1890]." In Margo Culley. *A Day at a Time: The Diary Literature of American Women from 1764 to the Present.* New York: Feminist Press at the CUNY, 1985. 165–178.

1980   **Bell, Anne Oliver, ed.** *The Diary of Virginia Woolf [1882–1941],* Volume 5. New York: Harcourt, 1984. index.

Woolf described her diaries as "diamonds of the dust heap." (*See also* #1981.) The text for the final volume was taken from Diaries XXV–XXX. On Sunday, January 19, 1936, she wrote, "I went up to an elderly stout woman reading the paper at The Times Book Club [a circulating library] the other day. It was Margery Strachey. What are you doing? I said. Nothing! she replied. 'I've got nowhere to go & nothing to do.'" On Saturday, March 8, 1941: "Just back from L.'s [husband Leonard] speech at Brighton. Like a foreign town: the first spring day. Women sitting on seats. A pretty hat in a teashop—how fashion revives the eye! And the shell encrusted old women, roughed, decked cad[a]verous at the tea shop. The waitress in checked cotton. No: I intend no introspection. I mark Henry James's sentences; Observe perpetually. Observe the oncome of age . . . " She died on March 28.

1981   **Nicholson, Nigel, ed.** *The Letters of Virginia Woolf [1882–1941],* Volume 6. New York: Harcourt, 1980.

Here are Woolf's last years, 1936–1941, when she was aged 54–59, titled "Leave the Letters Till We're Dead." (*See also* #1980.)

1982   **Workman, Ann Hill.** *Part-Time Lady.* Bergenfield: A. Deutsch, 1986.

Marketed as a book of humorous personal narrative, Workman recounts her mid-life office employment experiences in Belfast as a part-time typist. The book was distributed in large-print edition by J. Curley in 1987.

Oral History
See also Chapter 10: History (1845–1867).

1983   **Chamberlain, Mary,** 1947– . *Fenwomen: A Portrait of Women in an English Village.* London: Routledge & Kegan Paul, 1983. il.

First published in 1975 by Virago. Chapter 10, "Old Age." Mary Chamberlain is a founder of the London History Workshop. Her social and oral history of the women in an isolated English village of the Fens (Gislea, Cambridgeshire) provided the basis for Caryl Churchill's Broadway play, "Fen."

1984   **Faulkner, Audrey Olsen, et al.** *When I Was Comin' Up: An Oral History of Aged Blacks.* Hamden: Shoe String Press, 1982.

Here are thirteen oral histories of African Americans who migrated from the South to the Northeast between 1915 and 1960. Most were aged, poor, black women who settled in Newark, New Jersey. Having experienced isolation, poverty, and oppression in the South, they found crowding, relatively high wages, and ambivalent white behavior in the North.

1985   **Geiger, Susan N. G.** "Women's [oral] Life Histories: Method and Content [review essay]." *Signs* Winter 1986 11(2): 334–351.

1986   **Litwin-Grinberg, Ruth R.** *Lives in Retrospect: A Qualitative Analysis of Oral Reminiscence as Applied to Elderly Jewish Women.* U of California, Berkeley, 1982. 33/01A.

1987   **Ryant, Carl.** "Comment: Oral History and Gerontology." *Gerontologist* February 1981 21(1): 104–105.

1988   **Smith, Anne,** 1944– . *Women Remember: An Oral History.* London and New York: Routledge, 1989. il.

Smith's interest in women of her grandmothers' generation led to her creation of these biographical studies of the history of six such women, chosen at random among British women, whom she interviewed.

1989   **Susie, Debra Anne.** *In the Way of Our Grandmothers: A Sociocultural Look at Modern American Midwifery.* Florida State U, 1984. 46/03A.

1990   **Wilson, Emily Herring.** *Hope and Dignity: Older Black Women of the South.* Philadelphia: Temple U Press, 1983. il.

Maya Angelou provides the foreword and Susan Mullally photographs for this "celebration" of twenty old, Southern (mostly North Carolinan) African-American women. Pauli Murray appears in the epilogue. Some reviewers have responded that there is just too much nice warm glow here, referring to biographies that portray trust in white persons.

USES AND CRITICAL STUDIES OF BIOGRAPHY

1991   **American Antiquarian Society.** *Guide and Index to Women's Diaries.* New Canaan: Readex Corp., 1984.

Volume (or segment) 1 consists of "New England Women" and is a Readex Microfilm Collection from the files of the American Antiquarian Society. It includes eight diaries on twenty-two reels of microfilm. Subject indexing accesses such considerations as "widowhood," "aging," etc.

1992   **Cline, Cheryl,** 1954– . *Women's Diaries, Journals, and Letters: An Annotated Bibliography.* New York: Garland, 1989.

Identified are published, "private writings of appreciable length." Anthologies and family collections are included. Indexing is international in scope, although most are in English, with subject-indexing (*see* "aging," "mother-daughter," etc.) as well as authors, professions, and locations.

1993   **Cruikshank, Margaret.** "A Note on May Sarton." In Monika Kehoe, ed. *Historical, Literary, and Erotic Aspects of Lesbianism.* New York: Haworth, 1986. 153–156. *See also* #1963, #1964, #1965; Chapter 12.

1994   **Culley, Margo.** *A Day at a Time: The Diary Literature of American Women from 1764 to the Present.* New York: Feminist Press at the CUNY, 1985. bib.

A useful introduction to the functions and form of women's diaries, *A Day at a Time* considers "older" women. Although not indexed, there is a useful bibliography.

1995   **Goodfriend, Joyce D.** *The Published Diaries and Letters of American Women: An Annotated Bibliography.* Boston: G. K. Hall, 1987. index.

Recent publications (e.g., Caldwell, Culley, Lifshin, Payne, Sorel) have furthered the goal of documenting American females' past by making more widely known to researchers, students, and teachers the diaries and letters of the nation's women. Goodfriend intends to provide a comprehensive guide to the most readily accessible of those that have been printed. Entries for personal documents available in printed form are arranged chronologically by the initial date of composition, from 1669 to 1982. Some of the subjects accessed are: children and adolescents, courtship, death, divorce, marriage, middle-aged women, old age, separation, single women, and widows.

1996   **Hale, Noreen.** *Present and Retrospective Learning Needs Elicited from the Autobiographies of Ten Women over Age Sixty.* Indiana U, 1981. 42/08A.

1997   **Heilbrun, Carolyn G., 1926– .** *Writing a Woman's Life.* New York: Norton, 1988. bib, index.

"The pattern of men's lives suggests that at fifty they are likelier to reveal their egoism than their hidden ideals or revolutionary hopes" (p. 124). Heilbrun designates 1973 as the turning point for modern women's autobiography (Sarton's *Plant Dreaming Deep*). Her subjects are fiction and poetry writers. Chapter 7 is about women authors in the last third of life.

1998   **Hoffman, Leonore, 1929– , and Margo Culley, eds.** *Women's Personal Narratives: Essays in Criticism and Pedagogy.* New York: Modern Language Association of America, 1985. bib.

A section is devoted to using personal narratives in the classroom. Appendices include "Writing Exercises," "Editing a Woman's Diary: A Case Study," and a selected bibliography.

1999   **Huff, Cynthia.** *British Women's Diaries: A Descriptive Bibliography of Selected 19th Century Women's Manuscript Diaries.* New York: AMS Press, 1985.

One of the subjects considered is widowhood.

2000   **Woodward, Kathleen.** "Instant Repulsion: Decrepitude, the Mirror Stage, and the Literary Imagination." *Kenyon Review* 1983 5: 43–66.

2001   **Woodward, Kathleen.** "Reminiscence, Identity, Sentimentality: Simone de Beauvoir and the Life Review." In Robert Disch, ed. *Twenty-Five Years of the Life Review.* Binghamton: Haworth, 1988. 25–46.

2002   **Woodward, Kathleen.** "Simone de Beauvoir: Aging and Its Discontents." In Shari Benstock, ed. *The Private Self: Theory and Practice of Women's Autobiographical Writings.* London: Routledge, 1988. Chapter 4.

12
Fiction and Poetry by and About Women as They Age

She had always been an unashamed reader of novels, but if she hoped to find one which reflected her own sort of life she had come to realise that the position of an unmarried, unattached, ageing woman is of no interest whatever to the writer of modern fiction.

Barbara Pym, 1913–1980, *Quartet in Autumn* (1977)

CRITICISM AND USES OF FICTION AND POETRY
See also Chapter 10; Chapter 11.

2003 **Dowling, John.** "Moratin's Creation of the Comic Role for the Older Actress." *Theatre Survey* May-November 1983 24: 55–63.

2004 **Eddy, Beverly Driver.** "The Dangerous Age: Karin Michaelles and the Politics of Menopause." *Women's Studies* September 1992 21(4): 491–504.

2005 **Fallaize, Elizabeth.** *The Novels of Simone de Beauvoir.* London and New York: Routledge, 1988. bib, index.
    Professor Fallaize's study of Simone de Beauvoir's (1908–1986) five novels and one short story collection is primarily focused on her as a writer of fiction. Her writing on such subjects as existentialism, women, and, in particular, old age illuminates her novels. Works considered here are *She Came to Stay, The Blood of Others, All Men Are Mortal, The Mandarins, Les Belles Images,* and short story cycles *When Things of the Spirit Come First* (#2188) and *The Woman Destroyed,* which includes *The Age of Discretion.*

2006 **Gullette, Margaret Morganroth.** *Safe at Last in the Middle Years: The Invention of the Midlife Progress Novel: Saul Bellow, Margaret Drabble, Anne Tyler, John Updike.* Berkeley: U of California Press, 1988. index.
    Gullette's history of the idea of the middle years of life in the nineteenth and early twentieth centuries by such novelists as English Margaret Drabble (1939–) and American Anne Tyler (1941–) concerns contemporary images. These authors consider

women in relationship to adulthood, aging, celibacy, divorce, misogyny, and power, as mothers of protagonists, and as daughters.

2007   **Heilbrun, Carolyn G.** "Middle-Aged Women in Literature." In Grace Kesterman Baruch and Jeanne Brooks-Gunn, eds. *Women in Midlife.* New York: Plenum Press, 1984. Chapter 3.

2008   **Hoder-Salmon, Marilyn.** *A "New-Born Creature": The Authentic Woman in "The Awakening": Novel to Screenplay as Critical Interpretation.* U of New Mexico, 1983. 45/08A.

2009   **Holloway, Karla F. C., and Stephanie Demetrakopoulos.** "Remembering Our Foremothers: Older Black Women, Politics of Age, Politics of Survival as Embodied in the Novels of Toni Morrison." In Marilyn J. Bell, ed. *Women as Elders: Images, Visions, and Issues.* New York: Haworth Press, 1986. 13–34.

2010   **Horn, Barbara.** "Beyond Hags and Old Maids: Women Writers Imagine Aging Women." In Jo Alexander, ed. *Women and Aging: An Anthology by Women.* Corvallis: Calyx Books, 1986. 63–67.

2011   **Janeway, Elizabeth,** 1913– . "Midlife Crisis." In her *Cross Sections from a Decade of Change.* New York: Morrow, 1982. 294–306.

2012   **Johnsen, Norma.** *The Hair Wreath: Mary Wilkins Freeman's Artist Fiction.* U of New Hampshire, 1989. 50/06A.

2013   **Kapelovitz, Abbey Poze.** *Mother Images in American-Jewish Fiction.* U of Denver, 1985. 46/06A.

2014   **Keating, Gail C.** *Sarah Orne Jewett's Experiences with Mentoring and Communities of Women.* Temple U, 1987. 48/04A.

2015   **Kenney, Catherine McGehee,** 1948– . *The Remarkable Case of Dorothy L. Sayers.* Kent: Kent State U Press, 1990. index.
    English poet, playwright, novelist, and writer of detective and mystery stories Dorothy Leigh Sayers (1893–1957) transformed the modern detective story into a serious novel of social criticism. In *Unnatural Death* (a Peter Wimsey book), she introduced Miss Climpson in a chapter titled "A Use for Spinsters." Kenney considers Sayers's views on the situation of women (Chapter 7, "Unnatural Death and the Testimony of Superfluous Women") and her work as a lay interpreter of Christianity.

2016   **Lassner, Phyllis.** *Elizabeth Bowen.* New York: Barnes & Noble, 1989. bib, index.
    Lassner's scholarly feminist analysis of the life and work of twentieth-century Anglo-Irish writer Elizabeth Dorothea Cole Bowen (1899–1973) has relevance for women and aging. Bowen's novels of manners and sensibility revise traditional notions of female character. *See also* Lassner's *Elizabeth Bowen: A Study of the Short Fiction* (New York: Twayne, 1991).

2017   **Lydon, Mary.** "L'Eden Cinema: Aging and the Imagination in *Marguerite Duras.*" In Kathleen Woodward and Murray M. Schwartz, eds. *Memory and Desire: Aging Literature Analysis.* Bloomington: Indiana U Press, 1986. 154–167.

2018   **Nett, Emily M.** "The Naked Soul Comes Closer to the Surface: Old Age in the Gender Mirror of Contemporary Novels." *Women's Studies* 1990 18(2/3): 177–190.

2019   Noling, Kim Hunter. *The Self-Dramatizing Matron in Shakespeare's Romances.* Cornell U, 1985. 46/01A.

2020   Raines, Helen Howell. *The Moving Sphere: Margaret Drabble's Novels of Connection and Contradiction.* U of Denver, 1985. 46/09A.

2021   Reichardt, Mary R. *A Web of Relationship: Women in the Short Stories of Mary Wilkins Freeman.* U of Wisconsin, 1987. 48/08A.

2022   Reuter, Jeanette, and Michele W. Zak. "Erik Erikson and Doris Lessing: Psychological Theory and the Female Novel of Development." In Ann Mae Voda, et al, eds. *Changing Perspectives on Menopause.* Austin: U of Texas Press, 1982. Chapter 12.

2023   Rosen, Janice, 1955– , ed. *Independent Women: The Functions of Gender in the Novels of Barbara Pym.* New York: St. Martin's Press, 1988. index.
        English novelist Barbara Pym (1913–1980) enjoyed early commercial success, but her work languished unpublished for decades because her (gender-related) subjects were deemed uncommercial. *See* #1957 and #1958.

2024   Satz, Martha. "Less of a Woman as One Gets Older: An Interview with Margaret Drabble." *Southwest Review* Spring 1985 70: 187–197.

2025   Sherman, Sarah Way. *Sarah Orne Jewett: An American Persephone.* Hanover: U Press of New England, 1989. bib, il, index.
        Sherman received a U of New Hampshire Book Prize for her exploration of the mother-daughter myth of Demeter and Persephone in Victorian women's culture and her use of it to interpret the life and work of Maine writer Sarah Orne Jewett (1849–1909), best known for her 1896 book, *The Country of the Pointed Firs.*

2026   Sokoloff, Janice M. "Character and Aging in *Moll Flanders.*" *Gerontologist* December 1986 26(6): 681–685.

2027   Sokoloff, Janice M. *The Margin That Remains: A Study of Aging in Literature.* U of Massachusetts, 1985. 46/12A.

2028   Stanley, Arthur Andrew. *Mary Lavin's Widow Stories.* U of Georgia, 1982. 43/06A.

2029   Sucher, Laure, 1942– . *The Fiction of Ruth Prawer Jhabvala: The Politics of Passion.* New York: St. Martin's Press, 1989. bib.
        In this book and in her Ph.D. thesis, Sucher considers such topics as Jhabvala's tragicomic treatment of female sexuality. Born in Germany in 1927 and educated in England, Jhabvala went to live in New Delhi in 1951 following her marriage to an Indian. As a writer, she has been compared to Dorothy Parker. Her *A Room with a View* screenplay won an Academy Award.

2030   Thompson, Christine K. *Content and Technique in Dorothy M. Richardson's "Pilgrimage."* U of Oregon, 1984. 45/07A.

2031   Waxman, Barbara Frey. "From Bildungsroman to Reifungsroman: Aging in Doris Lessing's Fiction." *Soundings: An Interdisciplinary J* Fall 1985 68(3): 318–334.

2032   Wyatt-Brown, Anne M. "From Fantasy to Panthology: Images of Aging in the Novels of Barbara Pym." *Human Values and Aging Newsletter* January-February 1985 6(3): 5–7.

DRAMA

See also Chapter 8: Media; Image; Stereotypes (1635–1679).

2033   **Berry, David Chapman,** 1942– . *The Whales of August: A Play in Two Acts.* New York: Dramatists' Play Service, 1984.

Originally a play, this title is perhaps better known as the film with Bette Davis, Lillian Gish, and Ann Sothern. It is about two elderly sisters facing the challenge of giving up their family home and independence.

2034   **Fugard, Athol.** *The Road To Mecca: Suggested by the Life and Work of Helen Martens.* New York: Theatre Communications Group, 1985.

Winner of the 1988 New York Critics' Best Foreign Play, the story of a widow fighting to retain control of her own life despite attempts to retire her to a nursing home is set in a small South African town.

2035   **Jacobs, Ruth Harriet,** 1924– . *Button, Button, Who Has the Button?* Durham: Crones' Own Press, 1988. (Crones' Own Press, 310 Driver, Durham, NC 27703.)

Dr. Jacobs's self-published drama with poetry is distributed by this small press. The play is a series of loosely connected scenes in which women aged 20–80 and of diverse backgrounds speak to each other about their sorrows, joys, fears, and hopes. It ends with the cast joining in a "womanchant" of celebration. Sociologist-gerontologist Jacobs is an advocate for old women.

2036   **Keatley, Charlotte.** *My Mother Said I Never Should.* Portsmouth: Heineman/ Methuen, 1988.

Winner of the 1987 George Devine Award, this play is about growing up and growing old—four generations of women living and partially living in Manchester and London, England.

2037   **Koelsch, Patrice.** "The Crystal Quilt." *Heresies* 1988 6(3): 31. "Coming of Age" issue #23.

2038   **Lister, Rota H.** "Bibliography of Canadian Plays About Older Women." *Resources for Feminist Research/Documentation sur la Recherche Féministe.* July 1982 11(2): 238–240.

2039   **Shaffer, Peter,** 1926– . *Lettice & Lovage.* New York: Harper & Row, 1987.

Shaffer's comedy had its first performance at the Theatre Royal, Bath, in 1987 and reached the Globe Theatre in London. Maggie Smith as Lettice Douffet and Margaret Tyzack as Lotte Schoen recreated their roles in New York. This published (and tamed) version contains a "significant rewrite": in the English version, the two middle-aged women were left to blow up a select list of modern architectural monstrosities!

2040   **Uhry, Alfred.** *Driving Miss Daisy.* New York: Theatre Communications Group, 1987.

Screenplay published by Script City in 1988. Play and film span twenty-five years in the life of a Southern, white Jewish woman, "Miss Daisy," and her relationship with the African-American chauffeur her son has hired.

2041   **Wasserstein, Wendy,** 1950– . *The Heidi Chronicles & Other Plays.* New York: Harcourt Brace Jovanovich, 1990.

"Uncommon Women and Others" (first published in 1978); "Isn't It Romantic" (1985); and "The Heidi Chronicles" (1988). Wasserstein's plays often relate to women moving and being moved into middle age.

Novels and Novellas

2042   **Adams, Alice,** 1926– . *Second Chances.* New York: Knopf/Random, 1988.
Death and dying, friendship, and sexuality are major elements in the interrelated lives of several elderly women and men in this novel set in a contemporary U.S. small town.

2043   **Adams, Alice,** 1926– . *Superior Women.* New York: Knopf/Random, 1984.
In the manner of Wasserstein's *Uncommon Women and Others* (#2041), five women, friends since their 1943 Radcliffe College days, recount their experiences of forty years.

2044   **Aldridge, Sarah,** 1911– . *Madame Aurora.* Tallahassee: Naiad, 1983.
Aldridge, whose pseudonym is Anyda Marchant, is one of the founders of Naiad Press. She is considered the doyen of lesbian novelists. *Madame Aurora* is a historical romance.

2045   **Aldridge, Sarah,** 1911– . *Misfortune's Friends.* Tallahassee: Naiad, 1985.
"What is Mrs. Henshaw's influence on the young lesbians in her life? Why is she always present in times of need . . . and what is the real tie between her and Althea's aunt?" *Misfortune's Friends* is a historical romance.

2046   **Alford, Edna,** 1947– . *A Sleep Full of Dreams.* Lentzville: Oolichan Books, 1981.
The story is told through the eyes and thoughts of a young nursing home employee as she struggles to "see" the old old women—two former prostitutes, a compulsive hoarder, and others.

2047   **Allen, Charlotte Vale,** 1941– . *Dream Train.* New York: Atheneum, 1988.
Anne, in her mid-70s, and her husband are on the Orient Express, celebrating their fiftieth wedding anniversary. The hero of this romantic novel is Joanna James, a young journalist who meets and is influenced by Anne.

2048   **Ariyoshi, Sawako,** 1931–1984. *The Twilight Years.* New York: Kodansha/Harper, 1984.
Written during her middle age, Ariyoshi's novel about a middle aged daughter-in-law caring for a senile old man was translated from Japanese by Mildred Tahara. Originally titled *Kokotsu No Hito,* it was popular in 1972, awakening people to the seriousness of aging.

2049   **Arthur, Elizabeth,** 1953– . *Binding Spell.* New York: Doubleday, 1988.
Ada Esterhaczy is an old Hungarian herbalist. A variety of interesting people consult her: Russian professors visiting in Indiana, a sheriff, a would-be witch, a psychologist.

2050   **Asimov, Isaac,** 1920– , et al, eds. *Senior Sleuths: A Large-Print Anthology of Mysteries and Puzzlers.* Boston: G. K. Hall, 1989.
Fifteen fictional detectives and American and English authors are represented in this select collection. They include Agatha Christie's "The Case of the Perfect Maid"; Dorothy Salisbury Davis's "Mrs. Norris Observes"; Helen McCloy's "The Pleasant Assassin"; and Charlotte MacLeod's "Journey for Lady G."

2051   **Astor, Brooke,** 1903– . *The Last Blossom on the Plum Tree: A Period Piece.* New York: Random, 1986.
May Sarton referred to this American novel of the 1920s about a "May-December romance" as "a charming bubble of a light novel." The title is derived from

the Chinese proverb, "He who sees the last blossom on the plum tree must pick it." It refers to possibly the last chance for romance for two widows, as well as the impending stock market crash.

2052   **Atwood, Margaret Eleanor,** 1939– . *Bodily Harm.* New York: Simon & Schuster, 1982; published in 1981 in Canada by McClelland & Stewart.

Canadian novelist and poet (*see #2169*) Atwood contends that Canadian literature reflects Canadians' tendency to be willing victims and survivalists. And she is concerned with the need for women to assert their individual identities. This allegorical novel concerns a middle-aged Canadian journalist who undergoes a cancer-related mastectomy and her personal restoration.

2053   **Azpadu, Dodici,** 1942– . *Saturday Night in the Prime of Life.* Iowa City: Aunt Lute, 1983.

Azpadu's novel concerns two aging women, Nedie and her lover Lindy, and the male-dominated Sicilian culture that affects the women who exist inside and outside it.

2054   **Baird, Marie-Terese.** *The Birds of Sadness.* New York: St. Martin's Press, 1986.

Melanie is a 78-year-old woman whose strength is attributed to her father. When her granddaughter becomes pregnant with an illegitimate child, she joyfully prepares for the birth; when the granddaughter decides to abort the pregnancy, her grandmother is dismayed.

2055   **Barker, Pat,** 1943– . *The Century's Daughter.* New York: Putnam, 1986.

Eighty-four-year-old Liza has worked all her life and now experiences the stresses of being old, alone, and a British working-class woman. She refuses to leave her slum residence, from which she and her parrot Nelson have been evicted. Social worker Stephen is responsible for persuading and removing her to an old age home.

2056   **Barker, Pat,** 1943– . *Union Street.* New York: Putnam, 1982.

The year 1973 in England was particularly hard for people on the street. This novel portrays seven women living in poverty—a chapter for each, although they are interrelated. The oldest is 76.

2057   **Benjamin, Ruth,** 1934– . *Naked at Forty.* New York: Horizon Press, 1984.
Middle-aged woman poet finds self-fulfillment.

2058   **Bennett, Mary Lou.** *Murder Once Done.* Menlo Park: Perseverance Press, 1988.
In this mystery three elderly women cope with murder in Oregon.

2059   **Berk, Ann.** *Fast Forward.* New York: Doubleday, 1983.

Yet another contemporary middle-aged woman is foisted off as "liberated" as she complies with society's expectations to be all things to all people much as in the past.

2060   **Bernays, Anne F.,** 1930– . *The Address Book.* Boston: Little, Brown, 1983.

Alicia Baer (in some ways like Bernays) lives and has a good job as an editor in Boston. Spouse of a well-known Harvard surgeon, parent of an adolescent daughter, owner of the address book, she is offered an attractive New York–commute job. Bernays is the author of *Professor Romeo* (Weidenfeld & Nicolson, 1989), a Cambridge, Massachusetts, college teacher whose fictional portrayal was about sexual harassment of female students.

2061   **Birmelin, Blair T.,** 1939– . *The Dead Woman's Sister.* New York: Schocken, 1985.

Old Miss Evelyn Duvenek and her sister, Elsie Marie, live on the Upper West Side of Manhattan—"recluses" isolated among many people in an old apartment house. When Evelyn finds Elsie Marie dead, she ventures into the corridor and is befriended by neighbor Mrs. O'Connell. A "visiting homemaker" and a "welfare mother" are also involved.

2062 **Blackwood, Caroline,** 1931– . *Corrigan.* New York: Viking, 1984.
For three years, Mrs. Blount has been a grieving, possibly selfish, widow. This is the clever story of what happens to change things and who catches on to the deception involved.

2063 **Braverman, Kate.** *Palm Latitudes.* New York: Simon & Schuster, 1988.
One of these three Los Angeles Latinas is aged Marta Ortega. Divided into chapters from each woman's perspective, *Palm Latitudes* provides mother-daughter, grandparent, intercultural insights into their lives.

2064 **Breeze, Katie,** 1929– . *Nekkid Cowboy.* San Antonio: Corona, 1982.
Breeze is a middle-aged wife and mother whose first book is a historical novel of Texas in the 1920s, centering on a strong-minded old woman.

2065 **Bridgers, Sue Ellen,** 1942– . *Sara Will.* New York: Harper & Row, 1985.
Middle-aged Sara Will Burney lives with her widow sister. A distant relative accompanied by his teenage unwed-mother niece and her baby arrive on the scene. Sara overcomes her fear of "love," and they become a three-generation family.

2066 **Brookner, Anita,** 1928– . *The Debut.* New York: Simon & Schuster, 1981.
Publishers Weekly's description is revealing: "Few of her colleagues or students have even a notion that Dr. Ruth Weiss, a buttoned-up, fortyish spinster professor of literature, publishing sections of her endless thesis . . . has known emotion as great as that of the fictional French heroines." The British edition of this first novel is titled *A Start in Life.*

2067 **Brown, Rita Mae,** 1944– . *Bingo.* New York: Bantam, 1988. il.
Nickel Smith (43) works for the local newspaper. She tells us about sibling rivalry in Pennsylvania as her aunt Louise (86) and mother Julia (82) vie for Ed (70), the new man in town.

2068 **Bruggen, Carol.** *Crumbs Under the Skin.* London: A. Deutsch, 1984.
This writer lives in England, has been employed as a teacher, and has had several plays broadcast on Radio 4. Her first novel is a fantasy about middle-aged English psychiatrist Judith. Bruggen has been compared to British writer Muriel Spark (1918–), who has achieved recognition primarily as a novelist (*The Prime of Miss Jean Brodie*, 1962) whose forte is satire blending comedy and horror.

2069 **Burr, Bettz.** *Blue Ladies.* New York: Seaview, 1980.
This first novel is about three middle-aged women associated with the "female ghetto" of an East Side Manhattan art museum directed by Dr. Robert Patrick.

2070 **Calisher, Hortense,** 1911–1972. *Age.* New York: Weidenfeld & Nicolson, 1987.
In their 70s, New Yorkers Gemma and Rupert have been happily married for many years. But the knowledge and fear that one of them will be left behind dominate them. Their separate journals, or diaries, constitute this short novel. Gerontologist Mary Sohngen's review provides two pages of good reading (*Gerontologist* April 1988 28[2]:

282). It was Calisher who wrote, at age 61, "In the zoo of the social sciences is where the muskglands of humanity are removed—for study. A novel doesn't study—it invents. Inevitably, it represents" (*Herself*, 1972).

2071   **Carrington, Leonora,** 1917– . *The Hearing Trumpet.* San Francisco: City Lights Books, 1985. il.

Originally published in 1974 in French as *Le Cornet Acoustique*. Gerontologist Mary Sohngen, who has written about the images of old persons in contemporary literature, considers this an example of the "protagonist as rebel" novel. Marian Leatherby, 92, causes a rumpus in an old ladies' home.

2072   **Chase, Joan.** *During the Reign of the Queen of Persia.* New York: Harper & Row, 1983.

Gram, also known as the Queen of Persia, is raising a second generation on an Ohio farm.

2073   **Christie, Agatha Mary Clarissa,** 1891–1976. *Five Complete Miss Marple Novels.* New York: Avenel, distributed by Crown, 1980.

"Writing at a time when few women worked at jobs that would bring them into contact with any members of the public, much less murderous ones, Christie did not have access to recently popular methods of explaining an amateur detective's involvement in crime; she did, however, have available stereotypes of women, and used them to her advantage. Miss Jane Marple, an elderly spinster, is garrulous and nosey, a near caricature of a gossipy old lady . . . [Dame Agatha] employs and criticizes (by mocking) gender stereotypes. Miss Marple's intelligence and the threat she poses to the guilty [and to male authority figures], allowing themselves to be deceived by appearances . . . and by conventional attitudes toward old, unmarried women . . . [are] feminist elements in the Marple novels that deserve notice; the most significant of these is the valorization of precisely those feminine qualities ridiculed in the stereotype of the irrational, intuitive, gossipy spinster. Christie shows the advantages women's ways of thinking may have: Miss Marple's interest in people is not mere nosiness, but evidence of a lifelong study of human nature to which she has brought, and through which she has cultivated, acuity, insight, intelligence, and imagination" (Maureen T. Reddy. *Sisters in Crime: Feminism and the Crime Novel.* Continuum, 1988. 19–20). This collection consists of *The Mirror Crack'd* (published in Great Britain as *The Mirror Crack'd from Side to Side*); *A Caribbean Mystery; Nemesis* (the final and often considered the best Marple mystery; her refusal to be negated by age confirms her heroism, making the book significant despite the misogyny expressed about rape); *What Mrs. McGillicuddy Saw!* (published in Britain as *The 4:50 from Paddington*); and *The Body in the Library*. Television and motion picture plays starring Helen Hayes and Angela Lansbury have been made of these.

2074   **Desai, Anita,** 1937– . *Clear Light of Day.* New York: Harper, 1980.

The setting is Indian society of the early 1940s. Tara and her diplomat spouse are making a periodic visit to the Old Delhi family mansion that houses her older sister—the novel's main character, middle-aged, single Bim—and the youngest brother, Baba. Their eldest brother has been able to move away.

2075   **Dodd, Susan M.,** 1946– . *Mamaw.* New York: Viking, 1988.

Zerelda Cole James Samuel is also referred to in the literature as Zereld James. She survived numerous childbirths on a nineteenth-century Missouri farm, the horrors of war, eviction, widowhood, exile, prison, children's deaths, and her second husband's aggression, senility, and institutionalization. Outlaws Frank and Jesse James were two of her children. This historical novel is based on that life.

2076   **Douglas, Ellen,** 1921– . *A Lifetime Burning.* New York: Random, 1982.
Douglas's sometimes pseudonym is Josephine Haxton. As in her *Apostles of Light* (1973), the setting is a small Mississippi town. A 60-year-old college teacher reveals herself in a diary-like journal written to her children.

2077   **Drabble, Margaret,** 1939– . *The Middle Ground.* New York: Knopf, 1980.
Drabble is an English novelist, educated at Newnham College, Cambridge, where she took a double first in English. Highly thought of in her native country, she has also achieved success and awards in the United States. The literary establishment praises her unique style; feminist critics add that she portrays female experiences honestly. Her women are often attractive and intellectual, but there is much more to them— For example, Kate Armstrong, a middle-aged, divorced "working mother," an achiever living in contemporary London. Very little actually happens *to* her in the course of this novel of encounter.

2078   **Drabble, Margaret,** 1939– . *The Radiant Way.* New York: Knopf, 1987.
Drabble's 1975 *Realms of Gold, The Middle Ground* (#2077), and *The Radiant Way* form a series about women's middle years. Here, the novel covers five years in the lives of three women who meet at Cambridge University in the 1950s.

2079   **Eberstadt, Isabel.** *Natural Victims.* New York: Knopf/Random, 1983.
Middle-aged Sis Melmore is a beautiful and rich widow and mother—considered a "natural survivor" in this lengthy (480-page) novel.

2080   **Engel, Marian.** *The Year of the Child.* New York: St. Martin's, 1981. Published in Canada with the title *Lunatic Villas.*
Harriet Ross is a middle-aged, divorced writer working to support a houseful of her and others' children. Elderly Mrs. Saxe moves into Lunatic Villas, the name of Harriet's Toronto house.

2081   **Ferguson, Patricia.** *Family Myths and Legends.* London: A. Deutsch, 1985.
The bitterness that can accompany caregiving in a matriarchal environment is portrayed in London. As the novel opens, Joan is in the kitchen contemplating the murder of her mother.

2082   **Figes, Eva,** 1932– . *Ghosts.* New York: Pantheon, 1988.
Figes is a British feminist author of German birth, educated in England. After working as a publisher's editor and translator, she became a full-time journalist, reviewer, and writer of both fiction and nonfiction. This novel takes a nameless old woman through a series of experiences including mother-daughter relationships and physical changes of aging.

2083   **Figes, Eva,** 1932– . *The Seven Ages.* New York: Pantheon, 1986.
A midwife whose ancestors speak to her through voices has returned to their cottage to consider generations of their women. Kate, one of her daughters, is an obstetrician continuing the tradition.

2084   **Figes, Eva,** 1932– . *Waking.* New York: Pantheon, 1981.
Gerontologist Mary Sohngen, who has written about the images of old persons in contemporary literature, considers *Waking* an example of the "protagonist as victim" novel. Seven brief interior monologues trace stages in life from childhood to neglected old age and solitary death.

2085   **Flagg, Fannie,** 1944– . *Fried Green Tomatoes at the Whistle Stop Cafe.* New York: Random, 1987.

American comedian and actor with origins in the South, Fannie Flagg is also an accomplished humor writer. The Rose Terrace Nursing Home in Birmingham, Alabama, houses narrator Mrs. Cleon "Ninny" Threadgoode, who becomes friends with middle-aged Evelyn Couch, a visitor experiencing a difficult menopause. Excerpts from the weekly newspaper of 1929 provide background for Ninny's stories. *Fried Green Tomatoes* has been made into a motion picture with Jessica Tandy in the role of old Ninny and Kathy Bates as middle-aged Evelyn.

2086   **Florey, Kitty Burns,** 1943– . *The Garden Path.* New York: Putnam, 1983.

Forty-nine-year-old "earthy" Rose Mortimer has a gay 29-year-old son. Her daughter, 27, teaches both of them "forgiveness."

2087   **Forbes, Delores Florine Stanton,** 1923– . *Don't Die on Me, Billie Jean.* New York: Doubleday, 1987.

The author of this Crime Club novel (whose pseudonyms are Forbes Rydell and Tobas Wells) is an American mystery writer. This one is about "two sweet old ladies" and a "little" female dog retired to St. Martin.

2088   **Freydberg, Margaret Howe.** *Katherine's House.* Woodstock: Countryman Press, 1986.

The novel within a novel works around the quandary of whether or not to sell the ancestral home that is Katherine's house. It is a quandary for her because she has allowed herself to become one of the older women accustomed to accepting others' opinions without protest. Katherine is 49 years old and separated from the husband.

2089   **Gallie, Menna.** *In These Promiscuous Parts.* New York: St. Martin's Press, 1986.

Small-town life in Wales is the setting for this Joan Kahn book about older women. The title derives from Rudyard Kipling's *The Elephant's Child*: "Do you happen to have seen a crocodile in these parts?"

2090   **Gilliatt, Penelope Ann Douglas,** 1932– . *Mortal Matters.* New York: Coward-McCann, 1983.

Gilliatt is an English critic, writer of novels (*The Cutting Edge*), short stories ("Come Back If It Doesn't Get Better"), biography, and the "Sunday Bloody Sunday" screenplay. She grew up in Northumberland, where this novel begins. Her documentation note refers to sources that included Dame Christabel Pankhurst's *Unshackled*, Annie Kenney's *Memories of a Militant*, and Helen Blackburn's *Woman's Suffrage*.

2091   **Gilman, Dorothy,** 1923– . *Mrs. Pollifax and the Golden Triangle.* New York: Doubleday, 1988.

We first met widow and grandmother Emily Pollifax in Gilman's 1966 *The Unexpected Mrs. Pollifax.* A series of adventures working for the CIA have followed. By 1988, she's Emily Reed-Pollifax, "senior citizen."

2092   **Gordon, Mary,** 1949– . *Men and Angels.* New York: Random, 1985.

Although *Men and Angels*'s hero, Caroline Watson, is a fictional middle-aged American painter, author Gordon drew on the lives of artists Cecilia Beaux, Mary Cassatt, and Suzanne Valadon.

2093   **Gray, Francine du Plessix,** 1930– . *World Without End.* New York: Simon & Schuster, 1981.

"After the age of forty there isn't much to live for except friendship," says one of the characters. Gray is an American writer of fiction and nonfiction; her most recent nonfiction book is *Soviet Women: Walking the Tightrope* (Doubleday, 1990).

2094   **Hayes, Helen, 1900–1993, and Thomas Chastain.** *Where the Truth Lies.* New York: Morrow, 1988.

The main character, Halcie Harper, is in her 80s. She solves a Hollywood crime and explains that she can do so because she has played Miss Marple so many times. *See also* #2073.

2095   **Heath, Catherine.** *Behaving Badly.* New York: Taplinger, 1985.

Middle-aged Bridget's husband leaves her for a younger woman. Author Heath was born in London and teaches English literature. Her dialogue here has been praised by the *London Times* "as artfully artless as that of Barbara Pym."

2096   **Hershey, Olive.** *Truck Dance.* New York: Harper & Row, 1989.

"Feisty" middle-aged Wilma Hemshoff of East Texas leaves her philandering husband and grown sons for a trucker's life. "It's better than fixing fries." And she wanted to be size 12 again. Said to be a novel of a woman's self-discovery, "A week past her 44th birthday with a lot of highway behind her, she was more lonesome than she'd ever been in her life."

2097   **Howard, Maureen, 1930–** . *Expensive Habits.* New York: Summit Books, 1986.

Author Howard is an American novelist and teacher who lives in New York City. Hero Margaret Flood is a celebrated novelist dying of heart disease in New York.

2098   **Hull, Helen Rose, 1888–1971.** *Islanders.* New York: Feminist Press at the CUNY, 1988.

Women are the "islanders." This edition includes an afterword by Patricia McClelland Miller. It is the story of Ellen Dacey, who, in 1927 when *Islanders* was originally published (by Macmillan), was a model unmarried woman—caretaker to parents, siblings, and subsequent generations. Feminist Hull taught English composition at Wellesley and Barnard (women's) Colleges and wrote novels and short stories during summers. It is interesting to compare her 1927 novel with the 1984 work by Jaanus, who also teaches at Barnard (*see* #2099).

2099   **Jaanus, Maire.** *She.* Garden City: Dial Press, 1984.

Successful professor, older (40) woman/younger man. Jaanus is a Barnard (women's) College English faculty member. It is interesting to compare her 1984 novel with the 1927 work by Hull, who also taught at Barnard (*see* #2098).

2100   **Johnson, Pamela Hansford, 1912–1981.** *A Bonfire.* New York: Scribner, 1981.

Johnson was an English broadcaster and versatile writer of psychological novels and literary studies, although she is probably most known for having been C. P. Snow's spouse. This novel sees middle-class, sheltered daughter Emma Sheldrake through three marriages from 1924 to 1937.

2101   **Jolley, Elizabeth, 1923–** . *Foxybaby.* New York: Viking, 1985.

Author Alma Porch has arranged to serve as an instructor at a sort of Australian reentry summer school run by Miss Peycroft, who speaks in stereotypes. "'I am so glad' she said glancing back at Miss Porch with a mixture of approval and doubt, 'that you seem to be a twinset-and-pearls sort of person, so reliable. . . . I was afraid that being an authoress and perhaps something of a feminist you'd wear hob-nailed boots and a man's hat pulled down over your eyes. Why is it . . . that Wimmins Libbers keep those terribly ugly hats on all the time, even at mealtimes?'" And there are objections to Alma's plans for the course. "'I realize,' Miss Peycroft said, 'that it is from Goethe and therefore beautifully written but we . . . simply cannot invite . . . mature age students from the more . . . well-to-do suburbs, to come to The Better Body Through The Arts Course and throw that at them . . . '" (pp. 21, 24).

2102   **Jolley, Elizabeth**, 1923– . *Miss Peabody's Inheritance.* New York: Viking, 1984.

Australian writer Diana Hopewell corresponds with Miss Peabody, a London spinster. A story-within-a-story evolves as Hopewell involves Peabody in her current novel.

2103   **Jong, Erica Mann**, 1942– . *Parachutes and Kisses.* New York: New American Library, 1984.

Jong is an American poet and novelist, author of the bestselling *Fear of Flying* (1973), a picaresque novel of Isadora Wing's sexual adventures, and *How to Save Your Own Life* (1977), in which Isadora leaves her husband for a new man and Hollywood. In the intervening years, she has married him, had a child, and separated from him. Now 39 and afraid of love, she no longer loves to write, her only income source as a single mother, and casts about, trying everything, including another younger man.

2104   **Jong, Erica Mann**, 1942– . *Serenissima: A Novel of Venice.* New York: Houghton Mifflin, 1987.

Jessica Pruitt is an American actress in her 40s attending a Venice film festival. A Shakespeare devotee, she has appeared in a film version of *The Merchant of Venice*, and in this literary fantasy, invokes witch's power to wish herself back to the Venice of 1592.

2105   **Keane, Molly**, 1904– . *Time After Time.* New York: Knopf, 1984.

Old people can be cruel to each other, as Keane illustrates in this spectacle of sisters April, May, and June existing in a decaying Irish manor house with their brother, Jasper, and their pets.

2106   **Kogawa, Joy.** *Obasan.* Boston: David Godine, 1981.

Oba means aunt in Japanese; with *san*, it can become auntie or middle-aged woman. This novel based on Canadian evacuation and relocation of Japanese during 1942–1945 is narrated in 1972 by aunt Emily Kato's 36-year-old niece.

2107   **Lessing, Doris May**, 1919– . *The Diaries of Jane Somers.* New York: Knopf, 1983–1984; and London: Michael Joseph, 1984.

British novelist and short story writer Lessing grew up in Rhodesia and moved to England in 1949. Despite her disclaimers of feminism, many women readers have been inspired by her books. Her (Jane Somers's) diaries consist of *The Diary of a Good Neighbour*, in which she is middle-aged, followed by *If the Old Could*, and they are about the problems of older women and sex, loneliness, and the generation gap.

2108   **Lessing, Doris May**, 1919– . *The Good Terrorist.* London: J. Cape; and New York: Knopf, 1985.

The good terrorist is Alice Mellings, who housemothers a group of London radicals who have taken over an abandoned building. She winds up doing all the dutiful homey things for which she held her middle-class mother in contempt, making herself indispensable and invisible, earning a sense of belonging by denying her own sense of self. This satire is also about death.

2109   **LeSueur, Meridel,** 1901– . *Winter Prairie Woman, 2d ed.* Illustrations by Sandy Spieler. Minneapolis: Midwest Villages & Voices, 1990.

Written when she turned 90, *Winter Prairie Woman* is a six-part story of the end of a very old woman's life. She must leave the Midwestern farm where she has lived all her life because it is falling apart around her, but she goes forward, welcoming death as a new start.

2110   **Lindau, Joan,** 1944– . *Mrs. Cooper's Boardinghouse.* New York: McGraw-Hill, 1980.

May Sarton describes this novel "full of tenderness . . . how rare these days." In it, 10-year-old Kate helps old Mrs. Cooper run her Missouri small-town boardinghouse.

2111   **Lively, Penelope,** 1933– . *Moon Tiger.* New York: Grove Press, 1987.

Lively was born in Cairo, Egypt, and spent her childhood there during World War II. *Moon Tiger* is about Claudia Hampton, a former war correspondent, who recalls her experiences as she dies of cancer.

2112   **Lurie, Alison,** 1926– . *Foreign Affairs.* New York: Random, 1984.

American writer Lurie is also a Cornell University professor of English. She won a Pulitzer Prize for *Foreign Affairs.* In it, she tells the stories of Vinnie Miner, age 54, and Fred Turner, 29—both American academics on leave in England from the same institution—in alternating chapters and a variation on the older woman/younger man.

2113   **Mandel, Sally,** *Portrait of a Married Woman.* New York: Bantam, 1986.

New Yorker Maggie Hollander, 38, is the much novelized wife and mother who has it all. Having given up her art to marry, she is now offered a designer job and meets a man in art class.

2114   **Marshall, Paule,** 1929– . *Praisesong for the Widow.* New York: Putnam, 1983.

Sixty-four-year-old New York widow Avey Johnson departs an expensive West Indian cruise for her African heritage and adventures that include an elderly man and a close look at her life.

2115   **Mason, Bobbie Ann,** 1940– . *Spense and Lila.* New York: Harper, 1988. il.

Also available in large-print edition. Lila and Spence are separated for two weeks when she is hospitalized for cancer surgery, but their marriage sees them through.

2116   **McCaffrey, Anne,** 1926– . *The Year of the Lucy.* New York: Tom Doherty/St. Martin's Press, 1986.

The story begins in the United States in 1961. It is about Mirelle Martin—illegitimate, wife-mother, would-be sculptor—and Lucy—long-gone friend who years ago had encouraged Mirelle in her aspirations.

2117   **McCauley, Sue.** *Other Halves.* New York: Penguin, 1985.

New Zealand journalist McCauley's first novel is autobiographical, about two of society's outcasts and an older woman/younger man.

2118   **McCorkle, Jill,** 1958– . *Tending to Virginia.* Algonquin Press of Chapel Hill/ New York: Random, 1987.

Ginny Sue is pregnant, unhappy, disillusioned with her husband. She turns to the women from other generations in her life, including her grandmother and newly retired mother.

2119   **McCoy, Maureen.** *Summertime.* Las Cruces: Poseidon Press, 1987.

Jessamine Morrow, 85, departs the retirement home with another inmate in this novel of three generations of Midwestern women.

2120   **Miner, Valerie,** 1947– . Freedom: Crossing Press, 1985.

A statement by the author follows the last page: "Writing is for me a social act at the beginning and at the end. I think fiction emerges from an imaginative collectivity of writers and readers rather than from solitary genesis." May Sarton has said about this novel, "Two wonderful old women whose relationship is feisty, tender and deep. No fluff about senior citizens here." And Marge Piercy, "Both of the women, Chrissie and Margaret, are sharply sketched, eccentric, easy to identify with. . . . " There are no stereotypes of women or of old women, and both are feminists.

2121   **Mitchell, Gladys,** 1901– . *The Death-Cap Dancers.* New York: St. Martin's, 1981.

Mitchell is a writer of detective novels whose work has been described as wittier and more original than that of Christie or Sayers. Dame Beatrice Lestrange Bradley, an aged psychiatrist in the manner of Miss Marple, solves a crime that has baffled police.

2122   **Montero, Rosa,** 1951– . *The Delta Function.* Translated and with an afterword by Karl Easton and Yolanda Molina Gavilan. Lincoln: U of Nebraska Press, 1991.

This translation of Montero's *La Función Delta* is in the University of Nebraska Press's European Women Writers series. It is the story of 60-year-old Lucia, dying of cancer. She fears being alone, being abandoned, and dying. In the hospital, she begins a diary or journal that recreates herself as she was thirty years earlier in 1980, for the present is the year 2010. Montero was born and raised in Madrid, the setting of this novel. Although she explores many of the old taboos—homosexuality, women's and old people's sexuality, and death by choice—she disassociates herself from writers of feminist novels.

2123   **Moore, Katharine,** 1898– . *The Lotus House.* New York: Schocken, 1983; and London: Allison and Busby, 1984.

In Moore's first novel, published when she was 85, Letty Anderson purchases the house where she spent some of her childhood. Moore has also written children's books and nonfiction including her twenty-two-year correspondence with Joyce Grenfell (1910–1979), *An Invisible Friendship* (#1930), and *Cordial Relations: The Maiden Aunt in Fact and Fiction* (London: Heinemann, 1966).

2124   **Moore, Katharine,** 1898– . *Moving House.* London: Allison and Busby, 1986.

Moore's second novel is also about senior women in Great Britain, and also concerns their housing. Both (*see* #2123) appear in *The Katharine Moore Omnibus* (Schocken, 1987).

2125   **Moskowitz, Bette Ann.** *Leaving Barney.* New York: Holt, 1988.

Widow Tessie carries on their bookstore business, deals with a condescending geriatrician son-in-law, and copes with funds missing from the accounts in this humorous mystery novel.

2126   **Moulton, Elizabeth.** *Fatal Demonstrations.* New York: Harper, 1980.

Like Sylvia Plath, Moulton had been a finalist in the *Mlle.* magazine guest editor competition while in college. She returned to writing in mid-life with this, her first published novel. A historical novel, it begins in 1970 and surrounds elderly Boston widow Isobel Greenough Storer's memories. The title relates to the Sacco and Venzetti case (they were executed in Massachusetts in 1927) and the Kent State University "riot" in 1970.

2127 **Naylor, Gloria.** *Mama Day.* New York: Random, 1988.
Abigail (73) and Mama Day Miranda (80) are Manhattanite Cocoa Day's grandmother and great-aunt. They see each other during vacations at home on a Georgia island that has magical powers.

2128 **Novick, Marian.** *At Her Age.* New York: Scribners, 1985.
Molly Vorobey (75) and her daughter and grandchildren reject Florida life and return to New York.

2129 **Oates, Joyce Carol,** 1938– . *American Appetites.* New York: Dutton, 1989.
In this novel of the late 1980s, Ian and Glynnis McCullough are an upper-middle-class, middle-age (he is 50) American couple. She is into cookbooks, and they have a college-age daughter, Bianca. "Existence, [he] playfully argued, often before audiences, is a matter after all of how you define your terms" (p. 5). And then Ian kills Glynnis, inadvertently, as it were. Oates is an American award-winning writer of poetry (e.g., *Invisible Woman: New and Selected Poems, 1970–1982.* Ontario Review Press/Persea Books, 1982), criticism and reviews, short stories and novels, as well as a professor of English.

2130 **Oates, Joyce Carol,** 1938– . *Solstice.* New York: Dutton, 1985.
After her divorce, middle-aged Monica Jensen aims to throw herself into her new teaching job. She becomes involved with famous local artist Sheila Trask.

2131 **O'Marie, Carol Anne.** *The Missing Madonna.* New York: Delacorte, 1988.
O'Marie is a nun writing about two 70-year-old nuns attending an Older Women's League convention and attempting to solve the mystery of an old friend's disappearance. There are too many unnecessary references to "old," and the humor is sometimes at a woman's expense.

2132 **Perrin, Ursula,** 1935– . *Old Devotions.* New York: Dial Press, 1983.
The lives of two former college roomates, now middle-aged, have differed. Isabel, the storyteller, is a divorced "failure"; Morgan is a suburban housewife.

2133 **Piercy, Marge,** 1936– . *Braided Lives.* New York: Summit/Simon & Schuster, 1982.
Said to be semiautobiographical, *Braided Lives* is about the narrator, Jill, now middle-aged and a successful writer, and her lifelong friendship with cousin and friend Donna.

2134 **Pym, Barbara,** 1913–1980. *An Academic Question.* New York: Dutton, 1986.
Pym's unpublished novels included *An Academic Question*, which has been absorbed with *Quartet in Autumn* (1977). She did not title it, referring to her "academic novel." In it a library administrator in academe "was rather an old-womanish young man and the three of us [women office workers] tut-tutted and chatted cosily about the state the papers were in without making the slightest attempt to tidy them up" (p. 145).

2135 **Pym, Barbara,** 1913–1980. *A Few Green Leaves.* New York: Dutton, 1980.
In her final novel, finished shortly before her death of cancer and published posthumously, Pym wrote about anthropologist Emma Howick—in her 30s—and an

Oxfordshire village such as the one where she shared a cottage with her sister. "At the mention of 'stress' Martin was at once on the alert. Although his main field of study and interest was geriatrics, he was well aware of the importance of giving full attention to *all* his patients, for even the young middle-aged would one day be old persons. Besides, he was interested in and puzzled by Emma, who did not seem to fit into any of his pre-arranged categories" (p. 209).

2136   **Pym, Barbara**, 1913–1980. *An Unsuitable Attachment*. New York: Dutton, 1982.
        Written in 1963, when Pym was 50, this novel was rejected by Cape, which had published her six previous novels, and by two other publishers. Although she stopped writing for many years, she continued despite herself to keep writer's notebooks and her diary (*see* #1958). The restricted lives of her characters are now recognized as timely and well drawn. Hazel Holt edited this unfinished novel for publication. An older woman/younger man are a part, although not the main theme. The full texts of Pym's work are at the Bodleian Library.

2137   **Raskin, Barbara**. *Hot Flashes*. New York: St. Martin's, 1987.
        Several middle-aged women who have been best friends gather following the death of Sukie Amaram. Diana examines Sukie's diary.

2138   **Rich, Virginia**. *The Baked Bean Supper Murders*. New York: Dutton, 1983.
        Mrs. Eugenia Potter is a widow in her 60s, observer of life, and hero of this mystery series. Other titles are *The Cooking School Murders* (1981) and *The Nantucket Diet Murders* (1985).

2139   **Rowntree, Kathleen**, 1938– . *The Haunting of Willow Dasset*. Boston: Little, Brown, 1989.
        This "family novel" is essentially about Sally, a young girl, and the memorable summers spent at her grandfather's farm. But as she matures, she recognizes that the picture was imperfect: three elderly aunts, for example, are portrayed as comic—one, called Great Aunt Pip, as a flirt.

2140   **Rubens, Bernice**. *Birds of Paradise*. London: Hamilton, 1981; and New York: Summit Books, 1982.
        Ellen Walsh and Alice Pickering, both 63, are old friends and next-door neighbors. They celebrate their widowhood by taking a Mediterranean cruise and encounter a rapist on board.

2141   **Rule, Jane**, 1931– . *Memory Board*. Tallahassee: Naiad, 1987.
        Diana and David Crown are twins. Diana, a retired gynecologist, has lived her life with Constance, who now suffers from Alzheimer's Disease. After years of separation, David seeks his sister out.

2142   **Sanders, Joan**, 1924– . *Other Lips and Other Hearts*. New York: Houghton Mifflin, 1982.
        Jasmine "Jas" Redland is a writer. She abandons her husband of twenty years for a "voyage into Mormon culture and country." The author grew up in Utah.

2143   **Sarton, May**, 1912–1995. *Anger*. New York: Norton, 1982.
        Sarton is a popular writer established in several forms: autobiographical works, novels dating back to 1946 and *Bridge of Years*, and poetry are available in large print. *Anger* is about the marriage of a Boston couple, banker Ned and singer Anna.

2144   **Sarton, May,** 1912–1995. *The Education of Harriet Hatfield*. New York: Norton, 1989.

Harriet, 60, opens her dream-women's bookstore following the death of her lesbian lover.

2145   **Sarton, May,** 1912–1995. *The Magnificent Spinster.* New York: Norton, 1985.

The magnificent spinster is Jane Reid, a teacher and mentor of the narrator. Of it, Sarton has written, "I have come to see that *The Magnificent Spinster* is a flawed novel, and not my best, though it is not a total failure. Of course the big hurdle was to write about Anne Thorpe—Jane Reid in the novel—without probing in a way that could offend relatives and friends. . . . The reviewers blame me for a 'goody goody' character who is not believeable. And . . . because she is apparently asexual. . . . I am not sorry I wrote this novel, the last big novel I imagine I shall manage to write. It was very hard work indeed and twice I nearly gave it up. But I am rather detached from it now and look forward to trying a novel not based on a real person and to give my imagination free rein" (#1963: 149–151).

2146   **Sawyer, Corinne Holt.** *The J. Alfred Prufrock Murders.* New York: Donald I. Fine, 1988.

"Feisty" is the word reviewers usually use to describe Angela Benbow, a widow who has moved into crafts and detecting. Other familiar aspects frequently built into retirement community life about four women in their 70s include a quiet librarian, gossip, and confusion.

2147   **Schaeffer, Susan Fromberg,** 1941– . *The Injured Party.* New York: St. Martin's Press, 1986.

Wife and mother Iris has been hospitalized with depression. An old and terminally ill lover arrives on the scene, but her husband does not protest as he observes Iris's response.

2148   **Siddons, Anne Rivers.** *Homeplaces.* New York: Harper & Row, 1983.

Middle-aged Micah Winship has been successful as a journalist living in New York City since fleeing the South of her youthful civil rights activism. She returns to her father in his illness.

2149   **Smiley, Jane.** *At Paradise Gates.* New York: Simon & Schuster, 1981.

Anna Robison, 72, tends her dying husband and reviews their life together in this novel of three generations of women of an American family.

2150   **Smith, Evelyn E.,** 1927– . *Miss Melville Regrets. Miss Melville Returns. Miss Melville's Revenge.* New York: D. Fine, 1986, 1987, 1989.

Middle-aged and not married, New Yorker Miss Susan Melville first appears as a hit woman. In her *Return,* she is a successful artist and solves a double murder. And in the satirical *Revenge,* she has taken on a Charles Bronson character–like role, doling out justice to unrepentant criminals protected by diplomatic immunity. The author is American science fiction writer Delphine C. Lyons.

2151   **Somerville, Edith De,** 1858–1949, **and Martin Ross,** 1862–1915. *The Real Charlotte.* New Jersey: Rutgers U Press, 1986. bib.

Edited by Virginia Beards, this edition includes notes, a further-reading bibliography, and a Somerville and Ross chronology. First published in 1894, before their "Irish R M" stories, *The Real Charlotte* is about nineteenth-century Irish women, in particular, Charlotte and Francie, and the relationship of social class and inheritance. Somerville was Irish novelist Anna Oeone; she wrote with Martin Ross, pseudonym of her cousin Violet Florence Martin.

2152 **Stein, Toby,** 1935– . *Only the Best.* New York: Arbor House, 1984.

Stein teaches drama at the High School of Performing Arts, and history at Barnard (women's) College and Columbia University. This is her novel of middle-aged Jewish-American women.

2153 **Stone, Alma,** 1914– . *Now for the Turbulence.* New York: Doubleday, 1983.

Born in Texas, the author lives in New York City, the setting in which two old sisters and their support group friends struggle to maintain their independence. *Now for the Turbulence* has been described as "black sly humor," but is it? The title is derived from the announcement on the air flight from Miami to New York.

2154 **Sullivan, Faith.** *Mrs. Demming and the Mythical Beast.* New York: Macmillan, 1984.

Larissa Demming narrates this story of releasing one's mythical beast— middle-aged women's sexuality. Writer Sullivan has been compared to writers Erma Bombeck and Jean Kerr.

2155 **Sullivan, Faith.** *Repent, Lanny Merkel.* New York: McGraw-Hill, 1981.

According to her publisher, Sullivan lives a serene suburban life in Los Angeles. For some reason, Laura Stanley Pomfret, 42 years old, former cheerleader, now happily married housewife, must confront "an indiscretion of her irrepressible youth" at her twenty-fifth high school reunion . . . and before then, shed ten pounds.

2156 **Tagliavia, Sheila.** *An Arrangement for Life.* New York: Harper & Row, 1980.

Born and raised in Toronto, the author lives in Italy with her husband and three children. This "finely textured and complex novel that, speaking softly, chronicles the transformation of a woman's life" set in upper-middle-class Italy, is about middle age and marriage.

2157 **Tan, Amy,** 1952– . *The Joy Luck Club.* New York: Putnam, 1989.

Four Chinese-American daughters in their 30s and their mothers, born in China and in their 60s, speak for themselves (except for one daughter whose mother has recently died) in this fiction. Also available in audiocassette form.

2158 **Taylor, Valerie,** 1913– . *Prism.* Tallahassee: Naiad, 1981.

For Eldora, life began at 60, when she met Ann, who has retired. The author, a feminist lesbian grandmother, has been writing short stories and novels since she was 8 years old.

2159 **Tell, Dorothy.** *Murder at Red Rook Ranch.* Tallahassee: Naiad, 1990.

In this Poppy Dillworth Mystery, 65-year-old Poppy is working on her first major case in her new career as a private investigator.

2160 **Togawa, Masako,** 1933– . *The Master Key.* New York: Dodd, Mead, 1984.

Simon Grove translated *Oinaru Gen'-Ei* (literally Grand Illusion), a well-known Japanese novel from the 1950s.

2161 **Tyler, Anne,** 1941– . *Dinner at the Homesick Restaurant.* New York: Knopf, 1982.

Anne Tyler has been called the chronicler of the modern American family. She considers herself a Southerner. In *The Clock Winder* (1972), a character says, "Don't tell your father . . . but it's a fact that from the day they're born until the day they die, men are being protected by women" (p. 142). Tyler's ninth novel begins with Pearl Tull's recollections of 1931, and ends in 1979 on the day of her funeral. Matriarch Pearl is 85 and dying—she is also angry and abusive.

2162   **Uno, Chiyo,** 1897– . *Confessions of Love.* Honolulu: U of Hawaii Press, 1989.

Portions of Phyllis Birnbaum's translation have appeared in different form in *New Yorker* and other magazines. Chiyo Uno went to Tokyo in 1917 and wrote popular, autobiographical "confessions," this relating to Seijii Toho (1897–1978). (*See also* #2190.)

2163   **Weldon, Fay,** 1933– . *The Life and Loves of a She-Devil.* New York: Pantheon, 1984.

Weldon is a well-known feminist, British novelist, and playwright. She wrote the first *Upstairs, Downstairs* scripts and adapted *Pride and Prejudice* for British television. She is also known for her participation in the criticism of publishers' exploitation of writers. In this satire-fable, fat Ruth in a bad marriage wants justice and revenge against husband Bobbo and his girlfriend Mary, power, and money. (These are the Roseanne, Ed Begley, Jr., and Meryl Streep characters of Hollywood's version.) Patricia Waugh has referred to the book as contemporary feminist gothic and to Ruth as "another heroine who believes that, given the impossibility of changing her culture, she may gain acceptance within it only through changing herself. This means, specifically, changing her body" (*Feminist Fictions,* pp. 189–195).

2164   **Weldon, Fay,** 1933– . *The Rules of Life.* New York: Harper, 1987.

It is the year 2004, and the British Museum is now a Temple of the Great New Fictional Religion. Gabriella Sumpter, three months dead, reviews on remind (i.e., as a ghost) her sixty-one years as a professional mistress.

2165   **Wesley, Mary,** 1912– . *Jumping the Queue.* New York: Penguin, 1983.

Throughout her life, Wesley had written and discarded fiction because she considered it unworthy. But as a widow, she found it necessary to realize income, and *Jumping the Queue,* her first novel, was published in 1983 when she was 71. In it, Matilda Poliport, recently widowed, has decided to "end it all." It also appears in her *The Camomile Lawn* (1984). Her work encompasses the experiences of women as they age.

2166   **Wesley, Mary,** 1912– . *Not That Sort of Girl.* New York: Viking, 1987.

Wesley's fifth novel is about Ned and Rose. Fifty years later and after the funeral, Rose looks back on her life and her lover.

2167   **Wolitzer, Hilma.** *Silver.* New York: Farrar, 1988.

As their twenty-fifth wedding anniversary approaches, Paulie makes serious plans to leave her unfaithful husband, Howard, only to become his caregiver when he suffers a heart attack.

2168   **Zeidner, Lisa,** 1955– . *Customs.* New York: Knopf, 1981.

Zeidner is an American writer of poetry and fiction. In this novel, former child prodigy and musician Jennifer's friendship with a wealthy "bag lady" is opposed by friends. Mildred Howell sits down next to Jennifer in Grand Central Terminal and gradually takes over. This is also a story about suicide.

Poetry

2169   **Atwood, Margaret Eleanor,** 1939– . *Selected Poems II: Poems Selected and New, 1976–1986.* New York: Houghton Mifflin, 1987.

Canadian Atwood has been a writer since she was a child. She first made an international reputation as a poet. She is also a writer of marvelous short stories, articles, and novels (*see,* for example, #2052).

Bradstreet, Anne Dudley (1612–1672). *See* #2176.

2170   **Chandler, Janet Carncross,** 1910– . *Flight of the Wild Goose.* Watsonville: Papier-Mache Press, 1989.

These poems, written as Ms. Chandler approached 80, celebrate life and include consideration of relationships between old women and men.

Dickinson, Emily Elizabeth (1830–1886). *See* #2176.

2171   **Elkind, Sue Saniel.** *Another Language.* Watsonville: Papier-Mache Press, 1990. il.

Elkind discovered poetry as a form of self-expression when she was 64, a time many consider "old age." This largely narrative poetry appeals mainly to old women. It is accompanied by Lori Burkhalter-Lackey's photographs. *No Longer Afraid: Poems* (Roanoke: Lintel, 1985) is another short collection of Elkind's work.

2172   **Fortner, Ethel Nestelle.** *Nervous on the Curves.* Laurinburg: St. Andrews Press, 1982.

More than two hundred of Fortner's poems have appeared in small-press magazines and anthologies. This is one of her published collections. For other poems, *see Women and Aging: An Anthology by Women* (#71).

2173   **Goodison, Lorna.** *I Am Becoming My Mother.* London: New Beacon Books, 1986.

Goodison is an African-American writer of poetry and fiction, often with a Caribbean setting.

2174   **Lifshitz, Leatrice H.,** 1933– , ed. *Only Morning in Her Shoes: Poems About Old Women.* Logan: Utah State U Press, 1990. index.

Lifshitz has edited this collection of twentieth-century American poetry about aged women and another by twentieth-century American women authors, *Her Soul Beneath the Bone: Women's Poetry on Breast Cancer* (Urbana: U of Illinois Press, 1988).

2175   **Mandel, Charlotte, et al, eds.** *Saturday's Women: The Eileen W. Barnes Anthology.* Upper Montclair: Saturday Press, 1982.

Works of twentieth-century American women were generated through an open competition to publish a first collection of poems by women over age 40. This anthology consists of poems by fifty-three of the entrants.

2176   **Martin, Wendy,** 1940– . *An American Triptych: Anne Bradstreet, Emily Dickinson, Adrienne Rich.* Chapel Hill: U of North Carolina Press, 1984. bib, index.

The poetry collected here is about patriarchy and autonomy versus dependence. Anne Dudley Bradstreet (1612–1672) is considered the first American woman poet. On her rural Massachusetts farm and while raising eight children, she wrote poetry, most published after her death. By contrast, Emily Elizabeth Dickinson (1830–1886)'s life was ruled by her father. Adrienne Cecile Rich (1929–) is a contemporary American feminist and poet. Her nonfiction has also been successful. When she was awarded the 1974 National Book Award, she rejected it as an individual, but, with Audre Lorde and Alice Walker, Rich accepted it on behalf of all women (*see also* #2181).

2177   **Martz, Sandra, ed.** *"When I Am an Old Woman I Shall Wear Purple": An Anthology of Short Stories and Poetry, 2d ed.* Watsonville: Papier-Mache Press, 1991. il.

The first edition of this literary collection of writers on the subject of women and aging was also published by Papier-Mache, in 1987.

Oates, Joyce Carol, 1938– . *See* #2129.

2178   **Ostriker, Alicia Suskin,** 1937– . *Writing Like a Woman.* Ann Arbor: U of Michigan Press, 1983. bib.

"To say 'poetess' is and always has been a gentle insult. . . . In the future our poetry, literature and art may become genderless. I do not mean sexless, or asexual: something like bisexual or androgynous . . . " (pp. 146–147). These essays on the question of why fear governs women's poetry are about twentieth-century American women poets and their work.

2179   **Ray, Mary Ellen James.** *A Pause for the Menopause.* Los Angeles: Rising Tide Publishing, 1984. il.
Rising Tide is a subsidiary of Womankind Books, located at 5 King Street, Huntington Station, NY 11746.

2180   **Reti, Ingrid.** "Reality?" "At Sixty-One." "Duologue." Poems. *J of Women & Aging* 1990 2(2): 47, 91, 109. "Women, Aging, and Ageism" issue.

2181   **Rich, Adrienne Cecile,** 1929– . *Your Native Land, Your Life.* New York: Norton, 1986. bib.
Rich is an American poet and author of the classic feminist prose *Of Woman Born: Motherhood as Experience and Institution* (New York: Norton, 1976; 10th Anniversary Edition, 1986) and poetry *Snapshots of a Daughter-in-Law: Poems, 1954–1962* (New York: Harper & Row, 1963; Norton, 1967). This collection, which she has also recorded, is autobiographical in a way. "In these poems I have been trying to speak from, and of, and to, my country. . . . I believe more than ever that the search for justice and compassion is the great wellspring for poetry in our time, throughout the world . . ." (*see also #2176*).

2182   **Searles, Jo C.** "Inventing Freedom: The Positive Poetic 'Mutterings' of Older Women." *J of Women & Aging* 1990 2(2): 153–160. "Women, Aging, and Ageism" issue.

2183   **Spektor, Mira Josefowitz.** "Untitled." "Sonnet." Poems. *J of Women & Aging* 1990 2(2): 33–34, 67. "Women, Aging, and Ageism" issue.

2184   **Throne, Evelyn.** *Of Bones and Stars.* Tampa: American Studies Press, 1981. "Herland" Series #1.

2185   **Viorst, Judith,** 1931– . *Forever Fifty and Other Negotiations.* New York: Simon & Schuster, 1989. il.
Also available in large-print edition. Viorst is a *Redbook* magazine contributing editor and has written children's books. These poems are in the "laugh at ourselves" genre.

SHORT STORIES

2186   **Arnold, Marianne.** "The Old Woman." In Floyd Salas, et al, eds. *Stories and Poems from Close to Home.* Berkeley: Ortalda, 1986. 101–104.

2187   **Ballantyne, Sheila.** *Life on Earth: Stories.* New York: Simon & Schuster, 1988.
See especially "Key Largo" and "You Are Here" in this collection of ten short stories.

2188   **Beauvoir, Simone de,** 1908–1986. *When Things of the Spirit Come First: Five Early Tales.* Translated by Patrick O'Brian (from *Quand Prime le Spirituel*). New York: Pantheon, 1982. "Marcelle," "Chantal," "Lisa," "Anne," and "Marguerite."

2189   **Briskin, Mae,** 1924– . "Two Women, One Child." In her *A Boy Like Astrid's Mother.* New York: Norton, 1988. 140–153.

2190   **Chiyo, Uno,** 1897– . "Happiness." In Phyllis Birnbaum, translator. *Rabbits, Crabs, Etc.: Stories by Japanese Women.* Honolulu: U of Hawaii Press, 1982. 133–147.

2191   **Clausen, Jan,** 1950– . "Yellow Jackets." In her *Mother, Sister, Daughter, Lover: Stories.* Trumansburg: Crossing Press, 1980. 102–114.

2192   **Fisher, Mary Frances Kennedy,** 1908–1991. *Sister Age.* New York: Knopf, 1983; and Random House, 1984.
        This collection of fifteen story-essays about aging was originally published in 1964. Sister Age was Ursula von Ott in Zurich, a "nagging harpy." *See also* especially "Mrs. Teeters' Tomato Jar" and "A Kitchen Allegory." "M F K Fisher on Aging" is among the short readings included in *Word Play Word Power: A Woman's Personal Growth Workbook* (Berkeley: Conari Press, 1989) by Kimberley Snow.

2193   **Freeman, Judith,** 1946– . "What Is This Movie?" In her *Family Attractions.* New York: Viking, 1988. 113–136.

2194   **Freeman, Mary Eleanor Wilkins,** 1852–1930. "Old Woman Magoun." In Susan Koppelman, ed. *Between Mothers and Daughters: Stories Across a Generation.* New York: Feminist Press at the CUNY, 1985. *See also* Freeman's "Mistaken Charity" and "Old Lady Pingree." In Susan Cahill, ed. *Among Sisters: Short Stories by Women Writers.* New York: New American Library, 1989.

2195   **Fremlin, Celia.** "The Bonus Years." In her *A Lovely Day to Die and Other Stories.* New York: Doubleday, 1983. 113–128.

2196   **Fremlin, Celia.** "The Holiday." In her *A Lovely Day to Die and Other Stories.* New York: Doubleday, 1983. 99–112.

2197   **George, Diana Hume.** "'Who Is the Double Ghost Whose Head Is Smoke?' Women Poets on Aging." In Kathleen Woodward and Murray M. Schwartz, eds. *Memory and Desire: Aging, Literature, Psychoanalysis.* Bloomington: Indiana U Press, 1986. 134–153.

2198   **Gerber, Merrill Joan.** "At the Fence." In her *Honeymoon.* Urbana: U of Illinois Press, 1985. 19–29.

2199   **Gerber, Merrill Joan.** "Straight from the Deathbed." In her *Honeymoon.* Urbana: U of Illinois Press, 1985. 30–41.

2200   **Glasgow, Ellen Anderson Gholson,** 1874–1945. "The Difference." In Susan Koppelman, ed. *The Other Woman: Stories of Two Women and a Man.* New York: Feminist Press at the CUNY, 1984. 167–190.

2201   **Grekova, I.,** 1907– . *Russian Women: Two Stories.* Translated from Russian by Michel Petrov. New York: Harcourt Brace Jovanovich, 1983.
        Grekova, also known as Miss X, is Yelena Sergeyerna Ventsel, doctor of science and mathematician.

2202   **Higgins, Joanna.** "The Courtship of Widow Sobcek." In John Gardner, ed. *Best American Short Stories, 1982.* New York: Houghton Mifflin, 1982. 37–53.

2203   **Kensington Ladies' Erotica Society.** *Ladies' Own Erotica: Tales, Recipes, and Other Mischiefs by Older Women.* Berkeley: Ten Speed Press, 1984. il.
        Kensington is an affluent community adjacent to Berkeley, California. The writers are a group of over-age-40 ladies who dedicated their book affectionately to the memory of their "patron saint," Judd Boynton, who introduced " . . . a group of unassuming women

who can teach us men much." The Kensington Ladies and their erotica differ from *Pleasures: Women Write Erotica*, published the same year by Doubleday and edited by Lonnie Garfield Barbach, which is a compilation of twentieth-century American women authors' perceptions.

2204   **Koppelman, Susan, ed.** *Between Mothers and Daughters: Stories Across a Generation.* New York: Feminist Press at the CUNY, 1985. *See also #2194 and #2221.*

2205   **Koppelman, Susan, comp.** *Old Maids: Short Stories by Nineteenth-Century United States Women Writers.* Boston: Pandora Press, 1984. bib.
        Koppelman provides an introduction and afterword. Contents: "Old Maids," "The Fortune Hunter," "Mary and Ellen Grosvenor, or The Two Sisters," "Aunt Mabel's Love Story," "Old Maidism Versus Marriage," "Fruits of Sorrow, or An Old Maid's Story," "An Old Maid's Story," "The Two Offers," "Number 13," "One Old Maid," "An Ignoble Martyr," "Louisa," and "How Celia Changed Her Mind."

2206   **Koppelman, Susan, ed.** *The Other Woman: Stories of Two Women and a Man.* New York: Feminist Press at the CUNY, 1984.
        Eighteen stories of adultery and its response span one hundred years of short fiction by American women writers. They include Charlotte Perkins Gilman's "Turned" (1911); Ellen Glasgow's "The Difference" (1923); and Alice Walker's "Coming Apart" (1980).

2207   **Lessing, Doris May,** 1919– . "An Old Woman and Her Cat." In Irene Zahava, ed. *Through the Eyes: Animal Stories by Women.* Freedom: Crossing Press, 1988. 91–107.

2208   **LeSueur, Meridel,** 1900– . *I Hear Men Talking & Other Stories.* Linda Ray Pratt, ed. Albuquerque: West End Press, 1984.

2209   **Lynch, Lee,** 1945– , ed. *Old Dyke Tales.* Tallahassee: Naiad Press, 1984.
        Lynch's syndicated column, "The Amazon Trail," appears in newspapers across the United States.

2210   **Marshall, Joyce,** 1913– . "The Old Woman." In Margaret Atwood and Robert Weaver, eds. *Oxford Book of Canadian Short Stories in English.* New York: Oxford U Press, 1986. 92–102.

        Martz, Sandra. *See #2177.*

2211   **Mason, Bobbie Ann,** 1940– . *Love Life: Stories.* New York: Harper & Row, 1989.
        Sixteen of Mason's stories of love in youth, middle age, and old age set in Kentucky have been collected here.

2212   **McKillip, Patricia A.,** 1948– . "Baba Yaga and the Sorcerer's Son." In Jane Yolen, et al, eds. *Dragons & Dreams: A Collection of New Fantasy and Science Fiction Stories.* New York: Harper, 1986.

2213   **McKillip, Patricia A.,** 1948– . "The Old Woman and the Storm." In Robin McKinley, ed. *Imaginary Lands.* New York: Greenwillow, 1986. 25–35.

2214   **Muller, Donna Nitz.** "The Old Woman's Blessing." In Jonis Agree, et al, eds. *Stiller's Pond: New Fiction from the Upper Midwest.* St. Paul: New Rivers Press, 1988.

2215   **Oates, Joyce Carol,** 1938– . "Queen of the Night." In her *A Sentimental Education: Stories.* New York: Dutton, 1980. 1–33.

2216   **O'Brien, Edna,** 1931– . "The Widow." In her *Lantern Slides: Stories.* New York: Farrar, Straus, Giroux, 1990. 33–50.

2217   **Paley, Grace,** 1922– . "Dreamers in a Dead Language" (11–38); "Friends" (73–89); "Listening" (199–211); and "Ruthy and Edie" (115–126). In her *Later the Same Day*. New York: Farrar, Straus, Giroux, 1985. "Dreamers in a Dead Language" also appears in #2222.

2218   **Petesch, Natalie L. M.,** 1924– . *Soul Clap Its Hands and Sing*. Boston: South End Press, 1981.

   These sixteen very short stories are usually about women, e.g., "Shopping."

2219   **Pollard, Jean Ann,** 1934– . "Old Woman." In Charles G. Waugh, et al, eds. *Haunted New England*. Dublin: Yankee Books, 1988.

2220   **Sanford, Annette.** *Lasting Attachments*. Dallas: Southern Methodist U Press, 1989.

   The Press's Southwest Life and Letters series includes this collection of short stories well suited for young adults as well as old people. The stories are about every-day events in the lives of average people, most of whom are old.

2221   **Schockley, Ann Allan,** 1927– . "A Birthday Remembered." In Susan Koppel-man, ed. *Between Mothers and Daughters: Stories Across a Generation*. New York: Feminist Press at the CUNY, 1985. 285–293.

2222   **Sennett, Dorothy,** 1909– , **ed.** *Full Measure: Modern Stories on Aging*. St. Paul: Graywolf Press, 1988.

   As a woman then in her 70s, Sennett had difficulty persuading established American and English writers to appear in a collection about aging. Then the gate-keeper publishers resisted such a manuscript, although most of the stories are by and about men. The women authors are Arthenia J. Bates, Carol Bly, Hortense Calisher, Na-dine Gordimer, Joyce Carol Oates, Grace Paley, and Jean Rhys.

2223   **Sennett, Dorothy,** 1909– , **with Anne Czarniecki, eds.** *Vital Signs: International Stories on Aging*. St. Paul: Graywolf Press, 1991.

   Sennett "attempts to defeat the stereotyping of old people (ageism) through the immediacy of the short story." The main character in each is a contemporary old woman or man. Most of these writers are from Australia, China, Japan, and Sweden, as well as a few from the United States. "In Hennie Aucamp's 'Soup for the Sick' an old white woman in South Africa attempts to transcend racism by her manner of dying; her will provides that if she can be buried beside a lifelong black friend, she will leave money for the building of a hospital. . . . Set in Budapest, Hungary, Mavis Gallant's 'His Mother' explores intergenerational relationships in a Communist society" (p. vii).

2224   **Solomon, Barbara H., ed.** *American Wives: 30 Short Stories by Women*. New York: New American Library, 1986.

   Originally published from 1852 to 1982, these stories by American women au-thors are about marriage.

2225   **Welty, Eudora,** 1909– . "A Visit to Charity." In her *Collected Stories*. New York: Harcourt, 1980. 113–118.

2226   **Welty, Eudora,** 1909– . "A Word Path." In her *Collected Stories*. New York: Harcourt, 1980. 142–149.

2227   **Woolf, Virginia,** 1882–1941. *The Complete Shorter Fiction of Virginia Woolf*. Susan Dick, ed. New York: Harcourt Brace Jovanovich, 1985. bib.

   Some of these forty-five pieces had not been previously published. Dick's edit-ing is outstanding. They date from 1906 to 1941 and display the evolution of Woolf's methods and themes; e.g., "Mrs. Dalloway in Bond Street" grew into *Mrs. Dalloway*.

13

Women Studies and the Aging of Females: Locating Additional Sources

We are anonymous—graphed but not acknowledged,
a shadowy presence—hinted at but never defined.

Janet Harris, 1915– .

Bibliographic Support: 2228–2237
  Review articles
Researching: 2238–2260
Serials, Data Bases, Abstracts, and Indexes
  Serials
  Special topical or thematic issues of periodicals
  Indexes

BIBLIOGRAPHIC SUPPORT

Throughout Women and Aging: A Guide to the Literature, *books*
providing significant bibliographic support are indicated by inclusion
of "bib" in their citations. A doctoral dissertation usually includes a
literature review. Particularly useful is the review article, review essay, or
bibliographic essay. A bibliographic essay is a critical article on the literature
of a subject, usually written by a recognized expert and especially useful
in planning literature searches, keeping up to date, and knowing the
state of the art. It may focus on an aspect of the subject, on publications
of a defined period of time, etc.; criticism is an important part. A list of
review articles, chapters, etc., included in the guide concludes the Biblio-
graphic Support section of this chapter; they are also identified within
the collection.

See also this chapter: Researching (2238–2260); this chapter: Review articles (following
2237); Subject Index.

2228   **Borenstein, Audrey,** 1930– . *Older Women in 20th-Century America: A Selected*
Annotated Bibliography. New York: Garland, 1982, index.
        Dr. Borenstein provides a basic bibliographic tool for scholarly and popular re-
searching of women age 40 and over. Eight hundred titles from the social and behavioral sciences (mainly social sciences) as well as the humanities, most published in the
1960s and 1970s, are included. *See also #2230.*

2229   **Coyle, Jean M., comp.** *Women and Aging: A Selected, Annotated Bibliography.* New York: Greenwood, 1989. index.

Because of the many duplications, there are far fewer than the 622 numbered units in this bibliography. Periodical articles are not included in the subject or author indexes. Annotations are one or two sentences paraphrasing titles. Dr. Coyle is president of a gerontological consulting firm.

2230   **Dolan, Eleanor Frances,** 1907– , **and Dorothy M. Gropp.** *The Mature Woman in America: A Selected Annotated Bibliography, 1979–1982.* Washington: National Council on the Aging, 1984.

"Mature" here refers to middle-aged and old women. The 425 listings are arranged alphabetically by author, with the intent of including nonliterary works not listed by Borenstein (*see* #2228) for the 1979–1982 period.

2231   **Hawley, Donna Lea, comp.** *Women and Aging: A Comprehensive Bibliography.* Burnaby: Simon Fraser U, 1985. index. Simon Fraser University (British Columbia, Canada) Bibliography series. Gerontology Research Centre 85-1.

The scope of Hawley's 128-page bibliography is "aged women."

2232   **Jaffee, Georgina, and Emily M. Nett, comps.** "Annotated Bibliography on Women as Elders." *Resources for Feminist Research/Documentation sur la Recherche Féministe* July 1982 11(2): 253–288. "Women as Elders" issue.

2233   **Mueller, Jean E., and Julie L. Moore.** "A Bibliography of Doctoral Dissertations on Aging from American Institutions of Higher Learning, 1981–1983." *J of Gerontology* 1984 39(5): 631–640.

For 1984–1986 coverage, *see* September 1987 42(5): 561–568, and so on. The compilation is divided into categories that include numerous sex/gender-related themes. Moore's "A Bibliography of Doctoral Dissertations on Aging from American Institutions of Higher Learning, 1934–1969" appeared in the *J of Gerontology* 1971 26(3): 391–422, with biennial supplements. University Microfilms of Ann Arbor, Michigan, (1-800-521-0600) distributes lists of dissertations awarded in various disciplines that include Gerontology and Women's Studies.

2234   **Porter, Nancy.** "The Art of Aging: A Review Essay." *Women's Studies Q* Spring-Summer 1989 17(1–2): 97–108.

2235   **Robinson, K.** "Older Women: A Literature Review." *J of Advanced Nursing* March 1986 11(2): 153–160.

2236   **Sunge, Jane.** "Bibliography on Social History of Elderly Women." *Resources for Feminist Research/Documentation sur la Recherche Féministe* July 1982 11(2): 241–251. "Women as Elders" issue.

2237   **Women Studies Abstracts.** New Brunswick: Transaction.

Regularly published since 1972 by editor-publisher Sara Stauffer Whaley and in recent years edited by Whaley, this indexing-abstracting service employs subject-headings that are logical and realistic. An international—with British emphasis—service abstracting since 1983 both books and journal articles is *Studies on Women Abstracts.* Abingdon, Oxfordshire: Carfax.

Review articles included in Women and Aging: A Guide to the Literature

#31 Olson, Amy Clarke. "Osteoporosis."
#314 Bowers, Barbara. "Women as Health Care Providers: Family Caregivers of the Elderly."

#354, #355 Leppa, Carol J. "Women as Health Care Providers."

#495 Steitz, Jean A. "Remarriage in Later Life: A Critique and Review of the Literature."

#587 Hayes, Christopher L. *Pre-Retirement Planning for Women: Program Design and Research.*

#693 Matthews, Anne Martin. "Canadian Research on Women as Widows: A Comparative Analysis of the State of the Art."

#905 Kercher, Kyle. "Causes and Correlates of Crime Committed by the Elderly: A Review of the Literature."

#975 Leavitt, Jacqueline, and Mary Beth Welch. "Older Women and the Suburbs: A Literature Review."

#1039 Goodman, Madeleine. "Toward a Biology of Menopause."

#1051 Huddleston, Donna Sue Tolley. "The Natural Menopause."

#1103 Perlmutter, Ellen Susan, and Pauline B. Bart. "Changing View of 'The Change': A Critical Review."

#1117 Stampfer, Meir J. "Menopause and Heart Disease: A Review."

#1135 Wilbush, Joel. "Menorrhagia and Menopause: A Historical Review."

#1200 Mansfield, Phyllis Kernoff. *Advanced Maternal Age and Pregnancy Outcome: A Critical Appraisal of the Scientific Literature.*

#1211 Van de Kamp, Jacqueline. *Pregnancy in the Older Woman: January 1983 Through December 1987: 327 Citations.*

#1464 McElmurry, Beverly J. "The Health of Older Women."

#1486 Swenson, Norma, "Women, Health, and Aging."

#1495 Verbrugge, Lois M. "Women and Men: Mortality and Health of Older People."

#1502 Zabrocki, Emily C. "The Health of Older Women."

#1569 Arber, Sara. "The Invisibility of Age: Gender and Class in Later Life."

#1675 U.S. Commission on Civil Rights. *Characters in Textbooks: A Review of the Literature.*

#1849 Feinson, Marjorie Chary. "Where Are the Women in the History of Aging?"

#1985 Geiger, Susan N. G. "Women's [oral] Life Histories: Method and Content."

#2234 Porter, Nancy. "The Art of Aging: A Review Essay."

#2235 Robinson, K. "Older Women: A Literature Review."

RESEARCHING

Doctoral dissertations are listed by subject matter throughout Women and Aging: A Guide to the Literature *as well as in the subject and author indexes.* See also *this chapter: Bibliographic Support (2228–2237); #2233. Tests, measures, scales, protocols, checklists, etc., used or referred to by these dissertation writers and other authors include:*

Age scales	(#1071)
Bem Sex Role Inventory	(#80)
Facts on Aging Quiz	(#1662)
Fishbein Model (sex role identity, gender)	(#558)
Geriatric Depression Scale	(#140)
Graduate Student Questionnaire (GSQ)	(#280)
The Health Assessment of Older Women Interview Guide	(#2260)

Life Satisfaction Index	(#1660)
Menopausal Symptom Checklist	(#1113)
Personal Views Survey	(#1535)
Rockport Fitness Walking Test in Females 65 and Older	(#57)
Rorschach Test	(#136)
Rosenberg Self-Esteem Scale (RSE)	(#280)
Self-Evaluation of Life Function Scale (SELF)	(#1535)
Social Attitude Scale of Agist Prejudice (SASAP)	(#1654)
Strong-Campbell Interest Inventory . . .	
Nursing Home Administrators	(#965)
Survey of the Quality of Life of Adult Men and Women	(#1868)
Tuckman-Lorge Attitude Scale	(#1662)
VO(2)Max Test-Retest	(#52)
Western Standard Retirement Path	(#609)

2238   **American Association of Retired Persons.** *Thesaurus of Aging Terminology: AgeLine Database on Middle Age and Aging, 4th ed.* Washington: National Gerontology Resource Center, American Association of Retired Persons, 1991.

Established headings include *Ageism, Displaced homemakers, Females, Menopause, Sex discrimination, Sex roles,* and *Widows.* This automated database provides citations from journal articles, books, government documents, reports, chapters, dissertations, and conference papers, as well as descriptions of federally funded research projects on aging since 1978, with selected coverage of earlier works. The Gerontological Society of America's list of "Data Resources in Gerontology: A Directory of Selected Information Vendors, Databases, and Archives" is also useful. The AARP's Women's Initiative has identified goals to initiate action to: ensure improved economic status of women; initiate action to ensure affordable, appropriate, and high-quality health and long-term care; promote better living conditions and address social needs; enable women to make informed decisions about matters affecting their lives; and heighten public awareness of the contributions women have made and continue to make to society. Its publications include *Fact Sheets* (e.g., "Facts About Older Women: Income and Poverty") and *AARP WIN,* a networking newsletter.

2239   **Antonucci, Toni C.** "Longitudinal and Cross-Sectional Data Sources on Women in the Middle Years." In Janet Zollinger Giele, ed. *Women in the Middle Years: Current Knowledge and Future Directions for Research and Policy.* New York: Wiley, 1982. 241–274.

2240   **Chatman, Elfreda A.** "Channels to a Larger Social World: Older Women Staying in Contact with the Great Society." *Library and Information Science Research* July-September 1991 13(3): 281–300.

2241   **Damon, Bonnie L., et al.** *Guide to 1980 Census Data on the Elderly.* Washington: U.S. Department of Commerce, Bureau of the Census. bib.

2242   **Giele, Janet Zollinger.** "Future Research and Policy Questions." In her *Women in the Middle Years: Current Knowledge and Future Directions for Research and Policy.* New York: Wiley, 1982. Chapter 6.

2243   **Glover, Peggy D.** *Library Services for the Woman in the Middle.* Hamden: Shoe String Press, 1985. bib, index.

Glover's recognition of women "in the middle" (ages 45–64) leads to such recommendations for public library collections as Emily Post's *Etiquette* and Don Sharp's *The New Woman Driver*. Her categories of needed resource information include cooking and entertaining, grooming, leisure activities, memory, money management, parents, pets, and resume writing. But she also identifies abuse, arthritis, cancer, death and dying, discrimination, displaced homemakers, divorce, housing, legal services, menopause, mental health, mid-life transitions, nursing homes, pensions, sexuality, and widows. Jane Porcino in her introduction describes some of the major transitions that mid-life women must make and the crises they meet. The failure of librarianship and information science to absorb and implement the insights of social gerontology was identified as early as 1971 (Elliott E. Kanner's U of Wisconsin Ph.D. dissertation, *The Impact of Gerontological Concepts on Principles of Librarianship*). Betty J. Turock's *Serving the Older Adult: A Guide to Library Programs and Information Sources* (Bowker, 1982) refers to "ageism in media" and provides guidelines for media analysis. Marianne Dee and Judith Bowen (*Library Services to Older People* [The British Library, 1986]) consider people in England over the age of 50 who have permanently left the workforce. Elaine Kempson and Dee edited *A Future Age: A Practical Handbook for Librarians Working with Older Adults* (The Association of Assistant Librarians, 1987), a brief collection of "how to" (in England) articles that recognize several special populations *other than women*.

2244   **Goldscheider, Frances K.** "The Aging of the Gender Revolution: What Do We Know and What Do We Need to Know?" *Research on Aging* December 1990 12(4): 531–545. Special issue on "The Demography of Aging."

2245   **Harris, Diana K.** *Dictionary of Gerontology*. New York: Greenwood, 1988.
Harris includes studies, organizations, and legislation in this basic tool. Female and gender-related words, terms, and proper nouns are considered. Definitions are accompanied by citations and references.

2246   **Herzog, Anna Regula.** "Methodological Issues in Research on Older Women." In Anna Regula Herzog, et al, eds. *Health and Economic Status of Older Women*. Amityville: Baywood, 1989. Chapter 6.

2247   **Herzog, Anna Regula.** "Physical and Mental Health in Older Women: Selected Research Issues and Data Sources." In Anna Regula Herzog, et al, eds. *Health and Economic Status of Older Women*. Amityville, New York: Baywood, 1989. Chapter 4.

2248   **Hess, Beth B., 1928– , and Myra Marx Ferree, eds.** *Analyzing Gender: A Handbook of Social Science Research*. Beverly Hills: Sage, 1987. bib, il, index.
This handbook is useful for research areas needing inordinate amounts of documentation, e.g., rape and other "sexual terrorism."

2249   **Long, Judy, and Karne L. Proter.** "Multiple Roles of Midlife Women: A Case for New Directions in Theory, Research, and Policy." In Grace Kesterman Baruch and Jeanne Brooks-Gunn, eds. *Women in Midlife*. New York: Plenum Press, 1984. Chapter 5.

2250   **MacQuarrie, Margaret Ann, and Barbara Keddy.** "Women and Aging: Directions for Research." *J of Women & Aging* 1992 4(2): 21–32.

2251   **Maddox, George L., et al, eds.** *The Encyclopedia of Aging*. New York: Springer, 1987. bib, il, index.
Articles include "Ageism" by Robert Neil Butler, M.D.; "Menopause: Biomedical Aspects" by Ruth Weg; "Menopause: Psychosocial Aspects" and "Older Women's Move-

ment" by Elizabeth W. Markson; "1981 White House Conference on Aging Issues" by Fernando M. Torres Gil; "White House Conferences on Aging" by William F. Laurie; "Widowhood" by Helena Znaniecka Lopata; "Women: Changing Status" by Angela M. O'Rand; and "Women's Retirement Movement" by Meredith Minkler and Robyn Stone.

2252   **Mathews, Virginia H.** "Libraries: Aids to Life Satisfaction for Older Women: A 1981 White House Conference on the Aging Background Paper." ERIC, September 1981. ED #215289. 97 pages.

2253   **Miller, Jeanne E.** "Sources and Uses of Qualitative Data." In Anna Regula Herzog, et al, eds. *Health and Economic Status of Older Women.* Amityville: Baywood, 1989. Chapter 7.

2254   **Nett, Emily M.** "A Call for Feminist Correctives to Research on Elders. *Resources for Feminist Research/Documentation sur la Recherche Féministe* July 1982 11(2): 225–226.

2255   **Nusberg, Charlotte, and Jay Soklovsky, eds.** *The International Directory of Research and Researchers in Comparative Gerontology, rev. and expanded, 1990 ed.* Washington: International Federation on Ageing, 1990. index.
    Details of hundreds of research projects and thousands of related bibliographic references are included in this reference book, which is also available on disk, formatted for WordPerfect.

2256   **Radcliffe College. Henry A. Murray Research Center.** *A Guide to the Data Resources of the Henry A. Murray Research Center of Radcliffe College: A Center for the Study of Lives.* Cambridge: The Center, 1988. index.
    An "Index to the Guide" is also available. Research relates to social conditions of women in the United States.

2257   **Ritcey, Sheila.** "Substituting an Interactionist for a Normative Model in Gerontological Research." *Resources for Feminist Research/Documentation sur la Recherche Féministe* July 1982 11(2): 220–221.

2258   **Seltzer, Mildred M., and Jon A. Hendricks.** "On Your Marks: Research Issues on Older Women." In Anna Regula Herzog, et al, eds. *Health and Economic Status of Older Women.* Amityville: Baywood, 1989. Chapter 1.

2259   **Sinnott, Jan E., et al.** *Sex Roles and Aging: Theory and Research from a Systems Perspective.* New York: Karger, 1986. bib, index.
    Lifespan study of roles is needed. The context of role-related responses should be examined. Chapters 3, "Adaptation Across the Life Span: Evolution, Future Shock, and Sex Roles" by Joan S. Rabin, and 10, "Methodological and Statistical Considerations in the Measurement of Sex Roles and Aging" by Michael Twindle.

2260   **Zabrocki, Emily C.** *The Health Assessment of Older Women Interview Guide Health Scoring Component: A Psychometric Evaluation.* U of Illinois Health Sciences Center, 1990. 50/10B.

Serials, Data Bases, Abstracts, and Indexes

The most recent information on a subject, especially in science, technology, statistics, economics, or politics—all particularly relevant to aging, gender, gerontology, and women—is likely to be found in journals, magazines, and newspapers; likewise subjects so new, obscure, or temporary that they are not covered by books. Interests and opinion trends of a given period can be traced easily, with recent periodical issues providing current information, and back issues a record of past ideas and their evolution, problems, and accomplishments. Parts of books are sometimes first published in periodicals. Professional literature is often challenged or updated in journals on subjects of concern to particular branches of knowledge and professions. Usually written by subject-specialists, they can keep attorneys, economists, educators, gerontologists, geriatricians, gynecologists and other physicians, scientists, political scientists, and others up to date.

There are more than 147,000 serials of all types from all over the world currently published in hundreds of subject areas. They include annuals, continuations, and conference proceedings issued irregularly or less than twice a year, as well as other forms.[1]

The collection of serials relevant to the subject of women and aging that follows consists mainly of journals, although it also includes some series, annuals, magazines, and newsletters. They have been selected for their utility in learning about females' aging and the associated potential and unique problems. A few recently defunct serials (e.g., *Broomstick*) are included because their back files continue to be useful and accessible. Commercial magazines clearly targeting women as consumers in terms of their age are not intentionally included.

Full information about each serial's frequency, publisher and sponsor (which may differ), starting date, circulation, whether subscription is part of membership, etc., can be found in current editions of such standard reference tools as *Ulrich's International Periodicals Directory* and *The Serials Directory*.[2] Although published in 1986, Hesslein's compilation, *Serials on Aging: An Analytical Guide*, is useful for its detailed annotations.[3] Reference books may also identify periodical indexes, abstracts, and citation indexes—if any—that regularly index all or part (called selective indexing) of the contents of each issue of a particular periodical. Some journals devote each issue to a theme; some publish occasional topical or special issues that may also be published as monographs (e.g., #1711). A list of special issues included in the guide concludes the list of serial titles.

A list of periodical indexes, citation indexes, and abstracting services most useful in accessing the contents of these serials and generally in the field of women and aging follows the special issues list.

Serials

1. Activities, Adaptation & Aging: The Gerontological Journal of Activities Management.
2. Adulthood and Aging. Springer Series on . . .
3. Ageing and Society.
4. Aegis: A Magazine on Ending Violence Against Women.
5. Affilia: Journal of Women and Social Work.
6. Age and Ageing.
7. Ageing International.
8. Aging. U.S. Administration on Aging.
9. Aging and Work. National Council on the Aging.
10. American Journal of Public Health.
11. American Woman: A Status Report. Women's Research and Education Institute Series.

12. Annual Review of Gerontology & Geriatrics. Springer.
13. Archives of Gerontology and Geriatrics. And Supplement.
14. ASCATOPICS: Aging/Geriatrics.
15. Bibliographies and Indexes in Gerontology. Greenwood Series.
16. Black Aging.
17. Broomstick: By, for, and About Women over Forty. (Defunct.)
18. Bulletin on Aging. United Nations.
19. Calyx: A Journal of Art and Literature by Women.
20. Canadian Journal on Aging/La Revue Canadienne de Viellissement.
21. Canadian Research Institute for the Advancement of Women Newsletter.
22. Canadian Woman Studies/Les Cahiers de la Femme.
23. Caring (National Association for Home Care, Washington, D.C.).
24. Catalyst: A Socialist Journal of the Social Services.
25. Celibate Woman.
26. Change (National Support Center for Families of the Aging).
27. Children of Aging Parents Newsletter.
28. Chronicle: Newsletter of the Crones Nest Project.
29. Clinical Gerontologist: Journal of Aging and Mental Health.
30. Connexions: An International Women's Quarterly.
31. Courageous Crones: A Web of Crones Newsletter.
32. Crossroads and Crossroads Legislative Report to Women.
33. Educational Gerontology: An International Bimonthly Journal.
34. Fifty Upwards Network: A Newsletter for Single Women in Midlife.
35. Focus on Women. Springer Series.
36. Friend Indeed: For Women in the Prime of Life.
37. Frontiers.
38. Frontiers in Aging. Human Sciences Press Series.
39. Gender & Society. Sociologists for Women in Society.
40. Generations: Journal of the American Society on Aging.
41. Gray Paper. Older Women's League Series. *See* #1617.
42. Health Care for Women International.
43. Hemlock Quarterly. National Hemlock Society newsletter.
44. Heresies.
45. HERS: Hysterectomy Educational Resources Newsletter.
46. Hospice Journal: Physical, Psychosocial and Pastoral Care of the Dying.
47. Hot Flash: A Newsletter for Midlife and Older Women. National Action Forum for Midlife and Older Women.
48. International Journal of Aging and Human Development.
49. ISIS: Latin American and Caribbean Women's Health Journal.
50. Journal of Aging Studies.
51. Journal of Applied Gerontology: The Official Journal of the Southern Gerontological Society.
52. Journal of Cross-Cultural Gerontology.
53. Journal of Education for Social Work.
54. Journal of Elder Abuse and Neglect.
55. Journal of Feminist Family Therapy.
56. Journal of Gerontological Social Work.
57. Journal of Gerontology. Gerontological Society of America.

58. Journal of Health Politics, Policy and Law.
59. Journal of Homosexuality.
60. Journal of Housing for the Elderly.
61. Journal of Women & Aging.
62. Journal of Women & Social Work.
63. Making a Difference. National Association for Lesbian and Gay Gerontology.
64. Maturitas. International Menopause Society.
65. Melpomene Journal: A Journal for Women's Health Research.
66. Memorandum: U.S. Senate Special Committee on Aging Annual.
67. Menopause Naturally and PMZ Newsletter.
68. Midlife Wellness: A Journal for the Middle Years.
69. Monthly Labor Review and Statistical Supplement. U.S. Dept. of Labor.
70. Ms. Magazine.
71. National Women's Health Report. National Women's Health Resource Center.
72. National Women's Studies Association Caucus on Aging and Ageism.
73. Network News: Newsletter of the Global Link for Midlife and Older Women. Women's Initiative of the American Association of Retired Persons and the International Federation on Ageing.
74. New Directions for Women. (Defunct newspaper.)
75. Older Lesbians Support Network Newsletter.
76. Osteoporosis International.
77. Psychology of Women Quarterly.
78. Psychotherapy Patient.
79. Pyramid: News Letter of the National Association of Widowed People.
80. Research on Aging.
81. Resources for Feminist Research/Documentation sur la Recherche Féministe.
82. Sage: A Scholarly Journal on Black Women.
83. Sex Roles.
84. Signs: Journal of Women in Culture and Society.
85. Smith College Studies in Social Work.
86. Social Security Bulletin & Annual Statistical Supplement. U.S. Social Security Administration.
87. Social Work: Journal of the National Association of Social Workers.
88. Sojourner: The Women's Forum.
88. Special Report on Aging: National Institute on Aging Annual. U.S. National Institutes of Health.
89. Wellesley College Center for Research on Women. Working Papers, e.g., #765.
90. Wise Woman.
91. Women & Aging Letter. National Policy and Resource Center on Women and Aging.
92. Women and Health.
93. Women and History.
94. Women and Politics.
95. Women & Therapy: A Feminist Quarterly.
96. Women of Europe. Commission of the European Communities.
97. Women's Health Perspectives: An Annual Review, 1–3. To be continued by Annual Review of Women's Health.
98. Women's Initiative Network: A Networking Newsletter ("AARP WIN").
99. Women's Studies Quarterly.

Special topical or thematic issues of periodicals

Arranged alphabetically by title, then chronologically.

American Ethnologist:
Special issue on medical anthropology. 1988 15(1).

Broomstick: Although defunct in 1995, many issues were topical and are available in libraries and resource centers. For example:
August 1980 1(9). Menopause.
November 1980 2(23). Death, dying, terminal illness.
May/June 1982 4(3). Marriage, family, aging relatives.
January/February 1983 5(1). Appearance, fat.
March/April 1983 5(2). Humor.
May/June 1983 5(3). July/August 1988 10(4). Religion, spirituality.
July/August 1983 5(4). Violence and abuse.
September/October 1983 5(5). Retirement and transitions.
September/October 6(5), November/December 1984 6(6). Feminism and older women.
May/July 1985 7(3–4). September/October 1988 10(5). July/August 1989 11(4). Disabilities.
September/October 1989 11(5). Reentry.
July/August 1990 12(4). Feminism and older women: Sisterhood.
September/October 1990 12(5). Widowhood, divorce, separation.

Canadian Woman Studies/Les Cahiers de la Femme:
Spring 1984 5(3). "Aging" issue.
Winter 1992 #12. "Growing into Age" special issue, Mary Sue McCarthy, et al, guest eds.

Connexions: An International Women's Quarterly:
1983 #7. "Young and Old Women" issue.

Culture, Medicine & Psychiatry:
1985 10(1). "Anthropological Approaches to Menopause: Questioning Received Knowledge." Special issue, Margaret Lock, guest ed.

Educational Gerontology:
March-April 1991 17(2). "Women, Education, and Aging" issue, Jeanne Gerlach, guest ed.

Generations:
August 1980 4(4). "Women and Aging" issue, Tish Sommers, guest ed.

Gerontologist:
August 1989 29(4). "Effectiveness of Caregiver Groups" Symposium.

Heresies:
1988 6(3). "Coming of Age" issue 1988 #23.

Journal of Homosexuality:
Spring/Summer 1986 12(2/3). "Historical, Literary, and Erotic Aspects of Lesbianism," Monika Kehoe, issue ed.
1990 20(3/4). "Gay Midlife and Maturity," John Alan Lee, ed.

Journal of Women & Aging:
1989 1(1/2/3). "Women as They Age: Challenge, Opportunity and Triumph" issue, J. Dianne Garner and Susan O. Mercer, eds.
1990 2(2). "Women, Aging and Ageism," Evelyn R. Rosenthal, issue ed.

1993 5(3/4). "Women and Healthy Aging: Living Productively in Spite of It All," J. Dianne Garner and Alice A. Young, eds.

1994 6(4). "Older Women with Chronic Pain," Karen A. Roberto, ed.

Ms Magazine:
January 1982 10(7). Mostly about aging: "Growing Up . . . and Up . . . and Up."

Network News: The Newsletter of the National Women's Health Network:
March/April 1984 9(2). "Midlife and Older Women: Taking Responsibility for Our Own Health."

Psychology of Women Quarterly:
December 1990 14(4). "Women at Midlife and Beyond" issue.

Psychotherapy Patient:
1990 6(3/4). "Psychotherapy and the Widowed Patient," E. Mark Stern, ed.

Research on Aging:
December 1990 12(4). "The Demography of Aging" special issue.

Resources for Feminist Research/Documentation sur la Recherche Féministe:
July 1982 11(2). "Women as Elders" issue, Emily M. Nett, ed.

Sojourner: The New England Women's Journal of News, Opinions, and the Arts:
September 1981 7(1). "Time Lines: The Years of Our Lives."

Southern Exposure:
May-June 1985 13(2–3). "Older Wiser Stronger—Southern Elders."

Women & Health:
Summer/Fall 1983 8(3/4). "Women in the Later Years: Health, Social and Cultural Perspectives," Lois Grau and Ida Susser, issue eds.

1985 10(2/3). "Health Needs of Women as They Age" issue, Rita Jackaway Freedman and Sharon Golub, eds.

1988 14(3/4). "Women in the Later Years: Health, Social, and Cultural Perspectives."

1989 13 (3/4). "Government Policy and Women's Health Care, the Swedish Alternative," Gunnela Westlander and Jeanne Mager Stellman, eds.

Women & Politics:
Summer 1986 6(2). "Women as Elders: Images, Visions, and Issues."

Women & Therapy:
1990 10(1–2). "Motherhood: A Feminist Perspective."

Women's Studies Quarterly:
Spring/Summer 1989 17(1/2). "Teaching about *Women and Aging*," Emily Abel, guest issue ed.

Working Age [AARP]:
November/December 1994 10(4). "Encouraging Women to Build Bigger Nest Eggs" "special issue on older women and the changing work force."

Indexes

Some periodicals publish indexes to their contents, but this self-indexing may be inconsistent, delayed, and create need for multiple searches. To aid in efficient use of periodicals, there are indexes to periodical literature, each regularly analyzing a group of periodical titles from a field such as education, gerontology, psychology, social welfare, or women studies by grouping articles from hundreds of different serials under subject-headings. This detailed breakdown, together with cross-references from one subject heading to another, aids in choosing one's topic and helps to focus (narrow) or develop (widen) a literature search. It is wise to identify and consult several appropriate indexes in order to locate the varied periodicals and information needed to provide documentation for research and writing. In the case of interdisciplinary women studies and aging, it is essential.

Periodical directories usually include the titles of any indexes accessing the contents of the periodicals they list. Periodical indexes usually list, alphabetically in the front of each index volume, the titles of the serials they regularly index. Many journals list, usually in the front of each issue, the title(s) of any periodical indexes, abstracts, and citation indexes that regularly analyze their contents. The computerized catalogs of many libraries now also provide this information. It can aid discovery of useful periodical articles and help with defining a topic.

Manual searching of some volumes of some hardcopy indexes, abstracts, and citation indexes can now be enhanced and even replaced by computer-assisted, online, and/or CD-ROM (compact disc-read only memory) searching. Indeed, there are some computerized database files (e.g., AgeLine, #2238) that have no exact printed equivalent. The title of a database file version may not always be the same as the title of its counterpart printed index, however. For example, *Social Sciences Citation Index* becomes Social SciSearch, *Psychological Abstracts* becomes PsycInfo, *Sociological Abstracts* becomes Sociofile, etc. Libraries currently contract with vendors of hundreds of online commercial databases and CD-ROMs.

The following list of tools includes conventional periodical indexes, abstracting services, ongoing bibliographies, and citation indexes that analyze the contents of recent and retrospective issues of periodicals relevant to the subject of women and aging. Full information about frequency, publisher and sponsor, starting date, title changes, etc., can usually be found in their preliminary pages. Not all abstracting services include "abstracts" in their titles; in the following list, titles have been enhanced to reveal this provision, e.g., #8. Some indexes provide brief annotations, e.g., #18.

In a few cases, what some may consider a less-than-ideal tool is included because it is the only one in its field with its provisions approaching our needs. Note that databases do not generally go back beyond approximately 1970 in their coverage, whereas printed indexes often do.

To access dissertations, biographical material, and literary essays (types of information not contained exclusively in periodical literature) one should also use such indexes as *Biography Index* and *BioBase, Dissertation Abstracts International* and its *Comprehensive Dissertation Index, Play Index, Essay and General Literature Index, Short Story Index,* and other indexing tools.

1. ABC POL SCI: A Bibliography of . . . Political Science and Government.
2. Abstracts in Anthropology.
3. Abstracts in English Studies.
4. Abstracts in Social Gerontology. Continues Current Literature on Aging.
5. Access: The Supplementary Index to Periodicals.
6. AgeLine. *See* #2238.
7. Alternative Press Index.

8. American History and Life [abstracts].
9. Applied Science and Technology Index.
10. Arts and Humanities Citation Index.
11. Bibliographic Index.
12. Biography Index.
13. British Humanities Index.
14. Business Periodicals Index.
15. Canadian News Index.
16. Canadian Periodical Index/Index de Periodiques Canadiens.
17. Catholic Periodical and Literature Index.
18. Current Index to Journals in Education. ERIC.
19. Education Index.
20. Excerpta Medica [abstracts]. Section 20/Gerontology & Geriatrics, etc.
21. Feminist Periodicals.
22. General Science Index.
23. Historical Abstracts.
24. Humanities Index.
25. Index Medicus; Abridged Index Medicus.
26. Index to Black Periodicals.
27. Index to Legal Periodicals.
28. Index to Periodical Literature on Aging.
    Index to Periodicals by and About Blacks. *See* Index to Black Periodicals.
29. International Political Science Abstracts/Documentation Politique Internationale.
30. Left Index: A Quarterly Index to Periodicals of the Left.
31. Lesbian Periodical Index.
32. Media Review Digest [abstracts].
33. MLA [Modern Language Association] International Bibliography [abstracts].
34. New Literature on Old Age.
35. *New York Times* Index.
36. Ny Literratur om Kvinor/New Literature on Women [bibliography].
37. PAIS [Public Affairs Information Service] Bulletin. PAIS International.
38. Philosopher's Index: An International Index . . . [abstracts].
39. Physical Education Index.
40. Psychological Abstracts.
41. Resources in Education [abstracts]. ERIC.
42. Science Citation Index.
43. Social Planning, Policy, and Development Abstracts.
44. Social Sciences Citation Index.
45. Social Sciences Index.
46. Social Work Research and Abstracts.
47. Sociological Abstracts. (Electronic version is Sociofile.)
48. Studies on Women Abstracts. *See* #2237.
49. Women Studies Abstracts. *See* #2237.
50. Work Related Abstracts.

Notes

Introduction

1. Butler, Robert Neil, M.D. *The Older Woman: Continuities and Discontinuities.* Washington: U.S. National Institute on Aging, 1979. p. 1.

2. Bahr, Howard M., and Gerald R. Garrett. *Women Alone: The Disaffiliation of Urban Females.* Lexington: Heath, 1976. p. 3. *See also The Sourcebook on Aging.* Wilmette: Marquis, 1979. p. 8.

3. ERIC is the acronym for the Educational Resources Information Center, a nationwide information system within U.S. academe sponsored by the federal government, useful to consult as a reflection of the status quo. Documents are indexed and accessible since 1966 by means of the ERIC thesaurus and two indexes, *Resources in Education* and *Current Index to Journals in Education.*

4. Harris, Diana K. *Dictionary of Gerontology.* New York: Greenwood, 1988. p. 117. *See* #2245.

5. Klemesrud, Judy. "Problems of Older Women Focus of Parley." *New York Times* October 26, 1983 III: 1.

6. Cook, L. *Off Our Backs* 1983.

7. Myers, Christopher. "Congress Impatient with the Way National Institutes of Health Confront Problem of Women." *Chronicle of Higher Education* March 13, 1991 37(2): A24. "Some lobbyists raised concerns that setting aside money for work on sex-specific diseases [e.g., lupus, osteoporosis—which are not confined to women, however] could begin to detract from the N.I.H.'s overall research effort."

8. McGuire, Rick. "Clinical Trials—Is Keeping Women Out of Research Studies Science or Sexism? What's the Deal?" *Arthritis Today* July-August 1991 5(4): 30–35.

9. Myers, Christopher. "Medical Researchers Pressed to Use Female and Minority Subjects." *Chronicle of Higher Education* July 10, 1991 37(43): A1, A20, A21.

10. Wheeler, David L. "Men Treated Differently from Women in Heart Cases, Studies Say." *Chronicle of Higher Education* July 31, 1991 37(46): A8. Wheeler reports in Research Notes that, according to the July 25, 1991 *New England Journal of Medicine*, two new studies by Harvard University researchers suggest striking differences between the ways physicians take care of women and of men who have heart disease.

11. For discussion of the gatekeeping concept, see Dale Spender's "The Gatekeepers: A Feminist Critique of Academic Publishing." In Helen Roberts's *Doing Feminist Research* (New York: Routledge & Kegan Paul, 1981); Dale and Lynne Spender's "Gatekeeping: The Denial, Dismissal, and Distortion of Women" (*Women's Studies International Forum* 1983, Volume 6); and Helen Rippier Wheeler's *Getting Published in Women's Studies* (Jefferson: McFarland, 1989).

Chapter 13

1. *Ulrich's International Periodicals Directory, 33d ed., 1994–1995.* New York: Bowker, 1993.

2. *The Serials Directory.* Birmingham: EBSCO, 1993.

3. Hesslein, Shirley B. *Serials on Aging: An Analytical Guide.* New York: Greenwood, 1986.

Indexes

All references are to entry numbers.

AUTHOR INDEX

Subject Index

About the Book

More than two thousand bibliographic entries and extensive cross-references make *Women and Aging: A Guide to the Literature* a valuable resource for anyone interested in women's studies, gerontology, and related subjects.

The guide includes journal articles, book chapters, essays, and doctoral dissertations as well as complete books. All book entries are annotated. Specific definitions, information regarding the relevance of topics, and related research interests are included throughout.

Each of the thirteen chapters begins with a list of topics covered, followed by the entries themselves organized alphabetically within each topic. An introductory chapter includes a helpful How-to; the concluding chapter provides guidance in researching a field.

In-depth subject and author indexes enable the user to identify specific areas of interest quickly and easily.

Helen Rippier Wheeler holds a doctorate in education and a master's degree in library science from Columbia University; her social science M.A. is from the University of Chicago. Her numerous publications include *Womanhood Media: Current Resources About Women* and *Getting Published in Women's Studies: An International, Interdisciplinary Professional Development Guide.* She is a feminist, a founding member of the Aging and Ageism Caucus of the National Women's Studies Association, and a member of the Berkeley Commission on Aging.

Robert N. Butler, M.D., is director of the International Longevity Center (U.S.) at The Mount Sinai Medical Center in New York City.